Intertexts

Intertexts

Writings on Language, Utterance, and Context

William F. Hanks

ROWMAN & LITTLEFIELD PUBLISHERS, INC.
Lanham • Boulder • New York • Oxford

ROWMAN & LITTLEFIELD PUBLISHERS, INC.

Published in the United States of America
by Rowman & Littlefield Publishers, Inc.
4720 Boston Way, Lanham, Maryland 20706
http://www.rowmanlittlefield.com

12 Hid's Copse Road
Cumnor Hill, Oxford OX2 9JJ, England

British Library Cataloguing in Publication Information Available

Library of Congress Cataloging-in-Publication Data

Hanks, William F.
    Intertexts : writings on language, utterance, and context / William F. Hanks.
        p.   cm.
    Collection of previously published (1986–1996) articles and essays.
    Includes bibliographical references and index.
    ISBN 0–8476–8740–6 (alk. paper). — ISBN 0–8476–8741–4 (pbk. : alk. paper)
        1. Language and culture—Mexico—Yucatán (State)   2. Discourse analysis.
    3. Indexicals (Semantics)   4. Maya language—Social Aspects.   I. Title.
    P35.5.M6H36   1999
    306.44′089′971452—dc21   99–16784
                                                                            CIP

Printed in the United States of America

♾ ™ The paper used in this publication meets the minimum requirements of American
National Standard for Information Sciences—Permanence of Paper for Printed Library
Materials, ANSI Z39.48–1992.

Contents

1

Introduction

The papers collected in this volume mark intervals along the way of an ongoing intellectual project. They represent successive attempts to formulate a few basic questions, viewed from several different perspectives. They are cumulative in the way that a series of markers along a path is cumulative, for anyone who walks from one to the next. That is, they map an itinerary, traversed over time. They are all directed toward questions of language and context. What do we mean by each of these terms? What does it mean to say that the two are mutually defining? That linguistic form is shaped, in part, by its joining to the actual contexts in which people speak and write, which are, in their turn, shaped by the meaning structures of language, the social? What are the "design features" of language and of verbal discourse that derive from and are resources for certain ways of thinking, acting, and communicating? What does language change reveal about broad historical patterns? What does the deeply social quality of language reveal about human sociality, and the capacity for culture? Can you separate language from context in the first place?

These questions are in some measure the inheritance that we received as part of a cohort of linguistic anthropologists trained in North America in the late 1970s and early 1980s. They descend from Boas, Sapir, and the Americanists, as well as European sociology, structuralism, and phenomenology. They arise out of the confluence of linguistics, anthropology, and, increasingly, history. And the papers could not have been written were it not for the work of other scholars, as I tried to reveal through the footnotes and references throughout. At the same time, my ways of formulating and dealing with such questions are rooted in an ethnographic setting, an exceptionally rich and vibrant culture, language, and history. All of the papers (save chapter 6) present analyses of Yucatec Maya. The reasons for this are several. First, because I am convinced that it is through understanding languages in their actual social complexity that we can best understand Language in general. And Yucatec happens to be the one I know best in the relevant ways. Second, because Yucatec provides exquisite examples of any number of important facts about language and social life, and this makes it heuristically invaluable. But the real reason is simply because Yucatec language, culture, and history have fascinated me from the beginning, and my apprenticeship to them has helped shape me personally and intellectually. The papers proceed from an unquestioned conviction that what they try to describe is intrisically beautiful and worth knowing in intimate detail. This joining of fascination in a world with a few basic questions has been for me what Weber (1946) called the "passion" or "frenzy" that drives science as a vocation.

THE APPROACH

One immediate consequence of this passion is that the papers are marked by a kind of empiricism, and this is the first step in sketching out the approach into which they fit. First there is the matter of the Maya and the apparently unlimited number of universes this term stands for, all interacting and emerging, and fully engaged in the complexities of today, just as much as in the complexities of a long past. It is equally obvious, if somewhat paradoxical, that these universes exist apart from any scholar such as myself, and yet, when I study them, what I see already bears the mark of my presence. One of the achievements of anthropology has been to lay bare some of the distortions implied by this so-called observer's paradox. It has never seemed to me, however, that because we cannot see other people as they "actually" are that we should therefore give up on the project of ethnography. Like any field-worker, I have stubbed my toes enough among Maya people, both physically and metaphorically, to be convinced that the objects of my passion exist apart from me. So in the first instance, the empiricism is what might be called "experiential." It is the premise that we derive knowledge from experiencing the world, not by immaculate perception but by engaging, by occupying the world, and leaving ourselves open to be occupied by it.

There is another aspect to this empiricism that arises out of the premise that concepts are themselves objects that we can study empirically. Knowledge derives not only from perceptual experience, but from reflection, rationalization, and interpretation— involving more of the body and more of the mind than is usually intended by the term "perception." And the innumerable ideas implicated thereby can themselves be empirically treated. Some of what will appear at first as theoretical discussion in the papers collected here is actually an attempt to treat theoretical concepts as empirical objects: to analyze them, perhaps even to *experience* them, as such. This fuzziness in the line between analysis and theory follows from the premise that the two are not ultimately distinct. They are *distinguishable* in analysis, just as highly local facts pertaining to a single culture are distinguishable analytically from general ones pertaining to all cultures. But there is no social theory that does not inform description of the world (even if it takes years to figure out how), and there is no description that is not beholden to theory (even if it tries to hide it). The challenge, therefore, has been to ground analytic theory as thoroughly as possible in a universe of facts. Facts, under this perspective, are objects, and objects are relational constructs. Hence, in the papers to follow, the objects analyzed include things like the body, metalanguage, texts, ritual altars, and space. Every one of these is a cover term for one or more networks of relations, and could justifiably be put in quotes. But the relationality is so pervasive that to do so would obscure the text, not clarify it. In any case, for readers familiar with semiotics of any variety, it is perhaps too obvious to belabor that, whatever the subject, the object is a nexus.

If this sort of qualified empiricism is part of analysis, it is also part of the worlds we analyze. To be blunt, the natives are empiricists, too. In saying this, I include us, anthropologists or not, insofar as we engage in "our own world," however this is defined. I also include Yucatec Maya people as I have come to know them, and in fact most of the people I have known, whatever their background. A qualified empiricism seems to be part of the practical attitude of everyday activities, even under apparently exotic conditions. It simply means that you pay enough attention to the world and to the ways in which it does or does not fit your view, so that you can act. In chapter 7, I describe some fairly exotic ritual objects, made by a shaman operating in a highly specialized context. Even here, the empiricism of his practices is no less sharp than the methods of a good ethnographer, no less a combination of percept with concept. It's just that he defines his objects differently, and focuses his observations on different points. In routine interactions, there is a wide range between the attenuated object-orientation of things like "hanging out" or resting, and the intensive observations that go into virtually any kind of work, skill or otherwise focused involvement. If anything, my experiences with Maya people, both contemporary (via ethnography) and colonial (via documents), have convinced me that they are very subtle observers. In short, empiricism belongs both to the worlds I describe and to the vantage point from which I describe them.

The same holds for rationality, which I take to be the premise that our engagements are guided by purpose, and our actions, in large measure, are means toward ends. We generally assume the ends to be feasible and take steps we estimate to be plausible ways of achieving them. For a linguistic anthropologist, this means simply that you do research and work out methods suitable to reveal myriad little truths about the culture you work in. You write in order to express, explain, convince. In the most general sense, the empirical commitments of ethnography are closely wedded to the idea that research is guided by reason, and reason implies argument. Anthropological argument proceeds from ethnographic description, where it is rooted, by way of inference and interpretation. This means that the most valuable statements are ones that could be shown to be false, and the best inferences are sufficiently explicit to be challenged. Sometimes, it is useful to formalize. To explain a fact of communicative practice is to relate it to other social and linguistic facts in its various contexts; to make assertions that could be wrong and to draw inferences that could be confronted. There is a tension between universalizing generalizations, which tend to erase the specificity of their objects, and particulate descriptions, which lose sight of generality. For the kind of research we do, that tension is irreducible, and neither kind of analysis is adequate on its own. Hence, for some readers, the papers may appear too general or parsimonious, too "ethnographically thin," while for others, the opposite will be true.

In this process, ethnography is more than mere data; it is a way of engaging in a different social world. And the interpretive frameworks of any anthropologist are *accountable* to those of the people whom (s)he describes. It is not that the two must be identical; it is perfectly clear that anthropologists make generalizations of a kind different from those of the people they work with. In fact, they often cut across the grain. But we must engage native frameworks in their plurality, from language and symbolic forms, through activities and positioned ideologies. In one sense, this is just practical, since there is no other way to understand them. At a more basic level, it is so because what we are trying to describe are processes of meaning production, and these always imply a combination of forms, actions, and ideologies. It is not enough to produce a model that "generates" the actions of natives as its output. Even if it were possible, this sort of extensional adequacy would leave unexplained what all the actions mean to native actors themselves. For this, we must attend to their intentions and motivational structures, and to the categories and relations that they themselves posit in the world. Punning on the word "motivation," we can say that a convincing analysis *motivates* a specific social fact by embedding it precisely in a larger social framework. Throughout the papers here, I have explored ways of motivating facts of communicative practice.

To describe social practices in terms of actors' motivations is to posit a baseline rationality that may be relativized to various kinds of aims, but that in each case assumes some means-ends relation. For speech, this implies a principled relation between linguistic form and communicative functions like referring, requesting, ordering, maintaining contact with an addressee, sheer expression, and so forth. It is also consistent with such apparently exotic aims as the exorcizing of a malevolent spirit from a place or person (cf. Chapters 7–8), the attempt to convert a colonized population (cf. Chapter 10), or the aim to display an authentic and politically effective identity (Chapters 4–5). In all of these cases, a large part of what I try to explain is exactly the forms of rationality and rationalization that Yucatec actors engage in. It should be clear that, for an anthropologist, the forms of rationality are many, and one need not adopt a wooden functionalism to describe them, nor need we assume that our brand of rationality is the measure of all others. It means simply that, when native speakers act and interpret one another, they typically engage in, or impute, motivations, thereby relating one another's actions to various ends. At the very least, to describe action in terms of instrumentality (Chapter 2), purpose (Chapter 3), strategy (Chapter 4), resistance and appropriation (Chapter 10) is to assume that agents are in one way or another, and in some degree, rational.

It is basic to the papers collected here that language is central in the constitution of action, both verbal and nonverbal. Intentions, motivational structures, means, ends, and entire interpretive frameworks are routinely formulated by native speakers in the course of everyday life. The universe of distinctions and equivalences sedimented in language are critical in defining these things, and indeed, speakers often express them in words (cf. Chapters 3, 5, 6). Even when unspoken, they are present as parts of the social habitus of the actor, and language is a fundamental element in the evaluative dispositions and "schemes of perception" of the habitus. For the same reason, the relation between language and the body is critical (Chapter 2). Deictics and demonstratives in a language like Yucatec show that corporeality pervades even the most mundane acts of referring. The study of deixis and routine reference can reveal aspects of corporeality and its relation to self-reflexivity that remain otherwise obscure. In other words, the close study of language provides exceedingly delicate evidence of these aspects of social practice. I would go further, and say that social practice can *only* be understood in a theory that includes language among its basic objects. Then again, language so understood is not an abstract system, but a modality for being in the world, already molded to the kinds of engagements it makes possible.

THE PAPERS

The papers explore a set of core concepts and it will be useful to flag them at the outset. The first two chapters focus on the analysis of indexical reference in ordinary conversation (Chapters 2, 3). Papers in Part II widen the scope to include aspects of discourse analysis and textual interpretation in different genres, written as well as oral. Those in Part III move into questions of historical interpretation, and the relation between colonial Yucatan and contemporary shamanic discourse. There is something idiosyncratic, or perhaps arbitrary, in this choice of topics; it goes back ultimately to the fascination I referred to at the outset. In another sense, the topics are not at all arbitrary, but highly motivated, first, because they are *thinkable* within current linguistic anthropology, but also because we have developed a vocabulary sufficiently precise to analyze them in detail. While the analyses do not fit snugly into an existing "paradigm," they respond to the work of others in the field. They are no less embedded than any of the discourse practices they describe. A second type of motivation is that the topics, concepts, and analyses correspond to interconnected parts of communicative practice, and are therefore cross-linked in various ways. Hence, most of the ideas I will flag here recur, in one way or another, in most of the papers. The difference is that the papers focus on different aspects, different combinations, or different empirical demonstrations of the concepts. The ones pertinent to Part I are: Indexical ground, Embodiment, Corporeal field, Copresence, Participation framework, and Metalanguage. I take these up in the order listed.

Deictic terms, like "this" or "that," have the deceptive appearance of establishing a transparent relation between word and thing, as though, to paraphrase Bloomfield, they were so simple that they could be glossed in gestures (1933:249). This appearance is indeed misleading, not the least because gestures turn out to be enormously more subtle and meaningful than Bloomfield assumed (and there is in fact an important cross-disciplinary literature on the topic). When one looks carefully at any deictic system, it turns out that, beneath a great deal of variation within and across languages, these terms all encode a single, elegant relational structure. In this structure, a referential function is joined to an indexical ground, in a way that the deictic denotes an object relative to the context of its utterance. So a term like "this" might encode "*the one* (referent) *proximal to* (relational predicate) *us right now* (indexical ground)". Or concretely, I denote the book near me as "this," and the one across the way as "that." Notice that if you take away the indexical ground, there is no way of identifying the referent, and there is no denotation. All you have left is "the one proximal to _____." Taken in isolation from a speech context, there is no way to associate the term "this" with an object, because there is no property of "thisness" that is shared by all those things it may properly refer to in speech. The property "proximal" is a likely candidate, but it is a pure relation—proximal to what? The minimal structure has three parts—the referent pole, the indexical pole, and the relation that binds them. Moreover, in this relation, the indexical element is backgrounded, whereas the referent is foregrounded. To interpret my utterance of "this" or "that" as denoting the book, you must relate it to context, but it is the book, not the context, which is the focal object. Hence, we say that context serves as the indexical ground of the reference. Having formulated this structure, the hard questions become: What are the relational features? And what do we mean by context? The papers here focus on the latter question.

One thing covered by context is surely the material setting of speech, whereby I include the bodies of speaker and addressee along with the perceptual connnections between them and the space in which they interact. Space is further inclusive of the social setting, the built environment (Chapters 3, 7, 9, 10), and the landscape (Chapters 9, 10). The challenge has been to deal with material realities in their concrete specificity, while simultaneously understanding them through the cultural and linguistic systems of native actors. What has most concerned me in these papers is precisely the ways in which context, including the body, is at once physical and conceptual, concrete and abstract, local and highly general, linguistically mediated and nonverbal, reflexive and irreflexive. So in Chapter 2, we will work through a series of embeddings of the human body as it is practiced by Maya speakers, moving from simple body coordinates and the perceptual field through domestic space and into some of the interactive fields in which coresidents and coworkers engage. Sometimes the focal object, sometimes the ground for other foci, the body is at once self-individuating and occupied by other social dimensions of space. Nearly all of the papers deal with space and spatiality in one way or another, but Chapters 3 and 7–10 do so directly: space as the field of reference (Chapter 3), as an element in various discourse genres (Chapters 5 and 6), as constituted through shamanic ritual (Chapters 7 and 8), and as an object of contention during the Spanish colonization of Yucatan (Chapters 9 and 10).

One element in this series of embeddings, which I consider basic, is the idea that "the body" is both reflexive and defined in relation to others. As will be evident from Chapter 3, Merleau-Ponty's concept of the *schéma corporel* has had a decisive impact on my thinking and underlies what I call the *corporeal field*. More than the body as sheer physical organism, it is these two aspects of bodily experience that are the most fruitful for the study of communicative practice. Merleau-Ponty's thesis was that the *schéma* is constituted out of three elements: the actual body posture of the individual, the entire range of other alternative postures that (s)he could have adopted at this moment, and the self-awareness on the part of the individual, of the former in relation to the latter. It is in a dynamic *prise de conscience,* a coming to awareness, that the schema is constituted. I argue that it is exactly this kind of bodilyness that is needed to properly analyze deictic reference. But for an anthropologist, Merleau-Ponty's schema is still too heavily centered on the individual. I needed a unit of description that incorporated its three elements, but with a basis in social interaction, not just the individual. This I call the corporeal field, where "field" is taken from practice theory and designates a social space of possible positions and position takings. The corporeal field is the reflexive actuality of bodily relations through which two or more interactants relate to each other. For face-to-face talk, it is obviously an interperspectival space (minimally encompassing an "I" and a "you"), with at least three subspaces: that of the Spkr, that of the Adr, and that which is common to them. The complexity of the field increases as the number of roles and coparticipants increases, and as we take into account the various asymmetries in their relations, both to each other and to the broader space of action (cf. Chapters 2, and 7–9).

Interactants who are engaged in the same corporeal field are *copresent* to one another. (I leave open for now the question of whether actors not in the same corporeal field can be said nonetheless to be copresent.) The idea of copresence here derives from Goffman, the ethnomethodologists, Schutz and, to a lesser degree, Merleau-Ponty. On the face of it, it just means that two or more actors are present in the same "space" at the moment of co-engagement (for linguistic purposes, at the time of utterance). In fact though, it is a good deal more complex, with several distinct features. *Spatial contiguity* is one of its typical features: the interactants are close together, under some relevant definition of what counts as close. But there is more to it than this, as you can see, if you consider that all the hundred-odd strangers in a subway train are "close," but few of them are engaged with one another in anything other than the specific avoidance patterns of urban anonymity. We do not want to say they are fully copresent if there is no mutual orientation. (Orientation that is not mutual is something less than full copresence, like the unnoticed overhearer surreptitiously listening to a speaker. Being unaware, this speaker is present to someone who is not present to him or her, and hence such cases are not true *copresence.)* Part of this mutuality is what Schutz called the "congruence of perspectives." You and I are different, but when I engage you, I assume that our perspectives are sufficiently congruent that, if I put myself in your position, the world will look to me more or less the same as it does to you. This is due to the assumptions that, for all intents and purposes, we share the same background common sense and are sufficiently alike that we apply it to similar effect. Chapters 2 and 3 explore this kind of congruence ethnographically, whereas Chapters 7 through 10 take up cases where it is lacking. They illustrate the fact that the degree of congruence between perspectives actually varies widely (just as does the definition of relative spatial proximity).

For Schutz, interaction requires not only congruence, but *reciprocity of perspectives* between parties. Reciprocity is neither similarity ("sharedness"), nor congruence per se, but the idea that interactants' perspectives are opposite, complementary parts of a single whole, with each oriented to the other. Hence, for me, I am "I" and you are "you," whereas for you, you are "I" and I am "you." The banal interchange of pronouns and deictics is one of the most pervasive expressions of reciprocity in speech. It works in part because both speaker and addressee are reflexively aware of themselves: to say "I" is to express this reflexivity as focus, whereas all of the second and third person (really nonperson) deictics express the same reflexivity, but as background. We saw this already with Merleau-Ponty's *schéma corporel,* which is the product of self-awareness. Part of the reciprocity is the additional postulate that you, the other, are also a self, which is to say, you are reflexive just as I am.

Hence, whereas the notion of being together is very simple, the phenomenal fine structure of it is quite complex. Copresence is defined by a series of gradual, logically distinct but experientially overlapping dimensions. A delicate ethnography of copresence, which is required by any description of communicative practice, has to describe these several coordinates. For one thing, they affect the use of linguistic forms in a precise and predictable fashion (Hanks 1990). For another, they are sites at which cultures differ and hence the social definition of routine experience is laid bare. To be copresent in a Maya interaction is both the same as and very different from, copresence among, say, English speakers. As the product of a *prise de conscience,* copresence is defined by human consciousness, against a horizon of social knowledge. At a sufficient level of detail, no two instances of it are alike (indeed, the very idea of a general definition of copresence evaporates). But in order to compare utterances within and across languages, it is necessary to simplify the phenomenal complexity. For the purpose of describing routine referential practices, we can do this by summarizing the various relations among interactants along a single dimension of relative symmetry. The more interactants share, the more congruent, reciprocal, and transposable their perspectives, the more symmetric is the interactive field. The greater the differences that divide them, the more asymmetric the field. Every dimension of copresence can also be a boundary between the interactants. In routine acts of reference and description in everyday talk, the field serves as the indexical ground, and speakers' choices of deictic terms respond systematically to differences in relative indexical symmetry (Chapters 2, 3).

It is striking that, even in nonlinguistic accounts such as Schutz's, the pronouns are used as handy labels for the positions that must be coordinated in a theory of copresence. It is just easier to think the present, and the copresent, using terms like I, you, this, that, here, there, now, and so forth, than to try and do so without them. Thereby hangs a larger issue. For the elements of copresence cannot be sorted out without carefully distinguishing between the participant roles and sectors (Spr, Adr, Other, Proximal vs. Distal portions of the corporeal field, etc.) and the actual persons occupying them. The distinction between roles and occupancies is familiar from social theory, but it takes on a special significance in any practice-based approach, such as mine. The reason is that roles can be described in a structural theory, whereas the occupying of them over time, the vacating of them, the contesting of them, in short the dynamic mapping of persons into roles that happens during activities, cannot. This requires a different approach in which we recognize that the relation between roles and actors is many-to-many and subject to rapid change (Chapters 2, 8), just as the relation between linguistic forms and roles is itself many-to-many and dynamic (Chapter 3).

These points were made forcefully by Goffman and subsequent studies in conversation, but they have yet to be fully integrated into general social theory. They show among other things that actors in the quick are exceptionally fluid in shifting between analytically distinct forms of engagement. For our purposes, two aspects of this are worth underscoring. First, if language is any indicator (and I believe it is), action can *never* be theorized from the egocentric perspective of the individual. It always arises out of the relation between the individual and a social matrix, including copresent others. It is impossible, for instance, to analyze speech accurately from the viewpoint of "the speaker," as is so common in received approaches outside the social sciences. Second, the apparently simple idea of the "here-now" is actually a locus of social embedding and lamination (to borrow Goffman's nice term)—a site in which multiple spatial frames are related with really impressive precision in even the most mundane of interactions (Chapters 2, 3, 5, 8, and 9). Hence, it is impossible to describe the "here-now" of social action with any plausible accuracy in a theory that assumes them to be transparent, as is the case with so many social theories. My claim is, therefore, that, *in principle*, neither a sheerly language-based approach, nor one deaf to language, could yield the truths demanded by social empiricism. As a preliminary way of keeping distinct these several differences, I use the terms participant frame (a configuration of roles) and participant framework (a frame in the course of unfolding, actually occupied by individuals). I know the terms are heavy, but I have found that the distinctions really do make a difference for both description and theory.

The last of the core ideas in Part I is metalanguage, and this ties in directly with self-reflexivity. By metalanguage I mean simply language about language, that is, utterances or entire discourses which individuate or comment on any aspect of speech or language. Over the past decades, this usage of language has become an increasingly important topic in linguistic anthropology, having been brought into modern research by Charles Morris, Roman Jakobson, Uriel Weinreich, Dell Hymes, and a variety of subsequent scholars including Michael Silverstein, John Haviland, Charles Briggs, and Benjamin Lee. In recent work, the metalinguistic capacity, which is universal to all languages, has been related to the expression of various social ideologies of language. The idea here is that any language provides its speakers with the symbolic resources necessary to formulate and express evaluations of the language (and of language in general), and these evaluations are typically positioned in just the ways we think of ideologies as being positioned. As one pursues the issues that arise in relation to metalanguage, they run in several directions. In sociological terms, it is one of the main vehicles through which social stereotypes are formulated and the interpretive frameworks that inform utterance reception are encoded. It is, in short, a direct route into common sense. In semiotic terms, it is an explicit form of reflexivity with real consequences for the organization of language. In linguistic terms, it provides some of the best evidence for the semantics of expressions, as well as a veritable gold mine of examples of indirect and quoted discourse. Culturally, metalanguage is as significant as is any other autochthanous form of self-interpretation. Compared to other kinds of self-expression, it can be even more revealing because the reflexivity is so formally precise.

In the papers collected here, several of these angles are pursued. Chapter 3 is directly concerned with the metalinguistic reflections of native Maya speakers on the meanings and uses of deictic expressions in their own language. I wanted to show both that when speakers reflect on deixis, they reason from interactive scenarios and not linguistic forms, and moreover, that their reasoning is coherent and revealing of how copresence is defined in this culture. In a less direct fashion, similar issues are at stake in Chapter 4, where the metalinguistic framing of "indigenous" expression is in play, Chapters 5–6, where metalinguistic framing is treated as a dimension of genre, and Chapter 10, where metalinguistic awareness is explored in relation to the colonial missionary attempt to convert native Maya people into bona fide Christians. These are all angles on what I take to be a fundamental human capacity for self-reflection, and reflection on the symbols through which we make ourselves. In other more sustained discussions, I have tried to show that metalanguage is a powerful tool in both linguistic and ethnographic analysis (Hanks 1990, 1996). At this point, I am convinced that the study of metalinguistic reasoning as such opens up hitherto unexploited resources for research into human cognition and linguistic systems, as well as interaction and the reception of speech and other forms of discourse (see here Lucy 1993).

Taken together, these six concepts—indexical grounding, embodiment, corporeal field, copresence, participation frameworks, and metalanguage—give a fair indication of the kinds of issues that arise from the study of deixis. Deixis provided an ideal focus for research on the relation between language form and context, the delicate covariations between them, the way multiple communicative functions are codified in forms, and the varieties of self-reflexivity that subtend even the most mundane acts of referring. Things like ritual language, political oratory, verbal deference, and specialized ways of speaking all provide florid examples of the social and cultural freighting of language. There also has been a great deal of excellent research in these areas. It seems, nonetheless, that mundane acts of reference and description hold just as much evidence for linguistic anthropology, and perhaps even more fascination. The unexceptional this and that of talk about objects, the expression of literal meanings, the degree to which apparently arbitrary facts of grammar turn out to be driven by aspects of social interaction, the ways in which language provides ready-made perspectives, and evaluative postures that speakers occupy through speech were the starting points for my work on deixis, and they remain the matrix for all of the papers collected here.

In a sense it is inevitable that a focus on utterances and interaction would lead to broader questions about discourse and textuality. After all, utterances are typically produced as part of an ongoing stream of speech, and references and descriptions are often part of longer stories. In any case, we need a way to distinguish among various kinds of language use, and if deixis really is as important as I think it is, then it ought to be pivotal in the construction of discourse more generally. Following these leads, the papers in Part II shift from face-to-face interaction to discourse genres. The two are intimately related, because many different genres are produced in the face-to-face, and a general approach to genres must take this into account (Chapters 5, 6). At the same time, they are different because many forms of discourse are precisely *not* face-to-face. In this case, the dynamics of copresence and corporeality shift to mediation via writing, print, and other forms of mediated distribution. When the papers move from spoken to written language, the vocabulary shifts: what started as indexical grounding becomes "centering," speaking becomes "voicing," understanding becomes "reception," and formal structure becomes "discourse organization." These and other parallel shifts reflect the embedding of indexicality in discourse, a phenomenon that varies according to the genres at hand. The idea of genre fulfills a practical necessity in description, providing a unit of organization and description larger than a single utterance, but smaller than the entire language. It also provides a natural point of entry for the study of style (and just as no utterance is without generic framing, no speech lacks style). As I worked through discourse interpretations of Maya documents, the consequences of style for even the most basic literal meaning became clear (Chapters 4, 5).

It is curious, and once again somewhat arbitrary, that for me the shift to discourse analysis was coincident with a shift from contemporary ethnography to historical interpretation. The move is easy enough to rationalize in retrospect: historical texts illustrate discourse under minimal conditions, because of the vast amount that can never be known of the context, and this makes it all the more necessary to be explicit about how we read. The consequences of different ways of reading are sometimes glaring, and this is heuristically useful for theory (Chapter 4). Then again, if the sort of practice approach I was trying to work out was really fruitful, it seemed reasonable to demand that it contribute to historical description, as well as to ethnography. Finally, there was the haunting ethnographic intuition that the forms of communicative practice I was observing in Yucatan had their roots in the colonial world. This is especially true of shamanism, which is sometimes misrecognized as a direct link to a pure indigenous past (whereas in fact shamanic practice is exceptionally porous and bears the mark of its colonial past). But aside from these justifications, there was the sheer beauty of the documents and the intriguing ambiguities of the voices they spoke. After a decade of work with modern Maya, the colonial materials provided a whole new perspective. Along the way, they forced me to rethink the idea of descriptive truth as it applies to utterances, cultural identity as it applies to the producers and receivers of texts, and structure as it applies to discourse genres, and not just to the texts that instantiate them.

One of the central empirical and methodological problems in working with colonial materials is the sheer partiality of what was written, what was saved, and what has lasted. Given my prior research in indexicality and communicative practices, the unavoidable problem was how to use such radically incomplete documents as evidence of broader social contexts. To this end, a variety of contemporary theories provided leads. The most relevant ones have in common the premise that linguistic form underdetermines conveyed meaning—that properly linguistic aspects of meaning are incomplete when compared to native speaker understandings. For instance, Grice's notion of implicature relies on the distinction between what a speaker (literally) says, and what (s)he thereby conveys, with the latter derived from the former via inference. Similarly, both schema-based cognitive semantics and situational semantics make appeal to context in deriving utterance meaning from properly linguistic meaning. In a more socially focused way, the analyses of conversational inference developed by John Gumperz and his students makes a parallel distinction between what a speaker says and the various conversational inferences that are drawn from it. In each case, the processes of implicature, inference, and working out of indirect or secondary effects involve what Roman Ingarden called "concretization" (1973:337FF). Notice that they all proceed from the observation that what is understood is typically greater than what is actually expressed in an utterance. In other words, the utterance (or text) is incomplete in respect of the meaning it will actually convey when received.

Ingarden's approach was uniquely productive on this point, since it focused on reading and written texts, and combined attention to discourse form with a phenomenological commitment to meaning as experienced. In other words, it bridges nicely the hiatus between Schutz and Merleau-Ponty on the one hand, and more formally based theories of language on the other. One of the basic ideas in Ingarden's approach is that the meaning of any literary work is not encoded or contained in the text itself, but rather derived by active readers as they engage the work. This derivation is what Ingarden called the "concretization" of the work, and it designates the relatively full joining of literal meaning, understood meaning, and the circumstances of the understanding. We say that the work is concretized in such and such a context, in order to denote the discourse as an actual token received by a reader/public. Ingarden observes that incompleteness is inherent and can never be overcome; the more you try to specify the total meaning of an utterance by adding detail and description, the more "blank spots of indeterminacy" you introduce, thereby requiring further interpretive work on the part of the reader. You can never increment literal meaning to the point that it fully specifies understood meaning. Ingarden's theory was of course developed to analyze literary texts, but I remain convinced that it is of central relevance to utterance description more generally.

It is not accidental, I think, that these several frameworks for discourse analysis are parallel. The basic idea of incompleteness is in each case an instance of indexical dependency. It is because texts contain hidden indexical components that they are incomplete when viewed apart from their concretization in a context. Or, one might say, it is because meaning is inherently incomplete that what we call "indexicality" is ubiquitous in speech. This is a further parallel to the more specialized embedding of indexicality in the relational structure of deictic reference. In all of these cases, the differences lie not in the presence or absence of indexicality, but in how it is related to form.

Once you make the move from studying discourse production in the present to studying historical documents—from speech to written text-artifacts—a number of things happen. The first is that you realize what a superabundance of meaning is generated in copresent interaction, precisely because so much of it is missing with a written text. For the same reason, you become aware of how many different kinds of meaning are in fact conveyable by a written text, and that texts, no less than utterances, are replete with meaning potential in a whole array of communicative dimensions. Indeed, the very relation of the written text to an oral utterance comes into focus. This is especially so for documents that we know were produced and received aloud, as is the case with colonial Maya. Some of the most gratifying aspects of colonial Maya documents has been the rich veins of orality in the language and the clear formal aesthetic (from poetic parallelisms through imagery and the overall structure of entire works). Also, because the texts were distributed, read, archived, and often cross-referenced in other texts, issues of intertextuality come immediately to the forefront. Indeed, when we take Ingarden's point that what we call a work is actually a history of concretizations, then the meaning of any historical document is the trajectory of its reception.

The first step in this trajectory is the making of the document itself, a production typically involving witnesses, scribes, and other institutional supports. Moreover, each text is an intertext, an object whose meaning potential was realized in the context of other texts, under certain discursive conditions. It is not always possible to recover the conditions, but a proper analytic perspective on discourse tells you just what to look for. The first wave of questions in this group of papers turns on the question: What kind of context is projected by individual texts and discursive series? The structure of indexicality and discourse centering are invaluable tools in answering this question, as are the precise participation frames that texts typically signal. You notice right away, for instance, that colonial notarial documents are typically dated, sited and in the first person, with named witnesses and higher powers invoked in conventionalized ways (I use the term "conventional" advisedly here; these are notarial standards.) These features contrast sharply with the entire corpus of hieroglyphic inscriptions, as well as the so-called native genres of prophetic history and ritual incantation. In place of a simple notion of the author (corresponding to the simple notion of the speaker), we get elaborate and genre-specific frameworks of participant relations. Moreover, the authorial voice spoken through these frameworks is often ambiguous in specific ways, showing a combination of apparently indigenous and apparently European elements. The difficulty of reading these texts is enormously useful in throwing open the question of what we mean by a speaker/author in the first place.

If meaning is fixed in the process of production, distribution, and reception, then we obviously need a way of describing the discursive fields through which these processes unfold. This is another productive side effect of historical interpretation, to force us out of a narrow focus on single authors or even author-addressee dyads. It is true that researchers working on copresent interaction broke away from the notion of isolated speakers more than two decades ago. (One thinks here of Goffman, Garfinkel, Sacks, Schegloff, Charles and Marjory Goodwin.) But they did so mainly by showing the need to subdivide the "speaker" into multiple roles and expand from dyads to various multiparty arrangements. Historical interpretation raises different questions: typically, at least some of the coparticipants in an intertextual trajectory are *not* copresent, either in time or space. Take letters produced by groups of Maya nobles in Yucatan, addressed to the Spanish crown or to some authority in Mexico, giving clear evidence of being produced in concert over a period of a month or so, involving people in different places and times (Chapters 4, 9, 10). The point of the historical materials is that they pose problems of mediation far beyond those usually associated with copresent talk (even though all talk is mediated, if only by language and gesture). For the same reason, they force us to get beyond notions like the "situation," "speech event," "face-to-face," and even copresence, in order to embed communicative processes in broader social fields. This is easier said than done.

A description of the discursive fields in colonial Yucatan must begin with the legal, institutional, and sociocultural divide between the Spanish sector and the Indian Republics. Colonial law made these distinctions, and the attempt to understand, organize, and convert the Maya into Christians was a centerpiece of the conquest. This immediately raises the problem of translation, since religious conversion in colonial Mesoamerica was conducted in the native languages, and the missionaries produced an enormous corpus of bilingual literature. The latter included such frankly metalinguistic works as dictionaries, grammars, primers, and descriptions of speech practices, as well as the scripts for prayers, sermons, sacraments, and other doctrinal discourse (Chapters 8, 10). But this corpus of missionary works is only the beginning of a broader discourse that bears the mark of translation. In the Indian Republics a wide array of genres were produced in Maya language, written in the Spanish-based orthography developed by the missionaries. One large class of such genres was notarial, consisting in bureaucratic and official documents reflecting the conduct of local government (Chapter 9). Alongside these were the more nearly "native" genres of "prophetic history" and ritual incantation. The main point for current purposes is that certain discourse features are common to the entire span of colonial genres, including those produced in both Spanish and indigenous sectors. In some cases the sectors are interwoven by discourse operators, such as the Catholic cross, which recur in all kinds of text (Chapter 10). In others it is more subtle, and turns on characteristic styles, features of format, and elements such as participant frameworks. Some of the most subtle examples of this are found in the progressive shifts in meaning of Maya terms to approximate the semantic values of the Spanish terms to which translators equated them. Hence, translation was implicated in changing the semantic patterns of Maya language.

The distribution of such elements serves as a primary form of evidence for intertextual relations, but also sheds light on the relations between sites of production, including the boundaries that separated them. For instance, the fact that the scribes who operated in the Indian Republics were trained in large measure by the missionaries is indicated powerfully by the commonalities of discourse style between missionary and notarial genres. The position of scribe, moreover, was a stepping stone to higher office in the Indian Republics, thus providing a series of connected positions through which individuals moved, bringing with them the kinds of linguistic change triggered by colonial social processes.

Running through these remarks is the related and unavoidable question of power asymmetries. The relations between Indios (the legal category of indigenous people) and Europeans in the colony were inflected with systematic differences in access to resources and the ability to use those resources. In some cases, but by no means all, these differences were resisted by indigenous actors. In others, indigenous actors take up positions within the very colonial structure of which they are the object (Chapters 4, 9, 10). Differences in power, and in its forms, also apply within both Indio and Euro sectors, both of which were internally complex. Focusing on the missionary project, to convert the Indios into Christians, one finds precise and elaborate hierarchies defined by the church and Spanish Crown, with regulations governing access to different positions. For instance, the native peoples participated in doctrinal pedagogy both as students and as teachers, but were unable to gain access to the monastic orders.

Among monastics residing in the missions, individuals were ranked as *frayle de confesion, frayle de missa, guardian,* and so forth, according to their ability to administer the sacraments and assume positions of leadership in the convent. The forms of power and authority embodied in the municipal and provincial governments were inscribed on discourse and had a pervasive impact on the production, distribution, and reception of texts. In some cases, features as apparently minor as the order of signatures and person references in texts respond precisely to differences in political position and generation (Chapters 9, 10).

One of the fascinations of the colonial discourse is its presence in contemporary Maya practices. Some of the salient features of style and phrasing that emerge in the sixteenth and seventeenth centuries are still attested in contemporary Maya (Chapters 4, 7, 8). One site in which this historical reproduction is most evident is shamanic practices. Chapters 7 and 8 are a first attempt to relate the precise forms of ritual practice of a contemporary shaman with the discourse of colonial Maya agents, as embodied in the corpus of documents. That the colonial authors were trained by Franciscan missionaries, of varying degrees of proficiency in Maya, lends a further irony (cf. Chapters 4, 5). One can see in modern shamanic prayer the traces of specifically missionary Maya, formulated in order to translate European doctrine into the native language. The translation practices of the colonial missionaries and their students helped to define the language from which shamanic prayer derives. Notice that this goes far beyond a notion of cultural syncretism, since contemporary shamanic discourse is not merely a combination of erstwhile European and Indigenous elements. It is the precipitate of a set of processes in which the two were already interacting and partly fused. It is also, of course, one of the sites in which presence and copresence and the body are defined for at least some contemporary Maya people.

Citations of data drawn from field research by the author follow two formats: one for audio recordings and the other for written field notes. For the former, in the citation (F.1.A.000), F abbreviates "field recording," 1.A the tape number and side, and 000 the footage at which the example occurs. For written notes, the citation (BB.1.100) abbreviates "blue book number 1, page 100."

REFERENCES

Bloomfield, Leonard. 1933. *Language.* New York: Holt.

Hanks, William F. 1990. *Referential Practice: Language and Lived Space among the Maya.* Chicago: University of Chicago Press.

Hanks, William F. 1996. *Language and Communicative Practices.* Boulder, CO: Westview Press.

Ingarden, Roman. 1973. *The Literary Work of Art: An Investigation on The Borderlines of Ontology, Logic and the Theory of Literature.* Translated by G. G. Grabowicz. Evanston, IL: Northwestern University Press.

Lucy, John A., ed. 1993. *Reflexive Language: Reported Speech and Metapragmatics.* Cambridge: Cambridge University Press.

Weber, Max. 1946. In *From Max Weber: Essays in Sociology.* Translated, edited, and with an introduction by H. H. Gerth and C. Wright. Mills, NY: Oxford University Press.

Part I

Indexicality and Referential Practices

2

Foundations of Indexical Context:
Social Mediations of the Body

Le mot 'ici' appliqué à mon propre corps ne désigne pas une position
déterminée par rapport à d'autres et . . . à des coordonnées extérieures,
mais l'installation des premières coordonnées, l'ancrage du corps actif dans
un objet.

M. Merleau-Ponty, *Phénoménologie de la perception*

INTRODUCTION

In acts of deictic reference, speakers integrate schematic with local knowledge. It is
critical to an understanding of deixis to recall that even very "local" elements of context, such as a speaker's own corporeal experience and perceptual field, are susceptible of schematization.[1] Various scholars have indeed argued that the body is among
the most fundamental zones of intersection between society and the biopsychologi-
cal individual. In its materiality and capacity for engagement, the body provides a
series of natural oppositions, a "raw material" in which collective categories and values are embodied (Comaroff 1985:7ff.; Turner 1980; Bourdieu [1972] 1977,
1980:120ff.). Body space has a schematic structure, just as does the deictic field, and
it is related to other spatial schemata by processes of analogy, homology, and transformation. Although deictics ground utterances in the local interactive process, being indexicals, they are nonetheless conventional resources that fit into a larger stock
of knowledge that Maya speakers share prior to any instance of use. Even in acts of
individuated reference to the immediate "egocentric" field of the speaker, these collective representations are available as public resources that speakers exploit. The role
of the body in reference is therefore not limited to either local or subjective aspects
of speech. To see this, let us briefly consider some different approaches to the notion
of a schema.

In most cognitive research, the term "schema" (pl. schemata, adj. schematic) is used
to designate a prefabricated conceptual structure that remains relatively invariant
throughout successive instantiations and that provides for holistic understanding of

19

some portion of reality. Agar and Hobbs (1985:415), for instance, summarize the concept as developed in artificial intelligence and psychology as "simply a convenient term to characterize some related inferences." What we are calling frames here are schematic constructs insofar as they organize inferences and have relatively constant structure. In a recent book, however, Mark Johnson has proposed a different approach to schemata, in which they are nonpropositional structures that connect concepts with percepts. Drawing on Kant's treatment of the imagination, Johnson sees these structures at play in organizing experience and comprehension in general. While they are also general in the sense of containing terms common to many experiences, schemata "emerge as meaningful structures for us at the level of our bodily movements through space, our manipulation of objects and our perceptual interactions" (Johnson 1987:29). That is, the relative abstractness of these structures is offset by the fact that they are part of our most concrete engagements with the world. This makes them dynamic rather than static (29) and becomes the basis of Johnson's discussion of understanding, imagination, and embodiment (Johnson 1987:173–93). Meaning and rationality, he says, are both embodied, to the extent that they are linked to image schemata and their extensions (190).

If Johnson's approach to schemata and embodiment developed out of his reading of Kant, it also derives from a reading of phenomenology, which he acknowledges but does not discuss explicitly. Merleau-Ponty ([1945] 1967) proposed that a fundamental part of our experience in the world is rooted in what he called our *schéma corporel*. His definition of this key concept differs from both cognitive notions of schemata and the human body, and from Johnson's appeal to embodiment, but it bears interesting relations to them. Since the work cited by Merleau-Ponty also plays a central role in Bourdieu's ([1972] 1977) early outline of a theory of practice, it is worth working through at least parts of it in some detail. Furthermore, when we consider modes of embodiment in relation to referential practice, Merleau-Ponty's approach will emerge as a powerful (antithetical) complement to the cognitive one and will provide a vocabulary for talking about aspects of deictic practice that go beyond mental representations.

It is important to appreciate from the outset that Merleau-Ponty's framework for the body was developed as a critique and an alternative to what he called "intellectualist" models. Most cognitive explanations of understanding fit this label insofar as they invoke mental representations and processes of inference (however automatized) as their basic terms. Merleau-Ponty used the idea of the *schéma corporel* as an alternative to mental representations, a way of asserting that there is knowledge *in* the body. Rather than a fixed data structure or even a component of the "imagination" (in Johnson's sense), the *schéma corporel* is the concrete, always changing self-awareness that actors have of their own bodily position in space. Merleau-Ponty phrases this reflexive component as "une prise de conscience de sa propre position," an intersensorial unity always grounded in the immediate experiential field of the actor. Rather than fixing the body in a set of inert categories then, the *schéma corporel* is dynamic, as is the body in motion. The key issue of generality is treated in this phenomenological framework not in terms of an abstraction away from experience but as a transposable concreteness (165): the *schéma* includes not just one's actual position but the sense of infinitely many other positions that are possible but not actually occupied. For instance, an actor sitting with legs crossed in a room has a preconceptual apprehension of his or her own placement but also a sense of the unquestioned possibility of changing position, shifting in the chair, standing and crossing the room, and so forth. As Merleau-Ponty put it, "le sujet normal a son corps non seulement comme système ouvert d'une infinité de positions équivalentes dans d'autres orientations. Ce que nous avons appelé le schéma corporel est justement ce système d'équivalences, cette invariant immédiatement donné par lequel les différentes tâches motrices sont instantanément transposables" ([1945] 1967:165). Both the actuality and the potentiality of spatial positioning, the *schéma* generalizes experience, not by abstracting concepts, but by transposing actual postures. (Transposability becomes a key feature of the habitus for Bourdieu.)

For Merleau-Ponty, the *schéma corporel* encompasses all body parts, unifying them into a single whole. This whole plays a dual role in spatial orientation. On the one hand, it is an active posture engaging the present task, putting the body itself in the world, "leaning towards" it to engage in a focused way. On the other hand, it is a ground, or to use the phenomenological term, a "horizon," relative to which other objects and spatial relations are grasped ([1945] 1967:117). Like other theorists in the phenomenological tradition, Merleau-Ponty sought to incorporate aspects of Gestalt psychology, and the duality of the body is partly due to its role as both figure and ground in Gestalt structures. This would suggest that in deixis, which we know to incorporate a referential figure on an indexical ground, the body plays both roles as well.

What can we derive from these different approaches to the role of the body in understanding? It seems obvious that referential practices, and particularly those involving deixis, put in play prefabricated cognitive schemata. The general relational structure of deixis, the categories of R values, pragmatic features, types of indexical grounds, and their standard combinations are all schematic resources for thinking and acting with language. The human body is part of this schematic order insofar as its perceptual, conceptual, and motor engagements are the basis on which structures are produced. The spatial schemata, for instance, presuppose the human body and provide terms in which to refer directly to its subspaces and orientation in the current surround. Deictic usage organizes inferences and contextualization processes. At the same time, preconceptual schemata like those proposed by Merleau-Ponty, and later by Johnson, are involved when speakers actually implement structures while communicating. That is, the actual indexical grounding of a deictic utterance and the individuation of a real particular in the role of referent. Here the duality and dynamism of the corporal schema interlocks with the structure of reference: the body is engaged minimally as ground or horizon for referring elsewhere and maximally as both ground and itself (or its parts) the figural referent. The intersensorial unity of the corporal schema is also in evidence in deixis, for, as we will see, perceptual and cognitive orientations receive the same dual engagement as does the spatial position of the body. In some cases, they are indexed as the ground from which objects are denoted, and in others they serve as both indexical ground and the figural referential objects themselves.

But even this combined approach to the corporeality of reference is incomplete insofar as it leaves out the intersubjective basis of the *schéma corporel* and also of the prefabricated schematic categories of the linguistic system. Speakers do not participate in communication as neatly bounded subjects but rather as parts of interactive frameworks, temporary occupants of relationally defined roles. Maya language encodes this sociocentrism in distinctions such as the relative asymmetry of all *-a’* deictics as opposed to the *-o’* forms, and the egocentricity of *way e’* 'here' and *tol o’* 'there', as opposed to the sociocentricity of *té’* 'there'. The interactive foundation of body space is a point on which both cognitive and phenomenological approaches are prone to break down. In arguing that the body is a ground of reference, one slips quickly into the assumption that the intersensorial unity in question belongs to just one person. In fact, as we will see in detail, the communicative process to which deictic reference is "posturally" adapted belongs to interactive frameworks in the first instance, and only secondarily to the individuals who occupy their subportions.

Thus we must look beyond the corporal schema as previously constituted and bring corporeality to the next level of the social space occupied by coparticipating parties to communication. The boundaries of corporeality, the limits on who can occupy what positions of social formations, the varieties of reciprocity (and their breakdowns) are all factors that lead us to posit a larger unit for the body, which we can call the *corporeal field*. Much of the present chapter is directed toward showing with ethnographic details how the *schéma corporel* of individual actors is subsumed and generalized through social relationships to encompass various interactive formations and processes. This chapter sketches the cultural definition of the living body in Maya, including its physical basis, actional orientation, and distinctive space. If there is a genuinely egocentric moment in deictic practice, it is linked to this space.

This chapter's discussion then places individual actors in the context of social relations around the homestead. The objective is to make it clear why we must look beyond the individual in order to account for regularities of referential speech. The marked status asymmetries among household members and their clear impact on language use are the themes of this discussion, which will lay the groundwork for the subsequent analysis of deictic space. There is a set of interactive genres that illustrate the consequences of social relations for conversational practice in Maya. The pragmatic conditions on who can engage in these genres, with whom, and under what conditions are part of the larger set of social conventions governing proper interaction among Maya. These in turn are reflected in the relative symmetry and asymmetry of the indexical ground of demonstrative reference. Thus, the idea of indexical symmetry, which may appear abstract or arbitrary in isolation, is a basis for relating aspects of utterance context with the differential rights and obligations of social actors engaging in the communicative process.

The final section returns to the question of how deixis is *embodied* in communication, and on the other hand, how communicative processes are embodied in deixis. We will discuss an extended example taken from recorded interactions in Maya. These show the interplay of many of the ethnographic phenomena described in the preceding sections of this chapter. More importantly, the examples will show how *schémas corporels* are produced in social situations according to the changing relevancies and positionings of the actors. The quasi-postural orientations in which Maya speakers engage during conversation derive, not from the order of prefabricated schematic concepts, nor from the locally variable *schéma corporel,* neither of which can account for the interactive adjustments inherent to ongoing practice. Rather, they drive from the interplay between these factors along with the (superindividual) corporeal field and the larger social field in which the interaction takes place.

The generalization of the corporal schema into a socially based field is part of another kind of generalization, one that involves the transposition of the indexical ground of reference from the body to more abstract aspects of communicative context. Thus, deixis can be grounded on previous discourse—as is clear in anaphoric uses—on fictional characters (whose corporeality can only be projected through memory or fantasy), or on aspects of utterance frameworks other than the body schemata. This brings us to a final point of broad significance to the study of referential practice, namely, the distinction between corporeality on the one hand and the more general phenomenon of embodiment on the other. Referential categories and practices can be embodied in aspects of activities that are not traceable to the body, just as the schematic structures involved in reference can be realized in aspects of sociocultural reality other than language. For instance, the schemata involved in deictic reference and in spatial descriptions in Maya are also embodied in such varied media as domestic floor plans, the principles according to which agricultural fields are bounded off, and the layout of shamanic altars. Disparate though these may appear, they are fundamentally related in Maya culture and serve to make the general point that, as Panofsky (1976) argued, visual and discursive production may be guided by a common set of controlling principles played out as mental (and bodily) habits.

CULTURE IN THE CORPOREAL FIELD

Materiality of the Body

The simplest representation of the human body in its physical aspect is the one used by shamans in ritual discourse.[2] The body is made up of the same elements as is the rest of the material world: a person's *wíinklil* 'body' is his or her *lú'um* 'earth'. One's breath and animacy are one's *-iik* 'wind'—also related to *yiik'al* 'force, heat of a fire, momentum', and *yiik'el* 'bees (of a hive), ants (swarming in the earth)'.[3] Like the earth and all animate objects on it, the human body has a *k'íinil* 'heat' of its own, evident in the opening and closing of pores, the passing of sweat, fever, anger, the coolness of relaxation, the chill of numbness, and numerous other bodily processes. This heat derives ultimately from the sun and must be held in a relatively delicate balance in order to safeguard the well-being of the individual. Through the double action of heat and the movement caused by the body's wind, the water of one's earth is transformed into *k'íik'el* 'blood'. These elemental relations are not wisely appreciated by nonspecialist Maya adults, although they are an important part of shamanic practices and descriptions. Most Maya people regularly attend to their corollaries: the balance of hot and cold is a ubiquitous concern in everyday life, as is the breath, the effect of wind on the individual, the flow of the blood, and the need for water. In the cures and other ritual discourse performed by shamans, these elements receive systematic representation and function as metonyms of the entire person. For instance, in the *tiíč'k'aák* 'divination', a diagnostic procedure, the divining crystals (*saástuún*) provide the shaman with a representation of the patient's earth, showing the location of any abnormal winds (Hanks 1984b,c). This is precisely the same mechanism that applies when the crystals are used to examine the "earth" of a homestead, thereby treating the body and the home as equivalent.[4] In the *saántiguar* prayer, in which an individual is blessed, and the *paá' 'iik'* 'drop wind' prayer, in which ill winds are exorcised, the earth of the person is presented, swept clean, and cooled (Hanks 1984c). The derivation of blood from water and the localization of distinct winds in different regions of the body are part of a larger system of specialized knowledge of body parts and processes. Shamans possess this knowledge as part of their technical specialization in health care for individuals, social groups, and their environment. It informs their schematic representations of the body, as well as their momentary orientations and understandings of particular bodies.

Animacy and Will

Beyond their bare material elements, human actors have two basic attributes that link them with other higher animates and that make it possible for them to engage in the world in a directed manner. These are the *-oól*, which covers roughly the will and the capacity for involvement and sensate experience, and the *-iík'* 'wind', understood in this context as 'awareness'. The term *-oól* also applies in standard usage to the heart of a tree, the sprouting center of a palm tree or plant, and the loaded ammunition in a rifle. It is inalienably possessed and when possessed by a human may be modified by any of a variety of adjectives including *kí'imak* 'happy', *siís* 'cold', *čokow* 'hot', *há'ak'* 'surprised', *naáy* 'becalmed', and *toh* 'straight (happy)'. The *-oól* can also be the object of transitive predications, such as *kušulik inwoól* 'it finishes my *-oól* (overwhelms me)', *kubèetik inwoól* '(s)he does my *-oól* (kids me)'. Other derivations include *kinwok'o-h'oó(l)tik* 'I beg (lit., weep *-oól-it*)', *kinwoó(l)tik* 'I want, wish', *yoólilil* 'on purpose, intentionally', *yah tinwoól* 'it pains me, I'm sorry', and *má' tuyoól yàan i'* '(s)he's not in his/her *-oól* (out of control, drunk or mad)'. The linkage between this aspect of the body and the actor's ability to formulate intentional action is a basic fact in Maya common sense, and references to the *-oól* are very common in daily discourse. At least one use of the term *-iik'* indicates that it too may stand for an individual's oriented awareness in his or her current context. When a person who is daydreaming or obliviously misperforming some task is called to attention by a superior, this is described as *tuk'á' asah yiik'* 'he snapped him out of it, got his attention (lit., reminded his wind)'. In most other contexts, the capacity for directed attention is derived from the *-oól* and associated most directly with focused gaze, to which we now turn.

Perceptual Field and Its Valuation

It is likely that, as Bühler (1982:126ff.) suggested, the senses of sight, hearing, and touch have a universal role in the micro-organization of social activities. Surely, normal communication requires the ability to perceive and be perceived. Yet this universal fact tells us nothing about how perceptual categories are mobilized, invested with significance, or how they are related to other forms of knowledge in human cultures and their communicative systems (Sahlins [1976] 1977). In Maya, there are two basic verbs of perceiving, *'ilik* 'to see (it)' and *'ú'uyik* 'to sense (it) (with any faculty other than sight)'. Both of these verbs are inherently transitive, that is, each implies an object. Although both may undergo passivization demoting the perceiver to a peripheral status 'It is seen (by me)', neither undergoes object demotion. There are no middle voice (objectless) forms for these verbs, although the middle voice is common elsewhere in the Maya verbal system (see Bricker 1978). In the case of *'ú'uyik* 'to sense', the mode of the perception depends entirely upon the object it takes.

Both of these verbs are associated with more than mere perception of objects. As in European languages, "seeing" in Maya is a typical metaphor for understanding, and speakers commonly ask their interlocutors if they "see" their point. An infant who shows quickness and awareness is said to have *saási yič* 'light (in) his or her eye'. 'See' in Maya also functions as a routine device for maintaining contact with an addressee. In this phatic function, the utterance *tawilik* ↑ 'Do you see? (get it?)' is very frequent in conversation and is subject to idiosyncratic phonological reduction, down to *talik, taik* (see Hanks 1983:116ff.). To "sense," on the other hand, is often understood to mean "to pay willful attention to." Checking on an addressee's attentiveness, speakers ask *tawú'uyik* ↑ 'Do you hear (it)?' This form does not collapse phonologically the way the corresponding one with "see" does, and it is (impressionistically) less frequent in conversation. This is perhaps because of the overtone of directivity often conveyed by the question, as in English "Do you hear?" "Are you listening to me?" when used to convey an order to pay attention. The utterance is power coded and therefore most likely to occur in asymmetric contexts where the speaker has the right to issue directives to the addressee. Parents scolding a child or friends calming down an angry or drunk companion might punctuate their speech with this question. The idea of paying aural attention to directive language without necessarily understanding it is aptly reflected in the Maya expression for 'attending mass', *ʔúʔuyik mìisa* 'to hear mass'. Moreover, a person said to *ʔúʔuyik tʔàan* 'hear speech' is understood to be reasonable, obedient, and respectful, while one who doesn't hear speech, *máʔa tuyúʔubʔik tʔàan,* is disobedient, rebellious, drunk, demented, in a rage, or otherwise intractable.[5] Thus the two basic verbs of perception also code understanding, the ability to "see" a situation, and attentive reasonableness, the ability to "hear, listen to it."[6]

There is another, less familiar association with vision in Maya, which foregrounds the agentive quality of gaze as a willful act. People and certain domestic animals are susceptible of conveying the "heat" in their own body to the body of an infant merely by gazing on the infant. This is particularly true of adult men sweating from physical labor, men or women shortly after sexual relations, and women menstruating, all of whom pose a real danger to any infant under about a year old. This phenomenon is known among the Maya as *ojo* 'eye', a familiar concept in Mesoamerican cultures where the hot-cold syndrome is found (Logan 1977; see Villa Rojas [1945] 1978: 386ff. and Hanks 1984c:134 for a fuller description of the Maya case). The illness results in diarrhea and possible dehydration of the child. It can be diagnosed by a shaman using crystals, who can see the excess heat in the infant's body and make hypotheses (on the basis of what he sees in the crystals) as to who gave the child the eye. This latter bit of information is crucial, because the fastest cure is to find the adult who caused the illness and have that person hold and touch the infant. The touching restores the child's own temperate body state, which calms the intestines. These things are known as a matter of common sense by adults, particularly mothers, and they motivate other patterns of behavior, such as covering infants with a mantle whenever they are in the presence of outsiders, to keep them out of sight.[7] Interestingly, while making visual contact is thus seen as a potentially effective act, aural contact is not. There are no objects or individuals that one can affect by listening to them, however fixedly and in whatever state of being the listener. An actor can *čʔehšikintik* 'cock one's ear (listening attentively)' as well as (s)he can stare, but the former has no recognized effect on the object, whereas the latter does. In prayer, shamans ask God to *sutk awič apaktikóʔon* 'turn your gaze to look on us', while the expression *paktik santo* 'looking at (a) saint' is an often heard oath of honesty (F.137.A.330). In both instances, directed gaze constitutes an effective bond between seer and object.[8] The term of gaze, *paktik* (verb) can be further modified to reflect anger, as in *ščʔeépaktik* 'to look angrily at from the side', *šleéʔpaktik* 'glare fixedly, angrily at', and *nunulpaktik* 'look up and down, side to side at (on the point of blows)'. One male speaker volunteered the revealing (if macho) hyperbole *tinšaáhšakčʔiíntik yeétel impàakat* 'I threw him down (to the ground) with my look' (BB.4.111).[9]

Bodily Orientation

The orientations and actional capacities of individuals, implicit in their physical states and processes, are given a more directly spatial representation in the ideas of *taánil/paàčil* 'front/back', *šnóʔoh/ščʔiík* 'right/left', and *yoókʔol/yàanal* 'up/down'. When applied to the human body (*schéma corporel*), the first axis is grounded in the visual field and normal forward locomotion of actors (see interesting discussions of body orientation in Bourdieu [1972] 1977; Bühler 1982:102ff.; Evans 1982:154ff.; Hallowell 1955; Talmy 1983). *taán* 'front' and *pàač* 'back' are noun roots that can also be possessed, as in *tintaán* 'to my front, in front of me', and *timpàač* 'to my back, in back of me'. Similarly, 'right' and 'left' can be possessed, as in *tinšnóʔoh* 'to my right' and *tinšč'iík* 'to my left'. The forms I have cited as 'up' and 'down' are actually invariably possessed relational nouns that could equally well be glossed 'over, atop' and 'under, below'. When the possessor is a human, they indicate the space above and below the person in the normal upright orientation—for a person lying face down on the ground, 'over' is to his back and under to his front. The center is not merely the body, then, but the body as it normally engages in movement and action (just as Merleau-Ponty's discussion of the phenomenal body would lead us to expect).

The spatial coordinates of bodily orientation also imply moral evaluations, and there is a strong association between up, front, and to the right as morally positive, and down, back, and to the left as morally negative. The vertical dimension is most systematically encoded in the cosmological premises and discourse forms of Maya shamans, where higher always implies more powerful and beneficent (Hanks 1984c). It is also a matter of common sense, however, appreciated by nonspecialists and reflected in daily expressions, such as *yàanal k'áaš* 'under the (wild and dangerous) woods', *yàanal haʔ* 'under water (describes an 'underhanded' deception)'. 'Front' and 'back' are, if anything, even more strongly associated with good and bad. Things from behind are dangerous, hidden, oppressing, while things in front are more likely to be benevolent, honest, and in clear view. The left hand is literally the 'angry' or 'sinister' one, being derived from the root *č'iík* 'angry, vicious' (as in swarming wasps and raging bulls). These aspects of corporeal orientation can be schematized as in figure 2.1.

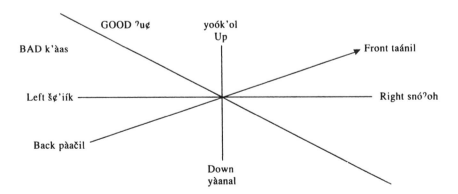

Fig. 2.1. Coordinates of body space.

Iknal as a Corporeal Field

In addition to the spatial coordinates and orientations described in the foregoing, there is one more concept that figures centrally in Maya speakers' commonsense grasp of bodily space.[10] This is the -*iknal* 'place', an inalienably possessed noun stem which denotes the proximal region around the object or individual functioning as possessor. When the possessor is human, the phrase conveys roughly 'in the company of X', or 'close to, alongside, with X'. It fits into a series of locational noun stems denoting the various social and personal spaces of an actor. These include one's -*otoč* 'house, abode' (inalienably possessed), *nah* 'house, fields, proximal region of', *kahtalil* 'homestead, residential compound', and the actor's several habitual workplaces, such as one's *soólar* 'yard, orchard', *paárseláa* '(irrigated) field', and *kòol* '(unirrigated) plot (*milpa*).' On one common reading, an individual's -*iknal* is equivalent to his or her *nah*, that is, the home or habitual place (BB.3.54; 12.B.630). Similarly, *kó'oš tinwiknal* 'Let's go to my place' is a routine way of inviting an addressee to come to visit one's home.

There is a second interpretation of -*iknal* in which it is not a fixed place that is owned the way a house is owned but a mobile field of action related to an agent the way one's shadow or perceptual field is. This is the sense linked to the bodily activity of a speaker. Although -*iknal* is usually possessed by a human noun, this need not always be the case, and one can speak of the -*iknal* of an animal, a tree, a well, or even a moving vehicle (as Man observed when discussing the term with me [BB.3.54]). Furthermore, the expression is vague as to where in the proximal zone of the object it refers, and there is no obvious sense that the orientational front of the object is a privileged referent of its 'place'. When used to refer to a place within one's homestead, the phrase *tinwiknal* 'in my place' is unambiguously interpreted in the bodily sense. Under face-to-face conditions, unless otherwise specified, the -*iknal* of either participant includes the other one as well. Hence, it denotes a joint interactive corporeal field containing reciprocal perspectives rather than an individual *schéma corporel*. When interactants are separated, and the current framework is relatively asymmetric, then the -*iknal* of a participant is typically egocentric, depending upon the perspective adopted. I have also attested uses of what appears to be a metaphorical extension from the bodily sense of the term, in which a speaker's -*iknal* was his or her habitual way of thinking or doing things.

The regional scope of one's -*iknal* 'place' is variable, as is the degree of remove at which speakers locate objects in vertical, horizontal, or lateral relation to themselves. Compared to the deictic *way e'* 'here', which is routinely used to refer to the entire homestead or work site, -*iknal* is interpreted more narrowly to denote the inner space of a single structure, such as the sleeping house. This inner space can be encompassed in a single visual field and is in practical reach of any adult within it. As Vic reasoned while discussing the meaning of the term -*iknal*, even if people standing inside a house are not mutually oriented, they are considered to be in a single -*iknal* so long as they are able to *hear* a single conversation (12.B.630). Bearing in mind the relation to per-

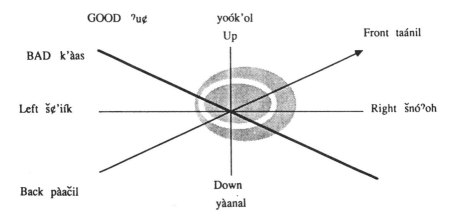

Fig. 2.2. Coordinates of body space with *-iknal* **(variable scope).**

ception, socially defined spatial boundaries, and shared body space, we can schematically represent the *-iknal* in figure 2.1 by adding a shaded zone around the point of intersection of the three orientational dimensions, as in figure 2.2. The shading should be understood to be situationally variable, according to the relative extent of the corporeal field in given contexts.

Corporeal Field and Centered Reference

There is a cliché in Maya that says that every person is a different world. People invoke this often when rationalizing perceived differences in character between individuals or misinterpretations of others' intentions. The thrust of the remark is that there are sharp limits on the degree to which one can know another person and share in his or her feelings. People interact on the basis of common assumptions and shared codes of proper conduct, summarized in the idea of *legalidad* 'legality, propriety', yet they are keenly aware that actors harbor hidden agendas, and that each person 'follows a different road'. The components of a person which most individuate him or her are the *tùukul* 'thought' and *náˀat* 'understanding'. Not only do people think differently, in ways knowable only through inference, but it is with their thought that they formulate plans, worry about things outside their current circumstances (the Maya equivalent for 'worry' is *sèentuklik* 'think intensely') and 'travel' through time and space without moving their bodies. Interlocutors cannot reasonably assume that they know each other's true agendas, or that they are really on the footings they appear to be on. These points were explained to me by three senior men on different occasions and are consistent with my own observations of how Maya people reason about persons, their motivations, and responsibilities. The people represented in this study are thus cognizant of the complexity of an individual's relation to his or her immediate actional context, and they are rarely inclined, in my experience, to take a person's representations at face value.

The physical existence of the body links it inextricably to the larger natural world through shared elements and processes of change in state, notably in terms of 'heat', 'wind', and 'dryness'. Individuals are taken to have different relative capacities for involvement, according to the states of their *-oól*, and their perceptual apparatus determines a unique field of sensate experience. Their ability to comment on their sensate experiences, which Maya speakers routinely do in the course of expressing opinions of most kinds, rests on the kind of reflexive *prise de conscience* that was fundamental to the *schéma corporel* as Merleau-Ponty defined it. Perception is closely related to the interpretation of sensory and other data, as well as the ability to participate reasonably in social interaction. The body defines an oriented egocentric space with an up, down, front, back, right, and left, in which the first term of each pair is morally superior to the second. This central place, at the intersection of the three axes, is also described as the *-iknal* 'bodily space'. The entire cultural construction of the body, which I have likened to Merleau-Ponty's *schéma corporel,* gives substantive content to the idea of "egocentricity" in Maya, because it constitutes the individual body in motion that we posit in the central role of speaker. But it is already evident that body space so defined is culturally saturated, and that through social interaction, it is routinely occupied by groups of coparticipating agents.

The Maya with whom I worked are keenly aware that individuals exist within networks of social relations, that they share knowledge, experience, and goals, that they are constrained by a common sense of acceptable behavior, and that they live out comparable life courses. The ideological commitment to the uniqueness of individuals holds only within a presupposed frame of social reference. This social frame unavoidably impinges on our understanding of verbal deixis, because it provides a basic set of common referents that speakers know they share as a matter of course. By situating the individual actor within a series of social relations, we prepare the ground for situating egocentric reference within the encompassing social field in which it occurs. As a preliminary indication of what is at stake, consider the category *-iknal.*

A person's *-iknal* 'place' corresponds quite closely, on one reading, to his or her 'egocentric space' as discussed by Evans (1982); the immediate sphere of bodily activity, at the center of the vertical, horizontal, and lateral axes of space. Unlike paradigmatic egocentric space, the Maya *-iknal* may be possessed by inanimates (meaning 'around, near x') or by more than one interactant—one can speak of 'our *-iknal*' in a way that it would not make sense to speak of 'our egocentric space'. Furthermore, the *-iknal* may be interpreted as referring to an individual's home, not his or her present perceptual-actional context. In both of these ways, an individual, apparently egocentric place may be grounded in the social relations built upon coparticipation in the shared here and coresidence in the shared homestead.

The play between genuinely egocentric and sociocentric dimensions of context also emerges in deictic use. There is a categorial distinction between the two kinds of space in the locative adverbial roots, a fact which demonstrates the necessity of including the distinction in the universal repertoire of deictic oppositions. In the terminal deictics, the play between ego- and sociocentric frames shows up in the opposition between *-aɁ* and *-oɁ* terminals. The former indicate referents immediate to the speaker or newly introduced, and the latter indicate referents farther off or already known by both interactants. Thus, *-aɁ* marks assymmetrically available referents, such as parts of the speaker's own body, and *-oɁ* marks the common ground of shared knowledge. As Maya speakers can readily report, however, the asymmetric *-aɁ* forms are most properly used when the two interactants are already in a face-to-face relation, so that the addressee can perceive the precisely indicated referent. Thus, the asymmetry is a limited one which presupposes reciprocity of perspectives. The *-oɁ* forms, on the other hand, tend to be the ones mobilized when interactants are conversing over a distance or are separated by other physical or social boundaries.

This pattern of use has the consequence that egocentric space becomes an object of individuated reference in Maya speech just when there is a face-to-face relation already established between participants. Even though speakers talk over various kinds of remove, they make referential divisions in their immediate zone pretty much only when their addressee is close at hand. Thus, egocentricity comes into play in indexical reference under sociocentrically defined conditions.

THE *SOLAR* UNIT: SOCIAL RELATIONS IN THE HOMESTEAD

Comaroff and Roberts (1981) show that the Tswana conception of the house "embodies both a set of primary social values and elementary structural forms, along with the principles of their reproduction and elaboration" (49). This native conception is the point of origin of the value oppositions and structural elements contained in what Comaroff and Roberts call the constitutive order, to which they oppose the lived-in (experienced) universe (68). My claim here is different but related: the Maya household as a social organization embodies principles of segmentation, reciprocity, and asymmetry that are the basis of communicative patterns, particularly those which involve reference to or interaction in domestic space. In other words, the divisions and relations between coresident social groups are played out in spatial (and temporal) boundaries around the household, which in turn condition speakers' referential and other communicative practices. Alongside body space, domestic space is one of the core sources of schematic knowledge engaged in the conventional structure and use of deixis (cf. Friedrich [1964, 1970] 1979).

The basic residential unit in contemporary Yucatán is the *solar* 'yard, homestead', also commonly called *kahtalil* 'homestead' when it is located in a rural area. Residence units range in size from a single nuclear family, parents and children, to three, or rarely four, nuclear families related by descent through the males. Up to four generations may be represented in a single extended household, although two to three are apparently more common. As Villa Rojas ([1945] 1978:236) showed for east central Quintana Roo, Redfield and Villa Rojas ([1934] 1962:90) for Chan Kom, and Thompson (1974:27 ff.) for Ticul, contemporary households in Oxkutzcab are of several types, whose variation is partly accounted for by the developmental cycle of the family. Following Fortes (1958), Thompson proposes four phases in a single "temporal pattern": establishment of the autonomous household of a single family with a child; expansion, as the elder sons marry, bringing wives into the home and producing children; dispersion, as daughters marry out and elder sons gain financial independence, allowing them to move out and establish their own homes; and replacement, when the founding couple die and are replaced as heads of household by the remaining son and family. While far from invariant, this cyclic pattern sheds light on the homes with which we shall be concerned in this discussion.

One aspect of households that the developmental perspective clarifies is the obvious fact that they change over time. In 1977, for instance, DP and DA resided in a single *kahtalil* with their two youngest sons, both of whom are married, with one and two children, respectively. By 1985, the two sons had six children apiece and resided together in a single *kahtalil*, with DP and DA, the founding pair, now living in their own household nearby but not adjoining the sons. DP (the male head of the family) explained this move by saying that with twelve children around, there was no peace and quiet (an understatement to say the least). Similarly, in 1978, DC, a senior male whose estranged wife resides in Mérida, lived in a single *solar* in Oxkutzcab along with a seventeen-year-old unmarried son, whereas in 1985, the same *solar*, with additional house structures, is home to DC and all three of his sons, two of whom are married, with four children and one child, respectively. In terms of phases, the case of DP and DA appears to illustrate expansion, dispersion, and ultimate replacement of the senior couple by their eldest son as head of household. (Although replacement was motivated by expansion, not by death of the senior couple.) DC's home was in a state of dispersion in 1978 and was greatly expanded in following years, indicating that the order of phases is not invariant. Is and his wife, another Oxkutzcabeño couple, live in the (urban) *solar* they established shortly after marriage, sharing it today with their two sons, of whom the eldest is married with two children. Their original purchase of the house was explained to me as a necessity, because there was no room in the house of Is's father when they got married (BB.4.115). At the time, Is's younger brother was residing with his parents in the paternal *solar*, along with his wife and children, making it a three-generational homestead in the process of dispersing. Balim and Chio, two other adult men, currently reside in their own households with their wives and unmarried children, putting them at the early stages of expansion. Chio, whose oldest son is ten years old, is distinctly oriented toward this expansion and has recently acquired two plots of land adjacent to his own. He explained the acquisition as a way of preparing a place of residence for his son with his eventual wife. (The *solar* in which they currently reside is judged too small.)

Land is inherited through the male line, passing from father to son, and the *solar* is, under ideal circumstances, a sign of the persistence of the patriline. Chio's acquisition of lands for eventual transferal to his son is a common strategy, also employed by DP, who between the mid 1970s and 1985 systematically acquired rights over four plots of rural land, totaling approximately fifty mecates (a measure of surface area 20 by 20 meters), which he distributed among his three adult sons. These lands include mature fruit orchards and make up a considerable domain of family production as well as residence. On the other hand, DC's current situation illustrates the pitfalls of not acquiring land for one's sons, since his urban *solar* is his only land, measuring just three mecates. For lack of productive land, his two eldest sons have been forced to seek nonagricultural work as masons, tailors, and day laborers. Moreover, since the strip of the family plot belonging to DC proper will be passed on to his youngest son when he dies, the three brothers will be forced to live within the walls of a single *so-lar*. This prospect is disturbing to the two elder brothers and their wives, since the youngest is perceived to be dishonest and *k'asáʔan* 'rotten' (BB.4.67).[11]

Residence Patterns: *ʔilib'ȼil, háʔankab'ȼil*

From the perspective of the residence choices of newly formed married pairs, the Maya conventionally distinguish between two formations: (i) transitory uxorilocal residence, called *háʔankab'ȼ il,* from *háʔan* 'daughter's husband', in which the son-in-law resides temporarily with the parents of his wife; (ii) enduring patrilocal residence, called *ʔilib'ȼil,* from *ʔilib'* 'son's wife', in which the wife resides in the home of her husband's parents. Villa Rojas ([1945] 1978:238) documents that the former pattern was quite common in Quintana Roo, but it appears relatively rare in Oxkutzcab, as it was in Chan Kom (Redfield and Villa Rojas [1934] 1962:91 cite just one case out of 45 households). Among current Oxkutzcabeños, the son-in-law who resides with his wife's parents is considered either very docile, for submitting to the will of his parents-in-law, or in an unfortunate position (BB.4.58). DC recounted the problems he had had during his own period of *háʔankab'ȼil,* necessitated by the death of his own father; he had worked happily in the fields of his father-in-law "as a beloved son," but came into irreconcilable conflict with his mother-in-law, who persisted in undermining his authority over his wife. According to DC, the conflict ultimately caused the death of his wife, his first of three (F.140.B–142.B, recorded 2/2/87). Among the ten or so households with which I am familiar, there are no instances of uxorilocal residence, but eight include, or anticipate, patrilocal residence. Depending upon the number of sons in the family and how narrowly one defines the *solar* unit, such households may include between one and three or even four women brought in by marriage. In such cases, the husband's patrilocal household becomes the primary one with which the woman identifies. She thereby enters into a relation of subordination to the parents-in-law and ranking relative to coresident sisters-in-law. Ranking is apparently in terms of the birth order of their husbands, although in the cases with which I am familiar, this coincides with the relative age of the women.

While uxorilocal residence is apparently short-lived, patrilocal residence tends to persist, subject to independent processes of dispersion, because the residential *solar*

itself is inherited through the male line. In being incorporated, the new bride is sub-
jected to the evaluation of the more senior members of her husband's household, and
not all cases run as smoothly as the ideal. One woman told of having been rejected by
her husband's mother, who ended up accusing her of witchcraft and infidelity, both
of which she denied. She was forced to live with her own mother and to make her
cooking fire in her mother's kitchen, so as to avoid the other sister-in-law residing in
the husband's household. She eventually came to blows with her husband, who sided
with his coresidents, and they split up, leaving her to raise six children alone
(F.147.A.020). This example points up the potential stresses on the daughter-in-law
who is incorporated into the *solar* of the husband, even though it is the inverse case,
where the son-in-law is incorporated into the wife's parents' household, that is considered the most fraught with difficulty.

Head of Household

Every *solar* unit has a head in the person of the senior resident, usually male, who is
recognized as the highest authority in decisions affecting the household, whose name
is used to refer to the entire collection of residents and to whom the *solar* belongs
legally. Typically, the head of household is the eldest man, although in some cases it
is a widowed or divorced female. In female speech, it is usually the wife of the senior
male who is referred to as the head of household. The practice of using the name of
the head of household to refer to the whole group can be seen in examples such as the
following.
     Coming from Mérida to Oxkutzcab after having been away for a year, I met up
with the father of DP's coresident daughter-in-law. I asked him, *kuš tuún DP, biš anih*
'What about DP, how is he?' intending to refer to DP himself. The man responded
by describing the household members one by one, taking DP as a metonym of the
whole group of which he was head (BB.4.53). Maya speakers commonly use the expression *letióʔob don Hulano* 'them Mr. So-and so' to refer to the members of So-and-
so's household. The phrase combines plural marking on the pronoun with the apparently singular personal title. This combination would be ungrammatical if the proper
name were not interpretable as referring to a plurality of referents, since the pronoun
and name are automatically coreferential in this construction. On the other hand,
Toni refers to the household of her father as *nal inmàamah* 'my mother's place', and
Pilar refers to the home of her parents-in-law as *nal inswèegra* 'my mother-in-law's
place'. These usages are typical of the indexical pattern according to which women refer to the households by way of the senior woman.
     While "head" of household is defined by seniority and ownership, individuals ac-
tually exercise different degrees of authority around the house. DP and DA (senior
husband and wife) take a very active role in supervising the daily conduct of their two
youngest sons, both of whom are over thirty, with wives and six children apiece. The
sons reside in a *solar* given them by DP, and his exercise of authority includes often
daily walks through the house and kitchen of the sons, barking orders, and little crit-

icisms at the residents. DA follows a similar pattern in relation to her daughters-in-law, who are made to toe the line. DC, on the other hand, heads a household of three sons, two daughters-in-law, and five grandchildren, but does so with very little display of authority and an almost deferential avoidance of interfering. While DP and DA peruse the domestic space with impunity, DC gently enters his sons' homes only when beckoned or expected and expresses opinions about their actions, rather than telling them what to do. It is the sons, and not the father in this home, who set the tenor of daily life, even though they respect and defer to the father without protest when he does speak.

Is's place is another illustration of the same point, that heads of household may wield less than absolute authority. When I was discussing family history with him on February 2, 1987, he explained to me that he had forbidden his daughter to wear short pants outside the homestead, a practice he finds immodest, even though it is encouraged by grammar school teachers. Inside the *solar*, it was acceptable. Furthermore, he had told his coresident son to tell his wife and their children the same thing. So long as the wife and children are in the son's house (within the same walled *solar*), the son is charged with seeing to it that they dress properly, but when they pass through Is's house, *he* is the authority and can impose his will. Since his house is located directly in front of the main entrance to the *solar*, virtually everyone who enters or leaves comes under his gaze. This notwithstanding, he observed with a smile that when he is not there, for instance, when he stays at his *milpa* for several days at a time, the women do not follow his rules (BB.4.117). Were he to exercise the kind of force that DP does in his home, he would probably have told his daughter-in-law directly how to dress instead of telling his son to tell her.

Coresidents: Affinal and Consanguineal

Pulling together these observations on *solar* units, we can summarize the typical sets of coresidents as including the boxed portions of figures 2.3 and 2.4, the former showing consanguines and the latter affines. While all coresidents are normatively solidaristic, there is a special link between first-degree consanguines, particularly brothers and parent-offspring pairs. Offsetting this is the potential for competition and estrangement between brothers as they begin to inherit property.[12] DP's three sons appear to show a standard pattern, according to which juniors defer to seniors, and all stick together in relation to outsiders, yet they are indirectly critical of one another and less than totally trusting. For instance, MC once explained that if a man's brother were allowed to simply enter his home in his absence, the brother would surely seduce his wife, a morally repugnant but apparently plausible possibility. Thus brothers are individuals with whom one must be vigilant. DC's elder sons, as mentioned above, feel the bond of fraternal affection for their younger brother yet assert that he is a good-for-nothing whose presence in their household is a direct threat to the upbringing of their children.

Coresident affines, on the other hand, beyond the nuclear marriage pair, seem typically to have ambiguous relations. In particular, the relation between daughter-in-law and mother-in-law is prone to stress, while those between daughter-in-law and father-in-law, and wife and husband's brother, are based on avoidance. A daughter-in-law addresses her husband's parents (especially the father) rarely and only for specific purposes. While the mother may work daily with the daughter-in-law and develop obvious solidarity with her (like DA with Pilar, the wife of her son; they frequently work together and share a single kitchen), the father tends to address her only for the purpose of directing her behavior, and even then usually through her husband. Brothers, in my experience, almost never address or even acknowledge the presence of their brother's wife. Sisters-in-law are in a relatively symmetrical relation and may develop mutual affinity, but are ranked according to the relative age of their husbands and the length of time in the household. Thus, the primary affinal relations in the household are potentially troublesome and expected stress points in the social network. Secondary affinal relations, such as wife to husband's brother's children, or to husband's grandparents, are more variable and not subject to conventional avoidance.

Noncoresident affines, and in particular the wife's parents, are relatively distant relations whose presence is limited to periodic visits. One young wife explained that her parents had come to visit her in her husband's home just two times in the two

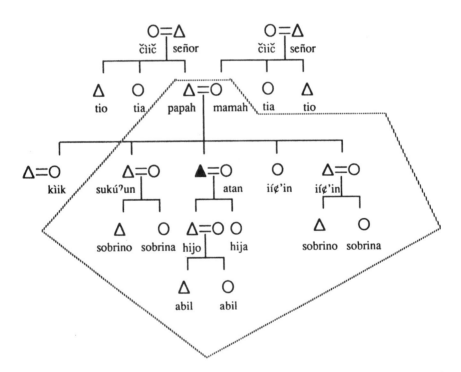

Fig. 2.3. Solar coresidents: consanguineal. Enclosed portion of figure indicates typical coresidents in a single extended household.

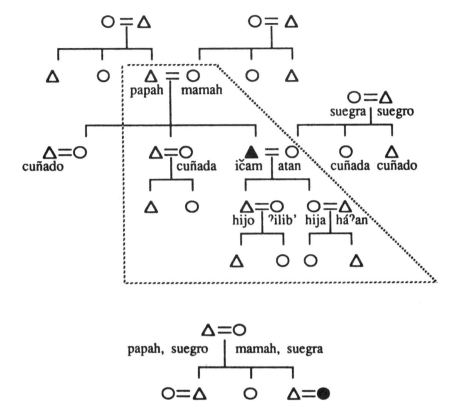

Fig. 2.4. Solar coresidents: affinal.

years of her marriage, even though they reside in Tekax, less than twenty minutes away by bus. Despite her deep affection for her father, he had not visited during that period, and she actually assumed that he had died and that her mother was hiding this fact from her to shield her from grief (F.137.A.210, 240). Another woman, a mother of six married for seven years, had not visited her parents for over a year, although they resided in Mani, just ten kilometers from Oxkutzcab. Her husband drives a truck which could easily provide transportation for visits, but they rarely go, except for the periodic *wàahil kòol* 'bread of (the) *milpa*' thanksgiving ceremony, at which the extended family and friends gather en masse. Typically, among these people, the relation between a woman and her parents is very diminished after marriage, and that between a man and his parents-in-law remains civil and somewhat distant.

Relation Terms for Household Members

Figures 2.3 and 2.4 are labeled with the standard Maya terms used to describe kinsmen, most of which agree with the usage reported in other ethnographic descriptions
(Redfield 1941:chap. 8; Redfield and Villa Rojas [1934] 1962:93; Thompson 1974:
31; Villa Rojas [1945] 1978:245). In the brief glosses in table 2.1, the first column
shows the canonical referential form which would appear in the possessive frame [*'in-
____*] 'my X'; unless otherwise indicated, the forms are inalienably possessed, mean-
ing that nonpossessed tokens in referential function receive special marking (to be described presently). The second column shows the "vocative" form used in addressing
the individual. The main formal difference between referential and vocative variants
is the tendency toward high pitch on the final syllable or rising final contour in voca-

TABLE **2.1** Relation Terms for Household Members

Referential	Vocative	Gloss
màamah	mámih	mother
papah, tàata	pápah	father
yùum	yuúm	father (esp. gods)
ʔìihoh, ʔìihah, pàal	ʔíihoh, ʔíihah, paál	son, daughter
čìič	čiči^ʔ	grandmother, either side
señor	señór	grandfather, either side
káʔaseñor	?	great grandfather, either side
àab'il*ᵃ*	paál	grandchild
káʔaʔàab'il	paál (?)	great grandchild
sukúʔun	sukúʔun	elder brother
kìik	kiík	elder sister
ʔiiɟ'in	ʔiiɟ'in	younger sibling (either sex)
tìiyo	tío	uncle (FBr, MBr, FSiHu, MSiHu)
tìiya	tía	aunt (FSi, MSi, MBrWi, FBrWi)
sóobrinóoh	sobríinoh	BrSo, SiSo, HuBrSo, WiBrSo, HuSiSo, (WiSiSo)*ᵇ*
sóobrináah	sobríinah	BrDa, SiDa, HuBrDa, WiBrDa, HuSiDa, WiSiDa
atan*ᵃ*	—*ᵇ*	wife
ičam*ᵃ*	—*ᵇ*	husband
swèegroh	swéegroh	husband's or wife's father
swèegrah	sweégrah	husband's or wife's mother
háʔaŋ	—*ᵇ*	daughter's husband
ilib'	—*ᵇ*	son's wife
kunyàadoh	kunyádoh	WiBr, SiHu
kunyàadah	kunyádah	BrWi, HuBrWi

*ᵃ*Absence of initial glottal stop / ʔ/ following possessive pronoun; presence of glottal stop in *ʔiiho*
indicates "hard" glottal, co-occurs with preconsonantal pronouns.
*ᵇ*Unattested.

tives. These are only the most standard terms, and their actual use is subject to various pragmatic conventions which we will not treat here.

In addition to these expressions, there are numerous common phrases that may occur possessed or nonpossessed, especially for spouses: *šnoh wíinik* 'wife (lit., fem. great human)', *šnuk t'uúl* 'wife (lit., fem. great rabbit)', *šbyèeyhah* 'wife (lit., fem. old lady)', *faáamilyáah* 'wife', *byèeyhoh* 'husband (lit., old man)'.

When used in the nonpossessed form to make reference, certain inalienably possessed relation terms are marked by the suffix *-ɛil*. These include mainly the first-order consanguineal terms for mother, father, all siblings, husband, and wife, as well as daughter-in-law and son-in-law. Recall that the terms for in-law residence also contain the suffix, *háʔankaʔ-ɛil* and *ʔiíɛʔin-ɛil.* Cf. *màama-ɛil* '(a) mother', *tàata-ɛil* '(a) father', *sukúʔun-ɛil* '(an) elder brother', *ʔiíɛʔin-ɛil* '(a) younger sibling', *laák'-ɛil* 'siblings', etc. The same suffix is used with the nonpossessed stem *yùun-ɛil* 'owner, lord', but with the specialized meaning 'Lord (God)'. While possessed *ʔu-yùum-il* is commonly used to refer to a human owner of property, the *-ɛil* form is restricted to spiritual lords and appears to convey a deferential, loving regard for the referent.

Rank and Seniority around the House

There are quite distinct status asymmetries among the members of a Maya household in terms of which individuals pay and receive deference. While the signs of deference in action are complex and often subtle, the principles of status assignment are evidently simple: elder is superior to younger, and male is superior to female. It is unclear to me whether generational precedence overrides age in cases such as an uncle younger than his nephew, and it is also unclear whether the relative age of brothers determines the relative rank of their wives or whether it is the age or length of time in the household that determines it. In the households under study, these dimensions coincided. Among brothers, age ranking is especially significant, with the younger normatively being obedient to the elder and avoiding all criticism of him. The strength of this bond is evident in the reticence of men to criticize their elder brother, their expected submission to his criticism, and their recognition that he has greater rights over collective undertakings than they do. A pointed example of this occurred on February 4, 1987, as I was making a floor plan of DC's *solar*, discussing the water tank in the yard with Lol, the younger brother of Man. The two brothers had built the water-tank together, a rectangular concrete box approximately 3 by 2.5 meters on the sides by 1.5 meters high. The tank lies partly on Lol's land and partly on Man's, and the water is shared property, just as the water from the hose at the front of the yard and the electricity are shared. But Lol explained that actually, since Man was his elder brother, the water tank was built more on his land than on Lol's. Even though the water seeks its own level and is used in common, the *sukúʔunɛil* gets a sign of respect, *ʔumpʼeéh respèetoh* (BB.4.62). Similarly, the precedence of male over female is reflected vividly in the expected submissiveness of wives to the will of their husbands, the acceptability of occasional wife beatings, and the expectation that husbands will circulate freely in the community, but wives will be either in their home or out on an errand sanctioned by their husbands. In elder sister–younger brother relations, it is uncertain to me which is considered superordinate, since it is their solidarity which is emphasized. In all asymmetric interactions, paying respect in word and attitude is called *çiik*, as in *k-in-çiik-ik⁹ impapah* 'I pay respect to my father'. This mode of speech is described briefly later in this chapter.

Social Zones of the *Solar*

As a social space, the *solar* is bounded off from the outside world and internally divided into areas corresponding to each of the nuclear families residing within it. I wish to make the more basic point that the social organization of residents is a fundamental part of domestic space. This has consequences for how speakers conduct themselves verbally around the house, as well as how they make reference to its subdivisions. To begin with, there are binding rules on how nonresidents enter a Maya homestead. They announce their presence at the outer entrance, by knocking on the door if it is within reach of the street and by calling out if it is not. According to native testimony and my own observations, it is considered rude and *sub'çil* 'shameful' to cross the outer threshold until told to by an adult resident (F.137.B.046), preferably the most senior individual present at the time. In urban households, where the front door of the main house is often right at the street entrance to the yard, women frequently place their sewing machines to the side of the front door, giving them a view of all who pass by, as well as those who enter. Visitors who enter are usually received in the main house, or at or just inside the front gate. For example, on February 2, 1987, I visited Is, whom I had known as an acquaintance for ten years. When I arrived at the door, his wife was sitting at her sewing machine in the doorway and invited me in, saying *⁹òoken don Wiíl!* 'Come in Don Will'. She offered me a chair directly in front of her machine and continued sewing as we talked. One of the children came through the house, and she told him to go tell Is that I was here. About fifteen minutes later, he showed up (BB.4.114). If, on the other hand, a group of strangers comes to the gate of the house, only one will properly enter, and the rest will wait outside.

When entering a multifamily *solar*, an adult of one family usually does not invite a visitor to enter the space of another, unless the visitor already has a privileged relation to the members of the house. In DC's *solar*, the practice is different, because DC is a *hmèen* 'shaman', who receives patients in his home on a regular basis. Patients, called *⁹ú⁹ulab* 'arrivers', routinely enter his yard and approach his front door (set back approximately thirty feet) *as they announce themselves*, rather than calling out and waiting for his response. All members of the household except the youngest children habitually respond, telling the patients to enter. A typical scenario occurred when one woman called out *tàal téelóo* 'Coming in theeere!' while tentatively entering the yard from the street. Margot, the senior daughter-in-law, responded by leaning outside the door of her kitchen, some fifty feet away, shouting *ʔòok en iʔiʔ* 'Go on in there!' the standard response. DC's front door was closed and he was nowhere in sight as the woman opened the door and slowly entered the house. She called out once again, using the same expression, but after entering, causing Margot to chuckle, since the 'there' in the greeting is appropriate when uttered from the gate, whereas the woman was already inside (BB.4.66, 82).

Except in cases like the foregoing, where the home of one *solar* member is a place of regular transaction with outsiders, it is the head of the immediate family—the husband or wife—who may bid one to enter. While there are virtually never walls or fences dividing the inner space of the *solar*, there are very sharply defined areas corresponding to the property lines of the males.[13] After the early years of marriage, each adult son is owner of his own section, and household members attend respectfully to the divisions. In DC's household, the total area is divided into three strips, belonging to him and each of his two oldest sons. Similarly, DP's *solar* is divided into four areas corresponding to him and his three sons. Chio's yard is divided in half between him and his older brother; even though the latter does not reside there, the land is his by inheritance and remains untouched by Chio. These divisions are not always apparent to outsiders, because they are marked only by inconspicuous boundary stones or sight lines between physical features, but they constitute real boundaries which constrain the circulation of actors in daily life.

The most immediate sign of the divisions is the fact that each marriage unit has its own *nah* 'house' where members sleep and store valuables, including the family *sàanto* shrine, hammocks, rifles, clothing, and important documents. Traditional Maya kitchens are in separate thatch structures, set within the yard behind the main houses. While one resident daughter-in-law may share the kitchen of the senior woman, relatively independent wives usually have their own kitchens, and this is the center of their personal domains.[14] The grouping of main house plus kitchen is the basic residential structure of the marriage unit within the *solar*.

The divisions between component homes in the household are evident in the paths taken by visitors. In DC's *solar*, each of his sons has his own entrance way, and visitors to one house do not cross through the yard of another, even when this is the most direct route to their destination. At about 9:00 A.M. on January 30, 1987, a *mestiza* (woman dressed in traditional huipil) appeared at the gate of DC's house and addressed Margot, the wife of Man. She had come to be fitted for an article of clothing that Lol was going to sew. As she came through DC's entrance to the yard, assuming she had arrived, Margot informed her that Lol's place was next door, saying:

(1)   má' way e' → té' tulaá' um p'eé nah o'
        'Not here, there at the other house.'

Although they are all within the same walled *solar*, the order of houses is (south to north) DC (head), Man (elder son), then Lol (younger son), side by side facing the street, such that the woman would have to walk through Man's courtyard to get from DC's house to Lol's. When Margot responded to her, the woman laughed, saying she did not even know which door to enter by. Rather than continue through the yard, however, she re-exited from the homestead and walked down to Lol's door by way of the street. I later told Lol of the incident, and he said the woman had responded in the natural way, since one does not just walk through someone else's yard (BB. 4.20;nF.137.B.015).

The internal divisions of domestic space constrain residents as well as outsiders. Physically mature males do not enter the kitchen of their brother's wife, nor of their aunt, without being invited by the brother or uncle. The motivation for this is the deep symbolic link between the *k'oób'en* 'kitchen' and the woman who tends the *k'oób'en* 'cooking fire' from which the structure gets its name. Nor does one enter the *nah* 'house' of another without invitation, since, as they say, someone might be dressing or bathing, and to enter would violate their privacy (BB.4.107). Women too are responsive to these constraints and generally remain outside others' living quarters, conversing with one another while working in the courtyard area. Children under about the age of twelve play and squall throughout the *solar,* crossing boundaries freely. In some cases though, such as DP's extended *solar,* different family units may have their own dogs, who stake out the family turf and constitute a very real impediment to perambulation, even for children (and turkeys and piglets).

The independence of marriage units within a single *solar* is based also on their relative economic independence from one another. In all of the households under study, the land is officially divided into parcels owned by the individual men, and the men work their own fields, orchards, or in other occupations apart from their siblings. They harvest separately and keep separate the money derived from selling produce at market. Domestic animals such as bulls, pigs, turkeys, chickens, pigeons, and goats are owned by individuals or married couples. Firewood, food, medicine, and miscellaneous household commodities are acquired and consumed by individual marriage units. To my knowledge, no tasks around the household are rotated among residents of different nuclear families; each family cares for its own parcel and its own affairs. Although there is much cooperation and an ethos of solidarity among coresident families, in virtually all joint undertakings, the separate contributions of the individual families are reckoned.

The separation between families in the *solar* is played out in myriad ways in the daily interactions of residents. As a temporary resident of DC's place for five weeks during 1987, I was able to observe in some detail how extended family members attended to their location and movement within the household, as well as to mine. Eating together is an important form of sociality in Maya culture, and I found that each brother and his wife wanted me, as honored guest, to eat in *their* kitchen, as reflected in the following extract from my field notes from January 29:[15]

> Sitting in the eating area (5) of Lol and Fi's place. Fi is ironing a shirt on the table next to me, while Lol and his friend play guitar and sing in the adjoining room (6). Fi has just

served me coffee and sweet rolls for evening *uk'ul* 'supper (lit., 'drink', used for both morning and evening meal).' She knows that I am waiting to have supper at Margot's table, but insists I have some there too. . . . Shortly later, Margot calls me next door to her table for supper. She poked her head into Lol's eating area (5), without entering. Shortly later, when I was sitting at Margot's table (1) over supper with DC, Fi appeared at the back door, and watched us without saying anything, nor entering. (BB.4.19)

In subsequent discussion, Fi assured me that she never cooks at the oven of Margot, and that even though the *solar* is one big family without any divisions, each family still has its own *-otoč* 'house' (F.137.A.529). That evening, the entire group ate together at the table of Man and Margot in celebration of my return. Fi breastfed her several-month-old infant at the table, but whereas she does this without covering her breast or the child when in her own home (even in my presence), here, in the company of coresidents, she covered herself, as she would were she "outside" (BB.4.47). In interactions with these families, as well as with DP's and a number of others, another fact became clear: when a guest, such as I, visits one home in the *solar*, this is not equivalent to visiting the entire *solar*. During my residence with DC as well as with DP, I was expected to visit the coresident families periodically in their own domains, to eat, wash up, or just converse in *their* house. Because women spend most of their time working in their own home and rarely go visiting without a recognized goal, a sleep-in visitor at a coresident house can go for days or weeks and hardly ever see the woman of the adjoining house. Particularly with third-level coresidents, who are on the other side of an objective divide, one might never lay eyes on the woman of the next house, especially if she is of childbearing age.

Despite their basic distinctness, marriage units cooperate and collaborate, overlaying their given social and sociospatial relations with bonds of joint interest and mutual regard. DC, Man, and Lol share the cost as well as consumption of electricity and municipal water in the household. They freely share tools such as machete, pick ax, chisel, hoe, hose, and knife (BB.4.28), although specialized tools like rifles, sewing machines, DC's divining crystals, and stereo recorders are not borrowed (cf. Villa Rojas [1945] 1978:241). They jointly construct various domestic structures like houses, kitchens, walls, and water tanks. Despite assertions to the contrary, Fi and Margot, like the sisters-in-law at DP's house, do occasionally cook for or with one another (F.137.B.160). For instance, on January 30, the entire group ate at Margot's table, but it was Fi who prepared the food at her fire next door (BB.4.26). As the single head of household, DC heats water for bathing on Margot's cooking fire and eats at her table daily (BB.4.86). While the two adult women currently wash laundry and dishes separately, in the past they shared a single *bateya* 'washing basin'. In DP's extended family, an analogous range of generalizations obtains, with the addition that the men coordinate their efforts to obtain irrigation water from the municipio and to transport produce from their fields to the market, some twelve kilometers away by paved road.

It is convenient to view residence patterns around Oxkutzcab in terms of three concentric circles. The first is the individual marriage pair with their offspring and possessions, the second the union of coresidents within a single walled *solar,* and the third the union of adjoining or adjacent *solars* of agnatic kinsmen. The first level marks the individual's "core" home, his enduring *-iknal* 'place'. This is where he is when he is home, or as the Maya say it, *kulá'an* 'seated'. At the second level of inclusion, coresidents of the *solar* share utilities and typically undertake certain collaborative projects together, such as building or repairing the wall around the household. They usually share a single courtyard through which members routinely pass, even if the living structures are not all oriented the same way to it. Some households at this level are more tightly integrated than others, but the ideal model is one of solidarity. This is the level of household corresponding to the beneficiary of the traditional Maya purification ceremony called *heéc lú'um* 'fixing earth'. The *solar,* as defined by the walled (or otherwise marked) perimeter, sets the limits of the space purified in the ceremony, and the residents of that space are the ones who pay for and benefit from it. The third level of inclusion is the most tenuous, since it encompasses both adjoining *solars* separated by a marked boundary and adjacent ones separated by up to hundreds of meters and perhaps several nonkin neighbors. What links the third-level set together is the bond of agnation between the heads of household. This usually implies solidarity and a common biography in which one or another of the households was the one from which all the brothers came.[16] Furthermore, it implies a ranking of the households by the age and generation of the heads, although it is unclear what role such ranking has in their relations. In DC's case, his current *solar* (second level) was in the possession of his parents when he was a boy. It was part of the same great tract of land that included his current yard, along with that of four neighboring *solars.* All but one of them has been sold off, and today, only the *solar* to the east belongs to an agnate, DC's older sister. Is's father and brother live in a *solar* around the corner from him, and they make a third-level group who collaborate and spend time together despite their physical separation. In acquiring plots of land around his neighborhood for eventual habitation by his son, Chio is in the process of building a third-level homestead out of his currently second-level one.

The density and affective quality of daily contact among third-level coresidents varies considerably, depending upon the individuals and their social relations. DC's sister, for instance, stops by to visit her brother's home several times each week, and DC is apparently always aware of her state of mind. Her two sons, who coreside with her in her *solar,* freely walk through DC's yard from their own yard behind it and greet their *primos* 'cousins' at their own back doors. Yet there is a mixture of estrangement in their relations, since the elder sister is considered delusional, only occasionally coherent (having been struck in her childhood by the wind of locusts), and the sons are considered violent and irresponsible. Milo is a third-level coresident with his younger brothers MC and VC, but they almost never set foot in his house and there are some mixed feelings between them and him.

Gender and the Division of Labor

There is a strict division between male and female activities around the home, with corollaries in the way adult men and women inhabit their living space. Some of the terms of this distinction have been mentioned in the foregoing, including the tendency of women to stay around their own home and their responsibility for food preparation and presentation and washing. Much of what I have been able to observe in Oxkutzcab fits in with or extends Redfield and Villa Rojas's ([1934] 1962:68) concise summary of division between the sexes in Chan Kom. Men do all major agricultural labor, both in the traditional *milpa* '(unirrigated) corn/bean/squash field' and in the mechanically irrigated orchards and leveled fields cultivated for commercial production. This includes selecting the plot, clearing and burning the forest, plowing or hoeing, planting, weeding, spraying, irrigating, tree splicing (*ingiertos*), and harvesting. Women occasionally get involved in harvesting in the orchards, where citrus, mango, avocado, and achiote (*k'ušub'*) trees are a main source of production, but their participation in other phases is nearly nil. On the other hand, women typically take produce to the market to sell and do much of the family shopping as well. At different times of the year and of their careers, men work as *naáhal* day laborers, particularly masons, mason's helpers, truck drivers, hired agricultural hands, pickers, and forest clearers. While women bring in sometimes very considerable income sewing or doing laundry, these tasks tend to be performed in their own homes and are not described as *naáhal.* Men typically work outside the residential *solar,* often in groups, in the open hot sun, performing heavy labor punctuated by periods of rest, such as the mid-morning *k'eyem* 'pozole' break, or cigarette breaks. Women work alone, around the house, ideally in the shade, at relatively lighter tasks from which they seemingly never rest. The building and repairing of domestic structures, including the house, kitchen, bird coop, pigsty, corral, wall, and fence and the laying of *šú'uk'* 'boundary stones' are all exclusively male activities. Only men bear arms for hunting, and only they participate in the offering of maize and meat to Maya y*unĉiló'ob'* 'lords' in the rain, thanksgiving, and purification rites (although it is the women who prepare the offertory food). Men, but not women, operate moving vehicles, bicycles, tricycles, and trucks, while women ride, usually on the back. At mealtime, women serve men but do not typically join them in eating. Men eat at a table, usually removed from the heat of the kitchen fire, while women remain within reach of the fire (cf. Nash [1971] 1975:293–96).

When a man is healthily engaged in work, he is said to be *čokow* 'hot', that is, forceful, potent, and invigorated by the heat of the sun. The sun hardens a man's body as he works, making him *maásisóoh* 'hard'. A woman when healthy is relatively cooler, and indeed, the description *čokow* usually implies sexual promiscuity when applied to females, especially *čokow póol šč'uúp* 'hotheaded girl, slut'. When pregnant or menstruating, women are relatively 'hotter', and are said to be *k'ohá'an* 'sick'. Women work in the shade and are typified as *suave* 'soft', *ʔoʔolkil* 'baby soft', *kukutkil* 'attractively chubby', and *k'àab' (il)* 'juicy'. Elderly women are said to *tithil* 'to dry', to be *tikin* 'dry'. When working in the orchards or extracting *sahkab'* 'calcified earth' from pits, men climb up trees and go underground, just as they walk *yàanal k'aàš* 'under forest' when hunting or going to their *milpa*. Women apparently never climb trees, rarely enter *sahkab'* pits, and do not walk in the forest unaccompanied. These various associations can be summarized by saying that women are linked to the earth's surface, which is, at its best, cool, moist, fecund, the ground in which plants grow. This might also explain the well-known fact that Maya women are much more prone to walk barefoot than men, and that the *k'oób'en* 'kitchen', a basically female space, is almost never given a concrete or tile floor even in modernizing households. Maya women stay on the ground.

Other specifically female tasks around the household include the management of domestic water—getting it from the well, storing it, heating it for bathing, washing with it, and watering domestic gardens, flowers, and animals. Women feed the dogs, pigs, and poultry, and occasionally tend the bulls, although this is seen as a properly male task.[17] They sweep, straighten, and weed around the home and courtyard, sew and iron domestic clothes, and care for the children. They maintain the flowers and candle in front of the family *sàantoh* 'saint shrine', as well as the domestic cooking fire (a smoky, onerous job). Insofar as the men build the domestic enclosures in which women spend most of their productive time, they can be said to be in an encompassing relation to them, perhaps the best symbol of which is the *k'oób'en* 'kitchen' encompassed by the *solar* walls and houses. Like the woman of which it is a metonym, the kitchen is private, wet (water is stored here), the locus of domestic fire and food. The man's *k'an če'* 'stool' on which he sits when eating is located in the kitchen, just as the placenta that nourishes an unborn child, also called the *k'an če'*, is located in the woman's *hobon* 'belly'. Eli, a thirty-year-old mother of six, mobilized these associations when she said, recounting her husband's sexual infidelities, *ʔoól impuúl uk'an če'* 'I almost tossed out his stool', meaning, 'I almost kicked him out of the house for good'.[18]

Beyond the Household

This chapter is based on an in-depth investigation of communicative practices among a small group of people in the municipio of Oxkutzcab, and my ethnographic descriptions have accordingly focused on the details of the households to which these people belong. Still, it would be misleading to stop the description at the household level without at least indicating some of the mechanisms by which households are integrated into the surrounding community. Here I will briefly indicate some that I have not investigated in depth but which would surely deserve more treatment in a fuller study of communicative practices. Perhaps the most obvious is the large commercial market in Oxkutzcab, where local farmers sell their produce, especially fruits, by the truckload to merchants from all over the Yucatán peninsula and beyond. The market is also the central shopping area and a convenient place to eat lunch, wait for transportation to or from all points, conduct any municipal business (the *palacio munici-*

pal is just across the street), or go to the doctor. Through the market, people regularly come into contact with new acquaintances and groups of actors from far beyond their own area of residence. Furthermore, they do so under conditions of unequal distribution of the wealth that flows through the market, a fact which establishes a whole order of socioeconomic asymmetry that has an important impact on people's communicative practices.

Linked to the market economy, many Oxkutzcabeños engage in wage labor in the agricultural sector (felling, weeding, picking), in masonry, fence making, transportation, and other occupations. Some of this is seasonal, fitting into the interstices of the growing year. Women routinely travel to market either in Oxkutzcab or as far off as Mérida, trading en route or bringing produce to trade in the markets. These occupations further extend the network of contacts and interlocutors sustained by typical adults, both men and women. Similarly, the network of roads and transportation that supports the regional economy cross-cuts the local divisions of household and town, linking people between towns. For instance, MC drives a truck between Oxkutzcab and the Cooperativa area as a full-time occupation. This brings him into repeated contact with households all around the area and as far off as Mérida, Chetumal, and Ciudad del Carmen. Similarly, most people have immediate relatives (siblings, parents, offspring) living in neighboring towns, such as Mani, Yotholim, or Tekax. On the whole, people's social networks are frequently quite far-flung and are mediated by economic, kin-based, or other social ties.

Also impinging on the local sphere of the household is the all-important *ejido* system of land distribution, in which members are divided into sections according to the locations of their agricultural fields. *Ejido* meetings and elections bring together large numbers of people whose lands are adjacent and who draw irrigation water from the same section of the municipal water system. The latter consists in a network of numbered electric pump houses that draw water for agricultural and household uses (flood irrigation in the orchards and shallow canal irrigation in the vegetable fields). Members of the same *unidad* 'section', called *socios,* often meet informally during breaks from work or while walking to or from their fields. Sitting in the shade, they discuss current plans or just shoot the breeze, developing sometimes long-term friendships, alliances, or antipathies. The sectional groups are also the primary beneficiaries of the *č'aá čaák* 'rain ceremonies' performed in late July and August.

These and other links between individuals and the larger social world must serve as an underexplored background for the focal communicative practices on which this study is based.

SYMMETRIC AND ASYMMETRIC INTERACTIONS AROUND THE HOMESTEAD

Given the foregoing, it will be clear that many of the interactions that take place (and some that do not) around the homestead are based on age, gender, or residence unit asymmetries between participants. In this section, I will sketch (i) the place of etiquette in domestic interactions, (ii) the concept of social symmetry as applied to verbal interaction in Maya, and (iii) an outline of some speech genres commonly used around the extended *solar.*

Orderliness in the Household

While Maya speakers highly value humor, affection, and spontaneity in speech, they are keenly aware that language use is governed by rules of propriety to which individuals should and must submit. The sense of propriety, called variously *legalidad* 'legality, properness', *cortiedad* 'courtesy', *respeto* 'respect', that which is *hač tubèel* 'right, correct', as opposed to *má꞊ patali꞊* 'no good', *helá꞊an* 'weird, off, strange, bad', permeates adult interaction around Maya households. Speakers defer to their status superiors, agreeing with, or at least not challenging, their assertions, following their directives if reasonable, addressing them only with certain titles or sometimes not at all. The impunity with which DP circulates in the domestic spaces of his sons is of a piece with his habit of telling them what to do and criticizing them when he deems it appropriate. The avoidance by men of their brothers' wives is constituted in part by their almost never speaking to one another. In short, talk around the house is part of the social organization of daily life, and it is governed by a linguistic etiquette focused primarily on who and where the participants are.

The orderliness of domestic interactions gives them a generic typicality according to which they are intelligible and repeatable.[19] DC's son Lol explained how the members of their household always show respect for one another, saying *diàarios tó꞊on e꞊→ yàan keiík ih* 'daily, we, we pay our respects (to one another)' (F.137.B.543). He went on to detail who can speak to whom and in what terms and then summarized with an affirmation of 'the system': *b'ey usistema k máan tó꞊on o꞊* 'that's how the system is that we go by' (BB.4.12). Margot, the wife of Lol's brother and hence his most distant *solar* mate, independently recapitulated nearly the same system in describing her own language use. In fact, the three homes sharing the *solar* are in many ways idiosyncratic, which makes this perceived regularity stand out. DC, a shaman, has a pet skunk living in his house and receives visitors at all hours. Man and Margot, with four children and a pet parrot named *Puto corrito* 'Nonstop faggot' (in imitation of his most common vocalization), see themselves as in a 'struggle to improve their lives' with education, cinder blocks, and Western health care. Lol and Fi, with their first infant, work together sewing clothing for customers, sing frequently together around the house as he plays accordion or guitar, and even sing with his male friend, a practice Man finds scandalous. An insomniac, Lol commonly plays the guitar and sings throughout much of the night. These idiosyncratic differences, which could be elaborated considerably, make even more salient the orderliness in relations among coresidents. Though less prone to discuss their own interactions, the adult members of DP's extended household are also scrupulous in their spoken treatment of one another and often invoke the idea of properness in discussing people's conduct. Hence, the schematic codes of conduct and divisions among actors are embodied in the frame spaces in which they communicate (actual and potential) and inevitably have an impact on the actual frameworks they produce in their interactions as well.

Symmetry and Asymmetry

Patterns of interaction among coresidents, like the spatial arrangement of domestic zones and structures, presuppose and help to constitute social relations around the household. Residents interact in accordance with their asymmetric status, gender, and immediate place of residence.[20] While there are no pronominal distinctions in Maya analogous to the indexical values of *tu/vous* in European languages, a kind of "asymmetric power pragmatic" is discernible nonetheless (cf. Brown and Gillman [1960] 1972; Errington 1988; Friedrich 1966; Silverstein 1976). Markedly asymmetric, nonreciprocal, interactive genres include *k'èey, laánk'èey* 'bawl out, criticize sharply', and *tusik b'èel* 'order around', which superiors address to inferiors. *eiik* 'pay respect to' and *ʔúʔuyik t'àan* 'obey' are often nonreciprocal, indexing inferior to superior, though not always. In addition to asymmetric genres, there are relatively symmetric ones, in which the structurally based status differences between participants are less salient or not in play; *eikbal* 'converse, conversation', and *baáš'al t'àan* 'play talk, joking' are two examples. Finally, there are other, more specialized ways of talking that may occur around the household and that are focused on the expression or elicitation of emotion: *pòoč 'i* 'to insult', *kikit'àan* 'sweet talk'.

These ways of speaking embody the play between symmetry and asymmetry among interactants and provide a bridge between the social-structural basis of participant relations and the linguistic forms of speech. As a set, they are less diverse than the Kuna linguistic varieties and languages described by Sherzer (1983), and all fall squarely within everyday Maya, as opposed to ritual speech. Whereas the Kuna varieties are ordered in Sherzer's description by relative formality, my overview of everyday Maya will be ordered in terms of the participant relations indexed by use of the genres. Like Sherzer, I rely on a notion of genre that combines formal features of message tokens along with aspects of the interactive field in which they are produced.[21] The description is illustrative rather than comprehensive. My purpose is to lay the groundwork for an account of demonstrative reference and address as verbal practices unavoidably linked to the play between participant symmetry and asymmetry. Accordingly, the discussion proceeds from asymmetric to symmetric genres, followed by an extended example of deictic reference in task-oriented speech at a work site.

Asymmetric Genres

Perhaps the most obvious example of asymmetric address is *k'eyik* 'bawl out' and *laánk'eyik,* its more intense counterpart. One of Eli's children is playing with food on the table as she tries to set it. Exasperated, she says loudly *tiít abaá téʔeloʔ ʔiího→* 'Beat it out of there, son! (lit., stretch yourself there, son)'. This is a mild case of *k'èey* speech in which the speaker verbally "shoves" the addressee to alter his behavior, clearly asserting her authority but not sustaining a confrontation. A more dramatic example occurred in DC's house, where the youngest brother Victor at one point stole some cassettes from my suitcase, which was stored in the elder brother's home. The senior men of the household, his father and two brothers, dragged him physically into his father's home, where they stood around him and told him to admit to his deed and return the cassettes. He stood mute, eyes downcast, as they *laánk'eyah, k'eék'eyah* 'blasted him verbally' in the overfast, tonally flat, falling final intonation contour of this genre,

(2)   ↓ -   - ↓
               » -   - »
        túʔuš t-a-¢'aá le báal oʔ → k'ub e báʔal oʔ ↓
        "Where'd you put the stuff? Hand over the stuff!' (BB.4.32)

This continued for nearly half an hour, during which Victor persisted in denying culpability, while his brothers raged that he was mocking them, *kaburlartikóʔon* 'you're making fun of us', that they would give him a beating, that they had taken note of his behavior, and that it was no damn good. He finally admitted his action and told how and when he had done it, but not before taking a verbal beating that included questioning his legitimacy as the son of DC.

   The most typical, if not the only, kind of speech addressed to domestic animals is *k'èey*, the directives used to shoo them away. There are different styles for different kinds of animals. Dogs, and only dogs, conventionally get the drawn-out bilabial ingressive sound made by pursing the lips and making a maximally loud and abrupt "kissing" noise, typically followed by the utterance *bikíh* 'No!' delivered overloud with extra stress on the final syllable. Chickens and turkeys get the repeating voiceless fricative sound *č+ č+ č+ č+!* with breathy offset for each segment, or the continuous, voiceless *hwúúšššš!* repeated several times. If the animals do not respond, a stick or projectile usually follows, an especially clear instance of the power asymmetry of the speech genre.

   A milder form of directing an addressee is what is described as *tusik b'èel* 'order road'. While *k'èey* implies a sharp or even furious delivery style, *tusik b'èel* refers mainly to the fact that the speaker is telling the addressee what to do. This can be done with attenuated requests (soft, overhigh pitch), instructions, or blunt directives, depending on the case. Adults describe it as a parental duty that a mother "order" her daughter, and a father his son, in order to teach them how to work properly. DP sits in the kitchen of his son's wife and corrects her every move, "Don't do it like that, do it this way". Leaving, he sees a piece of smoldering firewood by the kitchen door and barks from outside *má a na¢' ebáʔa tée hòol na aʔ* 'Don't leave this thing here by the entrance!' (BB.5.5). His utterances are all instances of *tusik b'èel*, which he sees as his right and responsibility towards his son's wife. On February 2, as DC was having supper at the table of Margot, a young, unmarried man arrived at the back door to request a *saán-*

tiguar treatment. He is a regular patient of DC's who commonly joins the family in conversation inside the house, and his unannounced appearance at the back door was treated as routine. Margot exercised her authority as senior woman of the house and told him tersely:

(3)   šén tol o'→taán uyuk'ul, šeén to ič nah o'
         'Go over there. He's having supper. Go over to the (other) house.'
         (BB.4.129)

The inverse of criticizing and ordering around is the respectful, deferential footing speakers adopt when engaged in *ćiíkil* 'pay respect' speech. This is evident when members of DC's household greet each other with their most proper address forms, *bweénos diías pápah* 'Good morning, father,' from son or son's wife to father; *bweénos días don Wiíl* 'Good evening, Don William' from child to father's *compadre* (cogodparent). Similarly, when a wife falls silent in a conversation joined by her husband, in effect giving him the floor, or a son assents to his father's statement even though he secretly disagrees with it, or a visitor addresses a resident from a respectful distance, these are acts of verbal respect. Just before lunch, Margot, who is my *comadre* 'cogodparent', a relation of reciprocal respect, called me to the table from the doorway of the room I was working in, leaning forward, smiling, almost whispering:

(4)   Margot: compádre → kó'ot en hañǎ
         'Compadre, come eat.'
         WH: kuš tuún DC?
         'What about DC?'
         Margot: ¢'úb'in t'ambi.
         'He's been called.' (BB.4.120)

Margot's demeanor and delivery style, as well as the fact that DC, the head of the household, had already been called to eat, showed her desire to 'pay respect'.

It is worth reiterating that this kind of speech, like the others, encompasses a range of utterance types and consists mainly in a footing that speakers adopt in talk, not a specific set of utterances or a kind of language as such. Being a sign of consideration, *¢iík* is also considered a proper mode of approaching strangers or reciprocating their address. Thus, while often a sign of nonreciprocal deference in an asymmetric relation, such as son to father, it may also be exchanged reciprocally as a sign of mutual respect.

To 'hear speech' in Maya, *'ú'uyik t'àan*, is to be reasonable, tractable, and above all, mindful of the rules set down by higher authorities. Around the house, subordinates who are ordered by their elders or spouses are expected to follow directions. An individual who proposes to do something likely to lead to trouble is expected to respond to a reasoned plea, even if it comes from someone structurally subordinate to him, such as a son or younger brother. These are cases of "hearing speech". It is the opposite when one is a *terko* 'pigheaded, stubborn' (cf. *terkiedad* 'pigheadedness') or *rebelde* 'rebellious', in which case words and rules go unheeded. Like signs of respect, *ʔúʔuyik t'àan* is in the clearest cases a nonreciprocal attentiveness one speaker pays to another, but it may also be seen as reciprocal when used to describe the general reasonableness of people who follow the guidelines of *legalidad* 'legality'.

Symmetric Genres

It would be wrong to suggest that Maya speakers constantly attend to their differences of status and experience in their everyday speech. There are strong bonds of affection, friendship, solidarity, and common experience that link interactants and put them on a relatively symmetric, reciprocal footing. There is an explicit sense among Maya speakers that both parties to an interaction should contribute to it, that to fail to contribute or to prevent an interlocutor from doing so is to violate the norms of sociability. Among the prototypically symmetrical genres of interaction, *çikbal* 'conversation, discussion, narrative' and *baášal t'àan* 'play speech, joking' are good exemplars. These are activities one engages in when visiting, sitting together over food or drink, when men smoke a cigarette together during a work break or just hang out together over coffee in the market, when women talk across the courtyard from their respective washbasins, and in the back of a truck when people are on their way to do errands. One is typically received in a Maya house with an invitation to *ʔòoken, héʔe b'áʔal akutal aʔ, kóʔoš çikbal* 'enter, here's something to sit on, let's converse', and people report, as well as evaluate, such exchanges as *haç'uç* 'beautiful' or *maʔ haç'uç iʔ* 'not beautiful' *çikbal*. The former is a source of *kíʔimak ʔóolal* 'happiness', *toh ʔóolal* 'contentedness', whereas the unwillingness to engage on this footing is a sign of estrangement or aloofness. Discussing an exchange I had had with another speaker, in which my interlocutor responded to my utterance by repeating it in slightly altered form, Man and Margot nicely illustrated the expectation of joint engagement as it applies to *çikbal*. I wondered if the other speaker was correcting me in altering my utterance or just agreeing with me by reaffirming it in slightly different form. They explained that she had been agreeing but naturally did not want to repeat my words verbatim, since to do so would give the appearance that I was talking to myself. There must be *cambios* 'changes' in the talk. Man want on:

(5)   tumèen kinnuúkik teč le héʔeš tawáʔalil eʔ↑ yan atuklik
             'because (if) I answered you just as you've said it, you'll think

             tinhùun kint'àan. Wá kuyúʔub'al le t'àan mèen ulaák'
             all alone I'm talking. If that talk was heard by another

             maák eʔ, yàan utuklik eʔ tèen pašik ↑ tèen ʔòok'ostik
             person, he'd think I'm the one playing (the tune), (and) I'm the one dancing
             to it (too).

k'abeét uhoók'ol ušeét'e
His (the other person's) part has to come out too.' (BB.4.108)

In order to have a conversation that is *tuúlis* 'whole,' there must be two different parts, each speaker contributing his own distinct part.

Maya speakers are known for their verbal humor, which includes a large repertoire of preexistent jokes and humorous stories, spontaneous puns, innuendo, hyperbole, caricature, and deception. Much of the spontaneous joking that punctuates conversation focuses thematically on sexual relations, slight misunderstandings of ambiguous circumstances, and incompetence imputed to the addressee or someone else. The speaker that has one over on the other is said to *meèntik uyoól* 'kid him, do (act on) his will'. While joking is apparently most intense among gatherings of men, it is also common between men and women, although not among coresident mixed pairs. It is considered inappropriate to engage in blatantly sexual humor or vulgar cursing in the presence of women, particularly senior ones, and "play speech" in its most elaborate forms tends (in my experience) to occur away from the residential portion of the *solar,* where the women and children are. This is not to say that there is no passing humor around the house, but that the range of devices used is restricted and the jokes understated. This may be because most of spontaneous "play speech" is a reciprocal activity in which each participant tries to entrap the other, twisting his or her words for humorous effect. There are sufficiently binding constraints around the household on who can address whom and on how that reciprocity is ruled out in most situations.

Two of DS's daughters-in-law, coresidents, were eating tacos in the market when I came upon them and stopped to *čikbal* 'converse'. We had known each other for several years, although not well. One of them offered me a plate of food, saying with a grin *hé°ela° witl, hé°el awó°oč a°* 'Here it is Will, here's your food,' at which the other burst into laughter. The implication of her utterance, including the grin, presentative gesture, and reference to feeding, was that she was mock offering her own body (not a provocative act in this context). JC, a man in his mid seventies, is locally famous for his relentless *baášal t'àan* and his willingness to turn conversation with almost anyone into a string of double entendres, such as when he is greeted *°oóla wiínik b'iš awanil?* 'Hi man, how are you ?' to which his response was for a time *laáyli walakbal e°* 'Still standing (erect).'

Men frequently exchange *baášal t'àan* in the brief greetings they trade outside the house when passing in the streets. A routine exchange might go as follows: AB, an adult man, is walking towards the market early in the morning when he sees TG, a familiar, passing on a bicycle. The exchange takes place as TG passes, without slowing:

(6)   AB: heéy TG! hábisken e°
        'Hey TG, will you take me along?' (= can you take my whole penis?)

TG: héˀeleˀ naáken iˀ
'Sure, get up (on the back of the bike)' (= sure, just try and jump
on me).

AB: hátaˀakeneˀ
'You'll shit on me.' (10/22/80)

Assume AB is carrying a load of firewood or produce on his back with a tumpline.
TG shouts in passing:

(7)   TG: maáreh, ˀal akùuč
             'Maria! your load is heavy (= your genitals are big).'

             AB: héˀelaˀ
             'Here it is (come and get it).'

             or AB′: héˀeš sùuk abisik teč eˀ
             'Like you're used to taking on (= you like men with big genitals).'

             or AB″: máˀ sùuk imbisik ten iˀ→màas sùuk ašbáˀal
             'I'm not used to taking it, (but) your girlfriend is (= I'm sleeping
             with your girlfriend).' (10/22/80)

Such play turns partly on the existence of a set of words and phrases that male speakers know have potentially double meanings, including *bisik* 'to take (be sexually penetrated)', *kučik* 'carry (be sexually penetrated)', *kùuč* 'load, genitals', *siˀ* 'firewood (erect
penis)', *kàab'* 'honey (semen)', *kèeso* 'cheese (female genitalia)', *čiwoól* 'tarantula
(vagina)'. When these terms, and many more, occur in speech, speakers have the option
of turning them towards their secondary meanings or taking them at 'face' or 'literal'
value. Thus, "play speech" is above all a response mode that consists in responding to
the humorous potential of the interlocutor's most recent utterance. Under its effects, discourse interpretation stays open to a whole universe of possible meanings that competent participants recognize but never state. VI once explained that this opening up is the
essence of *baášal t'àan*, but that it can be dangerous if one speaker takes offense (F.63.A).
The speech *kusatik ubaáh* 'loses itself, gets lost' in ambiguity and unstated interpretive
possibilities. More than a list of words with double meanings, play turns on the willingness to hear whatever is said for its humorous potential. This is surely one of the reasons that speakers find it very difficult to talk about *baášal t'àan* in the abstract, since it
is an interactive genre that presupposes chains of utterances by different speakers.

In VI's explanation, he cited examples of opening utterances, intended to initiate
playful interaction between men working together. His examples aptly illustrate the
trope of equating two referents as a way of indexing a set of unstated corollaries. Seeing
his co-worker's wife walking toward the market, a man says to him, *héˀ kimbin oˀ* 'there
I go', pointing to the woman. *túˀuš yaneč* 'Where are you?', the other responds. *héˀ*

kimbin hmàan o² 'there I go shopping', the first counters. At this point, the talk can proceed in the direction of play or of insults designed to provoke. The initial speaker has conveyed either that he is the addressee's wife, implying that the addressee prefers men to women, or that he is off following her for sexual favors. Alternatively, the first speaker could say, pointing to a dog, *hé²eleč o²* 'there you are', equating the addressee with an animal considered vile. In response, *hé²el a² pèek'* 'here it is. Dog!' making reference to his own body (or body part) and calling the addressee 'Dog'. This freewheeling reference to spouses and body parts is the antithesis of the highly respectful avoidance relations that men typically maintain with respect to the wives of their friends. Right after offering the above examples of openers, VI went on to explain that he had never set foot in the house of his best friend and co-worker Tigre, nor would he even so much as make reference to the existence of his wife. These avoidances are powerful constraints on speech, gaze, and spatial movement that are inverted in both play and insult.

Beyond 'play speech' proper, practical jokes that play on people's fear or ignorance are a favorite form of entertainment, even around the house. Man and Lol recounted with glee how they used to play tricks on their father when they were boys. Once they rigged up a string to DC's large *sàanto* crucifix, which stays on his altar, in front of which he performs most cures and all divination. They tied it so that while he was performing the *saántiguar,* with the patient looking intently upon the crucifix (as DC instructs them to do), they could make it wobble back and forth. Laughing hilariously, they told of how they had frightened an old woman who took it to be a sign of DC's tremendous power. Another time they set up loudspeakers under DC's altar and in the roof and used a borrowed microphone to confuse a patient who was sitting alone waiting for DC to return; they talked to her as if from out of the *santo.* A young man who visits DC often was startled the first time he saw me in the house and asked if I spoke Maya and who I was. Man and Lol spontaneously cooked up the story that I was DC's lost brother and that I had simply appeared one day out in the back yard. They strung him along for some time with this story, much to their enjoyment.

There is a traditional Maya story about a boy whose father died and for whom a vigil was kept in the family house (as is the practice). Known to be flippant, the boy was told by his mother to simply stand watch over the body, which was laid out on the table in its white mantle of death, and not say a word, while the others prepared for the ceremony. A mouse that lived in the roof, it turns out, came down and ran across the table; the boy tried to swat it, knocking over the candle, which set the mantle on fire, which in turn burned the body to a crisp. The boy never called for help, because he took literally his instructions to be quiet. This story, which many people find hilarious, combines the elements of unforeseen misfortune, communicative incompetence based on literal understanding, and a mechanical string of consequences. One of the most salient contexts in which I have heard the story recounted, with laughter, was in front of an actual corpse during a real life and death *velorio* 'vigil' at which some people were wailing, others sitting quietly, and others chuckling at the thought of a mouse setting fire to the *²ánimáas* 'dead person' (BB.4.140). DC was once listening to a long tale of misfortune told by a man who had come to him for advice. It appears that he and his brother had both had sexual relations with the same woman, who was now pregnant, and the man was gravely concerned to know whose responsibility the child was. He was quite upset and took the better part of an hour telling his story in detail. DC found it so humorous—so awry and ill conceived—that he laughed throughout much of the story, before telling the man that the responsibility was *his*.

INSTRUMENTAL SPEECH

It is appropriate to conclude this brief summary of everyday speech genres with an example of what we can heuristically call 'instrumental speech', although there is no such label in Maya (cf. Lyons 1977:826; Turner 1967:32ff.). I have in mind the task-oriented exchanges that take place between people working together—masons building a wall, women at work in the courtyard, men clearing trees together or digging canals in a field. The special interest of such talk for a study of indexical reference is obviously the relatively high proportion of deictic references, directives, and presentatives it contains by virtue of its focus on collaborative engagement. The interplay between preexistent status asymmetries between participants and the momentary footings they adopt in talk is especially clear in contexts in which the instrumental function is dominant.

Coresident males typically collaborate in at least some labor, like moving produce to market by truck, repairs around the household, and irrigating, provided their orchards or fields are contiguous. Ideally, senior fathers of adult men work and become partners with one of their sons, as is the case of DP and VC, who share a *parsela* and work jointly in DP's orchard, and Is and his father, who have made *milpa* together for the past twenty years. VI and his younger brother Gwal have worked side by side as masons for several years, and Man and Lol have worked together as masons, tailors, and on home improvements, as well. In the *heéꞓ lúꞌum* 'fix earth' and *wàahil kòol* 'loaves of the field' ceremonies, of which the beneficiary is the total (second-level) *solar* unit, the adult men collaborate in the preparation and execution of the ceremony, while the women jointly cook the meat, all under the close supervision of the shaman.

DP, VC, and I are working together hoeing out a canal along the back boundary of DP's *solar* (see fig. 2.5). Sitting on the edge of the canal, as I loosen the earth with a pick and VC hoes it open, DP tells me that he plans to plant a row of pepper bushes along each bank:

(8)   tiꞌ **e** kàanal k-**im**-b'èetik **a**ꞌ → káꞌa p'eé sùurko kén u-b'i seh →
        'In this ditch I'm making,   two rows will it take,

        ump'é **téꞌel a**→   **ump'eé tée bey a**ꞌ →
        one right here (pointing),   one like this here (pointing).

        káꞌa ꞓol pak'aál kén **in**-ꞓ'aáeh
        Two rows of plants will I put (there).' (2/18/87; BB.5.30)

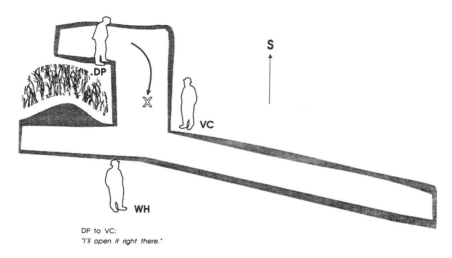

DP to VC:
'I'll open it right there.'

Fig. 2.5. Irrigation ditch: 'I'll open it right there.'

DP's first person singular reference to what **he** was doing, when actually he was sitting watching us work, was a clear instantiation of his rank as the head, not only of the current undertaking, but of the household in which we all resided and the *solar* in which we were working. Regardless of who wields the hoe, it is DP who is making a ditch to plant peppers.

To make reference to the different banks of the ditch, DP has selected Immediate deictic forms ending in the -*aʔ* terminal particle (boldface). Given our shared spatial context and the fact that all three of us were already engaged in the task, the Non-Immediate form *téʔeloʔ* 'there' would have been an equally proper choice of word. The use of either deictic presupposes the shared perceptual, spatial, and actional frame in which we were all located at the time. However, the act of defining the rows by pointing them out with this form is an **asymmetric segmentation,** which presents them as new information not already shared among the interactants. In fact, it was new to me, the addressee, although surely not to VC, also a ratified hearer. In the framework of its utterance, DP's reference to the anticipated rows of vegetables (in a place currently overgrown with weeds) produces a spatial division that will subsequently be part of the joint corporeal field of our labor. By choosing the Immediate, asymmetric deictic, DP puts himself in the role of defining his referents as his own, not as joint 'givens'. This way of aligning himself in relation to his referents is parallel to his use of the first person singular pronoun (boldface) to describe himself as the one doing things; both phrasings put him in the role of defining the agenda. VC, a respectful son, would no more make such a unilateral assertion in his father's presence than he would attempt to order him around. That is, though less obvious than some highly marked speech genres, the asymmetries of indexical reference also connect with the asymmetries of social status.

Shortly afterward, VC was bent over working on the canal with the pickax, when DP told him to dig out a *poseta* 'basin' in which to plant a bush. DP was standing almost directly over VC, within a meter of both him and the pocket of earth where the hole was to be dug (a circular basin about one meter across). As he spoke, he pointed to the west side of the ground and told VC to dig it out a little more (map BB.5.32):

(9)   **tían tée** čik'in **oʔ** →
            'There's where it is there on the west.' (2/18/87; BB.5.30)

Why has DP switched from the Immediate to the Non-Immediate locative deictic, even though the place he is referring to is less than a step away from him? He is still giving orders asymmetrically, by hovering over VC and telling him where to dig. VC was the one digging the *poseta* in his own most immediate activity field, but this was true of the previous utterance too. A clue to the difference is the utterance fraction *tían* 'there's where it is'. This is an anaphoric device indexing prior mention to the referent, indicating that both DP and VC are attuned to the location of the *poseta*, probably because they have talked about it before (although not in the immediately preceding talk and not in my presence).[22] Hence, DP has shifted his own *schéma corporel* from a focus on himself and his future projects (8) to the reciprocal zone of common knowledge established in previous discussion or shared awareness (9). Furthermore, while DP is the head of the *solar* and the primary authority in the plan to plant pepper bushes in the first place, it is VC who will perform the specific task of digging the *poseta*. What the choice of Non-Immediate deictic does here is put the referent in VC's activity space while indexing the *shared* background knowledge that he and DP have of the arrangement of the ditch. Despite the recognized status asymmetries between the two, this usage is a relatively **symmetric** one, because it relies on what the interactants share.

Another typically symmetrical usage followed shortly after, when DP judged that the job was done, looking at the site and saying:

(10)   **héʔel oʔ** ç'okáʔan **bey oʔ**
            'There it is, it's finished as is.' (BB.5.31)

This utterance is a standard way of bringing an activity to a close by summarizing it in a single deictic reference. Because the activity being summarized was a joint effort undertaken prior to the moment of utterance rather than a one-man performance anticipated in the future, the appropriate deictics are the relatively more symmetric, Non-Immediate *-oʔ* forms. (English is the same: one usually says 'There, that's that' to finish an activity, but something like 'Here goes, this is it' to begin.)

Moments later, DP was standing on the bank of a ditch connecting with the one we had just prepared, while VC was standing on the other side, opposite and several meters behind him (see fig 2.5). DP had just told VC of his plans to open up the second ditch, running parallel to the eastern portion of the one we had already done. It was an overgrown section of ground where there had been an irrigation ditch in the past. Directing his gaze and pointing at the overgrown ditch in his foreground, with his back to VC on the other side, he says:

(11)   **héʔ le** kánal tuún k-**inw**-áaik teč **aʔ**
          'Here's the ditch I'm telling you about.' (BB.5.31)

In this utterance, DP switches back to the **asymmetric** stance of characterizing the ditch entirely from his own perspective rather than including his addressee, VC. He once again produces a spatial segmentation not already accessible to VC and me: in fact, there was no canal in the place he pointed at, only a patch of ground where he anticipated one. This constitutes a shift in DP's *schéma corporel,* again isolating him and his prospective projects. Note that coincident with the switch in deictic adverb is a switch back into the first person singular subject 'I'. Maintaining his authoritative stance, DP went on to point out the spot, about three meters from him, between him and VC, where he would (tell VC to) open the ditch to connect it to the new one (see fig. 2.5). Facing VC, he said:

(12)   **k-in**-heʔik **téʔel aʔ**→
          'I'll open it right there.'

Correctly understanding this to be a directive, VC set about opening the not-yet-existing canal.

    Just after we had finished digging the long canal, DP and I were sitting side by side on the north bank, when he explained to me his plan to open yet another ditch in the undergrowth between the one where we were sitting and the far one that VC had just cleared (see fig. 2.6). There had previously been one there, but it had reverted to

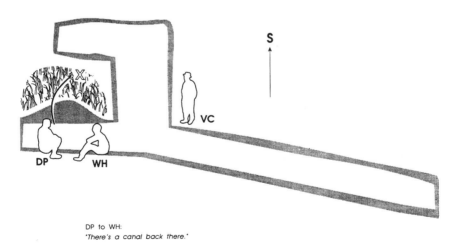

DP to WH:
'There's a canal back there.'

Fig. 2.6. Irrigation ditch: 'There's a canal back there.'

weeds. Between us and the weeds was a mound of earth piled on the bank of the near ditch, about three meters from us. Pointing over the pile, at the overgrown ditch about two meters behind it, DP said:

(13)   tumèen **té'el o**→ yan cánal **té'** pàačil **o'**
              'because there's a canal   there behind (the mound in front of
                                                us)' (BB.5.32)

Here he has switched back to the Non-Immediate, relatively symmetric deictics, and from first person 'I' to the impersonal existential statement 'there is'. The shift is partly due to the physical and perceptual distance between DP and the overgrown ditch, partly to the fact that the ditch is behind something, and partly to its having been there in the past. What is most important, however, is that DP and I are sitting together at an equal remove from the referent, momentarily engaged in *čikbal* from a common perspective on it. This is what most distinguishes this episode of reference from the preceding ones: DP is occupying a shared corporeal field with me, our respective gazes originating in the same subportion of the space.

Contrast these uses with two final examples, in which spatial reference is made to the region that includes the speaker and addressee without further segmenting any particular subportions of it. Fi, a young married woman residing *'ilib'čil* in the household of her father-in-law in Oxkutzcab, was telling me about her family in Tekax, a neighboring town. I inquired about the residences of her elder sisters, and she responded as in (14):

(14)   WH: kuš tuún akìik ó'ob'→ tú'uš yàan ↓
                  'What about your elder sisters? Where are they?'
              Fi: tían o
                  'They're there.'
              WH: tek'aš↑
                  '(In) Tekax?'
              Fi: tían tek'ašó'ob' e'→čeén tèen → **way e'**
                  'They're there in Tekax. I'm alone here.' (F.137.A.263)

The key word in (14) for our purposes is the boldface locative deictic, which refers to Fi's residence in Oxkutzcab, in contrast to the residence of her sisters in the neighboring town of Tekax (actually about twenty kilometers away along the main highway). Unlike DP's instrumental speech in which he marks out areas in the current surround for future work, Fi is narrating personal history to an outsider in her own home, and her spatial reference encompasses the whole of the household. Fi could have used the deictic *té'el a'* 'here, there', but her choice of *way e'* 'here' is motivated by the relatively great extent of the region referred to and (crucially) by the fact that she is occupying the region.

Similarly, when her husband Lol was recounting to me stories of local corruption, he interjected at one point:

(15)   sí le **way** aʔ→ paklan tòop
         'Yeah, around here, (everyone) screws each other.' (BB.4.12)

Just like Fi's utterance in the preceding example, Lol's makes reference to the local region without individuating any smaller place within it. The crucial factor is once again that Lol is a resident of the region he is describing. With the exception of transposed utterances the boldface deictic is *always* used to make reference to a zone occupied by the speaker at the moment of utterance; the home is a very common referent. Hence, whereas DP's instrumental utterances denote places distinct from, but in relation to, his own position in the joint field of labor, these two examples denote inclusive zones relative to the speakers' position within them. In both cases, the references are embodied in the speaker's current corporeal field, but the embodiment is different, and the role of the individual *schéma corporel* is accordingly distinct as well.

What then is the relation between the kinds of interactive alignments indexed in highly marked speech genres such as *kʼèey* 'bawl out' and *tusik bʼèel* 'order around', on the one hand, and the microalignments in evidence in routine acts of reference, on the other? They are at least partly governed by the same set of preexistent social relations, according to which a head of household can unilaterally speak down to, in front of, or behind any subordinate member, asserting in his or her own first person the authoritative word on what is going on and how it is to go. In an important sense, the asymmetry of telling a co-worker 'I am doing this right here' to describe the project in which both are jointly engaged is the same as the asymmetry of telling that person what to do. In the scenarios presented, DP's structural position as head of the household gives him the authority to adopt both an **asymmetric**, authoritative footing and a **symmetric,** solidaristic footing, according to his own communicative purposes. Like different physical postures, these footings embody dispositions to act in different ways: the former indexes, the nonshared, new, or "egocentric" status of the referent as belonging to the speaker alone, and the latter indexes, its shared, given, or "sociocentric" status. The former often involves the production of divisions that will subsequently be schematic, while the latter builds on already schematized divisions. By the same authority, DP routinely shifts between a solidary style of *éikbal* 'conversation', drawing on shared experiences and inclusive humor, and a power-laden style of giving orders and defining agendas.

This indicates a further element of the speech genres sketched here, which is worth emphasizing. In the course of about forty-five minutes around the work site, DP changed his indexical alignment many times; just four of them presented above. Similarly, he could easily switch between *éikbal* 'conversation', *baášal tʼàan* 'play', *kʼèey* 'bawling out', and *tusik bʼèel* 'ordering around' as many times over the same period. These conversational genres should be thought of as consisting of speech styles along with footing alignments that speakers combine and play off one another in sometimes rapid sequence. The changing symmetries and asymmetries of the framework of reference display the same quick mutability.

EMBODIMENT OF REFERENCE

What do these examples and ethnographic facts tell us about the general phenomenon of embodiment in language, and especially in referential practices? In the passage quoted at the outset of this chapter, Merleau-Ponty asserts that when a speaker uses the word 'here' in reference to his or her own body, something special takes place: the body is not individuated relative to any exterior coordinates but is actually "anchored in an object." This anchoring is the original establishment of spatial coordinates according to the phenomenologist, the means by which an actor takes up a position in the world. Recalling examples like (14–15), one has a sense that Merleau-Ponty was on to something basic, but that his statement is only partly true. Fi and Lol both make reference to zones whose distinctive feature is that they are actually occupied by the speaker at the moment of utterance. The two install themselves in this zone in the very act of making reference to it. DP also takes up a position forcefully in the utterances cited, yet he never makes reference to his own body. Instead, he indexes his corporeal field as a ground, of which VC and I were also occupants, and denotes bounded places in relation to it. While DP does not put his body in the canal when he makes reference to it, he nonetheless inevitably takes up a position relative to it and to his interlocutors. Just like the gaze that inhabits its object in Merleau-Ponty's opening remarks on the body ([1945] 1967:81ff.), indexical reference is a way of inhabiting the world and DP, Fi, and Lol all engage in it.

The first point then is that embodiment takes place not only when the body is the focal object referred to but, more pervasively, when the body belongs to the ground from which reference takes place. The relational structure inherent in indexical reference articulates both focal and backgrounded positions.

The second point has to do with the role of the individual speaker as owner of the *schéma corporel* that is the basis of embodiment. Here Merleau-Ponty's focus on the individual led him to overemphasize the isolability of the acting subject. In referential practices it is rarely the speaker as a single individual who makes up the ground. Recall DP's shifts in footing as he issued directives and predictions in his role as the head of the household. It is true that he focalized himself through first person singular reference and asymmetric locative deictics. Yet it was constantly relevant to his word choice that we were all working in the immediate area, that VC and I could see his referents once he pointed them out, that certain kinds of discussions had already taken place and were accessible by memory. The social mediation of reference is the necessary horizon without which subjects could not individuate themselves or the objects to which they have access. Fi (14) and Lol (15) necessarily take up a position in their home by the terms of their reference, yet they do so in relation to other places being discussed and to me, their addressee. Merleau-Ponty goes too far when he asserts that the body is the original anchor, which is not itself anchored in an "external" world.[23]

Study of referential practices leads to the conclusion that the two kinds of anchoring are two faces of the same process. The origo is not an individual *schéma corporel* but a corporeal field occupied by two or more coparticipating interactants. This means that the intersensorial unity that is basic to the phenomenological schema must be embedded in an "interperspectival" unity in order to serve as the ground of communication. Given the importance of talk in forming experience, it is unsurprising that the Maya term *-iknal* 'bodily space' is used to refer to both the intersensorial unity of a single speaker and the interperspectival unity of a corporeal field that includes others too (via coresidence in the homestead or coparticipation in the act of reference). Embodiment, even when it crucially involves the human body, cannot be treated from the perspective of an isolated speaker.

Discourse practices, such as the ones I have loosely called genres in this chapter, can also embody meaning and social relations. Here we refer to aspects of the sociocultural frame of reference that go beyond bodies in motion to include principles of rank and proper etiquette in domestic interactions, kinship relations, and divisions of labor by gender and age. These constitute **schematic** dimensions in the domestic field that cooperate with body space in grounding reference. Power-laden interactive genres such as scolding, bawling out, and ordering around (superiors to inferiors) and respecting and obeying (inferiors to superiors) embody social differences as part of their conditions of use. Play speech, particularly in its fast and dirty forms, is a relatively symmetrical genre of exchange, typically reciprocated among men away from the primary residential area of the *solar*. Task-oriented reference and description shows further, more subtle linguistic reflexes of social asymmetries. While not as obviously charged as some other genres, routine acts of reference are unavoidably caught up in the broader social field too. This is evident in the terms speakers select to identify referents, as well as the alignments they take up relative to their interlocutors.

Deictics, pronouns, and indexical referential expressions are among the fundamental referring items in all natural languages, while at the same time they conventionally index the interactants' egocentric, altercentric, or sociocentric footings. By combining in a single act the background frame of reference, along with the ongoing framework of coparticipation, deictic practice embodies individual *schémas corporels,* the interactive corporeal field, and the schematic structure of sociocultural context into a unified whole. Neither egocentric nor concrete, this enactment, which we can call "embodied reference," has little to do with the apparent self-evidence of pointing to the ground one stands on.

NOTES

Translations from Maya are in single quotes.

1. Stated in semiotic terms, even indexicals, which are defined by their actual contiguity with objects, come in conventional types. They are, as Peirce put it, "indexical legisigns." Thus an expressive particle in Maya like *bakaán* 'evidently, apparently', conventionally indexes that the proposition with which it occurs is unexpected or only apparently true.

2. Remarks on the esoteric knowledge of Maya shamans are based on in-depth experience with a single shaman in the region of this research, along with impressionistic observations of the practice of other shamans.

3. The perceived relation between swarming ants and the animacy of a person is perhaps also reflected in the description of rage in a person as *p'uúhul usìinik* 'his ants are stirred up, his Mongolian spot excited'. One adult female speaker explained that the *sìinik* is actually the Mongolian spot at the base of the spine, but that *p'uúhul* describes the swarming of ants (BB.4.134). According to the Cordemex dictionary, the former term meant 'pulse' during the colonial period. The verb *p'uúhul* is described in the Cordemex as "to make a din, cause a racket" and also denotes the collective hunts that Maya men conduct, in which they fan out in the forest making a racket to drive the game toward men posted along known paths. The analogy between the body with its nerves and pulse and the earth with its living inhabitants is patent here.

4. Nash ([1971] 1975:13) cites a close analogue in Tzeltal culture, in which body and homestead are symbolically equated. As in Tzeltal culture, Maya creation myths posit the derivation of man from earth in combination with God's breath.

5. Turner (1980:120ff.) describes a similar divide between hearing and seeing in Kayapo: the former is associated with passive understanding and conformity, a basic part of the political process, complemented by active understanding associated with seeing, speaking, and making things happen.

6. Cf. Tzeltal *ɂawai* 'feel, hear' used to describe a shaman's understanding of the messages in the pulse of a patient (Nash [1971] 1975:xxiii).

7. This point was driven home to me forcefully during my first fieldwork among Maya people in 1977. DP's family, with whom I lived and worked for three months, had a newborn son in the household (the first child of MC and Eli). The child, later to become my *ahijado* 'godchild', was kept in a hammock out of my sight, further covered with a white cotton cloth. At the time, the family lived in what I have labeled area III of DP's current homestead while I slept and ate in area I, then a small hut (*šáɂanih nah*) on the edge of the woods. It was nearly two months before I learned of the child's existence and only in my last week that I actually saw him. When I first saw him we had just returned to the house from the fields, where we had been weeding for several hours. We were filthy and sweaty in the August afternoon sun when DA came walking out of the house with an infant in her arms. She handed the child to me, to my shock, and told me to wipe the sweat from my arms and torso on the baby, then to walk around the yard carrying him in my arms, then to hold a pen in his hand and write on a sheet of paper. I followed her instructions and only learned at the end that I had just become the baby's *padrino* 'godfather' by the Maya rite of *heč meék'* (lit., 'fix-embrace', or perhaps 'forked-leg-embrace' after the position of the child's legs). Prior to that, the baby had been kept from my sight so that I would not inadvertently give it *ojo*, transferring my body heat to it by way of my gaze and thereby causing a thermal breakdown in the child. As DA explained it, the positions in which I carried the child were meant to ensure that he would grow into a man who stays cool while working under the intense sun (hence transference of sweat), a man not afraid to walk about the woods (hence meander around the yard under the trees with him), and a good student (hence writing). By having me touch the child upon first seeing him, DA neutralized the danger of my giving him *ojo* with my unaccompanied gaze.

8. The role of gaze in shamanic practice recalls Merleau-Ponty's ([1945] 1967:81ff.) striking discussion of gaze as a mode of constituting and actually occupying objects.

9. These terms were pointed out to me by three Maya speakers in the course of a conversation in which I was trying (unsuccessfully) to explain the peculiar look a woman had given me in the market. As I was reaching for ways to describe her look, they suggested the terms and demonstrated them as they did.

10. The following discussion is abstracted from a longer comparison of the concept of *-iknal* with the referential space of 'here' (Hanks 1993). The data on which my statements here are based include many attestations of uses of the term by native speakers, as well as extended discussions with several adults.

11. The youngest son is currently fifteen years old and known to steal, lie, and use vulgar language. The older brothers see this is a negative reflection on themselves and an eventual negative influence on their children.

12. Comaroff and Roberts (1981: chap. 2) describe a contrasting, more extreme case of tensions among agnates in the Tswana household, where agnatic bonds embody rivalry, hostility, and sorcery, in opposition to matrilateral bonds, which embody supportive and privileged relations. Unlike the Tswana, the Maya do not usually describe the agnatic bond in terms of its ambivalent characteristics but rather cite the prescription of solidarity.

13. The presence of an inner wall would surely be a sign of fractured relations. DC's older son, Man, speaking in bitter frustration of the behavior of his younger brother, Victor, said that if Vic grows up as a good-for-nothing and brings shiftless types to the house, Man would "slap up a goddamn cement and cinder-block wall" to keep him out. Is's wife, Bal, recounted the arguments she had had with SC, her neighbor to the east, over SC's turkeys wandering into Bal's yard. Bal got so fed up she wanted to put up a wall, to which SC objected violently (BB.4.101).

14. Thompson (1974:29) observed that in Ticul, sharing the kitchen of the senior woman was a sign of subordination to her, but this is not entirely accurate for the Oxkutzcabeño households that I know. In fact, in at least some cases, it is the most senior daughter-in-law who shares with the husband's mother, and this is a sign of alliance rather than subordination (the case of Pilar with DA).

15. The numbers refer to a layout sketch I made in my field notes. Room 1 is Margot's eating area, 5 is the eating area of Lol and Fi, and 6 the front receiving and work area of Lol.

16. My data are insufficient to indicate how many *solars* an individual family may go through and perhaps retain as property in the course of its career. In the case of DP's sprawling homestead, none of the currently inhabited areas was the childhood home of his oldest son, although rights over these lands have been gradually acquired by the family over some thirty years.

17. As men acquire *solar* space and move in the course of their careers, they commonly keep poultry and fowl, which they call simply *ʔinwàalak* 'my domesticated (animals)' in a *solar* separate from the one in which they actually reside. Balim kept his birds in a *solar* about 1 km away from the one in which he resided in 1979–81; Milo keeps his in a *solar* about 3 km away, in Yaaxhom; DP, while residing with MC and VC, kept his fowl in area III. In such cases, only the men go to feed the birds. They describe this simply as *kimbin tinsoólar* 'I'm going to my *solar*', letting context disambiguate between the *solar* where they sleep and the one where the birds sleep.

18. Cf. Comaroff (1985:56) for a partly parallel case of a close symbolic relation between the Tshidi woman's body and the house structure.

19. Nash ([1971] 1975:292ff.) makes an analogous demonstration of the schematic arrangement of activities and spatial arrays according to rank and custom in Tzeltal society.

20. My use of the term "asymmetry" in this discussion is guided primarily by two sets of readings, one focused on participant structure in verbal interaction (including the works cited in the text) and one focused on social systems more generally. Along these lines, Comaroff (1985:48) describes the symmetric relation between genders around the Tshidi household, as opposed to their asymmetric participation in the sociopolitical process beyond the household. Munn (1986:279–91) describes the role of asymmetry as a principle unifying objects of kula

exchange (necklaces and armshells), with their gender corollaries (female and male, respectively) and their motion corollaries (slow, enduring, arriving from the northwest vs. fast, arriving from the southeast). My focus here is naturally on the interactive and specifically verbal consequences of social asymmetries among household members.

21. These remarks abbreviate a longer discussion of the problem of speech genres presented in Hanks (1987a), where I suggest that the components of genre include the orientation of the speech form (i) to structures of power and authority; (ii) to the process of reception; (iii) to historically specific courses of action; and (iv) to the indexical centering of the performance in a field of participation. It is primarily the first and fourth that I focus on here.

22. Alternatively, the expression *tiʼ an téʼel oʼ* could be motivated by the shared orientation of the two to the task of digging the poseta, and so DP could be referring merely to the part of the task left to do without there having been any previous discussion of it.

23. Merleau-Ponty's attempt to derive everything from the self-possessed subject is no more distorting than the opposite claim, made by scholars such as Lyons (1977) and Gell (1985), that the actional orientations of deictic reference could all be translated into nonindexical Cartesian terms. Study of actual deictic usage in its cultural context leads away from the excesses of both objectivist and subjectivist semantics. What is needed is a combined approach in which the subject-object dichotomy is replaced with the relational terms of social practice.

REFERENCES

Agar, M. and J. Hobbs. 1985. How to Grow Schemas out of Interviews. In J. Dougherty, ed., *Directions in Cognitive Anthropology,* 413–31. Urbana: University of Illinois Press.

Bourdieu, P. [1972] 1977. *Outline of a Theory of Practice.* Cambridge: Cambridge University Press. Originally published in French.

———. 1980. *Le sens partique.* Paris: Les Éditions de Minuit.

Bricker, V. R. 1978. Antipassive Constructions in Yucatec Maya. In N. C. England, ed., *Papers in Mayan Linguistics.* University of Missouri Miscellaneous Publications in Anthropology no. 6, 3–24. Columbia: University of Missouri.

Brown, R., and A. Gillman. [1960] 1972. The Pronouns of Power and Solidarity. In Sebeok 1960, 253–76. Reprinted in P. P. Giglioli, ed., *Language and Social Context,* 252–82. New York: Penguin.

Bühler, K. 1982. *Sprachtheorie: die Darstellungsfunktion der Sprache.* Stuttgart: Gustav Fischer Verlag.

Comaroff, J. 1985. *Body of Power. Body of Spirit: The Culture and History of a South African People.* Chicago: University of Chicago Press.

Camaroff, J. L. and S. Roberts. 1981. *Rules and Processes: The Cultural Logic of Dispute in an African Context.* Chicago: University of Chicago Press.

Errington, J. J. 1988. *Structure and Style in Javanese: A Semiotic View of Linguistic Etiquette.* Philadelphia: University of Pennsylvania Press.

Evans, G. 1982. *The Varieties of Reference.* Edited By J. McDowell. New York: Oxford University Press.

Fortes, M. 1958. Introduction. In J. R. Goody, ed., *The Developmental Cycle in Domestic Groups.* Cambridge: Cambridge University Press.

Friedrich. P. [1964, 1970] 1979. Semantic Structure and Social Structure: An Instance from

Russian. In P. Friedrich, *Language, Context, and the Imagination: Essays,* 126–67. Stanford: Stanford University Press.

———. 1966. Structural Implications of Russian Pronominal Usage. In W. Bright, ed., *Sociolinguistics,* 214–59. The Hague: Mouton.

Gell, A. 1985. How to Read a Map: Remarks on the Practical Logic of Navigation. *Man* 20:271–86.

Hallowell, A. I. 1955. Cultural Factors in Spatial Orientation. In A. I. Hallowell, *Culture and Experience.* Philadelphia: University of Pennsylvania Press.

Hanks, W. F. 1983. Deixis and the Organization of Interactive Context in Yucatec Maya. Ph.D. diss., Department of Anthropology and Department of Linguistics. University of Chicago.

———. 1984b. The Interactive Basis of Maya Divination. Paper presented at the eighty-third annual meeting of the American Anthropological Association. Denver, Colorado.

———. 1984c. Sanctification, Structure, and Experience in a Yucatec Maya Ritual Event. *Journal of American Folklore* 97(384):131–66.

———. 1987a. Discourse Genres in a Theory of Practice. *American Ethnologist* 14(4):64–88.

———. 1993. Metalanguage and Pragmatics of Deixis. In J. Lucy, ed., *Reflexive Language: Reported Speech and Metapragmatics.* Cambridge: Cambridge University Press.

Johnson, M. 1987. *The Body in the Mind: The Bodily Basis of Meaning, Imagination and Reason.* Chicago: University of Chicago Press.

Logan, M. H. 1977. Humoral Medicine in Guatemala and Peasant Acceptance of Modern Medicine. In D. Landy, ed., *Culture, Disease, and Healing. Studies in Medical Anthropology,* 487–95. New York: Macmillan.

Lyons, J. 1977. *Semantics.* 2 vols. Cambridge: Cambridge University Press

Merleau-Ponty, M. [1945] 1967. *Phenomenologie de la Perception.* Paris: Editions Gallimard.

Munn, N. 1986. *The Fame of Gawa; A Symbolic Study of Value Transformations in a Massim (Papua New Guinea) Society.* Cambridge: Cambridge University Press.

Nash, J. [1971] 1975. *Bajo la mirada de los antepasados: creencias y comportamiento en una comunidad maya.* Mexico City: Instituto Indigenista Interamericano.

Panofsky. E. 1976. *Gothic Architecture and Scholasticism: An Inquiry into the Analogy of the Arts, Philosophy, and Religion in the Middle Ages.* New York: New American Library.

Redfield, R. 1941. *The Folk Culture of Yucatan.* Chicago: University of Chicago Press.

Redfield. R. and A. Villa Rojas. [1934] 1962. *Chan Kom: A Maya Village.* Chicago. University of Chicago Press.

Sahlins, M. [1976] 1977. Colors and Cultures. *Semiotica* 16:1–22. Reprinted in J. L. Dolgin, et al., eds., *Symbolic Anthropology,* 165–80. New York: Columbia University Press.

Sebeok, T., ed. 1960. *Style in Language.* Cambridge, Mass.: MIT Press.

Sherzer, J. 1983. *Kuna Ways of Speaking: An Ethnographic Perspective.* Austin: University of Texas Press.

Silverstein, M. 1976. Shifters, Verbal Categories and Cultural Description. In K. Basso and H. Shelby, eds., *Meaning in Anthropology,* 11–57. Albuquerque: School of American Research.

Talmy, L. 1983. How Language Structures Space. In H. L. Pick and L. P. Acredolo, eds., *Universals of Human Language.* Vol. 4, 625–54. Stanford: Stanford University Press.

Thompson, R. A. 1974. *The Winds of Tomorrow: Social Change in a Maya Town.* Chicago: University of Chicago Press.

Turner, T. 1980. The Social Skin. In J. Cherfas and R. Lewin, eds., *Not Work Alone.* Beverly
    Hills: Sage Publications.
Turner, V. 1967. *The Forest of Symbols.* New York: Cornell University Press.
Villa Rojas, A. [1945] 1978. *Los Elegidos de Dios: Etnografía de los Mayas de Quintana Roo.* Série
    de Antropologia Social, 56. Mexico: INI.

3

Metalanguage and Pragmatics of Deixis

INTRODUCTION

In performing an act of demonstrative reference, as in "*that's* it" (said pointing), a speaker produces a special kind of relation between himself or herself, an addressee, and the object of the point. One of the main ways in which natural language deictics differ from one another is in the kinds of relations they establish between participants and referential objects, familiar examples being Proximal to Speaker, Visible to Speaker and Addressee, Distal to Speaker, and so forth. Languages clearly differ in the kinds of relational features they encode (Anderson and Keenan 1985; Fillmore 1982; Hanks 1987, 1989), and the determination of these features is a central part of the empirical study of deixis. Beyond the identification of referents, however, demonstrative usage mobilizes a number of other relatively well-known functions too. These include ostensive presentations of a referent (Hanks 1984b), predication of identity or location ("There it is," "That's it"), direction of an addressee's attention ("There! [look!]"), along with other extra-referential effects (Levinson 1983:89ff.; Silverstein 1976). In many, though not all, cases of demonstrative reference, a crucial role is also played by the execution of bodily gestures simultaneous with the utterance, such as pointing, directed gaze, handing the object over, cocking the head, or pursing the lips (Sherzer 1973).

This unavoidable linkage of deictic functions to speech events is a powerful illustration of how language structure encodes aspects of the situational frameworks in which verbal interaction occurs. By *framework* in this context, I mean the immediate social field of space and time, perception, orientation, and participant engagement in acts of reference.[1] Because demonstrative reference may be linked to either antecedent or anticipated discourse, as well as to the simultaneous present, the framework of deixis must include the interactive process leading up to and following from an act of reference. Frameworks in this sense are what Cicourel (1985:172, 176) called *local productions*, emergent elements of particular settings, subject to revision over the course of interaction.

Alongside *frameworks* in this sense is the related concept of *frames,* which is also relevant to the description of deixis in language. The term "frame" is used in prototype and cognitive semantics to denote a set of lexical items whose members correspond to different parts of a single actional or conceptual whole (Fillmore 1978:165, 1985; Lakoff 1984). *Buy* and *sell* are parts of the same act of exchange, in relation to which both are understood. Insofar as these actional wholes, or event types, are reflected in the conventional resources of the language, they are *schematic,* as opposed to purely local, productions (Cicourel 1985:177). Schemata are prefabricated representations that structure the way actors perceive and interpret objects, events, and experiences. Although they are influenced by ongoing events, they are logically prior to, and function as guides in, any given event.[2] As Brown and Yule (1983:238ff.) point out, frames are usually viewed as "fixed data structures" that represent stereotypical situations. Thus, it can be said that frames are relatively static resources defined at the level of schematic structure, whereas frameworks are dynamic productions defined at the level of local usage.

Any theory that incorporates the ideas of frames and frameworks must address the relation between the two, whether from a cognitive, linguistic, or sociological perspective. How one formulates this relation will determine how one distinguishes the system of language from speech, and ultimately from the world in which it is used. Variously phrased, this has been a central preoccupation of recent linguistic theory, corresponding to the interface between semantics and pragmatics. By incorporating a family of concepts including frames, image-schemas, and prototypes, cognitive linguistics has inevitably redrawn the boundary between structure and use. This is evident, for instance, in Fillmore's (1985) undermining of the dichotomy between knowledge of language and knowledge of the world, as well as Langacker's (1984) outright rejection of the semantics–pragmatics division in cognitive grammar. In this chapter, I assume that there is a principled distinction between linguistic structure and situated use, just as there is between frames and frameworks, as I have defined them. Rather than privilege the distinction as a way of explaining deixis, however, my purpose is to examine in more detail the interpenetration of the two levels.

Various criteria are applicable to establish whether an aspect of use is part of the conventional linguistic code. These include, for example, the relative consistency of association between uses and forms, the grammatical consequences of a pattern of use, and the degree to which native speakers associate given forms with specific uses. For any aspect of conveyed meaning or function that arises in speech, the more consistently it is conveyed by a given form, the more grammatical evidence there is linking it to the linguistic distribution of the form, and the more readily native speakers associate it with the form, the more likely it is that it belongs to a schematic frame, and not only to situational frameworks.

This chapter bears mainly on the latter of these three criteria. It seeks to relate native-speaker awareness of the frameworks produced in deictic usage to the conventional frames mobilized in use. My goal is to demonstrate that, if properly analyzed, native accounts of language use can make a unique contribution to the study of pragmatics. It is usually assumed in linguistics that because native speakers are unconscious of much of the grammatical mechanism of their language, it follows that their naive descriptions can serve only as flawed clues to the system, best ignored or discarded in favor of other forms of evidence. One sees a similar orientation in the commitment of conversational analysis to "naturally occurring interactions" as opposed to hypothetical or stereotyped ones (Atkinson and Heritage 1984).

Common to both linguistics and conversational analysis is the observation that scientific study of language structure and use reveals an order of complexity far beyond what native speakers can describe. Although unquestionably accurate, this observation has obscured the equally important facts that native speakers do have relatively systematic ideas about language, that these ideas are an unavoidable part of pragmatic context, and that the expression of them in speech is itself a kind of direct usage. The interpretive frames that speakers share derive in large measure from their metalinguistic common sense, and the process of producing frameworks in actual use incorporates a significant metalinguistic component. One consequence of this for field work is that a frame semantics must take account of native metalanguage in order to locate the interface between schematic frames and local frameworks. The question then becomes how one goes about gathering and analyzing metalanguage in such a way as to maximize its positive contribution, while minimizing its potential for distortion.

Deixis provides a privileged case in which to explore the relation between frames, frameworks, and metalanguage. The relevant schematic frames are based on the actional wholes of demonstrative reference. They include the different deictic expressions corresponding to conventionally distinguished components of referential speech events. Whatever else is included, *I, you, we* (inclusive), *here, now,* and *this* are members of a single schematic frame, which might be called the proximal frame. Retaining Cicourel's (1985) terms, deictic subsystems in language are schematic templates made up of prefabricated categories through which local knowledge is articulated. The duality of such forms is a consequence of their being indexical, therefore local, yet also conventional types, therefore schematic. The idea that demonstrative expressions are organized into sets like the proximal frame is also reflected in the work of linguists and philosophers who analyze deictics by intertranslation, that is, by paraphrasing one form with others in the same language (Reichenbach 1947; Russell 1940; Lyons 1977). To paraphrase an expression, one uses the others in the same frame, as in "*here* is where *we* are *now*."[3]

The connection between deictics and metalanguage is a complex one. On the one hand, deictics could be viewed as metapragmatic devices insofar as they regiment the relation between a referential object and a pragmatic context relative to which it is individuated. Thus, a distal form such as English *that* signals (roughly) that the referent is in a relation of nonproximity relative to the utterance context, whereas a proximal form such as *this* signals a relation of relative immediacy. Through deictic usage, which is ubiquitous in speech, interactants continually monitor and qualify the linkage between what they are saying and the contexts in which they are doing so. It follows that the ability to use these forms appropriately is itself a metalinguistic ability, involving judgments of the fit between speech and context. On the other hand, while native speakers do not necessarily have well-developed theories about deictic frames as such, they do have elaborate ideas regarding the situational frameworks in which deictics are used. By working through these, drawing out the metapragmatic backing of the forms, we gather crucial information regarding both the conventional semantics and the pragmatics of deixis.

The empirical focus of the discussion is Yucatec Maya, a native American language of Yucatan, Mexico. We begin with a brief outline of three key concepts in the study of native metalinguistic awareness: metalanguage (in relation to object language), mention (in relation to direct use), and native typification (in relation to actual practice). In the next section we turn to the formal details of metalinguistic glosses which I elicited from Maya speakers in Maya. Treating metalanguage as a kind of use, I will show that speakers deploy the same grammatical resources in describing their language as they do in using the language in everyday interaction. It thus becomes clear that the relation between "naturally occurring direct use" and "elicited metalanguage" is not necessarily one of sheer division. To a considerable degree, the two overlap in the pragmatics of the language.

The linguistic commonalities between metalanguage and direct usage provide a grammatical scaffolding within which to explore the functional relations between the two. These are the focus of the next section, in which we examine what Maya speakers had to say about their language. Drawing on in-depth investigation of Maya deictic usage in a wide range of contexts, I found that speakers created metalinguistic glosses according to the same tacit assumptions which evidently guide their everyday language usage. Moreover, there was an intimate connection between what they told me about deixis, and how they managed their relations to me in the very course of elicitation itself. It conversing with me, they put into practice, so to speak, the same actional frames of deictic reference as they sought to describe.

This has two noteworthy implications. First, it suggests that metalinguistic elicitation as a field method can produce highly revealing results, provided it is conducted properly in the native language. The traditional notion that elicitation is inherently unnatural and distorting is based on an impoverished view of the method and an overemphasis on the disjunction between native views of practice and practice itself. Second, it is in metalinguistic descriptions that speakers provide some of the most direct evidence of their interpretive frames. If we assume an objectivist stance toward verbal interaction, then native views can never provide more than a deflected representation of the system. If, on the other hand, we assume an interpretive stance, such as that taken by frame semantics, then we would expect native talk about talk to reveal principles and schematic resources at play in a wide variety of contexts.[4] This is just what took place in my conversations with Maya speakers. Like other actors, they tend to reproduce in their statements about speech the very assumptions that guide them in the routine frameworks of interaction.

I emphasize the formal and functional connections between direct language use, or pragmatics, and native descriptions of use, or metapragmatics, because the two are traditionally kept apart. It would be inaccurate, however, to equate the two, and in discussing Maya metalanguage, I shall take pains to point out the ways in which it potentially distorts the intricacies of actual usage. In particular, speakers were inclined to accord significance to certain aspects of usage while overlooking others. Furthermore, there were inevitable differences between the actual conveyed meanings of deictic utterances and the descriptive terms in which speakers sought to portray those meanings. While it is crucial to take account of these discrepancies, they do not invalidate the method of elicitation. On the contrary, they reinforce the distinction between frames and frameworks, since the former are, by definition, schematic (therefore partial) constructs that are adapted and combined in situated speech. The main proposal of this chapter is therefore that native metalinguistic discourse is an essential part of pragmatics, because it is itself a kind of language use, and because it embodies the interpretive frames that guide everyday interaction.

METALANGUAGE, MENTION, AND TYPIFICATION

It is customary in semantics to observe a distinction between objects and the verbal expressions that may be used to refer to them. This division is clear in principle, and its application is simple when the object is a person or a bowling ball. When the object is itself a verbal expression, however, it may require considerable care to keep it distinct from its name. Consider,

> Here is the book.
> Here is adverbial.
> *Here* is adverbial.

The first sentence is (we will assume) a straightforward presentative, in the uttering of which the speaker directs the addressee's attention to a certain book, perhaps handing it over to the addressee. The second, if not nonsense, is a false statement, which asserts that my current location is adverbial in character. The problem with this sentence is corrected in the third, in which italics set off the name of the linguistic expression to which *adverbial* is properly attributed. The italics indicate that what they enclose is not a linguistic expression being directly used, but the name of an expression being mentioned. *Mention* will designate a mode of discourse in which a verbal expression is presented without being attributed to any speaker, usually for the purpose of commenting on it. One of the key features of this mode is that expressions in it are not subject to the normal appropriateness conditions that obtain in direct usage. This means that a demonstrative in the mention mode is not linked to the current event frame in which it is uttered, the way directly used demonstratives are. The speaker of the third sentence has not presented anything, nor made any claim about the current spatial or perceptual field.

When mentioning linguistic forms in written prose, one can try to be scrupulous in the use of italics and quotation marks, and keep the two modes of discourse distinct. However, the task is made difficult by the fact that mention is itself a kind of use, and some stretches of discourse may be ambiguous, or simultaneously mention and direct use, as in

> The meaning of *here* is the place where I utter "here."

The question is whether the material following the verb "is" in this sentence instantiates direct use or mention. It cannot be simply direct use, since it obviously bears a different relation to what precedes it than does the same phrase in

> This is the place where I utter "here" (as they unload the cargo).

Yet it is not simply mention either, since it is not the name of the deictic expression, but rather a rough gloss of its conveyed meaning. Any material that occurs in predicate position in a meaning statement such as this one is at least ambiguously mention, in that it bears on the language rather than on the extra-linguistic world. If we start from a distinction between use and mention, therefore, we must be prepared to recognize varieties of each, as well as overlaps between the two modes (see Garver 1965).

Speakers must manage the distinction between use and mention whenever they comment on, question, or make reference to linguistic form or meaning. These uses of language are *metalinguistic* in that they treat the language as an object of reference and description. It is a diacritic feature of natural languages that they may be used as their own metalanguage (Jakobson 1980 [1957]; Weinreich 1980). The italicized portions of utterances such as "What makes you say *that*?," " *This* isn't at all what I expected you to tell me," " *Now* that you've admitted it, don't you feel better?," and "Don't talk to me *that way*" all have a metalinguistic component. Although they do not *reproduce* linguistic forms, as do paradigm cases of mention and quotation, they nonetheless *refer* to events of speech, as is clear from the verbs of speaking with which they are used. Since references to and comments on language are part of routine usage, metalanguage falls within the scope of pragmatics even narrowly conceived (Levinson 1983: chapt. 1; Silverstein 1979). The practical task for speakers engaged in metalinguistic discourse is to formulate their statements in such a way as to keep clear the different levels that they must inevitably combine into an intelligible whole—use, mention, reference to chunks of language, and, as we will see, several other modes.

Vološinov (1986 [1929]:112–25) treated metalinguistic discourse under the rubric of reported speech, which he defined as both speech within speech and speech about speech. In the first case, like mention and verbatim quote, the original expression is reproduced in approximately identical form, rather than being rendered as an object of description. Vološinov saw reported speech in both variants as a central part of the social constitution of language, because it provides a kind of "document" of the ways in which speakers understand and evaluate their own usage, and that of their contemporaries. Because speakers do not talk exactly as they say they do, reported speech is an imperfect, sometimes distorting, representation of direct usage. Its value as a social datum is *not* a function of its accuracy with respect to that which it describes. Rather, it is a documentary expression of what speakers *think* they do. It is in this second sense that reported speech reflects the social evaluation of language, and leads to a consideration of linguistic common sense and ideologies.

A substantial part of native speakers' commonsense knowledge of their language is embodied in the ability to recognize and produce *typical* linguistic practice. This entails the ability to distinguish between relatively canonical uses of language and extended, or even idiosyncratic, ones. According to Rosch (1978:30), cognitive categories tend to become defined in terms of prototypical exemplars, which contain the attributes most representative of the category and least representative of items outside the category. Prototypical usage would correspond to those cases judged most typical of the relevant form, and most distinct from other uses. Thus, we could recognize a dwarf tiger, say of the size of a large dog, as a valid instance of the kind "tiger," while simultaneously recognizing the atypicality of the case. Fillmore (1978, 1982) is among several linguists who have adapted the concept of prototype to linguistic semantics, in an effort to account for both the variability of usage, and the fact that some aspects of the conveyed meaning of categories are more central to their definition than others. The dwarf tiger violates an English speaker's expectation of size, but this is a less severe anomaly than would be a specimen with spots instead of stripes, or quills instead of fur. Similarly, when a speaker uses a normally remote demonstrative expression, such as *way over there* (or its equivalent), in reference to an object actually within reach, we can recognize this as both atypical, hence contrastive, and yet fully intelligible.

This chapter examines a portion of the linguistic common sense of Maya speakers, as reflected in their descriptions of the meaning and use of spatial deictics. On the basis of metalinguistic discussions in Maya with native speakers, it is shown that these speakers have well-formed ideas about prototypical deictic usage, and that these ideas are crucially linked to the pragmatic frameworks that play a role in routine use. The individuals whose testimony is represented were all full-time Maya speakers, none of whom had received more than elementary formal education. All were accustomed to teaching and correcting me in Maya during at least three months prior to the metalinguistic discussion. The tenor of elicitation was kept purposely informal, one-on-one, usually at my home after work hours or at the work site during rests from labor. Questions were brief and open-ended, using standard Maya metalinguistic formulae such as *b'áˀaš u k'aát yáˀ al hèˀela* 'What does *hèˀela* mean (lit. want to say)?' and *báˀaš k u t'an ik hèˀela*? 'What does *hèˀela* say?'[5] The nonunderlined portions of these are among the simplest and least specific ways of asking what something means in Maya. Both of the metalinguistic verbs are transitive, taking a reported speech form as subject. In these two examples, the reported subject, which I will call the *target* of the gloss, is in the mention mode, reproduced without being attributed to any speaker or situation. Alternatively, it could be a description of speech (Vološinov's speech about speech), such as *le héˀ k aw áak oˀ* 'That which you're saying.' While I occasionally suggested an explanation in an effort to draw out more detail, my overall strategy was to question the obvious and obtrude only selectively on the response. The result was sometimes lengthy responses complete with anecdotes from daily activities, which I encouraged with backchannel and repeated inquiry.[6]

STRUCTURAL RESOURCES FOR METALANGUAGE IN MAYA

Maya speakers use a range of linguistic devices in formulating metalanguage, both in the course of everyday interaction and in response to queries about their language. These devices provide a set of resources for managing what Goffman (1981:128) called *footing*, that is, the alignment a participant takes up in relation to his or her utterance. Mention, quotation, and other forms of reported speech correspond to different footings, and Goffman's remarks are directly relevant to the study of metalanguage. He broke down the concept of 'speaker' into three distinct roles that usually coincide but can be separated in a variety of ways. The *animator* Goffman defined as the individual who actually utters a linguistic form; the agent of an act of phonation.[7] The *author* is the individual who has selected the words and sentiments expressed, whether or not he or she voices the utterance. The *principal* is that individual whose position is established, whose beliefs are told, by the utterance (see Levinson 1987; McCawley 1986 for further discussion). Although these three usually coincide in direct speech, it is easy enough to imagine a reporter quoting a speech by a press agent (animator) drafted by a speech writer (author) to represent the position of a political candidate (principal). Similar embeddings occur frequently in everyday Maya, as in English.

The structural devices that speakers use to signal their current footing in talk are what Goffman called *keys*. Keys index the shifts between different discourse modes, including for instance *direct discourse,* in which animator is author and principal; *mentioned discourse,* in which language forms are cited by an animator who may or may not be the author, but who speaks for no principal (insofar as he or she merely cites the language without attributing responsibility for it to anyone); and *quoted discourse,* where a speaker animates the utterance of another animator, who may or may not be author or principal. In everyday conversation, Maya speakers regularly key their current footing through five major devices: (i) lexical markers of the difference between hypothetical and real speech, (ii) verbs and particles of speaking, (iii) presentation of quoted speech as a topic for evaluative commentary, (iv) prosody, and (v) demonstratives and other shifters. It is worth emphasizing that the indexical grounding of demonstrative reference in discourse makes it a powerful resource for signaling a speaker's current footing. Consequently, metalinguistic glosses of deictics in Maya combine both direct and reported usage of the forms side by side, providing a unique opportunity to explore the functional structure of deixis in a multi-frame speech context. These five keying devices will be illustrated in the following discussion, with examples taken from elicited metalanguage.[8]

Hypothetical vs. Real Speech

One of the most commonly invoked distinctions in Maya metalanguage is the one between hypothetical verses vouched-for discourse, where these correspond to speech with no real principal verses speech of which the current animator is principal, respectively. In everyday talk with each other, Maya speakers shift often and fluidly between hypothetical discourse, created to make a point, lay out a rationale for some action, poke fun at one another, or just reason through a problem, and real discourse, presented as their own opinion, for which they take responsibility. In our metalinguistic discussions, hypothetical talk consisted of imaginary narrated events which were neither currently verifiable in the framework of our interaction nor subject to the normal assumption that objects and events referred to actually exist. Hypothetical discourse was a vehicle for presenting illustrative scenarios in which fictional characters took on the role of principal, addressing imagined interlocutors and performing imagined acts.

Among the devices used to key hypothetical speech are several special labels. These typically occur in initial position in a gloss, and key the onset of an example scenario. The discourse immediately following the key is to be interpreted as constituting a single framework, which commonly contains further embedded footings. Consider the bold portions of the following examples (where ↑, ↓, and → indicate rising, falling, and level terminal contours respectively).

(1) WH le beyoʾ ʾaálkabih binik
        So like that he took off running (what does it mean?)

     V   hmm wá **um p'eéh koómparasyon** → t aw il ik hwèeyas →
         Hmm, ↑ **for instance** ↑ you see footprints

         biš aw il ik ↓ nàaȼ' wá naáč→ le bey oʾ ʾaálkabih binik→
         "How do you see it? close or far (apart)?" "Like that, he went running
         (because prints are far apart)" [98.B.374]

(2) WH báʾaš u k'aát iy áʾal háʾaliloʾ
        What does háʾaliloʾ mean?

     V   **pór ehèemplo** k a hoók 'sik sìinko pesos→ hoóʾs u láak'
         For example you pull out five pesos. "Take out some more."

         mináʾan→ čeén háʾalilorʾ
         "There isn't (any more). That's just all." [6.B.163]

(3) DB le bey oʾ→ u tiʾáal u šul ik [...] mèen **mèen kwèen táa**
        That way (as you've said it), it's for finishing up [...] cause **assume**

         teč eʾ t a bin téʾe bey aʾ [...]
         you, you're going right over there like this, ... (continues) [98.B.374]

(4) DP **wá** k a k'aát ten eʾ→ kuš tuún pàabloh→túʾuš yàan
        If you were to ask me, "What about Pablo, where is he?"

         tíʾan óʾob téʾ tyotočaʾ
         "They're right over there in their house."

The material immediately following the underlined keys in each of these examples consists of a scene-setting descriptive remark, delivered in direct discourse—you see footprints, you take out five pesos, you're going along. In the case of the conditional clause in (4), the descriptive remark is the speech report "you ask me," which is flanked by the boldface particles.

In the first three examples, the keying phrase incorporates a Spanish borrowing. A *komparasyon* is a 'comparison' in that it offers a hypothetical scenario in some relevant way parallel to the topic currently at hand. *pór ehèemplo* 'for example' introduces an illustration. *mèen kwèentah,* which I have glossed loosely 'assume,' is very common in conversation, and is literally an imperative phrase 'make (the) account,' conveying 'let's say,' 'let's assume.' Each of these expressions can be combined with the Maya particle couplet *wá . . . e*ʔ, which is the standard way of marking If-clauses.

In three of the examples, what follows the descriptive setting is an instance of quoted speech. In these and other cases, the footing shifts involved in presenting such quotation are signaled only by slight shifts in prosody, if at all. Although V, DB, and DP animated this speech, its principals are fictional characters, an imaginary 'you' and 'I.' By using first and second person pronouns to create the scene, speakers chose to project themselves and me, their addressee, into the role of interlocutors in the hypothetical framework. This is part of a more global tendency on their part to use the current context of *our* interaction as the material out of which to create other interactive frameworks. We will return to this strategy below, in relation to demonstrative usage more generally.

Whereas hypothetical talk is tied to fictional principals, real talk is the responsibility of the current speaker. Even with quoted or reported speech, of which others are the principals, the current animator is responsible until further notice for accurate reproduction of the original utterances. Maya speakers cast most of their evaluative comments, immediately following the hypothetical scenarios, in real direct speech. Having animated the target expression under consideration, they commented on its appropriateness or conveyed meaning relative to the hypothetical framework. This shift back into real discourse they keyed with several recurrent constructions, as in (5–6).

(5)   WH kuš tuún <u>lel o</u>ʔ <u>bèeyl</u>?
                 What about <u>That's so</u>?

            DB <u>lel o</u>ʔ <u>bèey</u> → **pero** lel oʔ čeén u ¢ʼokbah tʼàan
                 <u>That's so</u>, but that one, it's just for terminating talk. [103.B.238]

(6)   V <u>má</u>ʔ<u>ah t in man ik le bey o</u>ʔ <u>o</u>ʔ → **ʔeskeh** máʔ ʔu¢ taw ič iʔ
                 <u>I don't buy the ones like that</u>. **It's that** you don't like it. [92.B.060]

Other Spanish phrases that index the shift from hypothetical to real commentary include *pwes* 'then' ([103.B.505]) and *kyere desìir e*ʔ 'it means (that)' ([6.B.100]).

Thus from the perspective of hypothetical and real speech, Maya metalinguistic statements typically project a hypothetical framework, in which both direct and quoted discourse are embedded, flanked by preceding and following real discourse. The openings of both hypothetical and real speech frames were often keyed by lexical expressions, with which speakers index their new footing. Such combinations of discourse modes and keys are typical not only of elicited metalanguage, but of everyday usage as well.

Report Forms

Report forms as used here refers to the lexical resources speakers mobilized to indicate that an immediately preceding or following utterance was an animation of the speech of another principal. This is more narrow than Vološinov's "reported speech," since it denotes "speech about speech," including the verbs and particles of saying that describe utterances, and that speakers used to frame their quotations as events of certain kinds, but it excludes the quoted "speech within speech" itself.

There are relatively few native verbs of speaking commonly used in modern Maya conversation, and performative usage, such as 'I (hereby) ask you X,' is rare in comparison with English. The most frequently encountered and least specific is *-á'alik* 'to say it,' which also occurs in the expression *uk'aát uyá' aleh* 'it means (lit. wants to say).' *t'àan,* the root for 'language, speech,' is also quite common, both in the transitive *t'anik* 'to mean (subject = a sign), to address someone (subject = a speaker)' and intransitive *t'àan* 'to speak (subject = a speaker), to be meaningful (subject = a sign).' *t'àan* was often used to refer to the initial utterance of an interaction, as in

(7)   DB   k u ¢'on ik č'iíč' le maák o ' → **k a t'àan ten**
        "Is that guy shooting birds?" **you address me.**

Both of these verbs of saying can occur either preceding or following a stretch of reported speech, which may be either verbatim quote or indirect discourse. Other verbs of saying include *paytik* 'to summons (someone),' *¢olik* 'to explain (it),' *¢ikbatik* 'to discuss, recount,' *nuúkik* 'to respond,' *k'eyik* 'bawl out,' *poč'ik* 'to insult,' and *tusik* 'to mislead, lie to.' Common Spanish forms include *koómprometerik* 'to commit one's self to (it),' *duúdàartik* 'to express doubt about (it),' *proónunsiartik* 'to speak (a language), to say' and *'iínbitàartik* 'to invite.'

In addition to verbs of speaking, there are two particles in Maya whose central function is to index reported speech. One of these is *bin,* usually glossed 'they say' or 'it is said.' This is invariant and apparently not inflected for person at all. It is used to report customary knowledge, as well as descriptive reports of actual utterances (what Vološinov 1986:130 called "referent analyzing indirect report"), as in *hé' bin u tàal e'* 'He says he'll come.' This particle is common in ritual speech and traditional stories (Hanks 1984a), but was virtually absent from the metalinguistic glosses speakers produced. A second particle commonly called the *quotative* is always inflected for person, indicates verbatim quotation of speech, or reperformance of some gesture, and occurs frequently in glosses. It always follows the quoted discourse and is inflected for the person of the principal to whom it is attributed, as in

(8)   DP   ti ? a tàah té ?el a ? **keč ti**? c̓áw é ?es ik ti ?
             "Come right here," **you say to him.** You've shown him (where to come).
             [1.A.80]

This form appears to be grammatically intermediate between a verb and a particle. Although it inflects for all three persons and takes a dative object, it cannot bear tense, aspect, or mode marking, nor can it be used as the sole verb in a relative clause, nor can it be questioned, negated, or adverbially modified in any way to reflect the kind of utterance it reports. It is extremely common in everyday Maya conversation, in which speakers routinely quote their addressees or other copresent individuals, imputing humorous utterances to each other as a way of playing, making fun, or even giving advice. Often speakers use it to re-present an interlocutor's utterance with a minor change in form, implying a totally different interpretation which usually portrays the interlocutor as laughable. In the glosses, it provided an efficient, semantically general way of shifting into quotation, thus taking over this one portion of the reported speech functions.

Quoted Topics and Direct Comments

Topicalization in Maya is indicated by fronting the topicalized phrase into S-initial position.[9] The end of the topic phrase is always (in this definition) indicated by a terminal particle, minimally *e*?, and usually set off from what follows by a slight pause or break in intonation. Commonly, speakers presented target forms in topic position, as mentioned forms on which they then commented, as in

(9)   WH   bá ?aš u k̓aát iy á ?al <u>hé ?el eč e</u>?
             What does <u>hé ?el eč e</u>? mean?

        DP   **le <u>hé ?el eč e</u>? o**?→ miš bá ?ah k iy á ?a ik
             That <u>hé ?el eč e</u>?, it doesn't mean a thing. [1.B.168]

(10)   WH   bá ?aš u kaát iy á ?al <u>tí ? ili o</u> ?
             What does <u>tí ?ili o</u> ? mean?

        DP   pwes **čeén <u>tí ?ili o</u>**? e?→ miš bá ?ah k u t̓an ik
             Well **just <u>tí ?ili o</u>**? (alone) says nothing.

In both of these examples, DP rejects forms I had suggested as meaningless. The bold portions are topic phrases consisting of the citation form in the mention mode, followed by a terminal particle. Immediately after the topic is DP's evaluative comment on it, as in

<table>
<tr><td>[Mention]</td><td>[Direct]</td></tr>
<tr><td>Topic</td><td>Comment</td></tr>
</table>

In the first example the topic phrase contains a presentative sentence, but is flanked by the NP demonstratives *le ... o'* 'that,' just as might be any other topical NP. This is consistent with Quine's (1951:26) observation that a stretch of mentioned discourse, regardless of its internal structure, functions as a single undifferentiated whole, or "hieroglyph," relative to the larger discourse in which it is embedded. The demonstrative *that* in this case lumps together the mentioned speech, and explicitly marks its anaphoric relation to what precedes it—DP is merely reanimating the citation form that I presented, leaving authorship and principalship squarely in my hands. It is my impression that this glossing strategy arose mainly in the context of negative judgments like these ones, where speakers were unwilling to impute what they considered to be an ill-formed utterance to even a hypothetical Maya speaker, laying the blame instead entirely on my linguistic incompetence.[10] In any case, the use of anaphoric deictics in references to preceding discourse and the topic–comment format are both standard Maya usages. They lend further evidence to the claim that these elicited glosses are valid exemplars of spoken Maya, rather than mere artifacts of an artificial task.

Prosodic Indexes of Footing Shifts

Maya conversation is marked by an abundance of expressive paralanguage, indexing shifts in footing, as well as other pragmatic effects. Very common features include pitch modulation (overhigh, overlow, falsetto), tempo (overfast, overslow, jerky rhythm), loudness (overloud, oversoft), and voice quality (breathy voice, tense articulation, creaky voice). Metalinguistic glosses were no different, and in many cases shifts between reported and direct speech were keyed only by paralanguage or use of marked final contours (↑,↓ rising and falling final contour; ^- -^ overloud; ↓— —↓ overhigh).[11]

(11)   DB k̂ū ȼ'on ik č'íí̂č' le maák̄ ô'→ k a t'àan ten→
            *"That guy's shooting birds," *you address to me.

                        ↑— —↑
        bey sùukil u ȼ'on k o'   ↑ <u>bey u ȼ'on k e č'íí̂č' o'</u>↓
        *"That's how he customarily shoots?" *<u>"That's how he shoots the birds."</u>
        [92.A.485]

The underlined portion is the target form that I had asked DB to explain for me. As it stands, the example starts off quoting a hypothetical utterance imputed to me, then shifts to direct delivery of the report formula 'you address me,' then shifts again to quoted hypothetical speech belonging to an unnamed principal, then produces the target utterance as a quoted response to the preceding hypothetical question. In the interlinear glosses, each of these key shifts is indicated by an asterisk. Note that with the exception of the report form, all remaining shifts are indicated in the Maya solely by prosodic features. The inferable interactive structure of the example is,

(11′)   UTTERANCE FORM   HYPOTHETICAL PRINCIPALS
              "That guy's shooting birds,"   you (WH) say to me (DB)
              "That's how he customarily shoots?"   I (DB) respond to you (WH)
              "(Yup,) That's how he shoots the bird(s)." you (WH) respond to me (DB)

The use of prosodic features like these is sufficiently central to metalinguistic speech to merit a separate study, but cannot be further explored here (see Gumperz 1982). The point for present purposes is that the shifts in footing so indexed fit into the repertoire of keying devices with which coherent multi-frame discourse is produced, whether spontaneously or in response to the questions of a foreign linguist.

Deictic Usage as a Key to Footing

The last major kind of verbal resource that speakers used to create metalanguage are the indexical–referential categories of person, nominal demonstratives, and deictic adverbs. As we have seen already, these linguistic elements are used to ground strips of discourse in interactive frameworks, both in everyday spontaneous conversation and in metalinguistic glosses. Because of their relational structure, binding unique referents to the actional contexts in which they are denoted, shifters are an ideal resource for laminating multiple frames in talk. In effect, in asking speakers what deictics mean, we ask them to make explicit the processes of contextualization whereby they routinely relate language to its situational framework. The transformation involved in such an exercise is basically one of foregrounding and describing what is normally backgrounded and automatic.

During metalinguistic conversations, speakers managed their interaction with me by using shifters in the standard ways. They assumed my participation as a 'you' and their own as an 'I', along with the full range of dimensions that make up a deictic frame—the perceptual, spatial, attentional, background knowledge, and temporal fields of our ongoing interaction. This is particularly evident in the use of shifters to refer to utterances, as in example (5) above and in a number of other cases. Often upon coming to the end of an illustrative scenario, the speaker would summarize it and reaffirm its properness, using a metalinguistic deictic token.

(12)   DB ... klàaroh tuún le bey oʔ
                  ... It's clear then like that [103.B.418]

Most summary statements were formulated with the deictic *bey, bèey* 'thus, in that manner,' like this one. This is the same form typically used to end narratives, 'that's how it happened, that's the way it was,' as well as to respond affirmatively to a statement, 'that's right, that's how it is' (see McQuown 1979).

The deictic framework of our current interaction was not only the ground from which hypothetical speech events were reported, but also became part of the reported events themselves. By using first and second person pronouns, along with proximal spatial, temporal, and nominal demonstratives, speakers mapped the current event framework (E^s) onto the example ones they created (E^{sn}). They rarely made up a purely hypothetical scenario, such as "Imagine one guy says to another out in the woods, 'Come here.' He'd be telling him to go to where he was." Instead, they showed a strong preference for examples such as "Imagine I say to you right in here where we are, 'Come here.' I'm telling you to come over here where I'm sitting." This strategy gave their examples an immediacy they would otherwise have lacked, keeping both of us involved as the principals of hypothetical utterances. More significantly, the practice of transposing the actual indexical ground into the hypothetical narrated framework ($E^s \rightarrow E^{sn}$) is further evidence that metalanguage is fabricated according to the same logic of use that underlies direct reference. The following is a typical example (曱- -曱 indicates tense articulation; ᵕ indicates fast transition; ≫ indicates extrafast; see note 11).

(13)   WH   <u>hé</u>ʔ <u>yàan té</u>ʔ<u>el a</u>ʔ → máʔaloʔ↑
                        What about <u>Here it is right here</u>?

            DP   <u>hé</u>ʔ <u>yàan té</u>ʔ<u>el a</u>ʔ ↓ m pʼeé báʔa taánka yan eč→
                        <u>Here it is right here</u>. It's a thing, you're outside,

                  ≫-   ↑- -↑   ↓- -↓
                  k aw áa ti e→ má a héʔ yàan téʔ el aʔ ᵕ↗ keč→
                  You tell 'im "Here it is right here!" ya say.

                  ↓-   -↓   ↑-   -↑
                  le kán aw áʔal eh→ púm→púm ᵕ↗ pʰúm ↓ k aw okol
                  When you say it, boom, boom, boom, you come in

                  曱 -   -≫   -曱
                  a čʼaá way ič nah eʔ ᵕ↗ k aw é es ik tiʔ↓
                  and get it here inside the house. You show it to him. [16.A.008]

This gloss was produced during a conversation inside the main sleeping house of my homestead, which I rented from DP. DP starts off re-presenting the target utterance, without specifying who is to be the assumed principal and without keying the report frame in which he begins. This frame is readily inferrable from the identity of his utterance with mine, which was reported, and it makes no difference to the example whether we assume him to be the hypothetical principal, or myself. What is important is that the utterance be assumed to occur just outside the door of my house, about 10–15 feet from our actual location, out of sight from us. I am cast as the hypothetical respondent who comes into the house where we are actually sitting and gets the object, whatever it may be. The retrieval and demonstration of the unnamed object reflects the presentative function of the utterance portion *hé° ela°* 'Here it is,' while the relation of proximity but noninclusion holding between the 'outside' and 'here inside' is a reflex of the locative adverbial *té° el a°* 'right here.'

In other words, this vignette explains the spatial relation encoded in the target deictics by way of homology between two event frames. DP postulates a deictic framework identical to the current one in all but the ways that he specifies. He presupposes the intelligibility of our current shared interactive framework, and uses this as a template from which to generate new ones. This is possible as a strategy only because our interaction in fact took place within a coherent indexical framework, organized by the same fields of perception, space, and knowledge as he was attempting to describe. Just as I have tried to point out the ways in which the language of Maya metalanguage draws on the same formal and functional resources as everyday speech, so too the use of deictics to anchor that metalanguage in the context of its production is a case of conventional frames used to produce a situated framework. In other words, the fact that DP formulates his description of Maya in Maya is of a piece with the fact that he projects himself, his current interlocutor, and the place of talk into the description. It is the inherently relational structure of deictic reference that allows him to manage this with the precision evident in examples such as (13).

The lesson for linguistic elicitation is obvious: the productive circularity in DP's linguistic common sense would be obliterated if our conversations had been held in any "contact" language other than Maya, or under any more closely controlled interview conditions. It was only by giving relatively free play to his and other speakers' ability to discuss their language in their language that I was able to observe their categorizations of our ongoing talk as it emerged. In this section, we have seen this circularity in some of the formal details of metalinguistic discourse. We turn now to the question of what these Maya speakers said about deixis, and how their portrayals compare with their actual usage.

COMMONSENSE TYPIFICATIONS OF DEICTIC SPACE

Because of their indexical component, relational features, and further pragmatic functions in routine use, deictic expressions can be seen as preconstituted signs corresponding to fairly complex actional wholes, as in the act of presenting an object to an interlocutor, simultaneously making reference to it, characterizing its current perceptibility, and directing the addressee's attention. Given a deictic expression, native speakers can make various deductions about the speech frameworks in which it could be properly used (cf. Silverstein 1978). The relative specificity of these deductions depends partly on the target form, since some deictics are more specific, or highly marked, than others. In my experience, Maya speakers have relatively elaborate ideas about deixis, which make up a coherent vision of the meaning and use of the forms.

In focusing on these ideas, we are no longer looking at the glosses as instances of direct use, as we were in the preceding section. Rather, native speakers' commonsense ideas about language and the practice of deixis guide, but do not determine, their actual usage, nor their actual interpretation of other speakers.

Their statements reflect a ready sense of what is *typical* usage, more than a considered assessment of the full range of ways they *actually* use the forms. Insofar as they reproduced many of the same assumptions in force in our current interaction, they looked past the individual differences between frameworks, and were able easily to generalize across tokens. The transposability of our current interactive framework into an indefinite number of other hypothetical ones is possible just because speakers have a common sense of the typical ways in which frameworks are the same. The fact that they know they can repeatedly perform "the same" utterance, or find themselves in "the same" situation more than once, is due largely to their practical sense of what is typical. Through typification, speakers transcend the absolute uniqueness of every utterance and every event.

At the same time, native speakers' focus on typicality had other entailments as well, the major one being that their glosses were highly selective as compared with analytic descriptions of usage. They overlooked or left out of their accounts many details, especially noncore aspects of indexical frameworks. Commonsense representations of language are partial, schematic, and contain differently weighted variables. Furthermore, they tend to be taken for granted by native speakers as that which is simply natural, leading to a portrayal of use that suggests more predictability and automaticity than is in fact the case. Thus, native common sense is not to be confused with actual usage, although it is a crucial part of the context in which such usage occurs. A further distorting aspect of the glosses is the fact that speakers' reports of conveyed meaning were usually formulated in nondeictic terms. Insofar as they equated the conveyed meanings of deictics with semantic descriptions, they necessarily deformed them, since the two linguistic subsystems are differently organized.

In this section, I will illustrate some of the continuities as well as discontinuities between what speakers say they do and what they actually do. The discussion is organized by the main metalinguistic themes that Maya speakers adduced in the glosses. For the sake of brevity, we will concentrate on the dimensions central to deictic space, holding aside the other components of the indexical field (Hanks 1984b, 1990). The relevant dimensions are perception, demonstrative gestures, and spatial contiguity.

Perceptual Dimensions of the Deictic Frame

The Maya deictic system contains a series of four stems based on the root *héʔel-* plus a terminal particle, *-aʔ* (Immediate, tactual), *-oʔ* (Nonimmediate, visual), *-bʼeʔ* (peripheral sensory), and *-eʔ* (an empty placeholder).[12] Elsewhere, I have described this series as Ostensive Evidential adverbials, because the first three are used predicatively for the acts of presenting or demonstrating a referent, and the latter conveys that the speaker is certain of the truth of the proposition in which it occurs, but without any current evidence (Hanks 1984b). The evidential basis of the category is reflected in

the clear focus of the forms on the sensory access that participants have to referents—
tactual, visual, auditory—olfactory or known for certain without current evidence.
The following glosses accurately display the centrality of perception in the native view
of these forms, and were in fact crucial evidence in establishing the perceptual basis
of this portion of the deictic frame.

(14)   DP   [...] um p'eé bá'ah <u>hé'b'e</u>→ 'eskeh u k'aát iy á'al e'→
                  [...] A thing (of which you say) "<u>There it is</u>," it means that

                  le k aw ú'uy ik→
                  it's (something) **that you hear**
            WH   hmm→
            DP   [...] tumèen kán inw á'al teč e' <u>hé'eb 'e'</u> wiíl→ 'eskeh→
                  [...] 'cause when I say to you, "<u>There it is</u>, Will!," it's that

                  má'a t inw il ik → miš teč e'→ [...] **wá taán k 'ik e'**→
                  I don't see it, neither do you. [...] (But) If **we see it,**

                  k inw á'a ik teč e' → má' hé'el o'o'
                  I say to you, "There it is of course!" [12.B.394]

(15)   DB   hé'el ó'ob a' → **a mač m ah**→ [...] wá má' **a mač m a e?**↑
                  "Here they are," **you've grabbed them,** [...] **If you haven't grabbed
                  them,**

                  hé' yàan hé'el o'
                  (then you say) "There they are right there" [19.B.094]

In (14), DP neatly equates a thing of which you would say "*hé'eb'e'* " with a thing
which you hear. This is in fact the most highly marked of the four Ostensive Evidentials,
and is only used to direct attention to referents the speaker can hear or smell but not see
at the moment of utterance. Auditory perception is by far the more common usage, as
when interlocutors are waiting for a truck to arrive, hear its roar in the distance, and point
out "Here it comes (*b'e'*)." This form is not used for demonstrating a referent within
sight or tactual reach of the speaker.[13] The verb *ú'uyik* actually ranges over touch, taste,
smell, and hearing, excluding only sight, which is described by *ilik* 'to see, look at.'
Within the Ostensive Evidentials, by contrast, *hé'eb'e'* is confined to nontactual, non-
visual perception. Thus, the deictic and the verb overlap on the dimensions of hearing
and smell, but fail to overlap on the sense of touch. The equivalence that DP asserts is
therefore only extensional, and is not matched by a sameness of encoded features.

In his second utterance, DP elaborates the distinction by specifying that neither
speaker nor addressee can see the referent. This negative condition recapitulates the
semantic opposition between *ú'uyik* 'to sense, listen to' and *ilik* 'to see, look at.' Although it is true that the target deictic is not used when the referent is visible, it is
equally true that it is not used in reference to spoken discourse, tactually available ob-

jects, or anticipated ones either. In his next utterance, he follows the same line of reasoning and says that if we *do* see the referent, then the deictic to use is *héʔeloʔ* 'There it is.' In other words: use *héʔebʼeʔ* when you 'sense' the referent; do not use *héʔebʼeʔ* when you and your interlocutor 'see the referent; use *héʔeloʔ* when both can see it. This account explains the difference between the two deictic stems in terms of the two verb stems. It accurately reflects the core function of covariation between deictic forms and perceptual events, but it over-automatizes this covariation. In the presence of shared visual access to a referent, DP's final scenario, *héʔelaʔ* and *héʔeleʔ*, as well as a number of other nominal and adverbial deictics, could be properly used. The entire account overlooks the roles of prior focus of attention, talk or common background knowledge, as well as the directivity conveyed by Ostensive Evidential utterances (Hanks 1984b). DP takes for granted that I can fill in these other aspects of usage, and focuses his scenarios narrowly on the core functions of the forms.

What most distinguishes the Ostensive Evidentials from other deictics in Maya is their constant association with acts of directed perception—not only the fact of interlocutors being in a state of sensory access to the referent, something which is relevant to much of deictic usage in the language, but the active directing of their sensory attention to it. These forms have the force of sensory directives—Take it!, Look!, Listen! The oppositions within the category of Ostensive Evidentials, while more complex than the three modes of perception, are nonetheless focused on perceptual differences. *héʔebeʔ* is pivotal in establishing perception as the dimension of contrast, since it is the most marked form, and invariantly indexes sensory access, whereas both *héʔelaʔ* and *héʔeloʔ* have other nonsensory uses as well (Hanks 1984b). Thus, what DP has done is construct his explanation in terms of the one dimension on which the target forms are most different from the rest of the deictic system, and most distinct from one another. This is what we would expect on a prototype account in which the perceptual features belong to the core of the category.

In (15), DB independently reproduces a segment of the perceptual field, starting from the most immediate Tactual form, which he equates with the act usually described by the verb 'to grab it, take it in hand.' Just as in DP's case, this is an extensional equivalence, since the semantic range of the verb is distinct from that of the deictic. Still, it accurately reflects the fact that the target form does not convey mere touch as a passive state of sensory access, but rather a seizing of the object, as an active execution. It goes without saying that a vast number of scenarios meet the negative criterion 'speaker does not grab the referent,' which DB offers right afterward. Proportionately many different deictics therefore *could* be used there. DB assumes, however, that the hypothetical principal lacks tactual but *does have* visual evidence of the referent. Under these circumstances, and holding constant the directive force of the utterance, *héʔreloʔ* is indeed the logical choice. Hence, DB takes for granted the perceptual dimension on which Vision is next best to Touch, and therefore *héʔeloʔ* is next best to *héʔelaʔ*. In markedness terms, what he has done is start from the more specific form, and characterize the following one by subtraction of the differential feature (in this case tactual access).

DB's performance is consistent with DP's in (14). Both take for granted the intelligibility of our ongoing conversation, once again constructing a metalinguistic gloss out of the coherent interactive framework of the elicitation. The Tactual form comes first sequentially, and establishes a directive–evidential frame. This is then carried over, just as frames are in spontaneous speech and narrative, with the one stipulation that tactual access is missing. Given a commonsense knowledge of typical deictic usage and frame maintenance, which was never called into question, these various tacit assumptions are available to speakers for unreflective use, and readily reconstructible after the fact.

Demonstrative Gestures

In Maya, as in most languages, there is a close association between different kinds of demonstrative reference and different communicative gestures. These gestures include the presentation of a referent by handing it over to an addressee, pointing to it manually with or without accompanying directed gaze, and cocking of the head to listen, among others. With some frequency, speakers glossed deictic forms by associating them with one or another gesture, as in the following:

(16)   MC hé ʾel a ʾ→ **k in tiíč'ik teč** →
                 "Here it is," **I extend it to you in hand.** [BB.1.73]

(17)   DP [...] bey šan **h ú ȼ'ík teč** um p'eé báʾal a kutal eʾ→
                 [...] also **he could give you** something to sit (on),

            k u liík l eʾ→ k y áaik teč eʾ kó ʾo ten té ʾel aʾ↓
            He stands up, he says to you "Come right here."

            ʾeskeh um p'eé báʾal **u mačk u ȼ'aá teč eʾ**→
            It's that a thing **he takes and gives to you**

            ká kulak eč iʾ→
            so that you might sit on it. [1.A.25]

In the first of these, MC describes precisely the maximally focal gesture of presenting a referent by extending it in the hand. This is roughly equivalent to the combination of taking an object in the hand and giving it to an addressee, as described by DP in the third line of (17). Note that these combine the tactual accessibility of gripping an object with the directivity of handing it over to an addressee, thereby obliging him to take it in turn. Other verbs of gesture that came up included *seéñalàartik* 'to signal, indicate' and *tuč uʾtik* 'to point out.'

All of these gestures involve the management of interactants' orientation in space, which is mediated by the social field of their mutual sensory access. This field is relatively symmetric and reciprocal in face-to-face interaction, where individuals can see, hear, and tactually engage a common context that includes themselves and each other.

In other circumstances, when the parties to talk are separated by perceptual barriers, say fifty meters of woods, or a house wall, the use of gestures obviously loses its communicative value. Speakers took this for granted and rarely bothered to say that their scenarios presupposed a face-to-face interaction, like the one we were engaged in, although this presupposition was in force unless otherwise indicated. As obvious as these examples may appear, they help us to determine the frames to which these forms correspond. There are several ways of summoning an addressee in Maya by using deictics, and not all of them require that the addressee be within range to receive the gestures cited in (16–17).

Spatial Contiguity

The contiguity and reciprocity between individuals in face-to-face talk is one of the canonical frames of deictic usage, but it is not the only one. Speakers routinely talk over boundaries of various kinds, and continue to use deictics in acts of indexical reference. For example, they may be involved in separate tasks on a work site that give them different visual and cognitive orientations while still allowing them to interact, or they may be separated by a social boundary such as a threshold, wall, or sector of the homestead, or traversing the forest in tandem at twenty meters apart from one another during a hunt, or passing one another on a path in the darkness. In less physical but no less relevant terms, the spatial field may be asymmetric due to individuals' different knowledge or rights over it, as in talk within the home or fields of one interactant, talk between a shaman and his patient at the foot of his altar, or talk between a senior woman and a child within her kitchen area (Maya *k'oób'en*). In these situations, interactants may share the same concrete context, but bear different social relations to it. These asymmetries should lead us to consider the spatial field of the deictic frame as something both variable and socially mediated. This came out in the way Maya speakers described it, as well.

(18)   DP   <u>kó ʔoten té ʔel a ʔ</u> → k'ab'eét náac̆' yàan tec̆ i ʔ
               "<u>Come right here</u>." He's got to be (already) close to you there. [1.A.061]

(19)   DP   [...] <u>way a tàal e ʔ</u> ʔoómen→ ʔeskeh laáyli t aw iknal kutàal e ʔ
               [...] "<u>Come here</u>, man!" It's that he still comes to where you are.
               [1.A.078]

(20)   DP   <u>hé ʔ yàan t aw iknal a ʔ</u>→ pero lel o ʔ k'ab'eét ti ʔanec̆ šan t yiknal i ʔ
               <u>Here it is where you are</u>, but that one, you've also got to be where he is.
               [19.B.100]

The first two of these examples occurred in the course of a conversation in which I was attempting to understand the difference between the expression *kó ʔoten té ʔela ʔ* 'Come right here' and *kó ʔoten waye ʔ* 'Come here,' both of which I had heard on several occasions. In (18), DP observes that the former is used when the addressee is already close to the speaker at the time of utterance. Note that this is not a statement about the *referent* of the deictic, which is the location of the speaker, but rather about the indexical *relation* between the interactants prior to the act of reference. Both of the target imperative clauses refer to the speaker's location at the moment of utterance, as DP reaffirms in (19). As he says, the addressee still complies with the directive by coming to where the speaker is, despite the difference in deictic. The series of exchanges from which these excerpts were taken was one of my first indications that speakers make reference to their own deictic space differently according to the relative immediacy of their addressee. Subsequent observations of direct deictic usage have corroborated this, indicating that the spatial field of deictic reference is not simply egocentric but sociocentric, mediated by the socially defined physical configuration of the participants.

In (20), DB also deduces the participant relation required in order for an act of deictic reference to be proper. In this case, the target form makes reference to the addressee's location, rather than merely indexing it. In the utterance "Here it is where you are," the speaker simultaneously commits himself or herself to two spatial propositions: (i) that the object of presentation (it) is within physical reach, susceptible of being touched, and (ii) that it is also located in the body space of the addressee. The first is conveyed by the deictic *héʔe . . . -aʔ* 'here it is,' and the second by the relational expression *tawiknal* 'in your place, where you are.' DB draws the unavoidable conclusion that since both participants are immediate to the same referent, they must also be immediate to each other.

In order to express his deduction, DB must make reference to the locations of the hypothetical interactants. This could be achieved theoretically with deictics, but it would require either prior description of the locations or a transposition. He could have said "You're both right here" or "You're right here and he's there," pointing to our current context as an icon of the hypothetical one. Instead, he opts for a nondeictic locational description. "You're there where he is." This description contains pronouns and demonstrative elements, but the spatial reference is identified primarily by the possessed NP *y iknal* 'his place.' The structure of the sentence is roughly as shown in (20′).

(20′) You're in his place too (in that case)

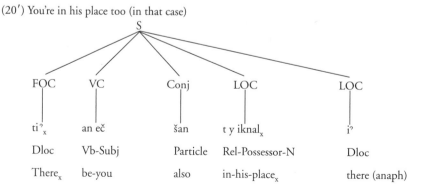

The subscripts on the initial demonstrative and postverbal locative phrase indicate that the two are obligatorily read as coreferential. This is a variant of the standard "split focus" structure (Hanks 1990: chapt. 10). The S-initial Dloc adds no deictic feature of immediacy or perceptibility, which would ground it in the current spatial frame. Instead, it is an empty placeholder for the postverbal locative, indicating only that the locative reference is focal. *tyiknal* 'in his place' identifies the location as a region including and proximal to the hypothetical addressee, 'him' (see just below). Thus this phrase is relational in the same way a deictic is: both denote zones of relative immediacy in relation to an interactant. Unlike a deictic, however, the ground of the relation 'in his place' is not the current speech event, but the narrated one, where the referent of 'his' exists. Furthermore, the ground (his) and the focal referent (place) are segmentally distinct in this expression, whereas in a deictic, they are signaled by one and the same form, as in "here" (our place).

In commenting on spatial deixis, native speakers often introduced the expression *-iknal* 'place' in an attempt to describe the actor-centric regions and relations that make up deictic frames. An understanding of the concept designated by this word is clearly part of Maya speakers' linguistic and interactive common sense. *-iknal* is an inalienably possessed noun stem that denotes the proximal region around the object or individual functioning as possessor. When the possessor is human, the phrase conveys roughly 'in the company of X,' or close to, alongside, with X.' It fits into a series of locational noun stems denoting the social and personal spaces of an actor. These include his *-otoč* 'house, abode' (inalienably possessed), *nah* 'home, fields, proximal region of,' *kahtalil* 'homestead, residential compound, home village,' and the actor's several habitual work places, such as his *soólar* 'yard, orchard,' *paárseláa* '(irrigated) field,' and *kòol* '(unirrigated) plot (milpa).' On one common reading, an individual's *-iknal* is equivalent to his *nah*, that is, his home or stable place ([BB.3.54]). Thus, in asking the question in (21), a speaker is asking 'whose home are you staying at?,' a question often posed to me.

(21)   maáš iknah yaneč→
         Whose place are you at? [12.B.630]

Similarly, *kóʔoš tinwiknal* 'Let's go to my place' is a routine way of inviting an addressee to come visit one's home.

There is a second interpretation of *-iknal* in which it is not a fixed place owned in the way a house is owned, but a mobile field of action belonging to an individual in the way a shadow or perceptual field does. This "bodily space" sense is the one invoked in the glosses of deictics, and it raises the question of whether *-iknal* is not a semantic descriptor of the very spatial frame encoded in the deictic system. Is my *-iknal* the same as my 'here'? This question can be addressed by way of three narrower ones: (i) Must the possessor of an *-iknal* be human, as the ground of deictic reference must?, (ii) Must it be an individual, or can it be a social group, as can the deictic ground? and

(iii) What is the regional scope of one's *-iknal*? Is the referent of our *-iknal* coextensive with the referent of our current 'here'?

Although *-iknal* is usually possessed by a human noun, as in the above examples, this need not always be the case. Two native speakers insisted when I asked them that it is perfectly proper to speak of the *-iknal* of an animal, a tree, a well, or a truck, stationary or moving [BB.3.54]. Furthermore, the expression is vague as to where in the proximal zone of the object it refers, and there is no sense that the orientational front of the object is a privileged referent. These speakers reaffirmed that when uttered within one's homestead, the phrase *tinwiknal* 'in my place' is unambiguously interpreted as the close personal space of the speaker, not the inclusive space of the homestead.

During a conversation with DP, I asked him several times the hypothetical question "Where is your *-iknal*?," assuming he would interpret it in the sense of 'home,' as in example (21) above. Instead, he took me to be asking the bizarre question "Where is your (current) place?," roughly equivalent to "Where are you right now?" Based on this interpretation, he rejected the question outright as incoherent. I could not sensibly ask about *his -iknal*, he explained, since we were face to face and therefore shared one and the same *-iknal*. Given that we were together, how could I ask him where he was? Hence, the shared spatial and perceptual frame of our interaction was the most narrow, least inclusive definition that he would accept. This fact suggests a close relation between this sense of 'place' and the social field of interaction.

Earlier in the same conversation, I had asked him to explain the sentence *hé⁷ kutàal le bá⁷ah tawiknal o⁷* 'Here comes that thing to where you are.' This would be a meaningful utterance, he explained, only if the speaker were separated from the addressee by about ten meters, and observed a moving object, such as an animal, directly approaching the addressee [12.B.575]. The motivation for this condition is that the utterance form makes reference to the addressee's *-iknal* as distinct from the speaker's, and such a segmentation would typically occur under conditions of physical separation between the two. This is consistent with the view that, unless otherwise specified, the *-iknal* of either participant in face-to-face talk includes that of the other. Hence it denotes a joint interactive space, rather than an individual zone. When interactants are separated, and the current framework is relatively asymmetric, then the *-iknal* of a participant is either egocentric or altercentric, depending upon perspective.

With respect to the regional scope of *-iknal* as compared with that of 'here,' DP made several revealing observations. Our conversation took place in the main house of my homestead, a one-room absidal-shaped, thatched, wattle and daub structure, which actually belonged to DP. Across the courtyard within the same household was a kitchen structure of similar shape, separated from DP and me by about eight meters, two orange trees, and the wall of the main house. At the time of our conversation, DA (DP's wife) was in the kitchen, out of sight and out of overhearing range. I asked DP whether DA could be said to be in our *-iknal* at present, and he responded,

$\uparrow$ _ _ $\uparrow$

(22)   DP   miná'an **t 'ikna** bey a' → hàah **way yan e'** →
             She's not in **our -*iknal*** like this. True, **she's hére,**

                $\uparrow$ _ _ $\uparrow$

           péro má' **t'iknal** i' →
           but not in **our -*iknal.***

    WH   b'a'an ten má' **t'iknal** i' →
           Why not in **our -*iknal?***
                        $\uparrow$ _ _ $\uparrow$
    DP   tumèen má' $\downarrow$ **way ič na** yan e' e' → [...]
           Because she's NOT **here in the house!** [...] [12.B.624]

The first response makes clear that DP typifies the deictic *way e'* 'here' as properly referring to a regional space large enough to include both a main house and its kitchen hut, whereas in the second response he interprets *-iknal* more narrowly to denote the inner space of a single structure. This inner space can be encompassed in a single visual field, and it is for all intents and purposes entirely within the reach of any adult within it. Pursuing the point, I then asked DP whether DA could be said to be in our *-iknal* if she were standing at the table across the room from us (approximately four meters). Yes, he said, as long as she was within the house. Even if there were ten people standing about inside the house, they would all be in our *-iknal*, because they would be able to *hear* our conversation. Thus, although the term has a more narrow scope than *way e'* when the two are contrasted, it is still associated with a perceptual and interactive space, when its possessor is human, just as are the deictics.

On a separate occasion, VI, another native speaker, equated *-iknal* in the first sense with an individual's house (*-otoč*), and in the second sense with his immediate *way e'* ([123.A.284]). The difference between VI and DP is that the former conceived a more narrow 'here,' bringing it down to the immediacy of *-iknal*, whereas DP insisted that unmodified *way e'* included a larger region. Offered the target phrase *té'e t in w iknal o'* 'There in my place,' VI rejected it outright, evidently taking it to be self-contradictory, on the reading of my *-iknal* as my current indexical space. You cannot be both *té'el o'* 'there' and at the same time *way e'* 'here,' he said. In rationalizing a metalinguistic judgment about 'my bodily space,' therefore, he tacitly equated it with the deictic space of 'my here.'

What then is the status of metalinguistic statements that define the proximal region of the deictic field, 'here,' in terms of the concept of an *-iknal?* There is clearly an intimate relation between the two in the common sense of Maya speakers. Several facts indicate a partial equivalence between them: (i) a speaker's current 'place,' like the speaker's 'here,' is typically shared with coparticipants and bystanders who share the same perceptual field; (ii) if two individuals are spatially or perceptually separated, then we can make proper reference to the distinct *-iknals* and the distinct 'here's of each; (iii)

-iknal, like spatial deictics, has a variable range, from the close body-space of an individual through his or her characteristic social spaces—home, fields, and orchards.

The dissimilarities between the two kinds of space are equally, if not more, important, (i) *-iknal* requires a superficial marking of its possessor, which may be an inanimate
object, whereas no deictic in Maya can be possessed, and none has an inanimate ground.
It is incoherent in Maya to think of the 'here' of a rock or a tree, whereas both of these
can have an *-iknal.*[14] (ii) The indexical field is resolvable into a large number of referential objects through the ready-made structure of relational features encoded in deictics. There is no corresponding lexical system to segment the internal space of an *-iknal,*
except for the mixed collection of vocabulary for body-parts, house-parts, trees, trucks,
and whatever else could be said to have a 'place.' (iii) The deictic field is inherently orientational because human actors have faces and limited fields of perceptual focus. The
-iknal has no orientation and cannot be modified so as to give it one. One cannot speak
of "the front, back, visible part" of an *-iknal,* nor of its foreground as opposed to background. Deictics convey precisely such segmentations. Finally, (iv) the overlap between
-iknal and 'here' applies only to the referential component of some deictics, leaving un-
accounted for the directivity, presentative, discourse cohesive, and other extra-referential functions that are central to deixis more generally.

What the similarity of the spatial deictic frame and the *-iknal* tells us is that descriptive glosses of deictic terms can reveal very significant extensional overlaps, but
they cannot establish intensional equivalence. There is no intensional equivalence between deictic and nondeictic terms in natural languages. Any attempt to reduce indexical expressions to descriptive paraphrases, whether in the context of commonsense
glosses or scientific theory, will inevitably deform them. In my estimation, the pairing
of *tinwiknal* 'at my place,' with *way e*ʾ 'here' is as close as we come to equivalence, and,
even here, the differences are critical to an accurate interpretation of either expression.
This does not mean that we should shun the sort of metalanguage that produced this
equation. Rather, we should abandon the attempt to find genuine equivalence, and
concentrate instead on disclosing the language- and culture-specific frames relative to
which speakers interpret speech. From this more realistic perspective, what matters
most is not the interchangeability of paraphrases, which is nearly always defeasible. The
main objective is rather to find a way into the circle of commonsense interpretation,
to reveal the frames on which native speakers draw in using and understanding their
language. Metalanguage, in this more realistic perspective, is an invaluable source of
evidence, whose potential remains abundantly underexploited in current pragmatics.

CONCLUSION

Where does native metalinguistic commentary fit into an overall account of deixis in
a natural language, and what can we learn from it?

Native metalanguage provides a wealth of evidence for the typical frames in relation to which deictic functions must be understood. Maya speakers *do* associate de-

ictics with routine interactive scenarios, and those embody spatial frames grounded in the perceptual, kinesthetic, and locative–spatial fields of interaction. These frames are *typical* in the sense of being schematic rather than precise in all details. They are variable in application, rather than determining necessary and sufficient conditions on proper usage. And they are focused on the core features of deictics, rather than treating all features equally. The common sense of what is typical in deictic usage guides routine practice, but does not determine it. It is part of what makes both interactive frameworks and speech repeatable, even though at a certain level no two events are the same. It is also part of the practical knowledge that speakers draw on in reporting and giving accounts of social events in everyday life.

The metalinguistic discourse reported here shows Maya speakers engaged in the task of creating narrative vignettes that embody local standards of proper speech. Asked to explain the meaning of deictic forms, they responded with ostensive definitions, in which token utterances were the exemplars. They conveyed, and in some cases even *said,* that proper usage is any usage similar to the one they were presenting. The local standard was represented in terms of prototypical pairings of utterance forms with interactive frameworks, thus giving powerful evidence that standards of deictic use are embodied in a practical knowledge of the interactional wholes into which acts of reference fit. Speakers have strong intuitions about deictic use, because they have strong intuitions about the interactive frameworks in which it occurs.

Throughout the preceding section, it was shown that speakers were selective in what they said about the forms, leaving out details of context and variation. Consequently, if we view the glosses as meaning statements, they can be shown to be in need of an indefinite number of revisions. By altering the scenarios of use, in just the way that the speakers altered our current context to come up with their examples, one can create a large number of distinct contexts, in which the conveyed meaning is different. Many if not most pragmatic components that speakers claim to be present in their own examples can be omitted, or what philosophers call "defeased." Most of the explanatory statements were at least potentially distorting, moreover, because the defining terms have different extensions and conceptual structure than the deictics to which they were applied. We saw this with verbs of perceiving, descriptions of gestures, and the pivotal concept designated by *-iknal* 'place, bodily space,' which is similar to, but distinct from, the designatum of *way e⁊* 'here.'

In each of these cases, what appears to be going on is that the descriptive statements, such as "We can't see it," are not being offered as paraphrase equivalents, for which they are obviously insufficient. Instead, they are highly selective descriptives of scenarios, and these scenarios are the real "meaning statements." What you are engaged in when you point out a referent is what you would normally be engaged in if you said "X." It is in virtue of their distinct relations to a single pragmatic framework that deictic and description can be said to be the same.

The intelligibility of the metalinguistic glosses shown here rested entirely on the commonsense intelligibility of the situation in which they were produced. Speakers' presupposition of *our* current interaction had two aspects: (i) They formulated their glosses in speech that was anchored in our mutual framework, thereby taking for granted my grasp of the spatial, linguistic, and interactive setting that we were in. (ii) They generated their hypothetical scenarios, in which target utterances would be embedded, by transposition of portions of the current conversational framework, using our situation as a stage and set of props with which to create examples. Thus, as Briggs (1986) showed in detail, the social situation in which elicitation takes place has a powerful and subtle impact on the form of responses produced.

The formulation of coherent glosses is a linguistic practice in which speakers create, and communicate within, a multiframe context. DP, MC, DB, VI, and other Maya speakers not cited here all demonstrated the ability to shift gracefully between speech attributed to hypothetical principals in a narrative, description of the narrative frame itself from our current perspective, and direct evaluative assertions about the embedded utterances. This kind of frame "lamination" is well within the range of everyday Maya pragmatics, attested for instance in storytelling. Metalanguage is a natural part of routine linguistic practice, made possible by the same resources speakers use every day. This is not to say that discussions about the meaning of utterance fragments like the ones here are routine. I have never heard two native speakers discuss the meaning of a deictic, nor have these forms ever, to my knowledge, been the focus of social scrutiny. Nonetheless, when quoting each other and reporting speech, which they do daily, they routinely perform actions of the same semiotic complexity as the glosses displayed here. Given the categorizations and different frames available right in the interview context, it is unsurprising that their common sense led them to start from there in explaining other contexts. This strategy shows up in the use of pronouns and demonstratives indexing our own interaction ('you,' 'I,' 'here,' 'there,' and 'this') as the constructive elements in hypothetical scenarios. One by-product of such use is that it reveals how speakers categorized their *current* situation, at the same time as they created new ones. They displayed their awareness of our perceptual, spatial, and orientational context by segmenting it and offering it as a standard. It would not be entirely false to say that they fabricated the framework of our interaction in the course of enacting other ones, just as they made up other ones on the basis of ours. By setting the standards of proper usage, the examples therefore became justifications of the ongoing practices of their authors.

The thrust of these remarks is that the line between metalinguistic and direct speech is a subtle one over which there are many transpositions. Both rely on linguistic common sense which is both *about* usage and *immanent in* it. In its schematic form, this common sense is embodied in prefabricated frames typifying actional wholes such as those explored here. Frames inherently categorize action and they may entail subtle distinctions such as the ones between the Maya notions of "bodily space" and "here." In its enacted form, common sense is embodied in the complex and rapidly changing frameworks produced in speech. The elicitation framework itself is a good illustration of this, for, as we have seen, it contains multiple laminations of frames among which speakers shift their footing with ease, and out of which they are able to generate indefinitely many new frameworks by selective transposition.

This ability to generate new frameworks rests squarely on native speakers' familiarity with conventional frames. It is not that they know these frames in a conscious way, but rather that they take them for granted and use them habitually and unreflectively. The tasks involved in elicitation force this largely backgrounded "knowledge" into the foreground, and in the process inevitably transform it. The metalinguistic verbalizations that result from this are not equivalent to the frames themselves, but they offer a privileged view on those frames. Precisely because frameworks consist of so many simultaneous factors, any one of which may be absent given the proper circumstances, it is impossible to infer from observations of usage which elements belong to typified frames, and which ones arise only out of the combinations of frames. In practical terms, it would have been virtually impossible for me to deduce the difference between perceptual and spatial proximity, for instance, by simply pondering examples. When speakers discussed usage in their own language, however, this difference came into sharp focus. As linguists develop better models of semantics and pragmatics, it is important to develop better research methods to go with them. The metalinguistic potential of natural languages and the commonsense ability of speakers to deploy that potential deserve a central place in this ongoing research.

ACKNOWLEDGMENTS

This chapter was written as part of a research project funded by the National Endowment for the Humanities, entitled "Language structure and communicative event, a study of the Yucatec Maya deictic system" (RO213474-86). I gratefully acknowledge this support. Earlier versions of the chapter were presented in seminars at the Center for Psychosocial Studies, Chicago, Illinois, and at the Centre de Linguistique Théorique at the École des Hautes Études en Sciences Sociales, Paris, France. I thank the members of both seminars for their critical comments, and particularly Bernard Conein, Pierre Encrevé, Michel de Fornel, Benjamin Lee, Richard Parmentier, Michael Silverstein, and Greg Urban, each of whom pushed me to clarify my position. Ellen Basso and Terence Turner commented on earlier drafts and helped me to frame the issues intelligibly. John Lucy and Charles Goodwin gave me extensive and very helpful written comments on the penultimate draft, for which I am most grateful. I am, needless to say, solely responsible for the result.

NOTES

Translations from Maya are in single quotes.

1. This choice of terms is derived mainly from Goffman's writings on frames and frameworks in interaction (1974, 1981), although I am attempting to distinguish the two in a way Goffman does not. In earlier versions of the chapter, I used *frame* in both senses, but found that readers were needlessly confused by the terminology, and I was unfortunately prone to equivocate between the two senses. Since the distinction drawn here seems well founded, even if it is difficult to maintain consistently, I have differentiated the terms.

2. See for instance Schutz's (1970: 96–122) discussion of typification and the "inner horizon" of memories and expectations that actors have about the typical properties of objects in the social world.

3. The goal of such paraphrases has traditionally been to reduce the indexical component of deictics to a nonindexical description, and phrase glosses in a logical metalanguage, rather than to intertranslate the forms. My point is that, regardless of their ultimate objectives, the works cited proceed by means of intertranslation. This procedure, I am claiming, rests on the existence of coherent frames in the sense developed here.

4. I use the term "interpretive" here in the sense that Fillmore (1985) uses it, not in the earlier linguistic sense of "interpretive semantics." Although the literature on frame semantics makes virtually no use of social theory, there is also a highly significant tradition of "interpretative sociology" deriving from the writings of Max Weber and Alfred Schutz. This literature addresses many of the same issues in social interpretation and typification, and has had an important influence on my treatment of metalanguage. For further discussion, see Hanks (1990).

5. Maya examples are cited according to the following conventions: italics when cited in the body of the text; target forms, which speakers were asked to gloss, are always underlined; English glosses of Maya forms presented in the body of the text are in single quotes; quoted forms are in double quotes; target forms are again underlined. Bold is used in numbered examples to draw attention to forms under discussion. Orthography is the standard one used by Mayan linguists, explained in McQuown (1979).

6. This chapter focuses on the kinds of observations speakers made of their usage, rather than on the relative frequency of association among factors in the glosses. Quantitative analysis, however, is entirely consistent with the approach taken here. Examples were selected from approximately thirty-five hours of audio-recorded metalinguistic interviews, collected between 1979 and 1986.

7. I will state Goffman's categories in terms of individuals, although it is clear that in many contexts it is groups that are involved.

8. Due to space limitations, I am unable to present in this chapter the evidence that these devices are commonly used in routine, nonelicited Maya. For this, the reader is referred to the copious examples in Hanks (1990) and the various sources cited therein.

9. A case could be made that topic phrases as I define them are actually free-standing sentence fragments that bear no syntactic relation to what follows them, but are pragmatically interpreted relative to the following discourse.

10. This is a power-laden speech strategy in that the speaker thereby flatly rejects both the acceptability of the citation form and any responsibility for coming up with a possible usage. DP was the most senior of all my Maya teachers, a "grand old man" with great-grandchildren, and was the most willing to contradict me directly in speech like that presented in the examples.

11. Paralinguistic symbols follow the system presented in McQuown (1979).

12. By 'empty placeholder' I mean that the *e'* terminal adds no information to the individuation of a referent, whereas the other terminals do. The loss of final *l* in the peripheral form is due to a regular deletion before consonant-initial suffix.

13. This assertion is oversimplified for the purpose of brevity. Examples are attested in which the referent is "indirectly tactual," such as the resistance of an object on the end of a line, and (according to John Lucy, personal communication) the first feeling of raindrops. The most common uses in Oxkutzcab, where this research was conducted, are nonetheless auditory. For extensive discussion, see Hanks (1990).

14. If one were to come across a sign at a dumpsite which read *pul waye'* 'Dump here,' or

a dirty truck with *p'o' lela'* 'Wash this' written in the dust on its hood, these apparently speak-erless deictic references would be interpreted relative to the reader's current field, or that of a reconstructible author. Such examples do not prove that inanimate objects can ground deictic reference without any human intervention, any more than they prove that a dump or a truck can issue an imperative.

REFERENCES

Anderson, Stephen R., and Edward L. Keenan. 1985. Deixis. In *Language typology and syntactic description,* Vol. 3, Timothy Shopen (ed.), pp. 259-308. Cambridge: Cambridge University Press.

Atkinson, J. M., and J. Heritage (eds.). 1984. *Structures of social action.* Cambridge: Cambridge University Press.

Briggs, Charles L. 1986. *Learning how to ask: a sociolinguistic appraisal of the role of the interview in social science research.* Cambridge: Cambridge University Press.

Brown, G., and G. Yule. 1983. *Discourse analysis.* Cambridge: Cambridge University Press.

Cicourel, Aaron. 1985. Text and discourse. *Annual Review of Anthropology* 14: 159–85.

Fillmore, Charles J. 1978. On the organization of semantic information in the lexicon. In *Papers from the parasession on the lexicon,* Donka Farkas, Wesley Jacobsen, and Karol Todrys (eds.), pp. 148–73. Chicago: Chicago Linguistic Society.

———. 1982. Towards a descriptive framework for spatial deixis. In *Speech, place and action: studies in deixis and related topics,* Robert J. Jarvella and Wolfgang Klein (eds.), pp. 31–59. New York: John Wiley and Sons, Ltd.

———. 1985. Frames and the semantics of understanding. In *Quaderni di Semantica* VI (2) (December): 222–54.

Garver, Newton. 1965. Varieties of use and mention. *Philosophy and Phenomenological Research* XXVI: 230–38.

Goffman, Erving. 1974. *Frame analysis: an essay on the organization of experience.* New York: Harper Colophon Books.

———. 1981. *Forms of talk.* Philadelphia: University of Pennsylvania Press.

Gumperz, John J. 1982. *Discourse strategies.* Cambridge: Cambridge University Press.

Hanks, William F. 1983. *Deixis and the organization of interactive context in Yucatec Maya.* Unpublished Ph.D. thesis, Department of Anthropology, Department of Linguistics, University of Chicago.

———. 1984a. Sanctification, structure and experience in a Yucatec Maya ritual event. *Journal of American Folklore* 97 (384): 131–66.

———. 1984b. The evidential core of deixis in Yucatec Maya. In *Papers from the Twentieth Regional Meeting of the Chicago Linguistic Society,* Joseph Drogo et al. (eds.), pp. 154–72. Chicago: Chicago Linguistic Society.

———. 1987. Markedness and category interactions in the Malagasy deictic system. *Chicago Linguistic Society Working Papers* 3: 109–36. Chicago: Chicago Linguistic Society.

———. 1989. The indexical ground of deictic reference. In *Papers from the Twenty-Fifth Annual Meeting of the Chicago Linguistic Society, Part II: Parasession on Language in Context,* pp. 104–22. Chicago: Chicago Linguistic Society.

———. 1990. *Referential practice: language and lived space among the Maya.* Chicago: University of Chicago Press.

Jakobson, Roman. 1980 [1957]. Metalanguage as a linguistic problem. In *The framework of language* (Michigan Studies in the Humanities), pp. 81–92. Ann Arbor: University of Michigan Press.

Lakoff, George. 1984. *There constructions: a case study of grammatical construction theory and prototype theory.* Berkeley Cognitive Science Report no. 18. Berkeley, CA.

Langacker, R. W. 1984. Active zones. In *Proceedings of the Tenth Annual Meeting of the Berkeley Linguistics Society,* C. Brugman and M. Macaulay (eds.), pp. 172–88. Berkeley: Berkeley Linguistics Society.

Levinson, Stephen. 1983. *Pragmatics.* Cambridge: Cambridge University Press.

    1987. Putting linguistics on a proper footing: explorations in Goffman's concepts of participation. In *Goffman: an interdisciplinary appreciation,* P. Drew and A. Woolton (eds.), pp. 161–227. Oxford: Polity Press.

Lyons, John. 1977. *Semantics* (2 vols.). Cambridge: Cambridge University Press.

McCawley, James D. 1986. Speech acts and Goffman's participant roles. *Proceedings of the second ESCOL.* Ohio State University Department of Linguistics.

McQuown, Norman A. 1979. A modern Yucatec text. In *IJAL NATS 3, Mayan texts 2,* Louanna Furbee-Losee (ed.), pp. 38–105.

Quine, W. V. 1951. *Mathematical logic.* Cambridge, MA: Harvard University Press. [Portions reprinted in *Readings in semantics,* F. Zabeeh, E. D. Klemke, and A. Jacobson (eds.), pp. 89–94. Chicago: University of Illinois Press.]

Reichenbach, Hans. 1947. *Elements of symbolic logic.* New York: Macmillan.

Rosch, Eleanor. 1978. Principles of categorization. In *Cognition and categorization,* Eleanor Rosch and Barbara B. Lloyd (eds.), pp. 28–49. Hillsdale, NJ: Lawrence Erlbaum Associates.

Russell, Bertrand. 1940. *An inquiry into meaning and truth.* London: Allen & Unwin.

Schutz, Alfred. 1970. *On phenomenology and social relations.* Helmut R. Wagner (ed.). Chicago: University of Chicago Press.

Sherzer, Joel. 1973. Verbal and nonverbal deixis: the pointed lip gesture among the San Blas Cuna. *Language in Society* 2: 117–31.

Silverstein, Michael. 1976. Shifters, verbal categories and cultural description. In *Meaning in anthropology,* Keith Basso and Henry Selby (eds.), pp. 11–55. Albuquerque: School of American Research.

    1978. Deixis and deducibility in a Wasco-Wishram passive of evidence. In *Proceedings of the Fourth Annual Meeting of the Berkeley Linguistic Society,* Jeri Jaeger et al. (eds.), pp. 238–54. Berkeley: Berkeley Linguistic Society.

    1979. Language structure and linguistic ideology. In *The elements: a parasession on linguistic units and levels,* Paul R. Clyne et al. (eds.), pp. 193–248. Chicago: Chicago Linguistic Society.

Vološinov, V. N. 1986 [1929]. *Marxism and the philosophy of language,* Ladislav Matejka and I. R. Titunik (trans.). Cambridge, MA: Harvard University Press.

Weinreich, Uriel. 1980. *On semantics,* William Labov and Beatrice and Weinreich (eds.). Philadelphia: University of Pennsylvania Press.

Part II

Genre and Textuality

4

Authenticity and Ambivalence in the Text:
A Colonial Maya Case

The Spanish conquest of Yucatan created a new discourse in which Maya and Spanish systems of representation were encompassed, interacted, and then produced hybrid cultural forms. The Maya nobility played an important role early on in this process, through their participation in both Spanish and indigenous sectors of colonial society. This paper explores the ambivalence of the nobility by analyzing their letters, addressed to the Spanish Crown, in Maya language. The hybrid character of these texts is demonstrated in the forms of royal address, the representation of the Franciscans and the secular clergy, and the network of intertextual relations linking the letters to a broader contemporary discourse. Mesoamerica, Maya, discourse analysis, colonial documents, native elites, Catholicism, missionaries

Like native elites in other colonial societies, the Maya nobility occupied an acutely ambivalent position in early colonial Mexico. They maintained systems of knowledge and action rooted in preconquest Maya society while at the same time holding office in the postconquest system of local government known as the *cabildo* (Farriss 1984:Ch. 8; Roys 1943). They were among the first converts to Christianity and became church instructors themselves (Collins 1977) while still carrying on indigenous forms of ritual practice outside the church. They were accorded special treatment by the Spanish Crown, allowed to dress as Spaniards, ride horses, bear arms, and be addressed as *don*. They were trained by the friars to be official scribes in the new colonial society. Yet access to these privileges depended on their ability to legitimate themselves before the Spaniards as genuine native nobles. They were the very symbol of an autochthonous system, yet at the forefront of acculturation. This paper explores the consequences of this ambivalence for communication in sixteenth-century Yucatan. It proceeds by way of discourse analysis of selected native language documents, taken first in relation to the broader social context of their production, and then to the semantic and rhetorical forms embodied in them. One major goal of the paper is to show how an account of ambivalence in discourse can lead to a deeper understanding of the forms of representation in colonial contexts.

Alongside the substantive focus of the paper is an equally important methodolog-

ical one, bearing on the interpretation of ambivalent documents. The difficulty of lo-
cating an authentic native perspective in a fundamentally equivocal context is obvious but has not stopped some scholars from positing a pure Maya voice, separated
from the Spanish by an "autistic disjunction" (Edmonson 1982:xx). I argue against
this approach to colonial society, by showing that it leads one to overlook or miscon-
strue ambivalence while searching for a purely indigenous system. This in turn ob-
scures the social value and meaning of the discourse in its contemporary context.

In order to make the point forcefully, it will be argued through a concrete case
study. In 1567, twenty years after the conquest of Yucatan, a series of letters was sent
to King Phillip II of Spain, composed in Maya and bearing the names of some eighty
Maya nobles. Seven were sent in February, one in March, and one in April. These are
among the first letters to appear in Maya language, and document the emergence of
a new discourse form. The linguistic ambivalence of the form, a lesser Spanish genre
cast in Maya, parallels the equivocal position of the signatories in colonial society.
Noting the Spanish influence in the letters, historians have judged them to be inauthentic—not true expressions of the native perspective, but rather Franciscan con-
coctions (Gates 1937; Tozzer 1941; Gonzalez Cicero 1978). At stake in this conclusion is not only the status of these particular letters, but more importantly the
methodology one uses in analyzing ambivalent documentary sources. Since many, if
not most, colonial documents are equivocal in present terms, the issues that arise here
are of relevance far beyond the Yucatec case.

The documentary value of these letters—and of the Nahuatl sources laid out in Anderson, Berdan, and Lockhard (1976)—is twofold. On the one hand, they refer to and
describe many aspects of the contemporary scene. Their value in these terms is a function of how well they correspond to the world they portray. In order to judge this, the
document and the object of description must be distinguished and compared. Is the text
true or false? On the other hand, the letters are also *part of* the world they describe, and
a second aspect of their value derives from this. They are the precipitate of an ongoing,
intensely conflictual process, involving many actors, both Maya and Spanish. In the
search for descriptive fact, scholars have overlooked the more basic questions of what
kind of communicative acts the letters embody, and to what ends. Even as descriptive
utterances, their value is "oblique" in the sense that they reflect the ideological horizons
of their authors (Bakhtin and Medvedev 1985[1928]:21), not an objective reality.

Yucatan in the 1560s was in the throes of a major crisis. Following a period of zeal-
ous and apparently successful evangelization by the Franciscans, it was discovered that
some native nobles continued to practice idolatry. With the aid of civil authorities in
the provincial capital of Merida, Franciscans under the Provincial Diego de Landa un-
dertook an inquisition in 1562 that lasted officially less than a year but is reported to
have continued unofficially for more than a century (Bricker 1981:20; Scholes and
Adams 1938, Vol. II:71–129; Tozzer 1941:78–83). In the latter half of that year, Francisco de Toral arrived in Yucatan as the first resident bishop and, being informed of the
Franciscan actions, immediately halted the inquisition and initiated an investigation.
There ensued a power struggle between Landa and Toral that involved Spanish civil

authorities, wealthy colonists and, inevitably, the Maya.[1] Segments of the native nobility suffered brutal humiliation at the hands of the friars in the inquisitorial process. Others were less directly involved in the inquisition but still became engaged in the subsequent disputes. Since well before the conquest, the native nobility had been fragmented into some nineteen independent states whose relations were in many cases hostile (Roys 1943, 1957). Given this context, it is clear that the very production of a letter to the king is an attempt to exercise the "symbolic power" to create appearances and belief, to confirm and transform the vision of the world (Bourdieu 1977:117, 1985). As with their knowledge of the Catholic moral order, the Maya nobles learned alphabetic writing from the friars as an instrument of conversion. Yet, from as early as the 1560s, they used these skills to constitute their own place in colonial society.

The discussion proceeds in five main steps. First, the letters are situated within the broader discourse context from which they arose and to which they were oriented. Next, they are shown to form an *inter*textual series on the basis of their graded incorporation of Spanish linguistic conventions. Following this, *intra*textual ambivalence is explored within the individual letters, first in the address forms to the king, then in the description of the Franciscan mission in Yucatan, and finally in a sweeping critique of the secular clergy. By moving from the level of the broader social field, to the intertextual series, to the intratextual rhetorical structure of the documents, I will demonstrate both the continuity of these orders and the key role of ambivalence in their organization.

AUTHENTICITY AND AMBIVALENCE IN THE NATIVE VOICE

The Maya letters of February and March 1567 lavish praise on the Franciscan fathers and entreat the Crown to send more quickly. The strong pro-Franciscan rhetoric of the texts has been seen as evidence that they were, in Gates's (1937:114) terms, "concocted by the friars to influence the king." Tozzer (1941:83, n. 350) concurs with Gates, as does Gonzalez Cicero (1978:110) in her study of religious affairs in sixteenth-century Yucatan. The evidence in support of this conclusion is initially compelling.

It is paradoxical that the letters praise Landa, who had directed the inquisition, rather than Toral, who put a stop to it. According to Tozzer (1941:81, n. 344) and Gonzalez Cicero (1978:127), Bishop Toral, upon his arrival in Merida, found two opposed factions: Landa, most Franciscans, and then-Alcalde Mayor Diego de Quijada on the one hand, and a few Franciscans, the wealthy Spaniards, and the secular clergy on the other. In letters to the Crown dated 1 and 12 March 1563, he condemned the ignorance and excesses of the Franciscans and requested that a new group of clergy be sent (Scholes and Adams 1938, Vol. II:34–41, 43). During the same period, he freed many Maya who had been incarcerated on charges of idolatry (19 February 1565 in Scholes and Adams 1938, Vol. II: 396). Over the next five years, he succeeded in having Quijada fined and imprisoned for having abetted the inquisition (Scholes and Adams 1938, Vol. II:363ff., cf. Toral to Crown 3 March 1564, Scholes and Adams 1938, Vol. II:68–73). In brief, Toral appears to have acted as a defender of the Indians. Gonzalez Cicero concludes, plausibly, that the 1567 letters, signed by Maya nobles and expressing affection for the Franciscans, must be a self-serving concoction of the friars. What they show is not the authentic sentiments of the Maya but their extraordinary malleability and the extent to which they were used by Toral's enemies (Gonzalez Cicero 1978:111, 194–95).

Not only do the Maya letters appear bogus for their support of the Franciscans, but they also look as though they were copied from a single Spanish template. Gates made this point and used it to argue that "Its [letter of 12 February 1567] value as a real expression of Maya sentiment is considerably invalidated by [it]" (Gates 1937:114). Tozzer (1941:83, n. 350) cites the existence of seven letters, all identical, dated 12 and 13 February 1567, clearly the same ones Gates refers to. To these should be added a considerably longer one dated 19 March 1567, bearing many of the same signatures as the others, also praising the Franciscans (Hanks 1985a; cf. Spanish version in Gonzalez Cicero 1978:232–35). Thus, the existence of eight letters of strikingly similar content, signed by some eighty Maya nobles and each corresponding to a Spanish version, appear to give further evidence of fakery.[2] Add to this the fact that the signatures of the seven February letters were obviously written by the scribe, not by the principals whose names are represented.

If the evidence of inauthenticity were not already compelling, there is another major piece. In a letter to the Crown, dated 12 April 1567 and signed by four native lords of Mani province, the sham is denounced explicitly, and the Franciscans condemned for their abuses (Zimmermann 1970:36–37). Surely, this squares better with the facts of Franciscan conduct than do the February and March accolades. There is no question in the received view, then, that the February and March letters are bogus, and that their value as expressions of Maya experience is vanishingly small.

On closer inspection, this commonsense reasoning becomes muddled. The similarity of handwriting in the texts and signatures of the February letters is evidence that a single scribe wrote them, but it is irrelevant to the more basic question of whether the principals authorized placement of their names. The signatures of the March letter are *not* all in the scribe's hand. The existence of Spanish versions of the letters fails to prove whether the Maya or Spanish texts came first, and may be explainable simply by noting that the Maya knew that Phillip II, their addressee, spoke Spanish and not Maya. A comparison of the two versions of the 9 March letter shows that the Spanish one is simplified with respect to the Maya (compare Maya version in AGI Mexico 359 with Spanish in Gonzalez Cicero 1978:232). It also is worth noting that the April repudiation by the lords of Mani also appears in Spanish, but no one has adduced this as evidence of inauthenticity.

As Zimmermann (1970) showed, there are actually two significantly different variants of the February letters, each with its corresponding Spanish gloss. It is only from the perspective of a reconstructed (but unattested) common text that the February letters can be spoken of as copies of a single one. The March letter is similar. All are addressed to the Spanish king, making partly identical petitions, praising the Franciscans in many of the same terms, bearing signatures of many of the same Maya nobles, and dated within five weeks of one another.

The letters also differ in significant ways, beginning with the fact that the February ones antedate the March one and can be seen as preludes to it. The February variants were twenty-nine (version I) and twenty-five (version II) orthographic lines in length, including text and final etiquette, and have between six and eighteen names of Maya nobles apiece (facsimiles in Gates 1937:114; McQuown n.d.; Zimmermann 1970: plates 30, 31). The March one is 138 lines long, with 26 signatures of Maya nobles plus four Spanish officials: Pedro Diaz de Monjibar and Gregor Rodriguez, *defensores* (defenders); Alonso de Arevalo, interpreter; and Geronimo de Castro, royal scribe. Eleven of the March Maya signatories also signed one or another of the February letters, but the rest are distinct. Unlike the February letters, the March one is followed by a twelve-line statement in Spanish by the scribe that identifies the provenience of the signatories and testifies to the authenticity of the document. Whereas the February letters praise the Franciscans, the March one also presents a detailed description of Spanish civil and religious authorities. There is also an extended critique of the secular clergy, a number of suggestions to the Crown on the governing of Yucatan, and a description of the exhaustion and anguish of the Maya. The February letters establish a channel of communication, and the March one builds on this, greatly expanding the message. In this light, the 12 April repudiation by the lords of Mani province can be read as an attempt to repossess the right to speak for "we here in Yucatan." It makes a competing claim to symbolic power in the name of a distinct Maya voice.

Gates reasoned that because there were multiple Maya versions of the February letter, with different signatories, the letter could not be a sincere expression of any one group. But this makes sense only under the assumption that a "letter" expresses a unique, individual point of view. There is no evidence that the Maya signatories viewed their communication in this way. Indeed, writing was not used for interpersonal correspondence in preconquest Maya society (Chi in Tozzer 1941:230; Roys 1943).

Assuming the necessary level of consensus, the alternative to seven nearly identical letters presumably would be for the principals all to sign a single copy, and be done with it. Why do they assert their allegiance one by one in parallel repetition instead of in unison? The evidence from other kinds of Maya writing and formal speech is that, within texts, repetition is a ubiquitous and culturally valued stylistic device in the Maya cultures.[3] Various of the books of Chilam Balam, native prophetic histories, also show unifying similarities alongside regional differences.[4] Neither stylistic repetition at the level of a single text nor recurrence of units of discourse across texts proves inauthenticity. It is more likely that the sevenfold repetition of the February letter was an authenticating device. It also permitted the signatories to differentiate themselves by groups while still taking up the same position.

Scholars have been quick to believe the April repudiation by the Xius and Pacabs of Mani province, but this letter is open to the same basic doubts as the others. Why is it in Spanish? Why does it also request more priests? The letter recapitulates Toral's stance vis-à-vis Landa, Quijada, and certain Franciscans. Did he therefore collude in its composition?

In fact, all of the letters are clearly part of a larger discourse that includes Spanish language communications. They share with the Spanish a common addressee in the person of the king, and they describe many of the same individuals described elsewhere in contemporary Spanish documents. They praise the Franciscans in terms similar to those used by Quijada in a letter to the Crown dated 15 February 1565 (Scholes and Adams 1938, Vol. II:170–71), and by the civil authorities of Merida to the Crown 16 May 1567 (quoted by Gonzalez Cicero 1978:194, n. 112). In a letter of 20 May 1564 addressed to the Crown, Quijada criticizes Toral for the economic burden he placed on the natives (Scholes and Adams 1938, Vol. II:83–84), a problem also raised, though less directly, in a letter to the Crown dated 16 October 1567 and signed by six Franciscans (Scholes and Adams 1938, Vol. II:378). The 16 May 1567 letter from civil authorities of Merida also criticizes the secular clergy for their greed and inability to speak Maya (cited in Gonzalez Cicero 1978:194). The very same criticisms are leveled in the Maya letter of 19 March, the same year. A thorough investigation of the contemporary Spanish documents would undoubtedly turn up many more specific features shared by Maya and Spanish texts.

The April letter from Mani has the appearance of "truth," because its signatories had borne the full force of Landa's inquisition. It is also self-serving, however, since it asserts the authority to speak for the Maya. Before granting this power of representation exclusively to one group of nobles, we should consider that whereas the April signatories had suffered the full force of the inquisition, the February and March ones (probably) had not. Instead, they were from Ceh Pech, Ah Canul, Ah Kin Chel, Chakan, Campech, and Chakan Putun provinces, none of which appears to have been the site of inquisitorial activities. This points up one of the basic errors of the traditional interpretation of this correspondence, namely the erroneous assumption that there existed a single Maya perspective against which to judge authenticity.

Another basic problem with the received interpretation is that it attempts to understand the Maya letters solely in the light of the Toral-Landa controversy. The inquisition of 1562 was so horrific and the subsequent recriminations so bitter, that historians have measured the Maya correspondence against these events. One need not deny the catastrophe, however, to deny it the privileged position of determining what is true. There was more going on among the Spaniards, among the Maya, and in their interrelations, than this one dispute.

The Franciscans during the years prior to 1562 had developed relatively close ties with many Maya, preaching the goodness and paternal affection of their Christian god (Gonzalez Cicero 1978:112–14) and standing between them and the depredations of the *encomenderos* (Gonzalez Cicero 1978:118). The ability of the early friars to speak and preach in Maya is well known, as is the fact that they first schooled the Maya in writing and Spanish and trained the official interpreters (Farriss 1984:97).[5] When they learned in the spring of 1562 that Maya continued to worship idols even after baptism, the Franciscans were revulsed (Landa in Tozzer 1941:75f.; Scholes and Adams 1938, Vol. II:71f.; cf. Farriss 1984:291f.). The initial evangelization of the natives gave way to a new phase of reaffirmation and maintenance of their Christianity (Gonzalez Cicero 1978:114; cf. Phelan 1970).

During the same time, Toral's assault on the Franciscans and their Provincial Landa was taking its toll. In September of 1562, the friars convened in Merida and decided to withdraw from many of the rural missions into the main churches of Merida, Mani, Valladolid, Campeche, and Izamal, while at the same time ceasing to administer the sacraments to a Maya population whom they no longer trusted to be true Christians (Gonzalez Cicero 1978:126). This all aggravated the need for more clergy to carry forth the conversion. Toral repeatedly appealed to the Crown that more Franciscans and clergy were needed (12 March 1563 in Gonzalez Cicero 1978:169; 17 October 1565 in Gonzalez Cicero 1978:184). Quijada (10 February 1565 in Scholes and Adams 1938, Vol. II:171) makes the same point, as do de la Torre to the Crown (4 May 1567), civil authorities of Merida to the Crown 16 May 1567 (cited by Gonzalez Cicero 1978:194, n. 112), and Franciscans to the Crown 16 October 1567 (Scholes and Adams 1938, Vol. II:378). In petitioning for more Franciscans, the Maya letters of February and March reflect the fact that, indeed, by 1567, there were few friars, and even they had cut off the Maya from access to the sacraments.

Over the course of Toral's time as bishop of Yucatan, he became increasingly isolated. He denounced Quijada, Alcalde Mayor as an abuser of Spaniards and Indians alike, and brought charges against him for having overstepped his authority in aiding the Franciscans in the inquisition. As early as 20 May 1564, Quijada was counterdenouncing Toral in correspondence with the Crown (Scholes and Adams 1938, Vol. II:83–84), saying that he was in collusion with the wealthy Spaniards, and that he was a tremendous economic burden on the Maya, from whom he extracted many goods and services (Gonzalez Cicero 1978:188; Franciscans to the Crown 16 October 1567 in Scholes and Adams 1938, Vol. II:378). He also supported a plan for graduating tribute according to individual wealth, which would further alienate him from the Maya nobility. In a letter of 10 February 1565, Quijada also complains of the clergy, who were said to be prospering under Toral, and alleged to maintain black slaves (Scholes and Adams 1938, Vol. II:171; cf. Gonzalez Cicero 1978:191).

It seems unlikely that Toral had very positive relations with the wealthy Spanish. He complained often of the poverty of the church and attempted to extract support from the Spanish *encomenderos.* But they apparently never complied and Cespedes did not provide the civil authority to impose the tithe in support of the church. Consequently, Toral censured the governor and civil authorities (Gonzalez Cicero 1978:111). He was embittered by the sense that his efforts were futile and that his inability to speak Maya cut him off from the native population (letter of 17 March 1566 to the Crown, cited in Gonzalez Cicero 1978:200). By holding the Franciscans in check, he helped to create the conditions for the secular clergy to play a more important role in the evangelization of Yucatan, thus contributing to the general weakening of the monastic orders in New Spain and Yucatan that was characteristic of the reign of Phillip II (Phelan 1970). Yet he condemned the clergy as self-interested and avaricious, lessons he had learned while serving as Franciscan Provincial in Michoacan (Gonzalez Cicero 1978:186). He was, ironically, a Franciscan himself and was probably antisecular by virtue of his belonging to this order (Phelan 1970:Ch. V).

The contradictions and isolation of Toral's position in Yucatan seem to have had a significant impact on him, and by March 1569 he requested permission from the Crown to renounce the bishopric (Gonzalez Cicero 1978:205). Given this trajectory, it is not surprising that none of the Maya letters express support for him. If the Maya nobles were paying any attention at all, they would have realized that Toral would not make an effective ally, besieged as he was, from all sides.

According to Toral, in March of 1564, there were only six seculars in Yucatan (Scholes and Adams 1938, Vol. II:68–73). One year earlier he had requested two dozen additional clergy (Gonzalez Cicero 1978:169), and in October of 1565 he requested fifty more.[6] He never got nearly as many as he sought, but he appears to have introduced eight to ten seculars despite his ambivalence about their general character (Gonzalez Cicero 1978:192–93). With the Franciscans on the wane, the role of these clerics as church representatives in Maya towns would have been proportionately greater than in the past. The Maya letter of 19 March 1567 mentions Toral only once by name, saying that it was he who brought the clerics. He was isolated from the Maya therefore, their relation being mediated by the almost universally despised secular clergy. By 1567, the situation appears to have deteriorated sufficiently to motivate a Maya critique of Toral, the secular clergy, Quijada, and the endless bickering, without assuming direct Franciscan interference. The March letter provides this critique.

One more major weakness in the received view is the implicit assumption that these documents can be evaluated in terms of their truth value as indicators of what was "really going on." Did the signatories truly love the Franciscans and despise the secular as they said, or was it a thinly veiled fake? On the grounds of evidence mostly external to the letters in question, I have argued that these things could be true. At this point, I wish to argue that the issue of truth is, in any case, not the central one. Truth versus falsity is a meaningful measure of descriptive statements, not of requests, orders, interjections, and so forth. If, for example, the point of the Maya letters were to establish a communication with Phillip II, to elicit his sympathy, to create an identity for the signatories, to persuade him to act in certain ways, or to claim the right to speak for "the Maya," then truth is less important than effectiveness. The received interpretation inappropriately singles out veracity as a criterion, without considering the nontruth functional aspects of the communication. This is symptomatic of a failure to see that these documents are not brute indicators of a reality that exists external to them. They are instead artifacts of communicative actions performed in a complicated, changing context.

AN INTERTEXTUAL SERIES

The existence of multiple versions of the February letter, along with the similarity between them and the March one, do not demonstrate inauthenticity. Rather, they demonstrate that the texts are concretely interrelated. This raises the important question of how these Maya letters fit into the broader discourse of Maya to Maya, Maya to Spanish, and Spanish to Spanish communication. These other communications are a central aspect of the context in which the letters were produced. They constitute an intertexual context.

Following Jenny (1982), "intertextuality" is a general term for a variety of relations among texts. Two texts may be linked to one another by concrete shared features, for instance, by reference to each other, by amplification (where one text elaborates on the other), by contradiction, or by reinforcement. They may also be related by common membership in a single genre within a given literary tradition (cf. Culler 1981:Ch. 5). Concrete intertextual relations often take the form of transpositions of segments of one text into another. The transposed element is necessarily modified as it is integrated into the new structure, and may or may not retain its recognizability as having originated from without. As a consequence, the presence of intertextual features in the discourse tends to break down the boundary between text-internal and text-external planes. Interpretation of the discourse cannot treat it as an isolate, but rather as part of a series of texts situated within a larger network. The intertextual context is also a key part of the field of action insofar as it provides objective resources for intelligible communicative performance.

The near-identity of the seven February letters is an extreme instance of intertextual linkage, so much so that one is tempted to see seven instances of a single text.

The two variants of the February letter seem to correspond to a dialect difference among their signatories (see Zimmermann 1970:plate 30 versus plate 31). Version I, from the northern region (Ah Canul, Ceh Pech, and Ah Kin Chel), shows 18 Spanish terms (23 tokens) (see Table 4.1). It is noteworthy that the Spanish borrowings are overwhelmingly nouns, religious in reference, as they are also in Version II from Chacan Putun and Tixchel provinces (see Table 4.2). This is consistent with what one finds in Nahuatl documents from the same period, and presumably reflects the predominant role of the friars in teaching literacy skills to the nobles (cf. Anderson et al. 1976).

TABLE **4.1** Spanish Terms in Maya Letter, 11 February 1567 (Version I)

Form	Gloss
yahaulil castilla	the kingdom [reign] of Castille
cristianoil	Christianity (2 instances)
frailes franciscos	Franciscan friars (2 instances)
doctrinas	doctrines (2 instances)
yalmah thanil dios	the spoken word of God
tuluumil castillae	in the land of Castille (2 instances)
tubelil dios	on the path to God
tuprovinç iail toledo	in the province of Toledo
frai [name]	friar so-and-so (4 instances)
cayumil ti dios	our lord in God (2 instances)
uchayan padresob	the rest of [the] fathers
tacristianoil pucç ikal	to your Christian heart
tu.ll.ukinil hebrero	on the 11 day of February
1567. años	1567 years
S.C.R.Mag	Sacred Catholic Royal Majesty

Source: Zimmermann 1970:32.

TABLE **4.2** Spanish Terms in Maya Letter, 11 February 1567 (Version II)

Form	Gloss
ti padreob	to [the] fathers
ti oc olal cristo	in Christian faith
padreob san francisco	San Franciscan fathers
udoctrina	their [his] doctrine
yalmah thanil dios	the spoken word of God
españa e	Spain
padreob san francisco	San Franciscan fathers
tubelil dios	on the path to God
españa e	Spain
frai [name]	friar so-and-so (3 instances)
hebrero 1567 habob	February 1567

Source: Zimmermann 1970:32.

There is a noticeable difference in the two versions in their respective uses of Spanish. Version I (with 19 tokens) has a third more borrowings than version II (13 tokens), partly due to its greater length (29 versus 25 lines). In four noteworthy cases, version I has a Spanish term where version II has a corresponding Maya one. *Cristianoil* (Christianity) in version I becomes *yoc olal cristo* (faith/will in Christ) in II; *tuprovinçiail toledo* in I becomes *tucuchcabil toledo* (from the province of Toledo) in II; *años* in I becomes *habob* (years) in II. Centered at the top of the page, version I has the expression of S.C.R.Mag, abbreviating "Sacred Catholic Royal Majesty," with the cross on the "Majesty." In exactly the same position, version II has the Maya expression *cicithanbil$_1$ cilich$_2$ noh ah tepal$_3$* (sacred$_2$ sweetly addressed$_1$ great majesty$_3$). In summary, version I displays a more extensive engagement in Spanish speech forms than does version II. This might correspond to different degrees of fluency with the language on the part of the principals involved. Alternatively, it could reflect a stylistic choice. By using key Spanish terms—for the divine king, the Christian faith, social space, and time—version I identifies itself as already within the Spanish frame of reference. Version II, with its elegant Maya formulations, identifies itself as authentically and nobly Maya.

The March letter is longer, with 138 lines, and shows proportionately more Spanish terms (64, see Table 4.3). They are still all nouns, but range over religious terms, place names and descriptions, the date, institutional titles and "official," Spanish-dominated, aspects of colonial society. As is evident from the tables, these foreign words are grammatically converted into Maya linguistic structures by inflection and derivation. Their presence in the discourse is a reflection of the interaction between native and nonnative frames of reference in the contemporary social context. The Maya nobles were already deeply engaged in Spanish discourse, and the gradience of incorporations, from least in version II of the February letter, to most in the March, forms an intertextual series. The increasingly elaborate use of Spanish is paired with an increasingly elaborate thematic development in the texts, from a religious focus, to a broad narrative account of the contemporary scene. As Bakhtin (1981:275) observed, the objects of description themselves serve to introduce into the discourse other descriptions in socially distinct, competing languages. Because the letters au-

TABLE **4.3** Spanish Terms in Maya Letter, 19 March 1567

Form	Gloss
ek padresob clerigo	black fathers clergy
ek padre(s)ob	black fathers (6 instances)
sant franᶜᵒ padresob	San Franciscan fathers (8 instances)
frai diego de landa provinç iail	Friar Diego de Landa Provincial
ti provinç iail	to the Provincial
obispo	bishop (2 instances)
obispo [name]	Bishop [Toral]
clerigosob	clergy
utibilil x̄p̄ianosob	the goodness of the Christians
doctrina	doctrine (2 instances)
missa	mass (2 instances)
evangelio ukaba tumen españolesobe	[the] gospel it is called by [the] Spaniards
doctrina x̄p̄iana ukabae . . . missa	Christian doctrine it's called . . . mass (2 instances)
cayumil ti dios	our lord in God (2 instances)
umehen dios	the son of God
tutan dios	before God
dios	God (3 instances)
uay ti provinç ia yucatan (lae)	here in [the] province of Yucatan (2 instances)
uay tuprovinç iail yucatan e	here in the province of Yucatan
uay ti ç iudad de merida. yucatan	here in the city of Mérida, Yucatán
tubolonpiç ukinil yuil març o	on the 19th day of the month of March
año de mil y quis y sesenta y siete	year of 1000 and 500 and 60 and 7
españolob	Spaniards
españolesob	Spaniards
defensorob	defenders
ufirmasob	their signatures
ajustiç ia yetel uchayan españolob	your Justice and the rest of the Spaniards
ajuszᵗo	your Justice
ajustiç ia	Your Justice (2 instances)
ucah juez	he [acts as] judge
yocç ic ubaob ti juezil	they insert themselves into [the] judgeship
agovernador ti don luis cespedes de obiedo	your Governor don Louis Cespedes de Obiedo
ti governador	to [the] Governor
oyador̩ loaysa	Oyador Loaysa
S.C.R.m̄	Sacred Catholic Royal Majesty

Source: Hanks 1985a.

thentically are engaged in their contemporary world, intertextual disparities in the context are played out as heteroglossia within the texts.

Beyond the incorporation of Spanish lexical items into the discourse, the letters also incorporated the overt features of the Spanish *carta*. At the top of each is the royal sign, Sacra Catolica Real Majestad, in abbreviation or unabbreviated Maya equivalent. While the elaborateness of the opening salutations differs across the letters, all have a clearly identifiable closing in which the king is revered and the date and place of provenance, along with the title of signatories, are given. The signatures are laid out after the closing and, at the bottom of the March letter, there is a testament of authenticity by the scribe. The script is neat, regular, and mostly free from abbreviations (cf. Anderson et al. 1976:33). Written on the top of the March document is "letter from the Indians to his majesty (it) is translated" in abbreviated Spanish. These features of format key the document as being of the generic type *carta*. Along with the lexical borrowings, they reinforce the perception that it is a Spanish discourse form. Accurate within limits, this perception should not obscure the fact that the genre is being transformed, and these *cartas* are quite unlike Spanish discourse in other ways. Anderson et al. (1976:30) said that sixteenth-century Nahuatl letters to the king displayed "essentially the polished rhetoric of old Tenochtitlan and Texcoco, the style of the orations of kings and priests in Sahagún." Of the present letters it can be said that they display the elaborated style of Maya literary and ritual discourse, in combination with the Spanish format and lexical items.

There is also extensive evidence that the letters are linked to Maya discourse traditions. One of the most obvious indicators of this is the fact that they are written in Maya language, according to its grammatical and semantic conventions. Moreover, the style—as well as the grammar of the discourse—is recognizably Mayan. The evidence for this assertion comes from a comparison of the letters with other linguistic artifacts in Maya languages. Comparison shows that they share characteristic features of "formal" Mayan discourse, found also in the Maya Books of Chilam Balam (Edmonson 1982), native chronicles (Barrera Vasquez 1984), prayer (Hanks 1984), and narrative. For example, they contain noteworthy semantic couplets, in which two immediately adjacent lines are identical except for one contrasting element, as in "we are humbled beneath your foot, we are humbled beneath your hand." Taken together, the two different parts of the couplet (foot, hand) stand for a third concept, in this case the whole person of the ruler.[7] Scholars have noted the importance of the semantic couplet as a literary device in Quiche Mayan (Edmonson 1968; Norman 1980; Tedlock 1983), Tzeltal Mayan (Becquelin Monod 1979, 1981), and Tzotzil Mayan (Gossen 1974; Haviland 1977), as well as in Yucatec Maya (Bricker 1974; Edmonson 1982), the language of the letters. The fact that they are partly formulated in couplets strongly suggests that the author(s) were familiar with this Maya literary convention. Not only the couplet, moreover, but also triplets and cases of extended parallelism are attested both in the letters and in other Mayan language artifacts.

These literary devices work together in the letters to indicate that the language has been formulated within Mayan aesthetic and rhetorical conventions. This in turn reinforces and authenticates the identity of the signatories as genuine Maya nobles. In relation to the display of Spanish elements in the same letters, the identification of the signatories as native is a rhetorical counterpoint. The dialogism between Spanish and Maya components of discourse is evident intertextually in the gradience of Spanish in the different letters. It is also present intratextually in the variation from section to section and in the basic tension within single sections of text.

Unlike the February letters, the March one presents a broad-ranging narrative account of the contemporary scene. Like the "novel" as described by Bakhtin (1981), it is a complex discourse form, built up in a variety of social voices. In an intensely affective rhetoric, the authors present themselves as the humble servants of God and the king, suffering greatly under the local colonial administrators, and anxious to become more perfect Christians. They take on the language of Franciscan mysticism to deprecate themselves as blind idolators and give evidence thereby of having already entered into the colonial dialectic of self-representation through an imposed language (cf. Comaroff and Comaroff

1986). They shift suddenly between this and a scathing denunciation of the secular clergy, formulated in elegant Maya literary language, and then back to an almost matter-of-fact voice in which suggestions are made to the king on how best to rule Yucatan. Although it would be impossible to encompass the whole of the March letter in this paper, one dimension that seems central is the stance taken up by the authors before the king.

The act of addressing the king in a language at least partly foreign is itself a display of the elite status of the signatories. The Maya nobility claimed foreign descent itself, prior to the conquest, and legitimated this claim through knowledge of the esoteric "language of Suyua," said to derive from the Toltecs (Stross 1983). By addressing the paramount, the speakers reproduced their noble status within indigenous society. They addressed Him as Ruler and Majesty, speaking up from below, and into the light from the darkness. The forms of royal address vary across the letters, and within each letter, in accordance with the immediate discourse contexts in which they occur. All of the letters begin with a salutation in which the signatories present themselves and explicitly establish their subordinate relation to the king. For the remainder of the text, the king is present, either as overtly signaled second person (you) or as the presupposed addressee to whom the rhetoric is directed. In the overt mode, he is always addressed in asymmetric terms; every second-person reference is accompanied by a reverential epithet. As the unstated object of persuasive rhetoric, he is appealed to in a variety of ways, including expressions of devotion, so that he might reciprocate by showing mercy. The forms of address reflect these shifts in footing and will be explored in the first set of examples.

The praise lavished on the Franciscans is formulated in terms of a series of reciprocal relations with the signatories, in which they share with them enduring love, a common language, the enlightenment of Christianity, and the familiarity of habitual accompaniment. The secular clergy, by stark contrast, are in all ways unreciprocal. They return hate for love, rage for devotion; they do not speak, they exploit. The contrasting relations set up between the Maya and the friars, as opposed to the seculars, form a paradigm that can shed light on the role of the king as well. By elaborately describing the goodness of Franciscan reciprocity while at the same time expressing total devotion to the king, the authors set up the presumption that he will reciprocate with favor. The alternative is embodied in the unreciprocating seculars. In this light, the final set of examples, which focus on the representation of the seculars, bears also on the overall logic of address. (I am indebted to Terence Turner for suggesting this perspective.)

STRUCTURES OF ROYAL ADDRESS

The March letter begins with an opening construction consisting of three parallel blocks of verse, followed by an isolated line. This is shown in example 1.[8] Note that each block, labeled I, II, III begins with *yoklal,* a connective expression meaning roughly "regarding, in consideration of, in favor of, because" (Barrera Vasquez, Bastarrachea Manzano, Brito Sensores 1980:979, cf. 601). It is a commonly attested phrasing device in the letters,

EXAMPLE **1** Opening Lines from Letter of 19 March 1567

Line	Block		Gloss
1.1	I	yoklal tumulcħabilon	For we [who are] gathered together
1.2		con chambel uinic	we simple men
1.3		canaate cayumil ti dios.	we understand our lord in God
2.1		yetel tech cech	and You You [who are]
2.2		noh ahau ah tepale	Great Ruler Majesty
2.3		yanix ti col ca Coclukeç lauac bal kananil	we wish too that you accomplish something necessary
3.1		tech xan	you
3.2	II	yoklal hach thonanoon	For truly we are humbled
3.3		taclacal yalan auoc yalan akab	we all beneath your foot, beneath your hand
3.4		hibahunon con batabob	however many we be, we [who are] chiefs
4.1		yetel canucteyilob	and our elders
4.2		yan uay ti provinç ia yucatan lae	[who] are here in the province of Yucatán
5.1	III	yoklal uay caluumile	For here in our land
5.2		ahotochnalonixan	we are natural born citizens too
5.3		coltic capatcante taxicin	we wish to recount it to your ear
5.4		cech ahaue	You Ruler
6.1		uchebalix acħaic unucul xan	in order that you take up its meaning too
6.2	IV	he tun cathan lae	Here then we speak
7.1	V	hach kanan uuilal	Truly there is great need
7.2		uay ti provinç ia yucatan	here in the province of Yucatán
7.3		Sant fran^co. padresob toon.	[of] San Franciscan fathers for us.

used to mark off the beginning of short sections of discourse, as in the blocks here.[9] In each block, the first two lines describe the signatories as "gathered together, simple (common) men" (lines 1.1–1.2), "truly humbled beneath your foot, beneath your hand" (lines 3.2–3.3), and "here in our land, natural citizens" (lines 5.1–5.2). These lines establish the total subjugation of the signatories to the royal addressee, joined with their status as legitimate *naturales*. The remaining lines of blocks I and III are grammatically parallel, each with a transitive verb with "we" as subject (1.3, 5.3) followed immediately by reference and address to Phillip II, plus the honorific epithets "you, you (who are) great ruler majesty" (2.1–2.2) and "your ear you Ruler" (5.3–5.4). The remainder of each block describes the goal of the letter, to get the king to reciprocate by acting in a certain way. Following the end of III is an isolated line framed by deictic particles, which present the letter itself as the speech of "we" (6.2).

Looked at as a whole, this construction of triplet plus isolated presentative establishes all of the critical deictic parameters of the communication, specifying in order: "We" (the addressers), "you" (the addressee), "here" (location of composition), and "this language" (the letter itself). These dimensions ground the event in social space and time and establish the relation of the nobles to the Crown in terms of communicative roles.[10]

Within each block, there is a tendency toward semantic and syntactic couplets, evident in the restatement of key phrases just twice, in parallel form. In each block, the first two lines describe the signatories in terms of a couplet. Lines 1.1–2.1 unite "gathered together" with "common." These jointly describe the nobles as a vulgar multitude in contrast to the exalted singularity of the Crown "you." The form *thonanoon* in line 3.2 means "humbled" in the palpable sense of domination beneath a crushing burden (see Barrera Vasquez et al. 1980:841). The verticality inherent in this image is elaborated in the canonical couplet "beneath your foot, beneath your hand." The ordered pairing of "foot-hand" to stand for a whole person is widely attested in Maya literatures (Becquelin Monod 1981; Gossen 1974:194–95; Norman 1980:395) and occurs not just here, but at the end of this letter also, where the nobles "reverently kiss the tip of your foot, the tip of your hand" (Hanks 1985a:lines 122–23; cf. note 7). Finally, the opening couplet of block III, lines 5.1–5.2, establishes the spatial nexus between the nobles, their land (*luumil*), and their natural homes (*otochnal*). This three-way relation is asserted at least partly in response to Crown policy of recognition of native status (*naturales*).

There are two more noteworthy couplets in these lines. The first occurs at lines 2.1–2.2 and consists of the dual pairing of *tech cech* (you you [who art]) with *noh ahau ah tepal* (great ruler majesty). The former are both second-person deictics used to create the addressee; the latter are nondeictic descriptors in apposition to the second person forms. The use of these descriptive epithets in address and reference to the king is common in both versions of the February letter and the March one, as well as in the *Yaxkukul Chronicle*, dated 1544, which recounts the history and boundaries of Ceh Pech province (Barrera Vasquez 1984).

According to glosses in the Motul dictionary and examples in other contemporaneous documents, *ahau* describes "ruler" or "chief" in a series of differentiated ranks. *Tepal*, on the other hand, means "majesty" or "glory," focusing more on the preeminence and abundance of the ruler than on his positional superiority (Hanks 1985b). The pairing of the two terms in descriptions of Maya lordship is attested in the Chilam Balam of Tizimin, as in examples 2 and 3 below.

In example 2, the pairing describes not the chief himself, nor the position of chief, but rather chiefly reign, in construction with the homologous pairing of *cab* (land [in undifferentiated sense of "earth"]) and *peten* (region, island [delimited area]). The proportion *cab:peten :: tepal:ahau* neatly captures the semantic likeness of *peten* and *ahau* as the segmented counterparts of *cab* and *tepal*. Immediately following this, the triplet *ah mahan x, y, z* places *tepal* (majesty) in construction with *pop* (mat) and *tz'am*

EXAMPLE 2 From the Book of Chilam Balam of Tizimin

Line		Gloss
1420	*Chehom uuich*	With wooden faces
1421	*t u cab*	in the land,
1422	*t u peten*	in the country,
1423	*t u tepal*	in the rule
1424	*t u y ahaulil*	in the lordship
1425	*Ah mahan pop*	borrowers of the mat
1426	*Ah mahan tz'am*	borrowers of the throne
1427	*Ah mahan tepal*	borrowers of the rule

Source: Edmonson 1982; line breaks and glosses retained.

EXAMPLE **3** From the Book of Chilam Balam of Tizimin

Line		Gloss
1270	*ti y ahaulilob*	in the lordships
1271	*ah bolon kin*	of the nine-day
1272	*ah bolon tz'am*	of the nine-throne people
1273	*t u tepal Ah Uuc Cha Pat kin*	in the rule of the 7 priest Cha Pat's days

Source: Edmonson 1982; line breaks and glosses retained.

(throne). The mat and throne appear to make up a traditional Maya couplet standing for chiefly rule (cf. Edmonson 1982:line 1256).

It is also noteworthy here that the verse form consists of a combination of couplets with triplets. In particular, the embedding of one couplet within another to yield an apparent triplet—[(A B) C]—is a structure type that recurs in the letters of 1567. In example 3 the same pairing is shown again, this time with *ahaulil* preceding *tepal*. Observe that, once again, the inclusive couplet formed by the two lines beginning with *ti yahaulil* and *tutepal* can be analyzed into an embedded pair (*ah bolon kin, ah bolon tz'am*) followed by a third (*ah Uuc Cha Pat Kin*). Hence, the same structure [(A B) C] is at play.[11]

The linking of *noh ahau* (great ruler) with *ah tepal* (majesty) in the opening lines of the March letter appears to be based on a traditional semantic couplet. The Chilam Balam of Tizimin shows it in reference to native lords and the Yaxkukul Chronicle shows it in reference (not address) to the Spanish king. From a semantic perspective, this joining of the ideas of articulated rule with abundant preeminence meshes with the duality of the Spanish kingship as worldly and divine. Recall that the insignia S.C.R.Mag̃ is glossed in version II of the February letter as *cicithanbil cilich noh ah tepal*, thus aligning the majesty of the king with his status as *noh ah tepal*. Unlike the March letter, which appeals to both aspects of the king, it is mainly the beneficent provider that is invoked in the February letters, with their appeal for mercy. Whereas the March letter has the dual epithet in its opening lines, the February ones have the single form *cech ah tepal e* (you [who art] majesty). The term *ahau* seems to appear only in passages that invoke the king as dominant ruler. Alongside this semantic motivation for the different address forms in the letters is another one, which derives from the immediate linguistic context. The dual form in the March letter fits into a larger verse construction in which there is a strong tendency toward couplets embedded within triplets. This tendency is missing in the corresponding lines of the February letters.

The last couplet illustrated in example 1 is the epithet for "we" in lines 3.4–4.1: "however many we be, we (who are) chiefs and our elders." Just like the royal address forms, the epithet begins with paired deictic reference (this time "we" rather than "you") and is completed with paired descriptive expressions. Whereas the "great ruler" and "majesty" characterize the same unique individual, "chiefs and our elders" describes two different groups of people. They are all included within the "we" of the signatories, but distinguished by status. *Batab* is usually glossed as Spanish "cacique," that is "chief" at the town level (see discussion in Farriss 1984: chapt. 8; Roys 1943,

1957). The *nuc₁ teilob₂* (principals, elders [lit. great/old₁ trees₂]) complement the chief in the governance of the town and appear to have had significant influence in the formulation of policy. This appeal to a native structure of authority carries forth the appeal to the king as ruler in the March letter; both are absent from the February letter. Furthermore, like the royal epithets, this one is embedded in an immediate verse structure in which the couplet dominates. Thus, the material form of the epithet encapsulates both the semantic-thematic focus on hierarchical rule, and the constructive dominance of the couplet within the immediate verse context.

We can glimpse aspects of the Spanish world in these lines, in the reference to God, the province of Yucatan, and the assertion of the native status of the signatories; but it is the Maya frame of reference that predominates. The symbols of rule and status, along with the formal symmetries of their statement come from Maya literary tradition. Within the dialogical tension between perspectives, the Maya encompasses the Spanish, transforming the *Rey* into *Ahau* and recasting the network of related concepts. The opening lines of the February letter strike a somewhat different balance.

Enlightenment and the Franciscan Mission

Several differences between the lines in example 4 and the corresponding ones in the March letter are immediately evident. There is no overriding triplet and no isolated presentative to separate the opening from the body of the text. The second block (lines 2.1–2.8) in example 4 goes directly to the central wish expressed in the letter, that more religious be sent to enlighten and teach the Maya. It is only after this, in the third block, that the relation between signatories and king is elaborated. There is no overt description of the signatories, nor of their submission to the king, just as there is no description of "here." Rather, "here" is the assumed but unstated place from which Castile is "far away."

Recalling the sequence of deictic references in the March letter, the contrast with the February one is striking. There is a marked paucity of overt first-person description in the first two blocks in example 4. Although "your vassals" in line 1.1 refers to the signatories, it is actually inflected as third-person plural (*ob*). The description of this plurality is not elaborated, as it was in the March letter. Similarly, there is little overt description of the royal addressee in example 4, save the almost perfunctory *cech ah tepal e* (You [who art] majesty) in lines 1.2, 2.2, and 3.6. The spatial matrix set up in the opening of the March letter is entirely lacking in the February letter. Finally, the language itself is nowhere commented on in example 4, whereas example 1 showed explicitly self-reflexive description in lines 5.3, 6.1, and 6.2. In all of these ways, the relation between the king and the signatories is more concrete and specific in the March letter than in the February letter.

While the first five lines in example 4 are almost totally lacking in verse parallelism, it becomes clear by line 2.1 that there is a remote parallelism between lines 1.1–1.2 and 2.1–2.2. *Lai tah oklal* in line 2.1 is an anaphoric variant of *yoklal* in line 1.1. In conjunction with the identical address forms in 1.2 and 2.2, this reinforces the perception that the two blocks are parallel. But it is a weak correspondence because, while the first block is in prose, the second is in measured verse.

EXAMPLE 4 Opening Lines from Letter of 11 February 1567 (Version I)

Line	Block		Gloss
1.1	I	*yoklal achinamob tulacal*	For all of your vassals
1.2		*-cech ah tepal e-*	-You [who are] Majesty-
1.3		*naata cacah ti yulolalil*	we understand willfully
1.4		*hibici unah tulacal*	how all is necessary
1.5		*uchebal ca lukulob e,*	in order that we be saved,
2.1	II	*lai tah oklal*	For that reason
2.2		*-cech ah tepal e-*	-You [who are] Majesty-
2.3		*bailcun a tumtic ychil auahaulilob*	would that you provide within your kingdoms
2.4		*yah bebeç ahulob,*	the ministers,
2.5		*ca utzac utichkakticob*	that they might illuminate
2.6		*yetel uç aç cunicob*	and enlighten
2.7		*yetel ucambeç icob*	and teach
2.8		*himac mabal yohmahob e;*	whosoever knows naught;
3.1	III	*bacx nachacoon*	Even though we be distant
3.2		*yetel tippanacoon*	and perceivable [from afar]
3.3		*yan ti yahaulil Castilla*	from the kingdom of Castilla
3.4		*ti lob e,*	notwithstanding
3.5		*canaatma tan olanil tamen*	we understand forthrightly [that] you do
3.6		*-cech ah tepal e-*	-You [who are] Majesty-
3.7		*baihi nedzanacoon yan e;*	as if we were close;

Source: Zimmermann 1970:32.

Note that beginning with the second half of line 2.3, there is a series of six lines, all measuring between six and eight syllables, all ending in *ob(e)*. The first two lines in the series, *ychil au ahauliloblyah bebecahulob* (in your kingdoms / its ministers) form a couplet on the basis of the end rhyme (*lob*) and of the partial grammatical parallelism between them as possessed noun stems that end in a [VI] suffix, (*il* in the former and *ul* in the latter). The next three lines (2.5–2.7) carry forth the *ob* end rhyme, but differ precisely from the preceding couplet. Rather than possessed nouns, they are all transitive verbs with identical inflections: *u-STEM-ic-ob*, where *u-* . . . *-ob* marks plural subject and object, and *-ic-* marks transitive incompletive aspect. Each is preceded by a connective element, "in order that" in the first, and "and" in the second and third. The final line in the series (2.8) carries the same plural *ob* in precisely the same metrical position (seventh syllable in the line), this time followed by the terminal particle *e*. This particle is isolated by the rhyme and meter scheme of the preceding lines, and its isolation emphasizes its function in bringing the verse series to a close. Combining with all of these structural links among lines is the presence of extensive alliteration in the vowels.[12]

Lines 2.1–2.8, therefore, illustrate what Tynianov (1981 [1924]) called a verse series, based on the combination of grammatical and sound parallelism. This series is more compact than any of those illustrated in example 1, because it is constructed with a larger number of smaller units arranged in more immediate proximity to one another. Furthermore, the almost total absence of parallelism in the preceding lines establishes a background against which the verse series emerging from line 2.3 is in stark contrast. These formal facts are inherently significant to the rhetoric of the letter, because they constitute a virtuoso display of artistic competence in Maya. They are in this sense authenticating devices.[13] The compact verse structure intensifies the request and its rationale while unifying them into a single bounded construct. Starting from recognition of the realm and its representatives (lines 2.3–2.4), it moves to a statement of the enlightenment derived from them. This simultaneously ratifies the association between the king's representatives and light, ignorance and darkness, while conveying the desire of the signatories to be taught. The Crown becomes the luminous center of space, Yucatan the dark, remote periphery, and the ministers the means of transforming darkness to light.

In lines 2.5–2.8 the semantic association between light and knowledge is neatly formulated in a triplet. As in earlier examples, this triplet is analyzable into a semantic couplet (illuminate, enlighten) within an encompassing couplet (illuminate, enlighten, teach), thus ([A B] C). The merger of light with knowledge is a familiar Maya theme, attested also in Quiche divination (Tedlock 1982:Ch. 7), modern Tzotzil oral literature (Gossen 1974:38–40), and modern Yucatec prayer performed by shamans (Hanks 1984). Similarly, both spatial remoteness and its association with darkness were discussed by Gossen (1974:Ch. 1) for Tzotzil.

Despite the intricately Maya literary style of the language in example 4, there is another reading of the passage on which it makes good Franciscan sense. This other reading dialogizes the text and relates it to a wholly distinct intertextual tradition. In his brilliant study of Franciscan mysticism in the New World, Phelan (1970:Ch. 6) showed that for the Franciscans, the Indians were spiritual children, capable of perfect salvation through faith. The New World was literally outside of the Old, a place where a more perfect Christianity could be achieved. Under the guidance of the Franciscans, the Indians would become citizens of the City of God, leaving to the Old World the City of Man. Phelan discusses the "twin apexes" of medieval Franciscan mysticism, the Apocalypse, and the sanctification of poverty (1970:Chs. 2 and 5). In preparation for the coming of the Millennial Kingdom, the Catholic monarchs were to preside over the extirpation of what Mendieta called "the three diabolical squadrons (of) 'perfidious' Judaism, 'false' Mohammedanism and 'blind' idolatry" (cited in Phelan 1970:13). The reference to blindness here brings up the dichotomy of darkness and light; the extirpation of idolatry—the Franciscan task in Yucatan—was an enlightenment to those who could not see. The perfection mentioned in line 1.5 of example 4, the enlightenment in lines 2.5–2.6, the teaching in 2.7—all of these are interpretable within the framework of Franciscan thought. This dialogism in the text is motivated by the social conditions of its production: it *does* reflect a Franciscan voice (among others), because this was a major part of the contemporary field of action.

The opening lines of the February and March letters also display several features of Maya literary style. Formal devices in example 1 included particle phrasing at the beginning of each block, syntactic, morphological, and semantic parallelism among lines, including the combination of couplets with(in) triplets. All of these features are attested in Maya literatures in one or another of Yucatec, Quiche, Tzeltal, and Tzotzil.

Example 4 from the February letter lacks the overall block structure of example 1, but adds a notably compact verse construction based on grammatical and semantic parallelism combined with rhyme, alliteration, and meter. In each case, the finely wrought language is a display of virtuosity, an indication that one of the voices it speaks is authentically Maya.

The Blackness of the Secular Clergy

A further example of ambivalence is the bitter denunciation of the secular clergy, who are first introduced as the "black fathers clergy" as shown in example 5. In the lines just preceding these, the Franciscan fathers (*sant fran.co padresob*) are said to be greatly needed in Yucatan.[14] For the remainder of the letter, neither the bishop nor the clergy break out of their status as dark forces antithetical to the well-being of the Maya. The full three-part epithet (*ek padresob clerigo*) occurs only in the first reference to the clergy, while the shortened form *ek padres(ob)* (black fathers) occurs eight times, and *clerigos* (clerics) occurs only three. All other references to the secular clergy (as opposed to the Franciscans) are pronominal. Thus, *ek padres(ob)* is by far the most common epithet for the seculars, as opposed to *sant fran.co padresob* for the Franciscans. To my knowledge, this is the only document in which a group of actors, Spanish or Maya, is described as "black." The uniqueness and prominence of the epithet are combined with its semantic contribution to the rhetorical assault on the clergy. It provides an organizing center for the critique of the clergy by drawing together the reprehensible properties attributed to them.

According to the *Diccionario de Motul* (folia 162r, 163, 163r in Martinez Hernandez 1929:343–45), *ek* at this time conveyed darkness and darkness of color as well as moral corruption, as in "*ek: eek* (a black thing). From this *paynum yekil a pixan tuuich Dios yokol chuuc tumen a keban* (greater is the blackness of your soul before God than charcoal because of your sins)" (folio 162r, English gloss translated from Spanish by author). While this association of sin with blackness of the "soul" is almost certainly derived from Christian ideas of spiritual purity and impurity, this citation demon-

EXAMPLE **5** From Letter of 19 March 1567

Line		Gloss
11.3	habla bacacix likul tac chi	Even though as appointed
12.1	hulci obispo tatuxchi	[there] arrived [the] bishop [whom] you ordered
12.2	frai fran.co toral ukabae	Fray Francisco Toral [is] his name
12.3	yulç ah caix uthoxah	he brought and he distributed
13.1	ek padresob clerigo	black fathers clergy
13.2	ucate ukabaobe	his lesser brothers [?] [are] their names
13.3	ca uuacunahob	then he posted them [stood them up]
13.4	ti canan cahob	as town curas
13.5	ychil cacahal	without our towns
13.6	yalabob uthan dios toon.	[that] they might say the word of God to us.

Source: Hanks 1985a.

strates that the association was already in place by the late sixteenth century. In combination with *ich,* meaning "eye, face, manner," it conveyed "a surly person who is standoffish and never shows a good face, nor wishes to converse." In combination with *chenan* (meaning undetermined), it conveyed "dark, frightening" (folio 163); *ek may* is glossed as "blind person." As a descriptor of individuals or states of affairs, *ek* appears to focus on the lack of sociability, lack of sight, and frightening darkness. Citing nineteenth-century sources, the *Cordemex* dictionary (Barrera Vasquez et al. 1980:149) adds to these senses the ideas of wildness (bravo) and standoffishness. According to Roys (1943), black paint was applied to the bodies of unmarried youths and common warriors going into battle, which is consistent with the marginality of the black clergy.

As a color, *ek* was associated with the west as opposed to *chac* (red) of the east. This directional corollary introduces further ones, including under (lower) as opposed to over (higher) and evil or ambivalent as opposed to good.[15] *Ek* (black) is also meaningfully opposed to *sak* (white) as a descriptor applied to Europeans. In the Chilam Balam of Tizimin, the coming of the white men with red beards from the east is described, as shown in example 6. Note that the arrival of the white men marks the arrival of (the) white god, evidently the sign of Christianity. It is in direct opposition to the prototype of white religion that the blackness of the clergy takes on its full force in the March letter. Furthermore, *ek* as darkness stands in opposition to *saasil* (light), whereby it represents the absence of enlightenment. Recall from the February letter that enlightenment was associated with the Franciscan mission in Yucatan. This complementarity is another indication of the intertextual relation among the Maya letters, including the April repudiation, which speaks of blindness and vision. It is also consistent with the strict antithesis between the Franciscans and the seculars as portrayed in the March letter. Consider the passage in example 7, in which several of the paradigmatic associations of *ek* are explicitly cited.

In the midst of a litany of criticisms of the seculars occurs the expression *ek uinic* (black man) (line 52.4), exactly the opposite of *sac uinic* (white man) of the Chilam

EXAMPLE **6** From the Book of Chilam Balam of Tizimin

Line		Gloss
1169	*u hun tz'it katun*	The first part of the Katun
1170	*ulic sac uinicob*	there arrived white people
1171	*ich can si ho*	heaven born Merida
1172	*u hetz' katun*	was the seat of the Katun
1173	*bee chac u mexoc*	so, red were the beards
1174	*u mehen kin*	of the sons of the sun,
1175	*sac uinicob e*	those white people
1176	*be okbac on ti tali ob*	so we wept at their coming.
1177	*ti likin u tal*	they came from the east;
1178	*ca uliob uay e*	then they arrived here,
1179	*ah mexob*	the bearded men
1180	*a pulob*	the guayaba people,
1181	*ti chicul ku sac*	and manifested the white God
1182	*uahom che canal*	standing on the tall pole.

Source: Edmonson 1982; line breaks and glosses retained.

EXAMPLE 7 From Letter of 19 March 1567

Line	Gloss
hex uCan ubelob	here too their ways are folded
50.5 *clerigosob lae*	these clerics
51.1 *hach kuxob toon*	truly they are hateful towards us
51.2 *tamuk uCaCalic capach*	whereas they oppress us (on) our backs
51.3 *cabeelte ti yotochob*	we do in (at) their homes
52.1 *lauac bal ca yalicob toon*	whatever thing they tell us (to)
52.2 *yoklal yantacob yotochob*	for they have their (individual) houses
52.3 *yanix upalilob*	and they have servants (slaves)
52.4 *ek uinicob*	black men
53.1 *yantacobix utziminob*	and they have horses
53.2 *.y. uthulob*	and rabbits
53.3 *he tun tucultalob*	moreover they reside
53.4 *ychil cacahalob e*	within our towns
54.1 *cacalah tzentob*	we feed the lot of them
54.2 *.y. ubal yotochob*	along with the things of their households
54.3 *maix bal ubolil*	and they pay naught
55.1 *maix tan cakatab tiob*	and we shan't ask them to
55.2 *yoklal çublaconob tiob*	for we are ashamed before them
55.3 *çahconix tiob xan*	and we are frightened of them also

Source: Hanks 1985a.

Balam of Tizimin. Just before this in the text, the clergy are described as *kux* (hateful, rancorous, abhorrent, that which causes pain) (Barrera Vasquez et al. 1980:425–26), and as oppressing the backs of the Maya (*CaCalic ca pach*) "forcing down (exigently) our backs." The latter reference to pressing downward is consistent with the vertical connotations of *ek* as west-under (see note 15), and recalls explicitly the relation between the Maya and the evil of idolatry, as stated just twenty lines earlier in the letter: *yoklal hach bulanoon tu-Cal-pach ciçin cuchi* (For truly we [were] mired *in the violent exigencies* of the devil) (Hanks 1985a, lines 23.3–24.1). The form *Cal-pach* is a compound of the same roots *Cal* (oppress) and *pach* (back) that occur in example 7, thus establishing the relational equivalence of the secular clergy and the "evil squadron" of idolatry. Later in example 7, the seculars are described as provoking shame and fear among the Maya. Although *ek* occurs only once in this passage, its pall covers the whole. The phrase *ek uinicob* (black men) is actually ambiguous in this context, and can be interpreted as either the African servants some of the clergy are said to have kept or the "black" clergy themselves (cf. Quijada to Crown 10 February 1565 in Scholes and Adams 1938, Vol. II: 170–71; Hunt 1976:42). While it may be that the secular clergy in fact wore black, therefore, their black habits are thoroughly revalorized within the rhetorical framework of the letter. It is the cultural loading of blackness that guides its appropriation in the discourse; hence the dark brown habit of the Franciscans is never mentioned.

Instead of readily discernible blocks of verse, this example illustrates a variety of poetic features that recur from line to line, but only occasionally coalesce into a dominant couplet or triplet. Most of the lines are between six and eight syllables long and correspond to a sentence. The coincidence of these facts creates the artifice of equivalence among the lines, based on quantity. Reinforcing this is the occurrence of twenty tokens of the plural marker *ob* in the course of the same passage. Recall that repetition of *ob* in final position in six- to eight-syllable lines was one of the poetic devices used also in the opening of the February letter.

Example 7 provides several illustrations of grammatical parallelism. Lines 51.1–51.2 could be read as a semantic couplet in which the two parts characterize the reprehensible conduct of the seculars. Note that the two lines are formally dissimilar. Lines 54.3–55.3 on the contrary are quantitatively regular at six, eight, eight, and six syllables respectively; grammatically parallel *maix X, maix Y, yoklal X (yoklal) Y;* semantically related (they don't pay, we don't ask them to; we're ashamed before them, we're afraid of them), and bound by the end rhyme (*tiob . . . tiob . . . tiob xan*) in the last three lines. The relative density of parallelism here reinforces the thematic unity of the segment; the unwillingness to pay for services rendered, the unapproachability and the provoking of shame and fear summarize the exploitative relationship of seculars to the Maya. It is in lines 52.2–53.2 however that verse parallelism combines most explicitly with the rhetoric of blackness.

Lines 52.2–53.2 consist of three sentences, each with the verb *-an* (to exist), *y-an-tac-ob* (there are [it-exists-collective-plural]), *y-an-ix* (there is/are also), *y-an-tac-ob-ix* (there are also). The identity of the verbs plus the alternation of inflections sets up a three-part syntactic frame in which the existence of five objects is asserted, one object per line in final position. Looking only at the first (leftmost) part of each line, there is an overlaid alliterative series *yo-ya-ya-ya-ye* (.y. abbreviates *yetel* [and, with]), to reinforce the grammatical parallelism. In the last half of each line (including all of line 52.4) are the five objects, all noun phrases ending in *ob* (plural), with three, four, four, four, three syllables respectively. The first two and the last two in the series are overtly possessed, marked by [y-] ~ [u-] (their, his, her, its). All four nouns are in exactly the same relation to their respective verbs, and to the clerics who possess them. This pattern leaves isolated, right in the middle, the epithet *ek uinicob* (black men), as the only noun phrase lacking possessive inflection, and unaccompanied by any verb or conjunction in its line. This foregrounds the entire construction and the epithet within as something distinct from what precedes and follows it. The motivation for this elaborate framing lies not in the formal construction itself, however, but in the semantic and symbolic values carried by *ek* (black).

The exquisite manipulation of the language in this passage sustains the display of Mayanness in the text. It has been closely worked according to indigenous conventions of formal discourse. Knowledge of these conventions was itself an indicator of the high status of the signatories within Maya society. Yet like all of the other examples, this one is ambiguously native. Numerous points of similarity between this letter and contemporary Spanish discourse indicate that they were formulated from within the same contemporary scene.

The passage is also imbued with the ever-present Franciscan perspective. While the meaning of *ek* can be explored within an indigenous framework, the possession of worldly objects, slaves, and domestic stock carries no standard negative overtones in Maya. It is from the perspective of the Franciscan vows of poverty that worldly possessions are intrinsically bad. In fact, the nobility is known to have traded in slaves, particularly in the provinces of the signatories (Roys 1943:68). When the clergy are berated for having or desiring wealth (for example, lines 91–94 of the same letter, Hanks 1985a), the criticism plays on the Franciscan assumption that wealth in all forms is antithetical to the spiritual mission of the church in the New World. What the letter shows, then, is a fusion of Maya and Spanish frameworks at several levels simultaneously, both deeper and more superficial than the meanings of the words.

CONCLUSION

The Spanish conquest of Yucatan created a new discourse, within which Maya and Spanish systems of representation were encompassed. In some cases, the two systems remain distinguishable from one another, while interacting within a single whole. This can be seen at various levels, from the occurrence of Spanish lexical borrowings in Maya sentences to the use of Maya language to write a *carta,* preach Catholicism, or pay allegiance to the Spanish king. In other cases, it is more difficult to assign forms of representation to one system or the other. Some elements may be common to both cultures, such as the cross as a ritual symbol. More often, it is impossible to sort out the two systems, because they are fused within the larger whole. This is the case with much of modern Maya ritual practice, which addresses a hybridized spiritual world, in a language merged from Catholic prayer and archaic Maya. The fusion of the two systems may be brought about through long-term interaction, but need not be. It can be performed creatively as well. The production of hybrid discourse is a pragmatic process that takes place in action. This process was already well under way by the 1560s in Yucatan, with the Spanish friars and native elites at the forefront.

Farriss (1984:98f.) presents an interesting example of cultural ambivalence in the career of don Francisco Uz, a hereditary chief (*batab*) from Mani province. Born in 1567, Uz held the position of Indian *gobernador* in two large towns in the area, learned to speak and write elegant Spanish, and became an official interpreter and senior aide to the Spanish governor. In the end, he was accused of complicity in the 1610 uprising in Tekax, Mani. Farriss suggests that his main crime was that he was too ambitious in manipulating the colonial system, and his success bred resentment. Dibble (1985) presents a complementary example from the same period in the Nahuatl region, where the works of Sahagún incorporated many elements of Nahuatl vocabulary and literary style. In writing his *General History of the Things of New Spain,* in Nahuatl, Sahagún became deeply familiar with native ritual practice, and language. In his evangelical writings he seldom mentioned native practices, but drew on them extensively in translating scripture and doctrine into the Nahuatl frame of reference. Like Uz and the signatories of the letters studied here, Sahagún contributed by his labors to a new, ambivalent discourse.

Previous analyses of the Maya letters of 1567 have fixed on the apparent failure of these documents to display the "native perspective." Their very transparency as a bid to shore up the Franciscans before the king reinforces the perception that they are not really Maya. The presence of Spanish throughout the documents at all levels seems to lead in the same direction. This line of reasoning overlooks some central facts. The native perspective is blurred because there was no unitary native perspective to express itself. Moreover, the addressee, many of the referents, and the format of the discourse itself were Spanish. If it were possible to produce a fully monolingual (monologic in Bakhtin's 1981 terms) expression under these circumstances, it is doubtful whether it would be intelligible to the addressee. In part, the heterogeneity of the language follows from that of the pragmatic field in which it was performed. This field included more than Spanish civil and ecclesiastical institutions. Accordingly, the letters cannot be understood solely in relation to the dispute between Toral and Landa, however important this was. Viewed in a broader discourse context that includes native language literature as well as a range of Spanish materials, they become more intelligible. By positing a pure native voice that is absent, one silences the native components that *are* in the language. Ambivalence takes on the appearance of inauthenticity.

I have argued in this paper that ambivalence in discourse is a corollary of the hybridization inherent in colonial contexts. While rooted in the broader social world, ambivalence takes on its distinctive forms in concrete communicative expression. In order to understand it, therefore, it is necessary to give an account of its specific realizations in discourse. We began this account by placing the Maya letters within their contemporary field, comparing them to one another, and to other written documents produced in the same context. This was the intertextual aspect of the analysis, in which the letters were viewed as members of a larger series, interconnected by generic features, transpositions, shared references, reinforcements, and contradictions. Intertextuality tends to break down the boundary between what is inside a text and what is outside it, giving it the appearance of a mosaic of parts derived from elsewhere. The ambivalence evident at the intertextual level is coupled by that at the intratextual level. Not only contemporary discourse in the collective sense was a hybrid, but particular instances were ambivalent as well. By detailed examination of segments of the February and March letters, it was demonstrated that the language itself is ambivalent in these texts. The address forms applied to the king reflect an indigenous logic of articulated rule and abundant prosperity, in combination with the Spanish framework of a unique Catholic monarch. The requests for Franciscans and the denunciation of the seculars obviously reflect a fusion of Franciscan and Maya systems of thought. These findings suggest the fruitfulness of bringing close discourse analysis to the interpretation of historical documents, including letters, but not limited to them.

If ambivalence is a general feature of sixteenth-century Yucatan, and not only of these letters, then it ought to arise in other forms of discourse as well. Like the nobility in the sixteenth century, "native" literature in anthropology has been seen as an icon of indigenous systems. It would be productive to reexamine native literary types, such as the Books of Chilam Balam (Edmonson 1982), the Ritual of the Bacabs (Roys 1965), and the native chronicles (Barrera Vasquez 1984), from the perspective of their ambivalence. Many apparently Spanish forms of discourse are also likely to be equivocal, particularly those produced by friars. With all of these materials, the main challenge is not to find the native, but to show how social interaction in the colonial world gave rise to new forms of discourse, and with them, new possibilities for action.

NOTES

Acknowledgments. Earlier versions of this paper were presented at the 1985 Annual Meeting of the American Society for Ethnohistory and the June 1986 faculty seminar in the Department of Anthropology at the University of Chicago. A portion of the argument was worked out in a paper presented at the 1985 Annual Meetings of the American Anthropological Association. I have benefited greatly from comments received on these occasions and also from other readers, including students and colleagues at the University of Chicago, an anonymous *AE* reader, and a list of others too long to appropriately produce here. I am grateful to these and solely responsible for remaining flaws in the paper.

1. My treatment of the immediate historical background of early postconquest Yucatan is necessarily selective. Cf. Farriss 1984, Roys 1957, Scholes and Adams 1938, and Tozzer 1941:78–83 and further references therein.

2. Jane Rosenthal has shown me strikingly similar letters, dated January 1562, written in Nahuatl, from Huehuetenango, Guatemala, and Mazatlan Soconusco, Mexico. Victoria R. Bricker has made a similar point (personal communication), observing that strong similarities among early documents in various native languages support the conclusion that they were produced from Spanish templates. Anderson et al. (1976) show numerous Nahuatl documents with similar features.

There is no doubt that the Spanish (particularly the Franciscans) had a fundamental role in the production of these native language texts. It does not follow from this that the texts are unequivocal Spanish productions, just as they are not unequivocal native productions.

3. The symbolic efficacy of repetition and parallelism in Maya literary and ritual practice is widely recognized and noted in Bricker (1974), Edmonson (1968), Gossen (1974), Hanks (1984), Roys (1965), B. Tedlock (1982) and D. Tedlock (1983).

4. The books of Chilam Balam are a genre of indigenous Maya documents, of which a number of instances are known. The genre is described in Barrera Vasquez and Rendon (1974 [1948]) and Tozzer (1977[1921]), and exemplified in Edmonson (1982) and Roys (1933).

5. The training of the Maya nobility in Spanish language, writing (both Spanish and Maya), and reading was conducted by the Franciscans in Yucatan, and is discussed in Collins (1977), Farriss (1984:96–97), and Lizana (1893 [1633]:46–56v).

6. The term Toral used in his request is "teatinos," which Gonzalez Cicero (1978:169) notes might refer to either "Jesuits" or members of an order founded by S. Cayetano de Thiene. She prefers the former interpretation.

7. It is almost certain that the pairing "foot, hand" derives at least partly from the Spanish, particularly Franciscan (?), convention of closing letters to the king with the expression, "we kiss your royal feet and hands." Cf. Anderson et al. 1976:30 for Nahuatl analog.

8. The presentation of textual examples is guided by the following conventions. Orthography and spelling follow the original, handwritten texts, facsimiles of which are in Zimmermann (1970) and Hanks (1985a). The symbol [C] is used in Maya examples to stand for glottalized [ts], written [ɔ] in the sources treated here. The line breaks and the separation into blocks are introduced here in order to help show grammatical and poetic phrasings. The original documents are written in the continuous line format of prose. In all examples, the numbering of the lines reflects both the original orthographic lines in whole numbers (1 to 7 in example 1) and the imposed verse phrases in fractions (.1 to .3 in the first line example in 1). Thus for instance, 7.2 may be read "the second phrase in the seventh orthographic line." Beyond this

heuristic utility, the numbering is arbitrary. Grammatical analyses rely on McQuown (1960) and the author's research.

9. Other connectives used frequently as phrasing devices include *yetel* (and, with), *tamuk* (whereas, however), *uchebal* (in order that), *ca utzac* (in order that), *lai tah oklal* (for that reason), *habla* (even though), -*ix* (and), and *xan* (too, also).

10. The use of deictic elements appears to be one dimension along which genres of Maya literary and ritual language differ. In books of Chilam Balam for instance, "here," "you," "now," and "we" (and so forth) are often obscured or left unspecified, making interpretation considerably more difficult. In shamanic prayer, they are precisely specified (Hanks 1984).

11. It is also noteworthy that the order *tepal, ahaulil* (2) is inverted to *ahaulil, tepal* (3). The ([A B] C) phrasing would be as follows: *ti yahaulilob ah bolon kin* (A); *ah bolon tz'am* (B); *tutepal ah uuc cha pat kin* (C).

12. Alliteration is also a common feature of modern Yucatec shamanic prayer (Hanks 1984). Cf. Roys (1965:xix) on its importance in the incantations in the ritual of the *bacabs,* and see B. Tedlock (1982:Ch. 5) on sound play in Quiche divination.

13. Other aspects of the texts that display or confirm the genuineness of the letters include frequent use of the intensifying particle *hach* (very, really); the confession of past offenses expressed with apparently heartfelt remorse (for example, lines 23–29 of the March letter); the appeal to intense affect in the relation of the Maya to the Franciscans (love, benevolence); the assertion of sincerity, as in lines 1–30 of the March letter; and the inclusion at the end of the March letter of a testimony in Spanish, attributed to the scribe, affirming the veracity of the document and of the identity of the signatories.

14. The Franciscan mission in Yucatan is expressed as, "say the word of God, say mass, instruct us in our language." This appears as a potential triplet in the text, analyzable into a couplet [say x, say y] followed by a third semantically related but slightly different line [instruct z]. A comparison of this with lines 2.5–2.7 of the February letter (example 4) reveals a striking similarity: "they illuminate, they enlighten, they teach." This too is a couplet, based in this case on the concept of light, followed by a related but distinct verb describing teaching. The clear parallel between the two letters on the statement of the Franciscan mission in Yucatan further demonstrates their intertexual relation. The fact that the wordings in the two are distinct but relationally homologous shows that what they share is not a stock of fixed expressions, but a more abstract logic of poetic representation.

15. The association of the directions with colors and qualitative characteristics is well known in Maya cultures. Cf. for example Edmonson (1968) on a colonial Yucatec, Hanks (1984) for modern Yucatec, Edmonson (1973:241) on the Popol Vuh (Quiche), B. Tedlock (1982:Ch. 6), and D. Tedlock (1983:149) on Quiche, and Gossen (1974:Ch. 1) on Tzotzil.

REFERENCES

Anderson, Arthur J. L., Frances Berdan, and James Lockhard, eds.
   1976 *Beyond the Codexes, the Nahua View of Colonial Mexico.* Berkeley and Los Angeles: University of California Press.
Bakhtin, M. M.
   1981 *The Dialogic Imagination.* Michael Holquist, ed.; Caryl Emerson and Michael Holquist, transl. Austin: University of Texas Press.

Bakhtin, M. M., and P. M. Medvedev
  1985[1928] *The Formal Method in Literary Scholarship, a Critical Introduction to Sociological Poetics.* Albert J. Wehrle, transl. Cambridge: Harvard University Press.
Barrera Vasquez, Alfredo
  1984 *Documento n. I del Deslinde de Tierras en Yaxkukul, Yucatan. Coleccion Cientifica, Linguistica 125.* Mexico: Instituto Nacional de Antropologia e Historia.
Barrera Vasquez, Alfredo, and Silvia Rendon
  1974[1948] *El Libro de los Libros de Chilam Balam.* Mexico: Fondo de Cultura Economica.
Barrera Vasquez, Alfredo, Juan Ramon Bastarrachea Manzano, and William Brito Sansores
  1980 *Diccionario Maya Cordemex.* Merida: Ediciones Cordemex.
Becquelin Monod, Aurore
  1979 Examin de quelques Paires Semantiques dans les Dialogues Rituels des Tzeltal Bachajon (Langue Maya du Chiapas). *Journal de la Societe des Americanistes* 66:235–63.
  1981 Des Pieds et des Mains: Analyse Semantique des Concepts en Tzeltal (Maya du Chiapas). Centre National de Recherche Scientifique, Paris. *La Linguistique* 17(2): 99–118.
Bourdieu, Pierre
  1977 Symbolic Power. In *Identity and Structure, Issues in the Sociology of Education.* D. Gleeson, ed. pp. 112–19. Driffield, England: Nafferton Books.
  1985 The Social Space and the Genesis of Groups. *Social Science Information* 24(2):195–220.
Bricker, Victoria Reifler
  1974 The Ethnographic Context of Some Traditional Mayan Speech Genres. In *Explorations in the Ethnography of Speaking.* Richard Bauman and Joel Sherzer, eds. pp. 368–88. Cambridge: Cambridge University Press.
  1981 *The Indian Christ, the Indian King, the Historical Substrate of Maya Myth and Ritual.* Austin: University of Texas Press.
Collins, Anne
  1977 The Maestros Cantores in Yucatan. In *Anthropology and History in Yucatan.* Grant D. Jones, ed. pp. 233–50. Austin: University of Texas Press.
Comaroff, Jean, and John Comaroff
  1986 Christianity and Colonialism in South Africa. *American Ethnologist* 13:1–22.
Culler, Jonathan
  1981 *The Pursuit of Signs: Semiotics, Literature, Deconstruction.* Ithaca, NY: Cornell University Press.
Dibble, Charles
  1985 Sahagún's Appendices. Paper presented at the 1985 Annual Meetings of the American Society for Ethnohistory, Chicago, IL.
Edmonson, Munro
  1968 Metafora Maya en Literatura y en Arte. Verhandlungen des XXXVIII Internationalen Amerikanistenkongresses, Stuttgart-München, 1968. Vol. 2, pp. 37–50.
  1973 Semantic Universals and Particulars in Quiche. In *Meaning in Mayan Languages.* Munro Edmonson, ed. pp. 235–46. The Hague: Mouton.
Edmonson, Munro, transl. and ed.
  1982 *The Ancient Future of the Itza, the Book of Chilam Balam of Tizimin.* Austin: University of Texas Press.

Farriss, Nancy M.
1984 *Maya Society Under Colonial Rule, the Collective Enterprise of Survival.* Princeton, NJ: Princeton University Press.

Gates, William
1937 Yucatan Before and After the Conquest by Friar Diego de Landa with Other Related Documents, Maps and Illustrations. Maya Society Publication No. 20. Baltimore, MD: Maya Society.

Gonzalez Cicero, Stella Maria
1978 *Perspectiva Religiosa en Yucatán, 1517–1571. Yucatán, los Franciscanos y el primer Obispo Fray Francisco de Toral.* Centro de Estudios Historicos, neuva serie 28. Mexico: El Colegio de Mexico.

Gossen, Gary
1974 *Chamulas in the World of the Sun: Time and Space in a Maya Oral Tradition.* Cambridge, MA: Harvard University Press.

Hanks, William F.
1984 Sanctification, Structure and Experience in Yucatec Maya Ritual Event. *Journal of American Folklore* 97(384):131–166.
1985a Transliteration and Translation of Letter of March 9, 1567. Maya nobles to the Crown (138 lines). Archivo General de Indias, Mexico 359.
1985b Rhetoric of Royal Address. Paper presented at the 1985 Annual Meetings of the American Anthropological Association, Washington, DC.

Haviland, John B.
1977 *Gossip, Reputation and Knowledge in Zinacantan.* Chicago: University of Chicago Press.

Hunt, Marta Espejo-Ponce
1976 The Processes of the Development of Yucatan, 1600–1700. In *Provinces of Early Mexico, Variants of Spanish America Regional Evolution.* Ida Altman and James Lockhart, eds. pp. 33–62. UCLA Latin American Center Publications. Los Angeles: University of California Press.

Jenny, Laurent
1982 The Strategy of Form. In *French Literary Theory: A Reader.* Tzvetan Todorov, ed. pp. 34–63. Cambridge: Cambridge University Press.

Lizana, Fray Bernardo de
1893 [1633] *Historia de Yucatan, Devocionario de Nuestra Senora de Izmal y Conquista Espiritual.* Mexico: Impreso Del Museo Nacional.

Martinez Hernandez, Juan
1926 Cronicas Mayas, Cronica de Yaxkukul. Merida.
1929 *Diccionario de Motul, Maya-Español Atribuido a Fray Antonio de Ciudad Real.* Merida: Talleres de la Compania Tipografica Yucateca, S.A.

McQuown, Norman A.
1960 Classical Yucatec (Maya). In *Linguistics.* pp. 201–47. Handbook of Middle American Indians, Vol. 5. Austin: University of Texas Press.
1963 Cartas del Archivo General de Indias (Unpublished collection of Maya language documents).

Norman, Will
1980 Grammatical Parallelism in Quiche Ritual Language. In *Papers from the Berkeley Linguistic Society.* Bruce Caron et al., eds. Vol. 6, pp. 387–99. Berkeley, CA: Berkeley Linguistic Society.

Phelan, John Leddy

1970 *The Millenial Kingdom of the Franciscans in the New World.* Berkeley: University of California Press.

Roys, Ralph

1943 The Indian Background of Colonial Yucatan. Publication 548. Washington, DC: The Carnegie Institution.

1957 The Political Geography of the Yucatan Maya. Publication 613. Washington, DC: The Carnegie Institution.

1965 *Ritual of the Bacabs: A Book of Maya Incantations.* Norman: University of Oklahoma Press.

Scholes, Frances V., and Eleanor B. Adams, eds.

1938 *Don Diego Quijada, Alcalde Major de Yucatan, 1561–1565.* Vols. I and II. Mexico: Editorial Porrua.

Stross, Brian

1983 The Language of Zuyua. *American Ethnologist* 10:150–64.

Tedlock, Barbara

1982 *Time and the Highland Maya.* Albuquerque: University of New Mexico Press.

Tedlock, Dennis

1983 *The Spoken Word and the Work of Interpretation.* Philadelphia, PA: University of Pennsylvania Press.

Tozzer, Alfred

1941 Landa's Relacion de las Cosas de Yucatan. Papers of the Peabody Museum, Vol. 18. Cambridge, MA: Harvard University Press.

1977 [1921] *A Maya Grammar.* New York: Dover Publications.

Tynianov, Yuri

1981 [1924] *The Problem of Verse Language.* Michael Sosa and Brent Harvey, transl. and ed. Ann Arbor, MI: Ardis Press.

Zimmermann, Günter

1970 *Briefe der indianischen Nobilität aus Neuspanien an Karl V und Phillip II um die Mitte des 16.* Jahrhunderts. München: Kommissionsverlag Klaus Renner.

5

Discourse Genres in a Theory of Practice

In order to analyze language use within a theory of social practice, it is neces-
sary to develop a coherent approach to speech genres. This paper contributes to
such an approach, by treating genres as elements of linguistic habitus, consist-
ing of stylistic, thematic, and indexical schemata on which actors improvise in
the course of linguistic production. The empirical focus is "official" Maya lan-
guage documents produced in 16th-century colonial Yucatan. The rise of novel
discourse genres in colonial society was part of the emergence of new, hybrid
forms of action. Mesoamerica, Maya, discourse analysis, social practice

This paper examines the concept of discourse genres, by way of analyzing a set of written texts produced by native officials in early colonial Maya society in Mexico. In their formal and functional details, the texts reflect a process of local innovation, blending Maya and Spanish discourse forms into novel types. They document the rapid emergence of new genres of language use, new types of action in colonial society. In describing such discourse, one is led to treat genres as historically specific elements of social practice, whose defining features link them to situated communicative acts. Central to the context of action were the massive changes being imposed on the Maya by the Spanish. Franciscan efforts to congregate the natives for the purpose of religious conversion had evidently begun as early as 1544–45, and were legalized by Royal Cedula in 1548 (Farriss 1984:161). In 1552, Oidor Tomas Lopez came to Yucatan and, through the well-known Ordenanzas, helped accelerate the forced congregation and reorganization of Indian communities (Cogolludo 1971[1654]:Bk. 5, XVI–XIX; Tozzer 1941:71, n. 318). It was in response to events such as these that local elites produced chronicles, surveys, and letters to the Spanish Crown.

The Lopez Ordenanzas dictated virtually all aspects of Indian life, including the form of town government, obligatory religious observance, prohibitions against slavery, fixed residence in a centralized town from which extended travel was not permitted, and strict regulations on marriage, on medical care, on feasting, and on group discussion in the evening. Of particular relevance to this paper were the provisions on residence of Maya nobles and *macehuales* (commoners). The first ordinance stipulates that "all caciques and gobernadores, principales and alguaciles [titles of municipal officials] of this said province shall reside and be in their own towns. . . . and shall not absent themselves from there for long absences . . . [more than] 8 days or so" (Cogolludo 1971: 391, trans. WFH). Immediately after this, it is ordered that each town shall have one "principal" per fifty inhabitants, this individual being the oldest and most venerated resident of the town (or section thereof). Since the religious instruction of the Indians is impeded by their residing in scattered homesteads around the countryside, it continues, all natives of this province shall congregate in the main towns, build permanent homes of stone therein, and cease agricultural production within towns, sowing their fields and maintaining their orchards on the outskirts. No native shall change town of residence without official dispensation (Cogolludo 1971:393). Farriss (1984:161) suggests that the Ordenanzas had the effect of contracting the Maya population geographically into existing nuclei, but did not "violate preexisting political boundaries or established relations within them." Emphasizing the disruptive effects of repopulation, Tozzer (1941:72, n. 319) cites the Relacion de Dzonot, which states that the area had been depopulated by force and the native town and orchards put to fire. The imposition of a new system of municipal and residential space is a central part of the background against which sixteenth-century Maya discourse must be understood.

During the same period, as the Spanish system of local government was imposed on Maya towns, forms of local leadership underwent major disruptive changes (Quezada 1985).[1] Both town-level *batab* (chiefs) and regional *halach uinic* (governors) came to be called "*caciques*," and many were named *gobernadores* (head of the town council) by the Spanish after 1552. Over the next ten years, the Spanish appointed the first *alguaciles* (petty officials) and scribes in Indian republics, opening up further opportunities for Maya nobles to achieve the legitimacy of official status in the colonial system (Farriss 1984:232–36). In the mid-1560s, in Quezada's view, the position of the *cacique-gobernadores* began to weaken as they were forced to share power with other officials in their respective republics. Quezada and Farriss agree that the role of *gobernador* was from the outset a divisive one in the Maya communities. It was incumbent on these officials to represent the interests of the Crown, not their town of residence, to collect tribute, suppress idolatry, oversee the treatment of *macehuales* (commoners), and impart justice (Quezada 1985:677). Eventually, the *caciques* were entirely displaced by appointed officials and ceased to have any effective authority in the republics.

The texts comprising early official Maya discourse were part of this conflictual process, and it is the *caciques, gobernadores,* and local officials whose names appear as signatories. The discourse displays emergent forms of representation, produced by local actors, in an apparent attempt to set at least some of the terms by which their social world would be regimented. As a result of the social field in which official Maya was produced, and to which it was addressed, the texts themselves contain a mixture of native Maya modes of representation along with Spanish bureaucratic and Franciscan doctrinal discourse. They include prominently the letters to the Crown, chronicles, and land surveys shown in Table 5.1, which make up the empirical focus of this paper.

The texts in Table 5.1 are all what Morson (1981:48) called "boundary works," that is, ambivalent discourse productions that are interpretable according to two (or more)

TABLE **5.1** Official Maya Documents[a]

Name	Date	Type	Provenance	Source
Yaxkukul 1	April 30, 1544	survey	Yaxkukul, Ceh Pech	Barrera Vasquez 1984:15–47
Yaxkukul 2	May 8, 1544	survey	Yaxkukul, Ceh Pech	Barrera Vasquez 1984:91–98
Chicxulub	1542	chronicle	Chicxulub, Ceh Pech	Brinton 1969:189–215
Mani	1556	chronicle	Mani, Mani	Tozzer 1941:43, 45, 58, 62 for description
Sotuta survey	Sept 2, 1600	survey	Yaxcaba, Sotuta	Roys 1939:421–433
Sotuta accords	Sept 6, 1600	agreements	Yaxcaba, Sotuta	Roys 1939:428–430
Letter to crown	Feb 11, 1567	letter	Mérida, Chakan	Zimmermann 1970:31
Letter to Crown	Feb 12, 1567	letter	Mérida, Chakan	Zimmermann 1970:31
Letter to Crown	March 19, 1567	letter	Mérida	Hanks 1986

[a]Name and type labels are heuristic; dates are the ones that appear on documents; provenance of document cited town, province.

distinct sets of convention, yielding two or more contradictory interpretations. Morson distinguishes sharply between the double decodability of boundary works and the fact that all literature is susceptible to various readings. In the former case, what is uncertain is not the status of a specific reading, but the entire frame within which interpretation should be set. The letters to the Crown, for instance, are partly governed by the conventions of Spanish official and religious discourse, and partly by those of Maya, in terms of which the message is quite different (Hanks 1986). Such works systematically encompass two or more distinct "texts," corresponding to different, even contradictory, readings. Produced in early colonial society, the conventions by which the texts were constructed were by no means fixed, and a comparison of them shows local innovations as well as widely shared features.

The novelty and ambivalence of early colonial Maya discourse raise analytic as well as interpretive problems. How shall we understand the relation between the linguistic form of such texts and the broader social and cultural world in which they were produced? What is a discourse "genre" in this context, and at what level is the concept to be defined? In a purely formal approach, genres consist of regular groupings of thematic, stylistic, and compositional elements. Generic types differ by the features or configurations by which they are defined, irrespective of the historical conditions under which the types come to exist and of the social values attached to them in a given context. On the other hand, genres can be defined as the historically specific conventions and ideals according to which authors compose discourse and audiences receive it. In this view, genres consist of orienting frameworks, interpretive procedures, and sets of expectations that are not part of discourse structure, but of the ways actors relate to and use language (Bauman 1986).

The conventions of genre help define the possibilities of meaning in discourse and the level of generality or specificity at which description is cast. Whether we read a text as fiction, parody, prayer, or documentary is a generic decision with important consequences for interpretation. Viewed as constituent elements in a system of signs, speech genres have value loadings, social distributions, and typical performance styles according to which they are shaped in the course of utterance (see Bauman and Sherzer 1974; Bauman 1977; Brody 1986; Gossen 1974; 1985; Hanks 1984, 1985; Sherzer 1983; and Tedlock 1983 for other Maya examples). The approach to discourse developed in this paper incorporates formal features, but locates genre primarily in relation to action in this second, historically specific way. The second part of this paper examines official Maya texts from this perspective, while proposing a set of four general dimensions in a practice theory of genre.

The analytic framework of this paper derives primarily from a synthesis of Bakhtin's "sociological poetics" with Bourdieu's theory of practice. The motivation for attempting such a synthesis is not only that these two scholars have proposed powerful, distinct, yet compatible theories of the relation between symbolic forms and social action, although this is true. Nor is it the impact these scholars have had on recent studies of language in culture, although this too is significant. The proposal of this paper is rather that, for the analysis of discourse, both "sociological poetics" and "practice" theory are insufficient when taken individually, but make up a coherent and revealing approach when combined. The former gives an inadequate account of the diachronic processes of discourse production, of the action-centric perspective of language users, and of the partial, open-ended realization of discourse forms in communicative practice. Bourdieu has written insightfully on each of these issues. On the other hand, Bakhtin's careful studies of formalist poetics, linguistics, and literary genres provide a nonreductive approach to verbal form, which will be necessary if practice theory is to come to terms with the linguistic processes embodied in action.

In his writings on language and social practice, Bourdieu has attempted to get beyond the dichotomy between complete, objective, rule-governed social forms and emergent, subjective, voluntaristic acts (Brubaker 1985). Analogously, Bakhtin sought to transcend the dichotomy between formalist objectivism and individual subjectivism. Practice for Bourdieu arises out of the interplay between the lasting dispositions to action that comprise "habitus," and temporality, improvisation, and the constraints inherent in any "language market" (Bourdieu 1982:656–62). As used in this paper, habitus comprises actors' abilities both to produce discourse and to understand it in relatively systematic ways, thereby encompassing both linguistic practice and native perceptions of it (Bourdieu 1984:170; Brubaker 1985:758–60). Itself the product of internalized divisions of social class, habitus includes principles of division and classification that are transposed across broadly differing fields of action (Bourdieu 1982:656, 1984:170–73). While not attempting to derive discourse directly from social class, this paper will argue that genres are an integral part of the linguistic habitus, that they exhibit the same dual relation to practice and native categories as sketched above, and that they are partly created through improvised, novel productions.

One of the central premises of Bakhtin's theory of discourse is that linguistic works have a structure of their own, whether they be single utterances or large-scale liter-

ary constructions. This means that the organization of a work is in some degree independent of both the world it purports to represent and the ideological perspective
from which it does so. Even would-be realist description is at best selective, a refraction of what it claims to portray. This refraction is effected primarily in the thematic
and stylistic construction of the work, which embodies ideological values rooted in
the broader social context (Bakhtin and Medvedev 1985 [1928]:21 [henceforth
BM]). No element can enter into the work purely on the basis of its form, without
importing its value coefficients with it. Actors take these values for granted, as a familiar background, an "ideological horizon," against which their acts are intelligible.
Human consciousness, for Bakhtin, comes into contact with reality only through the
mediation of ideology (BM 1985:7; Voloshinov 1986[1929]:86–88), and every
genre has its own value-laden orientation. At the same time, the work cannot be reduced to a reflection of ideology, since it is shaped by constructive principles specific
to discourse. Thus, even documentary surveys of political geography must be seen in
terms of the interplay between constructive discourse principles, social values, and
the objects described.

   In addition to their thematic orientation, works are also oriented toward the action
contexts in which they are produced, distributed, and received. Ideological creations
become part of practical reality by being realized in action and this entails adapting
them to concrete social circumstances. In this formulation, speech genres are seen as
both the outcome of historically specific acts, and themselves among the constituting
dimensions in terms of which action is possible. Genres then, as kinds of discourse,
derive their thematic organization from the interplay between systems of social value,
linguistic convention, and the world portrayed. They derive their practical reality
from their relation to particular linguistic acts, of which they are both the products
and the primary resources. What, in these terms, were the genres of sixteenth-century
Maya discourse, and what do they tell us about the idea of genre?

GENRES OF SIXTEENTH-CENTURY MAYA DOCUMENTS

Bakhtin distinguished what he called "primary" or simple genres, from "secondary"
or complex ones. The relation between the two is mainly a matter of relative inclu-
siveness. Secondary genres *include* primary ones, the way the novel as described by
Bakhtin (1981) includes virtually all other types of discourse through dialogism, direct quotation, reported speech, and so forth. In being absorbed into a secondary
speech genre, a primary one loses the directness of its connection to reality. Evidently,
direct, primary genres become oblique when incorporated into secondary ones, as in
the case of verbatim quotation embedded in a narrative frame. At least some of the
genres of sixteenth-century Maya documents are secondary in that they contain elements from several types of discourse, including quoted speech, descriptive narrative,
testimonial and persuasive rhetoric. This heterogeneity raises the question of how individual texts hang together as coherent wholes.

Bakhtin held that it is only at the level of the entire work that any genre can articulate with extralinguistic reality (Voloshinov 1986:99). On this point, as in his treatment of "finalization," he retained the formalist doctrine that literary works consist
of subparts integrated into a unified, heterogeneous whole. "Finalization" is the constructive process whereby a work becomes complete (Bakhtin 1986:76; BM
1985:130), and genres differ in the ways they specify completeness. Bakhtin distinguished three main kinds of finalization in discourse, according to the type of constructive principles involved: (1) thematic, (2) stylistic, and (3) compositional structural.[2] In narrative, thematic finalization (1) corresponds to story completion, while
compositional finalization (3) corresponds to plot completion (BM 1985:130). In
this gloss, "story" is the sequence of events (referents) making up the reality described,
and "plot" is the particular structuring of reference within the narrative. Bakhtin insisted on the "organic" relation between these two components in the utterance.

The three *kinds* of completeness distinguished by Bakhtin are further divided into
three distinct *levels* at which completion is achieved: (1) locally, in units such as
episodes, sections, and verse constructions; (2) at the more inclusive level of the whole
work; and (3) at the global level of the production and reception context in which the
discourse is concretized (cf. Vodichka 1982[1941]). In complex genres, like the Maya
letters and chronicles, local closure (1) is achieved in verse constructions, like those in
the February 1567 letters (Hanks 1986) and Yaxkukul document 1 (see example 4 below). In the clearest cases, verse constructions are balanced, compact, and closed in
on themselves, hence highly finalized in the sense of making a unitary structure (cf.
Jakobson 1960; Tynianov 1981[1924]:61, 88). One way in which the completeness
of a *work* is achieved (level 2) is through metalinguistic specification of genre within
the text itself. Yaxkukul document 1, for instance, characterizes itself as an *informacion de derecho* (statement of rights) (line 17, example 4), the March 1567 letter as a
"recounting to the ear of the king" (Hanks 1986), and Sotuta documents 2 and 3 as
conciertos (agreements). In the Chicxulub chronicle, section 36 (Brinton 1969
[1882]:213) contains the most explicit framing of the work as a "history." As these
examples show, "finalization" is not positionally linked to the *end* of a construction or
work, but pertains equally to the framing of the discourse, whereby it is unified and
set off from its context *as it unfolds.* The level of most concern to Bakhtin in his discussion of genres was the third one, at which the work is included in a process of production and reception (Bakhtin 1986; BM 1985:77). Colonial Maya genres display
common thematic, stylistic, and constructive features at each of the three levels.

Both Yaxkukul documents (Barrera Vasquez 1984), all three Sotuta documents (Roys
1939:421–33), and the letters of 1567 (described in Hanks 1986) share constructive
features that distinguish them from other kinds of discourse. They all bear dates of completion, along with the name of the place at which they were signed, signatures (or at
least names) identifying the authors and witnesses, explicit ending, and a relatively elaborate opening (except for document 1 of Sotuta, the beginning of which Roys does not
reproduce). Unlike the letters, the land documents from Yaxkukul and Sotuta, as well
as the Chronicle of Mani (see Tozzer 1941:n. 43, 45, 58, and 62), contain surveys of the

local area around the place of signing. Both Yaxkukul documents and the chronicle of Chicxulub (Brinton 1969:193–215) contain historical narratives that legitimate a set of Maya nobles as being from that area. The Chicxulub, like the Yaxkukul texts and the letters, is told in the first person, as well as being anchored to a here and now. All the documents under discussion contain assertions or report oaths of their own truth. Taken jointly, these constructive features are distinctive of the genres of early colonial "official" Maya. In particular, the deictic grounding of the texts in a specific "We, here, now" is a feature conspicuously absent from other types of native text, such as the books of Chilam Balam (Edmonson 1982) and the Rituals of the Bacabs (Roys 1965).

Another important characteristic of official Maya is the marked tendency of the texts to appear as part of an intertextual series. Groups of individual documents fit together into ordered sets, reflecting a hierarchical organization at Bakhtin's third level, superordinate to the individual work. Thus, Yaxkukul documents 1 and 2 are clearly related in that they issue from the same place, just eight days apart, both describe the placement of boundary markers to indicate the limit of the forest, and although they do not bear the same signatures, many of their signatories are clearly kinsmen in the Pech patriline. The Sotuta documents, partially reproduced in Roys (1939), are dated 2 September (document 1), 6 September (document 2), and 6 September (document 3), 1600. As in the case of the Yaxkukul series, the first document is the longest and most wide ranging thematically, and the following ones appear to have been provided in order to reinforce its legitimacy. The letters of 1567 also appeared in a series: seven similar versions of two main variants of one letter, dated 11 and 12 February 1567 respectively, followed by a longer and more encompassing letter dated 19 March 1567 (Hanks 1986). The appearance of these letters in a series was initially taken by scholars to indicate that they had been copied or otherwise faked. Viewed in light of the serial production of chronicles, it appears probable that this is a generic feature of early colonial Maya.

Serial production of works appears to derive from two modes of collective action, one the display of consensus, through mutually reinforcing renditions (as in the letters described in Hanks 1986:724), and the other the expression of discrepant claims, that is, as a vehicle for advancing contradictory or competing perspectives. In a letter of April 1567, nobles from the Mani area contradicted statements made in previous letters sent by other groups from northern and western regions. Similarly, the individual Sotuta and Yaxkukul surveys cite different boundary markers as defining the local area, although it is not clear whether they were contradictory, complementary, or just different. The discrepant claims made in the letters to the Crown clearly reflect conflicts among different individuals and groups of nobles struggling to secure their positions in relation to the colonial machine, a scenario consistent with other sources on the period (Farriss 1984:Ch. 8; Quezada 1985).

There are significant stylistic continuities across the texts, indicating that they were formulated within a coherent system of style (Hanks n.d.). It is typical of the chronicles, letters, and land surveys to contain a mixture of straightforward prose description, with at least some intermittent verse parallelism.[3] The most noteworthy parallelism is in Yaxkukul document 1 and the two letters of 1567. These originated from northern and western provinces, especially Ceh Pech, and display distinctive verse constructions apparently emblematic of the local nobility. The verse consists of mutually reinforcing repetition of the plural morpheme <*ob*>, quantitative equivalence of lines (six, seven, or eight syllables), alliteration, syntactic parallelism, and semantic parallelism (complementarity, near equivalence, part-whole relations). In each case, there is a relatively clean onset and coda to the verse series. In Yaxkukul document 1, the series lasts five lines and displays the verse pattern ABABA (see example 4), whereas in the letter of 11 February 1567, it runs six lines, and can be reasonably read as a couplet followed by a triplet and an isolated (dissimilar) line, or AABBBC (Hanks 1986:734). The 19 March 1567 letter breaks into verse at lines 52–53 and 54–55, the former a single sentence stated in five lines, and the latter four sentences in four lines, all bound by verse parallelism, but analyzable as two couplets, AABB (Hanks 1986:738).

These verse constructions are noteworthy because, while there is often evidence of metrical, rhythmic, alliterative, and grammatical parallelism in Maya discourse, it is relatively rare that they all combine into a balanced construction. More commonly, syntactic, semantic, and phonological phrasings coincide only in part or not at all. This results in highly cohesive discourse with numerous parallelisms, which fail to reinforce one another, and none of which dominates the others. Instead of clear instances of verse, one finds a relative tendency toward metrical, rhythmic, and grammatical-semantic redundancy, and instead of a clear scansion, one is forced to recognize many equally valid alternative phrasings. These factors lend significance to the compact verse constructions just cited, suggesting that they were local innovations in the development of official Maya genres.

Style is an integral dimension of prose as well as verse. One of the significant prose devices in colonial Maya is what I shall call "cyclic" description (cf. Fought 1985). Cyclic description is relatively free of the line-to-line parallels that sustain verse. Instead, the dominant device is periodic repetition, mostly in fixed order, of selected grammatical forms. While any short stretch of discourse in isolation appears to be merely linear description, when placed within the larger text, it emerges as part of a recurrent series of lines. More like a periodic refrain than a poetic parallel, this pattern can be represented as ABCDE . . . ABCDE . . . ABCDE . . . n. In the following example, taken from Yaxkukul document 1, lines 154–62 constitute a single cycle, which then starts up again at line 163. Looking at the entire second half of Yaxkukul document 1, this cyclicity organizes lines 111–284 exhaustively (Barrera Vasquez 1984:22–34). New cycles begin at lines 114, 119, 124, 131, 137, 143, 154, 163, 168, 175, 181, 186, 191, 195, 199, 203, 208, 216, 221, 230, 235, 240, 244, 248, 253, 259, 263, 267, 275, and 279. While Yaxkukul document 1 provides the best examples of this kind of cyclicity, the cyclic principle is in evidence in Yaxkukul document 2 (Barrera Vasquez 1984:92–93) as well.

(1) Textual example from Documentos de tierras de Yaxkukul, document 1 from Barrera Vasquez 1984:25–26. Line breaks and numbers retained from Barrera Vasquez except for adjustment at lines 157–59; analysis and gloss WFH; ## inserted to mark end of cycle;/in original:

154	nohol-tan	yn-bin-el	tzol pic-tun	
	Adv-Adv	Apro-Vi-sf	Vi	N-N
	Southward I go counting out (ordering) boundary stones.			
155	t-u-lac-al	u-bin-el		
	Prep-Apro-N-sf	Apro-Vi-sf		
	All (the way)	it goes		
156	la-tu-lah	kuch'-ul	t-u-chun	mul ac
	part-?-part	Vi-sf	Prep-Apro-N	N-N
	until	arriving	at the foot of	Turtle Mount,
157-8	y-an	u- / pic-tun-il		
	Apro-Vs	Apro-N-N-sf		
	(where) there is	the boundary stone.		
158-9	ti	c-in-patp-ic	ah cumkal-i	
	Dloc	Aux-Apro-Vt-inc	Agt N-trm	
	There I	leave off	(the) Cumkal people,	
160	ti-ix	c-in-ch'a-ic	in-yum	yxkil ytzam pech
	Dloc-conj	Aux-Apro-Vi-inc	Apro-N	Name
	there too	I pick up (am joined by)	my father	lxkil Itzam Pech,
161	ah	Sic pach'	y	u-kuch-te-el-ob
	Agt	Place Name	conj	Apro-V-N-sf-pl
	(who is)	from Sicipach	and	(along with) his counsellors.
162	ca-cath-il /	yn-bin-el	y-et-el-ob	
	Rdpl-Num-sf	Apro-Vi-sf	Apro-RN-sf-pl	
	Pairwise	I proceed	accompanied by them # #	
163	nohol-tan	yn-bin-el		
	Adv-Adv	Apro-Vi-sf		
	Southward	I go		
164	la-tu-lah	u-hok-ol	yok be	
	part-?-part	Apro-Vi-sf	prep N	
	until	it comes out	on (over) (the) road, (and so on).	

Although the cycles are clearly identifiable, they are not identical, varying somewhat in length, content, and order of elements. Each cycle begins with a statement of the direction of motion, as in lines 154 and 163, but what follows is subject to variation. With this caveat in mind, the internal composition of cycles may be said to consist roughly of the following information: (1) (inter)cardinal direction of motion in which the narrator ("I") is said to be proceeding while counting boundary markers (lines 154, 163); (2) name of the next goal or landmark toward which he is proceeding (lines 156, 164); (3) title or name of nobles who accompanied the narrator during this segment of his inspection, along with names of their town of residence (lines 160–61); (4) the location of the boundary markers relative to landmark wells, trees, road, or "corners" (lines 157, 166); (5) the place at which accompanying nobles leave off and new ones join him (lines 159–62).

The stem *tzol* is familiar to Mayanists from the calendrical system called *tzolkin* (day count). It is a commonly encountered stem in both colonial and modern Maya texts and dictionaries, with a range of meanings both verbal and nominal, including "count, order, series, succession, chronicle, explanation, explain" (see, for instance,

Barrera Vasquez et al. 1980:863); *pictun* are "boundary markers, regional division markers" (Martinez Hernandez 1929:folio 389r). The narrator describes his action, then, as "I go along ordering boundary markers," "dividing by marker." It is not accidental that this section of the document, which executes the counting out of boundary markers, is cast in cyclic prose, rather than verse. This is a reflection of the more general tendency for all acts of ritually significant "counting" in Maya to be done in predetermined cycles (Fought 1985; Hanks 1984). In other words, this section of the Yaxkukul land document displays a clear stylistic regimentation appropriate to the ritual (re)creation of social space. In support of this view, it is noteworthy that in the other land surveys, the surveyors are said to *place,* or *put down* boundary markers in order to divide the land, rather than count ones that were already there. This implies that the "survey" was a means of defining space, not merely describing it, by a process of counting out in regular cyclic fashion.

Cyclic prose style maximizes the iconic relation between the discourse, moving through a series of regular cycles, and the actual act of walking the perimeter of the area by following a series of boundary markers. It is this act that the discourse "counts out." In the Sotuta land survey, Don Juan (Nachi) Cocom and his principals also walked the perimeter of Sotuta, although there is little cyclicity in the discourse which reports the event. Rather, the places at which markers were laid down are simply listed, presumably in order of location (although this is not specified in the text). Locations are listed under the heading of "*Terminos y mojoneras*" (limits and mounds), and the first series is the water sources, "where crosses were placed" (Roys 1939:425–26). The discourse has a strong iconic component, not in cyclicity like the Yaxkukul documents, but in the use, within the written text of a graphic representation of the crosses. Thirteen Maltese crosses appear in the list, as illustrated in excerpt 2.

(2) Excerpt from Sotuta land documents (Roys 1939:425–26):

> *tisidzbic, tiiximche +, Tzuck, [. . .] cansahcab donde estaba una + cruz, [. . .]*
> Tisidzbic, Tiiximche CROSS, Tzuck, . . . Cansahcab where there was a CROSS cross.
>
> *Tixkochah donde estaba una +*
> Tixkochah where there was a CROSS

The three tokens of the cross displayed in excerpt 2 show three different syntactic incorporations of the symbol into the written text. In the first case, it appears without accompanying verbal description, implying that a cross was placed at the Tiiximche, but not stating this in words. The second instance of the symbol occurs within the noun phrase "a cross," illustrating what is also stated in the verbal discourse. In the third example, the graphic symbol *substitutes for* a lexical noun in the noun phrase "a ____." Hence, a graphic representation may entirely replace description or may be integrated into it as a reinforcement or partial substitute.

The linkage between linguistic form and the pragmatic force of discourse, which Bakhtin posited, is well illustrated by Yaxkukul document 1. Looked at as a whole, this text has three well-defined parts: (1) a declaration of the nature of the document itself as an authentic *informacion [de] derecho* (report of rights) (Barrera Vasquez 1984: line 17; Part 1 is lines 1–110); (2) a detailed account of the lay of the land and its subdivisions relative to landmarks (water sources, hills, trees, *tzuc* markers) around the Chacnicte well (lines 111–308); and (3) a public declaration of solidarity among the signatories (lines 309–483). The style of the language in each of the three parts is different, with occasional verse constructions in the first and third, but cyclic prose in the second. It is probable that this shift reflects the ritual force of counting out spatiotemporal divisions, a widely attested Maya mode of action whose main stylistic corollary is the cycle.

In summary, the two Yaxkukul chronicles, the Sotuta land surveys, the chronicle of Chicxulub, and the 1567 letters correspond to a single set of genres, which can be grouped heuristically under the rubric of early colonial "official Maya." All but the Chicxulub specify the date and place of formulation, names of principal author(s), and witnesses in the body of the text, along with signatures or a list of those responsible at the end, and a formulaic opening and closing. The Yaxkukul and Sotuta land documents contain surveys formulated with iconic signs—cyclic prose in the former and graphic representation in the latter. The Yaxkukul documents and the chronicle of Chicxulub contain historical narratives legitimating the principals as descendants of the founders of their respective areas. Common to all is a recurrent emphasis on truth, accountability, and the linkage between actors and the spaces they inhabit.[4] This linkage is expressed partly by the indication of deictic coordinates, providing a "here," "now," and "we" in terms of which to anchor the narrative to specific individuals in concrete contexts. Typical of letters and collective agreements is the tendency to appear in a series of distinct written texts, bearing different but contemporary dates and different but allied signatories. Not only were these works produced in a highly structured institutional setting, the *cabildo,* by entitled authors, the officials, but they were publicly witnessed by the elders and submitted to the record to become historical fact, as well. These features all enhance the authority of the texts and reinforce their official, binding character.

Official speech typically has the potential to make truth while imposing the terms in which actors must respond. Bourdieu observed that official language, especially when used to represent the social relations among members in a group, tends [to] "sanction and impose what it states, tacitly laying down the dividing line between the thinkable and the unthinkable, thereby contributing to the maintenance of the symbolic order from which it draws its authority" (1977:22). This is an apt description of official Maya documents and is consistent with Bakhtin's definition of a genre as "an aggregate of the means for seeing and conceptualizing reality" (BM 1985:137), as well as with his definition of the whole work as that which determines a response of a certain kind (Bakhtin 1986:76). By their capacity to unify and impose different perspectives on events, official genres have the inherent potential to transform the world as represented. Genres familiarize and naturalize reality, and different ones entail different views.

Official Maya discourse both presupposed and helped to maintain the legitimacy of the nobles within colonial society. Appointees of the Indian republics, *batab* (chiefs), and other *caciques* were engaged in a struggle to assert their authority over local affairs, as Quezada (1985) documents extensively from Spanish sources. It was only because the production of letters, surveys, and agreements was sanctioned by the Spanish that such texts could have the status of official documents. This was an objective limitation on the institutional value of the genres. At the same time, production of official documents was a way of exercising the authority vested in the nobles, of sustaining it, and of creating history "for the record." Written discourse became a vehicle for presenting the positions of local elites in their most convincing light. The frequent display of legitimacy and authenticity in the discourse is due to the importance and problematic status of these values in early colonial Maya society. In Bakhtin's terms, the encompassing "finalization" of discourse production and reception was defined partly in advance and partly in consequence of these genres. An accurate description of this process requires a closer examination of the place of genres in social practice, to which we now turn.

GENRE AS PRACTICE

Bakhtin attacked the formalist position that poetic language is a special system unto itself, and asserted instead that language acquires poetic characteristics only in concrete constructions. Genres and works are grounded in social practices of production and reception, rather than having an independent existence of their own. Viewed apart from the social ground, poetic forms and devices were at best only *potentially* poetic. Therefore, while abstract principles of discourse may relate works and genres as sets of objective possibilities, they become fully poetic only when embodied in concrete works (BM 1985:84). Bourdieu (1977:82–83) makes a parallel distinction between "habitus" and objective events. The former is "a system of lasting, transposable dispositions, . . . a matrix of perceptions, appreciations and actions." This corresponds to Bakhtin's conventional discourse forms and devices, which have inherent functional potential, but actual communicative force only when used. Bourdieu's "objective event" is the actual situated occurrence in which the system is realized, and which "calls for, or demands, a determinate response." For a theory of discourse genre, "objective events" unfold in the process of production and reception, in which generic works are constituted as the products and means of action (Bourdieu 1982:647).

Habitus has the inherent potential to generate homologous formations across different cultural fields, relating, for example, the calendars of cooking, daily tasks, times of day, and the life cycle in Kabylia (Bourdieu 1977:143–58). Different fields of action are organized by the same set of symbolic relations and modes of practice (rhythm of execution, sequence, duration, and so forth), with respect to which they are schematically equivalent. Bourdieu represents these equivalences as variant realizations of a single type of structure, summarized in his synoptic diagrams (Bourdieu

1977:Fig. 3–9). Being grounded in cultural schemata that recur across distinct fields of action, habitus is logically prior to any actual event of practice. At the same time, it is subject to innovation and strategic manipulation in practice, such that it is a product as well as a resource that changes over time.

Conventions of discourse organization are part of the linguistic habitus that actors bring to speech. Like the schematic calendars of Kabylia, routinized forms of poetic and narrative structure recur in a variety of different contexts. Works of sixteenth-century official Maya are schematically equivalent with respect to many stylistic, thematic, and constructive features. Insofar as we view genre as a recurrent grouping of such features, genres become part of the organization of habitus. They are the relatively lasting, transposable resources according to which linguistic practice is constituted. At the same time, they are produced in the course of linguistic practice and subject to innovation, manipulation, and change. A major question for sixteenth-century official Maya genres is the extent to which they were produced and transformed according to changing, local conditions, as opposed to merely instantiating preexistent structures. Being "boundary genres" derived from a fusion of Spanish and Maya frameworks, these texts document an ongoing process in which genres, and not only works, were being produced.

In the remainder of this section we will explore the linkage of Maya genres to some of the local conditions of their production, as a means of grounding them in situated communicative practices. The discussion proceeds in four main parts. First, the connection between these genres and the structures of power and authority to which they were addressed, through what Bourdieu called "regularization" and "officialization." Second, their orientation to the process of reception, including reported speech, metalinguistic framing, and persuasive rhetoric. Third, the actuality of genres, whereby they are embedded in historically specific courses of action, making them inherently open-ended rather than complete wholes. And fourth, the indexical centering of the genres in frameworks of participation (authorship, address, and witness), specific social spaces constituted as "here" and "there," and the historical duration over which the genres emerged as part of an unfolding "now." Taken together, these aspects of official Maya discourse illustrate core elements of a practice theory of genre, while raising new empirical questions for the study of discourse processes in colonial society.

Orientation to Dominant Structures, Regularization, and Officialization

Official Maya discourse displays a strong orientation toward Spanish ideology and institutional structures, but it would be wrong to conclude from this that the Maya were "already converted" and simply following the rules laid down by the conquerors. Rather, the display of hispanization in these works is at least in part a means of familiarizing them to the, primarily Spanish, addresses. The format, style, and thematic content of the documents all maximize the appearance that their authors honored the values of their conquerors and were themselves honorable. This involved, on the one hand, what Bourdieu (1977:22) called "regulation," whereby actors strategically make a show of their adherence to moral and ethical values of the group, in order to display their own impeccable character. On the other hand, the discourse is also "officialized," whereby it presents itself as a bona fide, witnessed document, authorized by specific, entitled actors. Both regularization and officialization are pragmatic processes that link individual works to dominant power structures. Both have a tangible influence on the linguistic forms through which genres are realized.

In works such as chronicles and letters to the king, the primary aims were apparently to reinforce the position of the principals (authors and witnesses) as representatives of the town *cabildo,* to influence Crown policy, and to establish the terms in which Indian Yucatan would be described. These goals are evident in several noteworthy officializing devices. All of the land surveys and the letter of March 1567 include a statement by named official(s) other than the primary authors that the contents of the document are entirely true. These same documents all bear the signatures of officially recognized witnesses, implying public consensus among the Maya nobles and elders as well as Spanish bureaucrats. Statements made in the texts are held accountable to public verifiable facts, through reference to specific individuals and locations by name. This is found particularly in the surveys and agreements, in the Chicxulub chronicle (sections 11, 32, 35, 39), and somewhat less in the March 1567 letter (and see Chi in Tozzer 1941:231). The elite status of the authors is displayed in the stylistic virtuosity of the discourse, which was emblematic of noble status among the Maya. The letters (Hanks 1986:735), Yaxkukul document 1 (see example 4 below), and the chronicle of Chicxulub (section 11 and see example 3 above) all show verse structuring (Hanks 1986, n.d.), and the land survey of Yaxkukul document 1 is cast in cyclic prose. Finally, both Spanish and Maya powers are invoked through reference, as a means of authorizing the discourse and increasing its effectiveness. This is found in all of the documents under study, as well as ritual language both colonial (Roys 1965) and modern (Hanks 1984). Thus, whereas Maya prophetic discourse apparently became historical fact by serving as a general guide for action (Bricker 1981:180), official discourse was designed to become fact by being accepted as a definitive record of specific actions performed under specific circumstances.

These texts also display the traces of second-order strategies evidently directed toward regularizing the authors in terms of what they took to be the desires and expectations of the Spanish Crown. For instance, the display of conversion is a kind of regularization. In their letters to the king, Maya nobles deprecated themselves in the terms of Franciscan morality, as idolaters mired by the devil, and took pains to display their reverent love of God and the king and their desire to be saved. Similarly, the assertion and display of peaceful solidarity among multiple, named witnesses (*testigos*) is a form of regularization, found in both letters and (at least the Yaxkukul) chronicles. It shows that the native nobles are tractable with the Spanish and prepared to exchange truth with them in front of witnesses. Insofar as the officializing devices outlined in the preceding paragraph brought the discourse within the scope of what the Spanish considered to be legitimate, they also contribute to regularization. Thus both modes of orienting toward dominant values and institutions have a broad impact on the constituting features of genres.

Reception, Reported Speech, and Metalinguistic Framing

Reported speech, for Voloshinov (1986:112–25), was a "pivotal" phenomenon in the social constitution of language. It is defined as simultaneously "speech *within* speech, . . . and speech *about* speech" (p. 115, emphasis added). Hence, the presence of reported speech in a generic work implies that the genre is secondary in Bakhtin's sense. Voloshinov's definition focuses on the interplay between verbatim reproduction of speech on the one hand, and description of it on the other. In the former, the utterances reported retain their autonomy and bring into the work the style and texture of the reported speech. In the latter, the reported speech is analyzed and transformed into a theme, formulated in the style and texture of the current (reporting) work. As Voloshinov makes clear in the subsequent chapters, and grammarians have long recognized, verbatim quotation and direct description are opposite poles on a continuum, which includes various intermediate steps as well, such as French "*style indirect libre*," indirect and "quasi-direct" discourse.

The significance of reported speech for a practice theory of genre is not only that it organizes a range of linguistic variants, but more importantly, that it is an "objective document" of the social reception of speech. In the forms of report, one learns of the "steadfast social tendencies in an active reception of other speakers' speech" (Voloshinov 1986:117). These tendencies are in play in overt dialogue between interactants, in reported speech uttered by a single speaker, and also in the inner speech of understanding. In each case, reception is the evaluation and investment of discourse with meaning, a key element in the historical actuality of signs, and in Bakhtin's idea of dialogism (Bakhtin 1981:301ff.; Voloshinov 1986:135). There is a material similarity between these "steadfast tendencies in an active reception," and Bourdieu's description of habitus as a lasting matrix of perception and appreciation. The link is not the concept of homology, but evaluation as a requisite to meaning.

Reported speech is not characteristic of the Maya land surveys, but does occur with some frequency in historical narrative (for example, in the books of Chilam Balam). In some cases, particularly in the letters, authors quote themselves as a way of framing their discourse, as in "we wish to recount to your ear, You Ruler, so that you can understand. Here then we speak: 'truly' . . ." (lines 5–6, letter of 19 March 1567). In the closing segments of official documents, the truth of the text is typically reasserted, and such assertions entail reference to the discourse itself, as in "*this* is true." Hence, they are metalinguistic frames that situate the work or some portion of it as discourse of a certain kind, with certain intelligible meanings. The clearest cases of quotation for current purposes are those where the utterance of some individual other than the author(s) is reproduced verbatim. The Chicxulub chronicle, for example, contains quoted speech attributed to Ah Naum Pech, in which he addresses the people of Yocolpeten, telling them of the arrival of Christianity and instructing them to embrace it, and supply the

Spaniards with food and other support (Brinton 1969:209, section 30). The quotation is interpreted initially relative to the context described, not relative to the context in which the description is performed (or read). A corollary of this is the fact that the tone and style of speech in the reported frame is distinct from that in the reporting because Naum Pech was addressing gatherings of his power equals and subordinates, whereas this chronicle as a whole addresses superordinate powers.

(3) Excerpt from Documentos de tierras de Chicxulub (from Brinton 1969:209, section 30). Orthography, punctuation retained from Brinton; glosses, line breaks WFH:

1. [. . .] *ca tuyalah Naum Pech ti umektan cahil*
    . . . then Naum Pech said to the municipal authorities
2. *ti tzucentzucil: "Oheltex, talel ucah hunabku [. . .]*
    from place to place: "Know (you all), One God is coming, . . .
3. *ca cici kamex, ma adzaicex katun yokolob . . .",*
    receive them, do not make war upon them . . ."
4. *bay tun ucibahob mamac dzaic katun*
    thus he spoke to them (and) no one made war on them,
5. *caix tulikzahubaob,*
    then they rose up,
6. *ca bin uyanteob Espanolesob,*
    then they went to aid the Spanish
7. *tuconcixtob,*
    they conquered (them),
8. *tu yet xinbaltahob dzulob' [. . .]*
    they toured with (the) foreigners.

The reported speech in line 2–3 is presented in what Voloshinov (1986:120) called "linear" style, namely direct quotation. On the other hand, the shift back into narrative is marked by a "pictorial" report, in which the reported discourse is described in the words of the narrator, not quoted (line 4). The narrative then elaborates on the reception of Naum Pech's public address, specifying that in fact, the people did go to the aid of the Spanish (line 6). Whereas Naum Pech's utterance is directive and marked by minor syntactic parallelisms, the summary report of it ("thus he spoke to them") merely states the proposition that the address took place. Hence, it illustrates what Voloshinov called "referent analyzing indirect report" (Voloshinov 1986:130–32). Right after this stylistic shift, the subsequent events are described in a series of parallel lines with two instances of the connective *ca* (then) (lines 5, 6), four derived transitive verbs (lines 5–8), and repetition of the plural morpheme <*ob*> (lines 5–8).

In other words, the embedded quote of Naum Pech's address shows its own speech style, appropriate to the context of its original production, whereas the embedding indirect report reproduces only the gross outline of the event and leads into a distinct style appropriate to the chronicle. The quoted speech is oblique in this context, since it is only relative to the descriptive frame, and not directly to the current utterance frame, that it is interpretable. This obliqueness notwithstanding, the incorporation of quoted speech also brings with it the authority of its original utterance, and so works to officialize the discourse in which it is embedded. Intermittent sound play in the chronicles and letters gives evidence that they incorporate further oral components, increasing the potential complexity of the genre while linking it to speech practice. Genres, for Bakhtin, "correspond to typical situations of speech communication and consequently also to particular contacts between the meanings of words and actual concrete reality under certain typical circumstances" (Bakhtin 1986:87). These contacts occur in the process of reception and are documented in reported speech.

A second way in which official Maya documents display an orientation to the social reception of speech is through their rhetorical style. Although the chronicles present themselves as true and factual *descriptions,* they are in some important ways *persuasive* as well. The Yaxkukul documents explicitly assert their own authenticity, certifying with signatures that the accounts are in fact what they appear to be (not just vehicles for some hidden agendas), and that what they state is true, not fabricated. (See Yaxkukul document 1 [Barrera Vasquez 1984: lines 61, 318, 359, 397, 428, 431]; document 2 [Barrera Vasquez 1984:91, 97]; Chicxulub documentos sec. 409 [Brinton 1969:214–15]; Sotuta document 2 and 3 [Roys 1939:428, 430].) Similar assertions of truth are common in the letters of 1567. These very assurances fit into the rhetoric of persuasion and identification, and thereby undermine the appearance of simple description. From this perspective, the officializing and regularizing devices described above also help regiment the reception of the discourse, making it intelligible and authoritative (Bourdieu 1982:649).

In addition to these broadly distributed devices, the 1567 letters to the king and certain kinds of ritual language display still other features directed toward influencing the action of a specific addressee (human or divine). These include (1) the use of imperative verbs or statements in second person that direct the addressee to act in a certain way; (2) the spelling out of a justification of why the addressee should follow the directive and fulfill the addressors' wishes; and (3) the appeal to intense affect, both positive and negative, in the addressors' relation to the addressees or some state of affairs.

Chronicles, surveys, agreements, and letters therefore contain a variety of indicators of the ways their authors interpreted speech and of the kinds of reception they anticipated for their own discourse. These devices necessarily overlap with the ones through which authors officialized and regularized their speech, since they are adapted to the same social context. The impact of these processes on discourse genres undoubtedly varies across historical contexts, but appears to have been quite deep in sixteenth-century official Maya. Central parts of each document reflect the successive adjustments through which the Maya attempted to interpret, adapt to, and manipulate their contemporary situation. These aspects of discourse connect not only individual works, but also the genres themselves to ongoing (changing) social processes. The genre categories labeled *carta* (letter), *informacion de derecho* (account of rights), and *concierto* (agreement) correspond to different genres of action and different modes of orientation to Spanish authority. Furthermore, there is sufficient variation on this point among works of each genre to indicate that the generic categories were changing rather than fixed (Hanks 1986, n.d.). In a real sense, then, these genres were being produced in practice.

Actuality and Incompleteness

The organic link between style, genre, and action that Bakhtin (1986) described is clearly evident in several sections of these texts. The opening three invocations in Yaxkukul document 1 (example 4, lines 3, 6, 8), as well as the interlocking description of the time and place of provenance in example 4, lines 20–24, all articulate with the act value of the discourse. Naming the king, the *encomendero,* and the governor, the authors take up a specific footing in relation to the Spanish, while at the same time demonstrating their own genuinely elite Maya identities, through the eloquence of the language. Later in the discourse, when the act context shifts from the presentation of the document itself (part I) to the actual survey of places (part II), there is a coincident stylistic shift. Address dominated by a kind of "speech tact" in which poetic parallelism is maximized, gives way to an iconic descriptive style, in which the order of elements in the text reproduces the spatial relations among objects referred to (see example 1 above). Bakhtin observed that the parallelistic style tends to arise in discourse in which there is dialogue with the reader (covert or overt) (BM 1985:95–96). The presence of verse parallelism in the opening frame of the chronicle, where higher powers are invoked, in contrast with its relative absence in the land survey, is consistent with this more general observation. Thus, even within the organization of individual works, shifts in the speech acts being performed are realized through shifts in linguistic style. This reflects the fact that the two are different aspects of the same utterance.

Practice as inscribed in time is always de-totalized, in that it remains unfinished and emergent (Bourdieu 1977:9). Hence, the unitary wholeness of genre, which is axiomatic in formalist approaches, becomes a problematic achievement in a practice-based framework. The idea of objectivist rules is replaced by schemes and strategies, leading one to view genre as a set of focal or prototypical elements, which actors use variously and which never become fixed in a unitary structure. The dimensions laid out in section 1 above are among the core ones in official Maya genres. Like schemes for Bourdieu's actors, genres according to Bakhtin (1986:78) are expertly used by speakers, even though they may be unaware of generic parameters.

In what he called the "historical actuality" of signs, Bakhtin claimed that the unity of discourse form and meaning is not fixed in objective grammatical structure, but is brought about through the social evaluation of discourse. This entails not only moral or aesthetic judgment, but the entire investing of the discourse with value, a process that takes place partly in reception and partly in composition (BM 1985:124). Hence, neither the genre nor the individual work can be viewed as a finished product unto itself, but remain partial and transitional. The actuality of discourse changes with its reception, and social evaluation is always subject to revision. Whatever the immediate pragmatic contexts of the land surveys, for instance, they continued to be cited as evidence in land claims well into the seventeenth century. The letters of 1567 are susceptible to different readings according to whether we view them as support for the Franciscans, as bids for influence, or as factual descriptions. Because they are at least partly created in their enactment, then, genres are schematic and incomplete resources on which speakers necessarily improvise in practice.

Indexical Centering: Person, Place, and Time

A key element in any practice-based theory of discourse is the grounding of generic works in their indexical context. Indexicality is a semiotic mode in which signs stand for objects through a relation of actual contiguity with them. In language, such signs include pronouns, demonstratives, and other "shifters," which relate utterances to their speakers, addressees, actual referents, place and time of occurrence. Indexical centering is a primary part of the interpretation of discourse because it connects the evaluative and semantic code with the concrete circumstances of its use. Furthermore, since such elements are discrete parts of discourse form, they nicely illustrate the embedding of speech context within the linguistic code itself. To say that generic categories derive in part from practice is to say that they embody indexical fields in potentially contrasting ways. Sixteenth-century official Maya genres embody a specific kind of public address by a collective speaker before witnesses, located in a carefully constructed "here" and "now."

Viewed as kinds of practice, genres are characterized by what Bakhtin called their "addressivity" (1986:95–96). Different genres correspond to different conceptions of the addressee, who may be an individual, a social group, contemporaries, successors, an unconcretized Other, or some combination of these. In the Chicxulub chronicle, Naum Pech's speech reflects a different footing in relation to his audience than that between the chronicle and its audience. As pointed out in example 3, this difference in addressivity has consequences for the discourse style. Similarly, letters, agreements, and surveys derive from different structures of address, implying subtly different fields of discourse practice.

Unlike the letters of the 1560s, which address the Spanish king in the second person, the native chronicles have no direct, overt addressee. The only instances of explicit address in these texts are reported speech, but there is an implicit structure of address involving witnesses as well as authors and an addressee. They are rich with references to colonial authorities, including God, the Spanish king, the Governor Francisco de Montejo (credited with the conquest of Yucatan in 1542), local authorities (by name and title), as well as witnesses and Maya elders. The elders are described as *nohxib* (great men) and *nucil uinic* (great persons), who were in the area before the arrival of the Spanish. Consider the following textual example, which makes up the first twenty-four lines of this document.

(4) Excerpt from "El documento de Yaxkukul, 1544" (Barrera Vasquez 1984:15–16). Line breaks (except minor change 20–21), numbers, punctuation, and word boundaries retained from Barrera Vasquez; glosses WFH. Orthography retained from Barrera Vasquez except substitution of [dz] where Barrera Vasquez has [ɔ] and simplification of barred letters:

1. *uay   tu   yotoch   cahal   yaxkukul*
    Dloc   Prep   Apro N   N-sf   Place name
    Here in the inhabited town of Yaxkukul

2. *tu   tabal   u probinsiail   meridad/de yucatan   lae*
    Prep   APro N   Apro N-sf   Place name   Dm
    in the dependency of the province of Merida Yucatan

3. *tu   kabaix   ca noh ahau   Rey   Ah tepal*
    Prep   Apro N-conj   Apro Adj N   N   Agnt N
    and in the name of our great ruler King majesty

4. *lay   yahau/lil   tumen   ca yumil   ti Dios*
    Dm   Apro N-sf   Prep Apro N   Apro N-sf   Prep N
    whose kingdom is made by our lord (father) in God

5. *lic   kabansic   yuchucil*
    Aux   V*t*   Apro N-sf
    whose power we name

6. *tu   kaba ca/   yum   Señor   encomidero*
    Prep Apro N   Apro N   N   N
    in the name of our lord Señor encomendero

7. *Gonsalo Mendes Cpn.   uay   tac   lumil   lae*
    Name   N   Dloc   Prep(Apro)   N-sf   Dm
    Gonzalo Mendes, Captain here in (our) land

8. *y   tu   kabaix   yuchucil*
    Conj Prep   Apro N-conj   Apro N-sf
    and in the name also of the power

9. *ca   yum   Señor   Dn   franco   de   montejo*
    Apro   N   N   Title   Name
    our lord Señor Don Francisco de Montejo

10. *gor/   y Cpn. gl.   Adelantado   aan   tumen   ca noh*
    N   Conj N   N   N   V*s*   Prep Apro N   Apro Adj
    Governor and Captain General Adelantado there by (order of) our great

11. *ahau   Rey ah tepal/*
    N   N   Agt N
    ruler King majesty

12. *de   su   magestad   y   tulacal   uinicob   noxibtacob*
    Prep   Poss   N   Conj Quant   N-pl   Adj N collective-pl
    of his majesty and all (the)   people elder males

13. *hotuckallob/*
    Quant-pl
    (who are) twenty-five

14. *layilob   cuxanilob   ti   ma   tac*
    Dm-sf-pl   Vb-stv-sf-pl   Prep   Neg   Vb-opt
    they were still (already) alive when (they₁) had not arrived

15. *Señor espanielesob   uay   tac   lumil/*
    N   N-pl-pl   Dloc   Prep(Apro)   land-sf
    Señor spaniards, here in (our) land

16. *lae   lay tumenel   lic dzaic   hunpel*
    Dm   Dm Prep-Apro-N-sf   Aux V*t*   Quant-NC
    For this reason we give (make) one

17. *ynformasionil derecho/*
    N   sf   N
    accounting a rights
18. *tu   tanil   batabob*
    Prep Apro N-sf   N-pl
    in front of (the) chiefs
19. *tzucentzucilob   tu   hunhunpelilob*
    NC-infx-NC-sf-pl   Prep Apro   Quant-Quant-NC-sf-pl
    from district to district one by one of them (at a time).
20. *uay tu/ hool   cacahob*
    Dloc Prep Apro N (Apro) N-pl
    here at the head of (our) towns
21. *tu   pach ca tocoy nailob*
    Prep Apro N   Apro Adj   N-sf-pl
    at the back of our abandoned houses
22. *lay tux cahantacob/*
    Dm Adv Adj-coll-pl
    where they (we and the elders) lived together
23. *ti ma   tac   espaniolesob*
    Prep Neg   V$_i$-opt   N-pl-pl
    when the Spaniards had not (yet) come
24. *uay tac   luumil   lae*
    Dloc Prep(Apro)   N-sf   Dm
    here in (our) land.

In attempting to identify the addressee of this document, it is necessary to observe a distinction between those *in whose name* it was produced and those *in front of whom* it was produced. Lines 3, 6, and 8 state that the utterance is performed in the name of "our great ruler of King majesty," "our father (lord) Señor encomendero Gonzalo Mendes here in our land," and "in the name of the power of our father Señor Don Francisco de Montejo, Governor and Capitan General Adelantado . . . and of all the great men (elders)." These are, by my analysis, the covert addressees whom the authors sought to influence.

There is a material similarity between this opening gambit and the sign of the cross. Both presence a superordinate addressee by the formula "in the name of" (literally identical in the Maya and in the Spanish "*en el nombre de*") repeated just three times with the named powers coming in the order Highest and singular (God the Father, Spanish king), subordinate and singular (God the Son, *encomendero* Mendes), and subordinate and plural (God the holy spirits, Governor Montejo, and the twenty-five Maya elders). Reference to an object "in its name" is a form of invocation, whereby the one named is made present in the utterance, just as an addressee is created in summons ("You there!"). This kind of address through reference is typical of ritual and other invocational discourse in Maya, both colonial (Roys 1965) and modern (Hanks 1984).

On the other hand, those *in front of whom* the utterance is performed, namely the *batab* (chiefs) in line 18, example 4, are among the witnesses who attest to the veracity of the expression, and thereby lend the legitimacy of their office to it. In relation to the superordinate powers invoked, the chiefs are party to the utterance, part of a collective addressor. Yet none of the signatories identifies himself as a chief, suggesting that in relation to the signatories (the primary "We"), the chiefs were addressees. Presumably, the discourse was worked out over a period of time under the primary authority of the *gobernador* and town council who signed it, then presented it before the chiefs and elders for ratification, and then presented it to the Spanish government as a joint statement. The witnesses are among the third set of referents invoked in the naming at the beginning, which suggests that they are covert addressees. Yet, the text states clearly that the opinions of the elders were taken "under oath" (*ti huramento*), and are accurately reflected in this document (Barrera Vasquez 1984: line 420ff.). This makes them party to the utterance in relation to the Spanish, while still part of the audience in relation to the primary "official" addressors. Although they are invoked just after the Spanish powers, they also figure explicitly among the signatories (Barrera Vasquez 1984:20–22, 45–46).

In addition to the ambiguity of the witnesses in relation to speakers and addressees, there is another transformation of the speaker. At the outset of the discourse, the primary "We" consists of what Farriss called the "first and second tier elites" of the local (Yaxkukul) Indian government, namely *gobernador* (mayor), *alcaldes, regidores* (councillors), and *escribanos* (scribes). The "great men and elders" also figure among those listed, although they are set off from the official functionaires (Barrera Vasquez 1984:17–18). After the opening section, which describes the conditions in which the document was produced, the discourse shifts from "We" to "I," from collective to singular speaker (Barrera Vasquez 1984:line 73). Much of the actual survey of the land is narrated in the first-person singular, with the Indian *gobernador*, Don Alonso Pech, as speaker. This is a reflection of a clear rank order among the primary addressors, corresponding to the hierarchy of positions in the Indian government. Each time the names or titles of these officials occur, they are ordered from highest to lowest in rank, and it is only the highest, the *gobernador*, who appears as a singular "I."[5]

Along with the speakers, audience, witnesses, and covert addressees, the first twenty-four lines of Yaxkukul document 1 also present a detailed description of the place from which the discourse issues. In lines 1, 7, 15, and 20–24 the "here" is successively described as the town of Yaxkukul, within the jurisdiction of "Merida," in the "province of Yucatan," "in this (our) land," and finally in the elaborate couplet construction, "here at the limit (head) of (our) towns, at the back of our abandoned homes." The root *hool* (mod. *hó' ol,* or possibly *hòol*) can be glossed as "entrance, end-point, top, head" (or "hole, entrance" for low-tone form) according to the context. In modern Maya ritual language, and I believe in this case, it refers to the superordinate member in a series, whether this be the uppermost, first, or ultimate. *ca-cab* can be interpreted either of two ways, as "our-land (Possessive Pronoun-N)" or as the unpossessed noun stem meaning "little town" (Martinez-Hernandez 1929:folio 60). From a semantic perspective, the latter reading is the more likely, and would imply that "here" refers to the superordinate place of which the others were divisions.

The second line of the couplet (line 21) is grammatically parallel to the first, being another locative phrase consisting of a relational noun, this time "at the back of" instead of "at the head of," possessed by a noun phrase referring to a social space, "our abandoned homes," instead of "(the) small towns." *pach* may be glossed as "outer surface, behind, after, ultimate in a series, upper back." *tocoy₁ -nail* is a compound noun combining "abandoned₁" and "house." There appear to be two separate couplets, the relational nouns in leftmost position and the possessing nouns to the right. *hool* and *pach* combine to describe the spatiotemporal provenance of the document (the current "here") as above, behind and after their small villages and abandoned homes. The adjective "abandoned" reinforces the sense of the old homes as things inhabited in the (preconquest) past, but now barren and left to rot (see Martinez Hernandez 1929: folio 425r).

These poetic equivalences reinforce the indexical centering of the signatories within Spanish social space, imposed upon them in the process of *congregacion* and in the publication of the Lopez Ordenanzas, sketched at the outset of this essay. The villages, like the old homes, are grounded in a past to be abandoned. These unstated but implicit messages make pointed sense when we recall that the *congregacion* was going on at this time (Farriss 1984:158–62). Furthermore, the signatories locate themselves atop and at the end of a historical process, which reinforces their claims to being "truly from here," and to having the right to speak for the collectivity.

The couplet in lines 20–21 is not isolated, but instead part of a larger verse construction that presents a single totalized description of the indexical "here-now" (lines 20–24). Several constructive factors reinforce this unit. Semantically, all five lines describe the same place "here" in a series of successive elaborations—"atop the villages, behind the old houses, where we used to live, when the Spanish hadn't yet arrived, here in our land." Lines 20 and 24 are the first and last lines of the construction and form a couplet themselves, each beginning with *uay t(i)* (here at), each with six syllables. In fact, the metrical regularity of this passage was remarkable and implies a different scansion, at six syllables (20), eight syllables (21), six syllables (22), eight syllables (23), and six syllables (24), suggesting a verse pattern ABABA. Within this pattern, the A lines all begin with deictic particles, which happen also to make an alliterative series *uay t(i)* and *lay tux*. The B lines both begin with the relational particle *t(i)* (to, at, when). Both B lines also make explicit reference to the past, whereas none of the A lines do, thus inserting time into the description of place. The repetition of the plural morpheme *-ob* in final position is carried over from preceding lines into the first four lines of this construction, which is then brought to a clear close with the nonrhyming deictic particle *lae*.

This verse construction may have been emblematic of the Yaxkukul region at this time, since quite similar constructions occur in the letter dated 11 February 1567 (lines 2.4–2.8) and in another one dated 19 March 1567 (lines 50–55). In these three cases, the lexical items in the verses are different, but the stylistic devices and overall template are notably similar (Hanks n.d.). All three documents were issued from the northwest provinces of Yucatan, with the involvement of individuals with the Pech patronym. This suggests that a regional style may have been emerging, although to demonstrate this would require further research. In any case, one would expect the emergence of such emblematic schemes in the process of discourse production, as a regular result of the transposition of homology within a speech community.

At a more inclusive level, lines 12–24 make up an intermediate verse construction embodying the elder witnesses, chiefs, and place of production as an indexical framework. The plural morpheme *-ob* occurs 13 times in the 12 lines in question, 5 times in lines 12–14 alone. This disproportion keys the discourse as (relatively) poetic while reinforcing an even rhythm and sound repetition. The first five instances of the plural (lines 12–14) are co-referential, all marking absolutive constructions that describe the elders. In less stylized speech, we would specifically not expect plural marking on both an adjective (*cux-an-il-ob*) and an adverb modifying it (*lay-li-ob*) (line 14). In contexts in which plural marking is not used as a poetic device, *-ob* seems to combine with *lay-li* rarely, and one would expect *layli cuxanilob,* or just *layli cuxanil.* Hence, its appearance here is motivated by the discourse context in which it occurs, not by the requirements of reference. These series contribute to the production of practice space, by the balance and cohesion they bring to the discourse.

There are two minor poetic series based on repetition of the syllable *tac,* in lines 12, 14, and 15, and later in lines 22, 23, and 24. The two series are identical insofar as the same three expressions recur in each. Whereas the same superficial form is repeated, there are three distinct grammatical elements involved. Lines 12 and 22 both have the collectivizing morpheme *tac* followed by the plural suffix. Lines 14 and 23 have the verb *ta(l)* (come) in the optative stem shape *ta-c,* both semantically plural but without the plural suffix, both preceded by the negative *ti ma* (when not). Lines 15 and 24 show yet another segmentation, namely *t-ac luumil,* derived from *ti-ca luumil* (to our land) by regular (morphologically conditioned) metathesis. (This instance could be analyzed alternatively as simply *tac,* a variant of the preposition *ti,* still distinct from the other two segmentations.) Within each series, the artifice of repetition backgrounds the grammatical differences among the forms, and foregrounds their cohesion within a single message. Between the two series, actual repetition foregrounds the significance of that message: our elders were here before the Spaniards, and this is therefore legitimate.[6]

Line 19 illustrates a slightly different case, in which two superficially different forms are grammatically parallel. The two descriptors of the *batabs,* "group by group" and "one by one" are both in distributive constructions, formed according to distinct patterns of derivation. The first shows the X-en-X pattern typical of some nouns and numeral classifiers, of which *tzuc* is one, meaning "pile, hillock" as a noun, and "towns, parts, districts, portions" as a numeral classifier (Barrera Vasquez et al. 1980:865–66). On the other hand, *hun* (one) patterns regularly as a numeral, forming the distributive on the X-X-NC pattern, just like the numerals 2, 3, 4, 5. . . . (?). I interpret *tzucentzuc-il* as a descriptor of the *batabs* in front of whom the document was produced (or declared). The *-il* suffix derives a predicate adjective from the distributive, with the added sense "(to be) from ____." It says that the chiefs were distributed by the districts from which they came. This is consistent with the standard definitions of the jurisdiction of the *batab* (Farriss 1984; Roys 1943). The *-il* suffix on *tu-hunhunpel-il,* on the other hand, is a different form (which just happens to be homophonous). This *-il* is the relational suffix, whose presence in this word is determined by the possessive relation. Hence, *u-* . . . *-il* is a single grammatical unit, meaning "it's ____." Given the standard interpretation of the classifier *p'el* as paired with inanimates, it is reasonable to suggest that this descriptor "one by one" describes not the *batabs* as individuals, but their jurisdictions. The two lines would then say roughly "in front of the chiefs, from their respective districts, one by one individually." All of these local-level parallelisms contribute to the stylistic and thematic centering of the discourse in its indexical context.

When we attempt to determine the temporal field within which these documents were produced, we confront a problem. Unlike segments of the Books of Chilam Balam (Edmonson 1982), or the medical prescriptions of the Ritual of the Bacabs (Roys 1965), the native chronicles are anchored to a time of production. Like the letters addressed to the king in 1567, they speak for a "now," specified by date, and a past in relation to it. The problem is how to interpret the dates, since there are inconsistencies that have led several scholars to posit scribal error. A number of chronicles were produced, or at least started, in the 1540s, but apparently finished only some twenty years later. Their common theme is the history and current boundaries of political centers along with their dependencies. They include (1) the survey portion of the Documentos de Chicxulub, which bears the date 7 February 1542, but which Brinton suggests was probably written twenty years later, on the grounds that it mentions events that took place as late as 1562 (Brinton 1969:189); (2) the Yaxkukul document 1, which bears the date 30 April 1544, but which Barrera Vasquez (1984:11), Martinez Hernandez (1926:33), and Roys (1957:47) agree was really produced closer to 1554, since it mentions Oidor Tomas Lopez, who arrived in Yucatan in 1552; (3) the Yaxkukul document 2 (Martinez Hernandez 1926; Barrera Vasquez 1984) also bears the date 1544, just eight days after version 1. The arguments in favor of a later date for Yaxkukul document 1 apply with equal force to document 2; and finally (4), the Cronica de Zotuta (document 1), partially reproduced in Roys (1939:421f.), recounts the survey of Sotuta undertaken by Nachi Cocom in 1545. In the closing frame, however, it is dated 2 September 1600 (Roys 1939:426; cf. Brinton 1969:256, n. 31). Unfortunately, Roys fails to reproduce the opening frame of the document, which may have contained a date. In any case, there is a discrepancy between an antecedent narrated time and the date at which signatures were affixed to the document. At least some of Barrera Vasquez's arguments for a later date on the Yaxkukul would apply equally well to this. If one posits scribal error, therefore, it remains to be explained why at least four different (sets of) scribes made such similar mistakes, despite which all the different witnesses attested to the accuracy of the documents.

Replacing the idea of fixed generic structures with that of strategic use of schemata, one can insert temporality and successive adjustments into the process by which chronicles were produced. At least two alternative explanations of the discrepancies in date are plausible. It could be that the documents were actually composed relatively late, but all present themselves as having been at least started much earlier, perhaps as a way of legitimating their authors' claims. In Yaxkukul document 1 it is explicitly asserted that the elders were "here" before the Spanish arrived. Under this reading, the dislocation of production time by claiming an earlier date, is a way of giving the texts authority.

It is equally plausible to hypothesize that the production of such official documents in fact developed gradually, beginning early and continuing through the sixteenth century. A natural corollary of this diachronic emergence is that the discourse of the chronicles is itself layered, containing strata produced at different times.[7] Such layering, and the recopying it often entailed, is a well-known characteristic of the Books of Chilam Balam and other native literary (and architectural) artifacts. Without further research, the actual period of production cannot be specified, but it appears that official Maya chronicles typically involved dislocated or transposed person and time frames.

This is suggestive of the "telescoping" that Bricker (1981:149–54) identified in Mayan and Spanish oral traditions. Events are telescoped when they are treated as equivalent despite their having occurred at separate times, as in the distinct events represented in the carnival at Hocaba, Yucatan (Bricker 1981:152). In Yaxkukul document 1, the date 1544 could be said to be telescoped into the (presumably later) time of completion. One major difference between the two cases is that, in Maya oral tradition, it is the calendar that determines what is telescoped into what (Bricker 1981:181). In the official documents, there is no evidence that dates were selected according to native calendric cycles. Moreover, oral tradition represents structural positions rather than individuals in Bricker's formulation (1981:8), whereas official discourse makes specific reference to many individuals, places, and events. This very specificity of reference is one of the core features of the genre.

Summary of Genre as Practice

At the outset of this section, it was suggested that conventional discourse genres are part of the linguistic habitus that native actors bring to speech, but that such genres are also produced in speech under various local circumstances. How does early official Maya discourse display the tension between these faces of the relation between practice and habitus? By officializing and regularizing their discourse, the principals brought themselves into line with aspects of the given social context, including the colonial government along with its contemporary representatives, as well as the Catholic morality imposed by the friars. At the same time, they contributed to the establishment of terms in which officialdom and regularity were defined, at least locally. They did this by combining and merging Maya representations with those of the Spanish, producing new blends and ambivalent types of linguistic expression (further explored in Hanks 1986).

By way of incorporating reported speech, metalinguistic framing, and persuasive rhetoric, these texts mobilize further aspects of the local habitus in order to regiment their own reception. Reported speech according to Bakhtin is an objective document of the social reception of discourse, while metalinguistic frames orient addressees and audiences, and persuasive rhetoric seeks to secure outcomes. Preexistent modes of reception, such as the literal realism of land surveys and claims of descent, the heartfelt sincerity of confession, and the reciprocal compliance to persuasion, were resources for the authors of these documents. But insofar as they combined such resources in new ways and reconstituted their relevance to new, hybrid genres, the texts also produced modes of reception. A similar process of production is evident in the indexical centering of official discourse within a hybrid address structure, including Maya and Spanish official witnesses. These same texts issue from dislocated spatial and temporal fields that encompass both pre- and postconquest society. Such dislocations are by no means arbitrary formal features, although they do have identifiable reflexes in discourse form. In all of these cases the duality between preconstituted social forms and novel improvisations is typical of the relation between discourse genres and practice.

CONCLUSION

How we classify sixteenth-century official Maya documents, and how we talk about discourse genres in general, depend upon the purpose of our classification. If the goal is to order works in terms of recurrent hierarchic groupings of units, then genres consist of structural categories within a cultural code. In the first section of this essay, official Maya was sketched as a generic category, subdivided by letters, chronicles, land surveys, and agreements. Further research is necessary in order to refine our understanding of this and other colonial discourse genres. Significant aspects of format, thematic content, and style are nonetheless common to works of official Maya and can be considered core characteristics of the genre.

Official Maya is a "threshold" genre in Morson's (1981:50) terms, that is, works within this category were created to be doubly interpretable. On the one hand, the texts fit nicely into contemporary Spanish categories such as *carta* (letter), *informacion de derecho* (statement of rights), and *concierto* (agreement). Such a fit was necessary in order that the works be "regular," translatable, and intelligible to their Spanish addressees. But native conventions also laid claim over official Maya in at least some of its features, and lead to another reading. For instance, the texts are written in Maya, showing indigenous forms of address, along with prose and verse styles common to other kinds of native discourse. It is also typical of official Maya works that they arise as part of an intertextual series of two or more versions of what seems to be a single template. This holds for the eight letters of February 1567, the two Yaxkukul chronicles, and the two Sotuta *conciertos*. This serial production is easiest to describe if we view generic categories as schematic devices that were adapted and altered in the different works and that take the form of analogies and homologies between them. Since schemata are always susceptible to further application, the genres remain open-ended and only partially specified. A further source of open-endedness is the process of reception and what Bakhtin called the "social evaluation" of discourse, namely how it was interpreted by contemporaries and descendants (cf. Bourdieu 1982:647).

Viewed as a set of principles immanent in practice, official Maya genres consist of modes of officializing, regularizing, and centering discourse in its contemporary indexical field. By invoking dominant ideological and institutional frameworks in order to legitimate their own claims, the authors sustained the appearance that they held to the same values as their Spanish addressees, that they were themselves legitimate, and that the discourse they created was authoritative. The indexical grounding of official Maya discourse is based on dislocated structures of address and temporal reference, in which local indigenous and European frameworks are blended. This is evident in the ambiguity of local Maya and Spanish witnesses, who were both an audience in front of whom the text was presented and, by ratifying its contents, joined the authors as collective principals.

Discrepancies between apparent dates of composition and events described in official Maya texts reflect an ambiguous time frame, also characteristic of the genre. Yaxkukul document 1, for example, claims 1544 as its "now," yet describes the arrival of Tomas Lopez, which actually occurred only eight years later. The Sotuta land survey records events said to have been performed in 1545, but has a closing date of 1600. In the former case, and possibly in the others, the time of production is telescoped with an earlier time reported on. These facts suggest that official genres were produced according to a principle of assimilation, whereby parts of the local audience were incorporated as principals and the present time of production was transposed into the past. Both appear to have been ways of lending legitimacy to the documents, through consensus in the one case and precedent in the other.

Although they appear narrow or even arbitrary in their linguistic detail, generic discourse schemata were as much part of the changing habitus of colonial Yucatan as were more obvious institutional changes, such as the imposition of *cabildo* municipal government, Spanish city planning, instruction in Spanish, and attendance at Mass. The Lopez *Ordenanzas* did not regiment verbal practice as closely as they did other aspects of Maya life, but the Franciscans appear to have had a fundamental impact on the discourse of the elites as early as the 1560s. Sixteenth-century Maya genres reflect a process of struggle over the terms in which social relations would be played out in colonial society. The struggle gave rise to new, hybrid improvisations, such as the Mani land conference of 1557, at which the boundaries of the area were officialized by agreement of chiefs from Mani and the neighboring provinces. According to Gaspar Antonio Chi, believed to be the author of the chronicle of Mani, the preconquest Maya observed no boundaries within provinces, but did maintain boundaries between provinces (Chi, in Tozzer 1941:230). The Mani conference, like the Yaxkukul and Sotuta surveys, was held in response to the Lopez Ordenanzas and to the radical transformations of the social landscape under way at the time. Yet, the Spanish premise of the conference and surveys did not preclude their being incorporated into the habitus of the Maya lords. In Mani, gifts were exchanged among principal lords, in the manner of the Maya nobility—five lots of 400 (*bakal*) cacao beans apiece, five cotton mantles of 4 breadths each, a string of red stones the length of an arm, and 1 score (*hunkal*) of jadite beads (Tozzer 1941: n. 58; see also n. 45 and 62). In the production of new forms of official action, the nobles reproduced their distinctness in relation to non-elite Maya society, reinforcing and in some cases creating, their privileged positions as officials in the *cabildo*. At the same time, they contributed to the ongoing process of making new Spanish realities intelligible by integrating them with already familiar Maya practices, something evident in ritual and other forms of representation as well (Bricker 1981, especially chapters 11–14). Different groups of nobles made different choices and improvisations, some apparently specific to a region or time, and others more widespread. The development of new genres was part of a process in which the new realities of colonial society were defined and familiarized, and the producers of Maya genres were struggling to set the terms of this familiarization.

Part of the effectiveness of symbolic forms lies in their capacity to become natural and to naturalize what they represent (Bourdieu 1977:164ff.). This process takes place largely through the use or replication of the form in practice, both as a resource for acting and for understanding. Colonial documents such as those discussed here are the products of practice, and the recurrence of identifiable discourse features in them is a trace of the development of new types of action. Viewed from the perspective of practice, genres are part of the naturalization of social experience. That genres like official Maya be made up of unstable blends of different kinds of discourse, only partly replicated through time, is a corollary of their being tied to practice in a changing field. It remains uncertain how fully the Maya chronicles, surveys, and letters achieved the immediate goals of their authors. What I have sought to show here is that they effectively contributed to the transformation of linguistic habitus and discourse practices in colonial Maya society.

NOTES

Acknowledgments. This paper developed out of a shorter one entitled "Symbolic Production and the Emergence of Genre," presented at the 1986 meetings of the American Anthropological Association in an invited session entitled "Language and Political Economy," organized by James Collins and Hy Van Luong. I am grateful for questions and comments received on that occasion, as well as written comments on intermediate drafts from Don Brenneis, John Comaroff, Nancy Farriss, Charles Goodwin, Michael Kearney, Shirley Lindenbaum, Robert Mestrovic, Rick Parmentier, Greg Urban, and an anonymous reader for *AE*. I have benefited greatly from discussion with members of a seminar on text structure held at the Center for Psychosocial Studies, Chicago, IL: Dick Bauman, Don Brenneis, Jim Collins, John Haviland, Judith Irvine, Ben Lee, John Lucy, Beth Mertz, Rick Parmentier, Greg Urban, Michael Silverstein, and Bernard Weissbourd. I am solely responsible for the result.

Abbreviations: Interlinear breakdown in textual examples uses the following abbreviations: Adv (adverb), Agt (agentive nominalizer), Apro (A set, prefixal pronoun), Aux (verbal auxiliary), coll (collectivizer), conj (conjunction), Dloc (locative deictic), Dm (demonstrative), inc (incompleive aspect), infx (infix), N (noun), part (particle), Pl (Plural), Prep (preposition), Quant (quantity), NC (numeral classifier), Num (number), Opt (optative-subjunctive mood), Rdpl (reduplication), RN (relational noun), sf (stem formative), trm (terminal), V_i (intransitive verb), V_s (stative verb), V_t (transitive verb), - (morpheme boundary).

1. Farriss (1984:227–36) presents a different interpretation of the transition from indigenous to colonial political systems, emphasizing the stability of the native elite and the great ex-

tent to which the Spanish system conserved the divisions of the Maya system. Farriss (1984:235, 242–43) and Quezada concur that it was the *gobernador*ship that most directly challenged the persistence of Maya political structures at the local level.

2. On the separation of these three elements see also BM (1985:79). The formalists came to distinguish them as aspects of the constructive significance of material (1) and device (2, 3).

3. Except document 1 of Sotuta, which Roys presents in Spanish only.

4. Chi (Tozzer 1941:231) states that prior to the conquest, public and legal proceedings were performed under oath in front of witnesses, suggesting a native source for this feature of colonial documents.

5. This account of the address structure of official documents is partial and omits the role of the scribe and Spanish officials in the actual production and distribution of the texts, as well as other aspects of what Goffman (1983) called the participation and production frameworks. These dimensions of context are an indispensable part of any full description of official genres, but will require more research to discern.

6. Because the repetition within each series is only superficial, it is lost entirely in translation. Although parallel forms are created, there is no repetition of information in the text, but instead a progressive accumulation of new information. Analogous series are attested based on the superficial identity of six distinct morphemes graphically represented by *ca(h)*, namely (in modern orthography) *káʔa* (two), *ká* (then [complementizer]), *ka* (we, our), *káʔah* (verbal auxilary: *future*), *kàah* (begin [intrns. vb]), and *kàah* (town, residence). In each case, parallelism helps create the artifice of a seamless discourse, inevitable and closed in on itself.

7. This layering is distinct from and logically prior to the overlays resulting from successive retranscriptions of the documents by later scholars and interested parties, a well-known philological problem illustrated by the Sotuta survey. According to Roys (1939:421), this survey as he presents it is excerpted from manuscripts copied by Pio Perez from another copy in the town of Tixcacaltuyu, itself apparently copied from the archives of Sotuta.

REFERENCES

Bakhtin, M. M.
    1981   *The Dialogic Imagination.* Michael Holquist, ed. Caryl Emerson and Michael Holquist, trans. Austin: University of Texas Press.
    1986   The Problem of Speech Genres. In *Speech Genres and Other Essays.* Vern McGee, trans. Michael Holquist and Caryl Emerson, eds. pp. 60–102. Austin: University of Texas Press.
Bakhtin, M. M. and P. M. Medvedev
    1985[1928]   *The Formal Method in Literary Scholarship: A Critical Introduction to Sociological Poetics.* Albert J. Wehrle, trans. Cambridge: Harvard University Press.
Barrera Vasquez, Alfredo
    1984   Documento Numero 1 del deslinde de tierras en Yaxkukul, Yucatan. Coleccion cientifica, Linguistica 125. Mexico: Instituto Nacional de Antropologia e Historia.
Barrera Vasquez, Alfredo, Juan Ramon Bastarrachea Manzano, and William Brito Sansores
    1980   *Diccionario Maya Cordemex.* Mérida: Ediciones Cordemex.
Bauman, Richard
    1977   *Verbal Art as Performance.* Prospect Heights, IL: Waveland Press.
    1986   Contextualization, Tradition and the Dialogue of Genres: Icelandic Legends of the Kraftaskáld. Paper presented at the Annual Meetings of the American Anthropological Association, Philadelphia, PA.

Bauman, Richard, and Joel Sherzer, eds.

  1974 *Explorations in the Ethnography of Speaking.* Cambridge: Cambridge University Press.

Bourdieu, Pierre

  1977 *Outline of a Theory of Practice.* Cambridge: Cambridge University Press. [French edition, 1972]

  1982 The Economics of Linguistic Exchanges. *Social Science Information* 16(6):645–68.

  1984 *Distinction: A Social Critique of the Judgement of Taste.* Richard Nice, trans. Cambridge, MA: Harvard University Press.

Bricker, Victoria R.

  1981 *The Indian Christ, the Indian King. The Historical Substrate of Maya Myth and Ritual.* Austin: University of Texas Press.

Brinton, Daniel G., ed.

  1969[1882] *The Maya Chronicles.* New York: AMS Press.

Brody, Jill

  1986 Repetition as a Rhetorical and Conversational Device on Tojolabal (Mayan). *IJAL* 52(3):255–74.

Brubaker, Roger

  1985 Rethinking Classical Theory: The Sociological Vision of Pierre Bourdieu. *Theory and Society* 14:745–75.

Chi, Gaspar Antonio

  1941[1582] Relacion. In *Relacion de las cosas de Yucatan, by Fray Diego de Landa.* Appendix C. Alfred M. Tozzer, trans. and ed. Cambridge, MA: Peabody Museum of American Archeology and Ethnology, Harvard University.

Cogolludo, Fray Diego López de

  1971[1654] *Historia de Yucathan.* Graz, Austria: Akademische Druck.

Edmonson, Munro S.

  1982 *The Ancient Future of the Itza: The Book of Chilam Balam of Tizimin.* Austin: University of Texas Press.

Farriss, Nancy

  1984 *Maya Society Under Colonial Rule.* Princeton, NJ: Princeton University Press.

Fought, John

  1985 Cyclical Patterns in Chorti (Mayan) Literature. In *Supplement to the Handbook of Middle American Indians,* Vol. 3. Munro S. Edmonson, ed. pp. 147–70. Austin: University of Texas Press.

Goffman, Erving

  1983[1979] Footing. In *Forms of Talk.* pp. 124–59. Philadelphia: University of Pennsylvania Press.

Gossen, Gary H.

  1974 *Chamulas in the World of the Sun: Time and Space in a Maya Oral Tradition.* Cambridge, MA: Harvard University Press.

  1985 Tzotzil Literature. In *Supplement to the Handbook of Middle American Indians, Vol. 3.* Munro S. Edmonson, ed. pp. 65–106. Austin: University of Texas Press.

Hanks, William F.

  1984 Sanctification, Structure and Experience in a Yucatec Maya Ritual Event. *Journal of American Folklore* 97(384):131–66.

  1986 Authenticity and Ambivalence in the Text: A Colonial Maya Case. *American Ethnologist* 13(4):721–44.

  n.d. Elements of Maya Style. Unpublished MS. # 1987. University of Chicago.

Jakobson, Roman
  1960   Linguistics and Poetics. In *Style in Language*. T. Sebeok, ed. pp. 350–77. Cambridge:
          MIT Press.
Letter of Maya nobles to the Spanish Crown, 19 March 1567. Archivo General de Indias, Mex-
          ico, p. 359.
Letter of the batabs to Spanish Crown, 11 February 1567. In *Briefe der indianischen Nobilität
          aus Neuspanien an Karl V um die Mitte des 16. Jahrhunderts.* Günter Zimmermann.
          München: Kommissionsverlag Klaus Renner.
Martinez Hernandez, Juan
  1926   *Cronicas Maya, Cronica de Yaxkukul.* Mérida, Yucatán.
  1929   *Diccionario de Motul, Maya-Español Atribuido a Fray Antonio de Ciudad Real.* Mérida:
          Talleres de la Compania Tipografica Yucateca, S. A.
Morson, Gary S.
  1981   *The Boundaries of Genres: Dostoevsky's Diary of a Writer and the Traditions of Literary
          Utopia.* Austin: University of Texas Press.
Quezada, Sergio
  1985   Encomienda, cabildo y gubernatura indígena en Yucatán, 1541–1583. *Historia Mex-
          icana* XXXIV (4, Abril-Junio): 662–84.
Roys, Ralph L.
  1943   The Indian Background of Colonial Yucatan. Publication 548. Washington, DC:
          Carnegie Institution.
  1957   The Political Geography of the Yucatan Maya. Publication 613. Washington, DC:
          Carnegie Institution.
Roys, Ralph L., ed. and trans.
  1939   *The Titles of Ebtun.* Washington, DC: Carnegie Institution.
  1965   *Ritual of the Bacabs.* Norman: University of Oklahoma Press.
Sherzer, Joel
  1983   *Kuna Ways of Speaking: An Ethnographic Perspective.* Austin: University of Texas Press.
Tedlock, Dennis
  1983   *The Spoken Word and the Work of Interpretation.* Philadelphia: University of Pennsyl-
          vania Press.
Tozzer, Alfred M., ed. and trans.
  1941   *Relacion de las cosas de Yucatan, by Fray Diego de Landa.* Cambridge, MA: Peabody
          Museum of American Archeology and Ethnology, Harvard University.
Tynianov, Yuri
  1981[1924]   *The Problem of Verse Language.* Michael Sosa and Brent Harvey, eds. and trans.
          Ann Arbor, MI: Ardis Press.
Vodichka, Felix
  1982[1941]   The Concretization of the Literary Work. In *The Prague School, Selected Writ-
          ings, 1929–1946.* Peter Steiner, ed. pp. 103–34. Austin: University of Texas Press.
Voloshinov, V. N.
  1986 [1929]   *Marxism and the Philosophy of Language.* Ladislav Matejka and I. R. Titunik,
          trans. Cambridge, MA: Harvard University Press.
Zimmermann, Günter
  1970   *Briefe der indianischen Nobilität aus Neuspanien an Karl V um die Mitte des 16.
          Jahrhunderts.* München: Kommissionsverlag Klaus Renner.

6

Text and Textuality

INTRODUCTION: DISCIPLINARY PERSPECTIVES

In recent years, the study of discourse has grown dramatically in anthropology and linguistics, generating a plethora of terms, concepts, and issues. A wide array of disciplinary orientations lies behind labels such as "text," "textuality," "discourse," "rhetoric," "narrative," and "poetic" (198). Here I focus on a limited range of issues in the organization and interpretation of text, working primarily with selected linguistic (34, 36, 54, 92, 118, 202), anthropological (17–20, 63a, 182, 188, 211), sociological (39, 76, 89, 90, 134), and critical (48, 73, 111, 123, 155, 161, 162, 205, 206) approaches. General overviews of these approaches, or collections of articles representative of them, can be found in the works just cited. Although research on text unavoidably touches on literacy and writing (38), language acquisition, education, and socialization (47, 89, 90, 153, 165), and political discourse and dispute (23, 29, 30), I do not address these topics directly in the following discussion. Rather, I concentrate on the status of text as sociocultural product and process, voicing in text, elements of textual organization, the relation of text to power in social contexts, some recent ethnographic studies of text, and certain further implications of this literature for social science.

It is helpful by way of introduction to consider the relation between the two terms conjoined in the title. When used as a mass noun, as in "text is composed of interconnected sentences," *text* can be taken (heuristically) to designate any configuration of signs that is coherently interpretable by some community of users. As vague as such a definition is, already it commits us to a certain line of inquiry. The term "sign" raises issues of *textual typology* [iconic, indexical, and symbolic (59, 157, 170); dense, replete (77, 155)], *medium* [including language, painting, film, music (150, 155, 201)], and *compositional units* [whether "text" must consist of more than one interconnected signs (202, 224)]. The qualifier "coherent" distinguishes text from an undisclosed array of other nontextual or anti-textual phenomena such as the senseless cacophony of a crowded street (as opposed to the senseful exchange of mutually oriented interactants), the random scuff marks on a public wall (as opposed to the intentionally executed lines of a drawing), or the noise of rush hour (as opposed to the concerted dissonance of a dramatic passage in a musical score). The fact of interpretability by a community of users locates text not so much in the immanent structure of a discourse as in the social matrix within which the discourse is produced and understood. It also signals a social orientation according to which text, whatever else it is, is a communicative phenomenon.

Textuality, on a first reading, is the quality of coherence or connectivity that characterizes text. On such a definition, this term is no more and no less vague than the first, since connectivity may be dependent upon the inherent properties of the textual artifact, the interpretive activities of a community of readers/viewers, or a combination of the two. It raises the further problem, however, to which I return in some detail below, of whether all texts are necessarily unified by textuality, or whether some kinds of texts may not contain within them significant anti-textual elements. That is, they may fail to have thematic, stylistic, or other kinds of unity, but still constitute a "text." I take the position that whereas the formal and functional properties of sign complexes can aid in the establishment of textuality, it is the fit between the sign form and some larger context that determines its ultimate coherence (see 7, 8, 73, 111, 123, 206, 218, 219).

Text and textuality, then, are part of a family of loosely interconnected concepts that includes at least the following (hyphens added): "Co-text" designates the accompanying discourse in a single text (34), the speech stream preceding and following an utterance-fraction (see 91, 92; on "endophoric," 142). "Meta-text" is any discourse that refers to, describes, or frames the interpretation of text (147). "Con-text" is the broader environment (linguistic, social, psychological) to which text responds and on which it operates. What might be called "pre-text" encompasses whatever prepares the ground for or justifies the production or interpretation of text. "Sub-text" focuses on whatever understandings or themes form the background or tacit dimensions of a text, inferable but not explicitly stated. The constellation of consequences and outcomes of producing, distributing, or receiving a text, whether intended and foreseen or not, might be thought of as an "after-text." The precise semantic shading and extension of the term "text" changes, depending upon which portions of this range of concepts one chooses to include.

Approaches to textual analysis can be differentiated according to the level(s) at which they constitute text as an object of study. From a linguistic perspective, text can be viewed as the realization of language in coherent, contextually interpretable speech. Thus, some linguists oppose "text-sentences" to "systems-sentences," stipulating that the former correspond to spontaneously produced utterances whereas the latter are the relatively abstract, decontextualized forms described in traditional grammar (34, 91, 140, 149). Linguists working in the tradition of Prague School studies in syntax, and functional linguistics more generally, have developed a number of significant principles of information structuring in verbal discourse. Using concepts such as functional sentence perspective, theme versus rheme, given versus new information, communicative dynamism, reference tracking, and referential hierarchies in discourse (37,

50, 51, 55, 65–67, 91, 92, 114, 132, 133, 194), these scholars have provided a detailed view of how information is introduced, maintained, and organized hierarchically in speech, and how, in particular, the structure of linguistic form interacts with the flow of information. From the perspective of this body of research, "text" is language form paired with its discourse interpretation. It is consistent with this view to postulate a textual "function" or "component" in the overall systematics of language, based on the inherent capacity of linguistic form to contribute to the production of text. We arrive by this route at the notion that textuality, like verbal style, is a functional property of language, pervasive in speech and conventionalized in semantic and syntactic structure. This literature has demonstrated, among other things, that ever more delicately defined aspects of linguistic form are motivated by functions defined at the level of discourse and hence text. The more general issue to which this speaks is the relation between grammatical systems and extra-linguistic principles, a mainstay of modern pragmatics (106, 140, 156).

A distinct view of discourse locates text not in language as a functional code, but in works as the individuated products fashioned when the code is put to use. A narrative, a poem, a traditional story, a novel, a myth, a newspaper headline, a conversational exchange, and a lecture have in common that they display specific features of format, including: beginning, middle, ending; compositional units such as episodes, scenes, sections, turns or stanzas; and genre categories, depending upon the case at hand. Discourse analysts have proposed various textual structures based on the overall architecture of a text, not only on the local management of information flow across adjacent sentences (9, 34, 109, 174, 179, 188, 192, 194, 198, 209, 210, 216, 217, 224). Looking only at the informational content of certain types of discourse, and not at their specifically linguistic properties, "story grammar" theorists have similarly proposed hierarchical structures that correspond to entire narrative works and are thus defined at a level distinct from that of sentential or even inter-sentential grammar (34 and citations therein). The difference between such units and the ones in a language-based view of text is significant. The "textual component" of a grammar, for instance, may consist of rules governing syntactic processes such as pronominalization (133) and clause nexus (67), but it is unlikely on any theory to contain rules for plot and character development, or units like episodes (216), genres (97), openings, or closings (140, 183). Principles pertaining to text-works bear on just such matters, subsuming text-language but going beyond it.

It should be pointed out that while text-language and text-works are distinct kinds of objects, there is significant overlap in the literature treating the two. The formalist notion of the verse series (212) and its development in structuralist poetics (36, 48, 106a, 118, 178a, 194) move in the direction of positing units larger than strings of grammatically connected sentences. Similarly, the Praguean concept of thematic progression relates the theme-rheme content of a series of sentences, thus positing higher level macro-structures (51; and see 215, 216). In structuralist aesthetics, the "functional systems" of works became a central object of analysis (9, 73, 74a, 115, 118, 161). Rather than a disjunction between textual language and text-works, then, there is a progression, which includes mid-level units larger than sentences but smaller than works.

As soon as one joins together the kinds of connectivity defined in discourse analysis with the notion of unitary text-works, it becomes interesting to explore the relation between the two. To what extent and under what circumstances can a work fail to display internal cohesion, being in effect a text without textuality? Can we define different genres of work in terms of different kinds of textuality displayed in their language; or vice versa, can we define types of textuality in genre-specific terms?

It is doubtful whether any approach to discourse that posits text-works can limit itself to the textual artifact alone, without taking the next step of situating the artifact in a broader sociocultural context (88–90). It is widely recognized that the role of context is central in defining the work as a complete, interpretively coherent object. Because of the interaction between grammatical structure and textual function, the form of a text can give many clues to its genre identity and proper interpretation; but the interpretation arises only in the union between form and context. For the propositional interpretation of discourse, it may be possible to make reference to limited aspects of context, although it is a matter of considerable debate just how limited interpretative frames are in scope (34, 64). Being much more concrete and inclusive units, text-works require for their definition correspondingly more global considerations of context. These encompass the processes of text production, what Bakhtin (8, 9) called the addressivity and responsivity of texts, canons of performance (17, 20, 107, 108, 187), modes of reception and response (123, 206), concretization (111, 113, 219), explication of institutional settings (38, 153), and particular literary histories (2). This extension into social history effectively reopens the question of what constitutes text: a certain kind of language, coherence as a work, or placement in a historical series? Concepts such as intertextuality (124, 131), genre (97), frame (64, 75, 101), and footing (76, 141) effectively mediate between works and larger historical contexts. They share with linguistic approaches the goal of explaining textual form but explicitly seek to relate form to its social context.

At another step removed from linguistic systems in the formalist tradition are the approaches to text grounded in critical and deconstructionist literary theory (22, 49, 52, 53, 164, 196). Deconstructionism grew partly out of a critique of structuralist approaches to meaning, and it poses a serious challenge to any theory of text based on coherence and connectivity. Rejecting the Saussurian concept of the signifier-signified bond as a fixed correspondence between signs and meanings (53a; 22:Ch. 7 & 8), deconstruction focuses on the nonfixity of meaning, and especially on the paradoxical, dissonant meanings of a text. Where a classical structuralist approach to text foregrounds the unity of text-works and the connectivity of textual language, de Man (52) foregrounds disunity in text and shows that texts unavoidably contain irresolved contradictions that ultimately undermine their own meanings. Rather than a quality of totality or intelligibility that accrues to the language or to the work, what develops is a hiatus between authorial intent and textual form, a space of indeterminacy that is filled only in the process of reading. It is important to appreciate that whereas structural models can give elegant account of contradictions by way of dialectal synthesis, critical literary theory refuses such a resolution to its contradictions. Rather than encompassing local disunities in a higher synthesis, it accords an irreducible role to disunity and locates the text in the process of its own deconstruction. This subversion of meaning is carried over into the texts produced by critics and philosophers as well, and becomes a basis for questioning both the divisions between these discourses and the possibility of ever fixing meaning.

The shift from a bounded linguistic artifact to an unbounded process of interaction among reader, text, and author has several consequences. One of them is to focus attention on the active engagement of a reader in constituting the text itself, thus raising interesting questions about reader response (206), reception (49, 123, 218), and the balance between what is said in text, what is unsaid but available, and what must be constructed (211:360ff., 459ff.). Another is to extend the notion of text far beyond its former boundaries, making, in effect, all of life an object of interpretation and hence a "text." Such a broad take on text can be integrated with (post)modern "interpretive" social sciences, which proceed from a similar questioning of determinacy and objectivism (41, 74b, 175, 176, 211). But a caution is in order, for to propose that interpretations are terminally indeterminate, while defining text in the most general possible terms, would be to risk losing one's object altogether (180). Stripped of its specificity, a text in the sense of a work can end up as an oddly residual instance of some more steadfastly vague phenomenon. A productive question from our perspective is the one Culler (49) asks—namely, what kind of semiotics of literature can incorporate the insights of critical and deconstructionist theory without carrying them to unproductive extremes? Alternatively, as illustrated in Said (181), the penetrating readings that emerge from critical theory can be used to reveal the divisive and contradictory logics of contemporary social reality.

Critiques of structuralism have emerged from a variety of other perspectives that have further implications for how one views text. Jameson (119, 120) argues for an approach at once more politically engaged in the contemporary world and more thoroughly historicizing in outlook. In articles on literary production, particularly in China (121), and on "Third-World literature" more generally (122), he examines the relation between political economic conditions, defined globally in a Marxist framework, and textual productions. The vast generality of Jameson's categories runs the same risk as do overly encompassing views of "text"—namely, that of reducing the specificity of any particular text or local tradition to a mere reflection of something else. In a very interesting critique, Ahmad (2) makes this point and illustrates it with remarks on the history of Urdu literature. Other approaches incorporating elements of Marxism also locate textuality within discursive formations, the latter being produced in practices of "articulation" (136), "dispersion" (68) and "linguistic exchange" (25, 26). These lines of inquiry can contribute significantly to an anthropological framework for textual analysis by exploring the ties between macro-level social processes and microlevel aspects of textual form (see also 3).

Given the impossibility of adequately discussing all of these perspectives in a short review, I concentrate on a relatively small portion of the problems they raise. It is my opinion that the textual issues most fruitful for anthropologists lie in the mid-range between formalism, which dwells on the forms, devices, and constructions of closed artifacts (codes or works), and what might be called sociologism, which dwells on the large-scale fields of production, distribution, and reception of discourse. The former makes productive use of linguistic models while failing, typically, to historicize its object, whereas the latter is richly historicizing but tends to yield reductive explanations of textual artifacts. From this combined perspective, the search for essential, transhistorical properties of "text" is futile. A better objective is the development of a revealing metalanguage in which to explore the specificities of given discursive formations and cultural practices in a variety of ethnographic contexts.

Part of this task is to devise a way of talking about text in various channels, or media, including writing, oral performance, painting, music, and other signifying practices (8, 12, 28, 63, 73, 129, 161:180ff.). The relation between poetry and painting has of course been a mainstay of critical theory [(77, 139); and brilliantly discussed by Mitchell (155)], and the social science literature on literacy and orality is burgeoning (38, 47, 78, 79). For the sake of brevity, the remainder of this review will focus specifically on verbal text without attempting to explore the concomitants of media and literacy. A longer treatment would have to address problems of format and channel in detail, since with language one confronts an entire array of texts—oral, written (alphabetic, syllabic, pictographic), transcribed, hieroglyphically represented, and translated into secondary codes such as Morse, drum, or whistle speech. The cognitive, aesthetic, social, and cultural corollaries of these different media vary equally widely, barring, for anthropologists at least, the simplifying assumption that all media are merely alternative realizations of a single text. Nor, for the same reason, is it justified to elevate one manifestation of textuality, such as the written word, to the level of a model relative to which all others are described. The appearance of objective constancy in written discourse is debunked by any approach that accords a constitutive role to interpretation (by a native audience or by an observer). Similarly, as most ethnographers of language recognize, verbal performance in social context is far from the ephemeris it might appear to be from an overly literary perspective.

The corpus of Maya hieroglyphs, for example, poses very important and interesting problems for the idea of verbal text, containing artifacts written in a mixed script interspersed with iconographic representations, found in "books" and on pottery, architectural structures, stelae, and even jewelry and bodily adornment (102, 127a). Similarly, the corpus of Maya texts produced after the Spanish conquest, written in the native language but using a modified version of the Spanish alphabet, consists of hybridized texts that include illustrations and discourse in various genres (61, 97, 98). These and similar corpora invite an analysis of the relations (contiguity, metonymy, homology, coarticulation, partial equivalence, etc.) that bind verbal texts to elements of their historical contexts (21).

KEY ISSUES IN TEXTUAL ANALYSIS

Cross-cutting these diverse approaches to text are a number of recurrent issues on which any viable theory of textuality must take a stand. One of these I will call the *status of the text*—that is, how one locates the textual object. For instance, it can be defined as a process of production, as a finished product (linguistic code or opus), as a means to or refraction of other (extratextual) ends, as a mode of understanding and responding (113, 206), or as a series of "receptions," inseparable from historical principals interacting with principles of evaluation (72, 73, 111, 218, 219). To a large extent, it was this issue of the status of text that ordered our summary of disciplinary perspectives. The key question was how different approaches objectify different aspects of the total textual formation. (That they do objectify is beyond question.) The status of text subsumes further, more specific questions that I address presently.

A second key question, overlapping with the first, is how theories deal with the phenomenon of *voicing in text*. This subsumes the relation between the textual artifact and the framework of production and participation from which it arises (76, 96, 101, 141). The distinctions among monologue, dialogue, direct, indirect, and quoted discourse (10, 147, 220), dialogism (7, 8), collaborative (40), cooperative (94), and one-person productions are also matters of voicing in my sense. They have to do with the reconstructible framework of participants for, to, and through whom the text speaks. The modern concern with the nature of the subject constructed in text is a problem in voicing, too, insofar as it rests on the relation between text and (a) constructed actor(s) (22, 49:32ff.; 164:Ch. 3; 189, 190). At the core of what Bauman (18, 19) calls the "performance" mode is the performer's special responsibility to perform with mastery (however this is defined in a given tradition). This responsibility puts him on a particular footing in Goffman's (76) sense, which constrains his alignments to the text, once again governing voice.

Approaches to text inevitably rest on some array of units and levels of textual organization, whether they do so explicitly or by way of unexamined assumptions. The kind of elements will differ, of course, according to how one treats the status and voicing issues. From a formal perspective, the problem is how text is phrased into segments arranged in some hierarchy based on inclusion, sequence, transformation, partial equivalence, and so forth (9, 109, 118, 193, 194, 208, 209, 213, 224). On the other hand, to separate literal from figurative aspects of meaning (52), narrative from story (9, 49), to distinguish among genres (56a, 97), and to foreground intertextuality (96, 124, 130, 131) all entail positing units and levels of organization. A performance-based theory will predictably isolate different sorts of units than a deconstructionist reading of a written text, for example, just as a Praguean poetics inevitably proposes units and levels utterly distinct from the ones on which a Marxist account like Jameson's (121) rests.

Finally, for anthropology the dimension of power in and of texts is of prime importance, linking up the textual formation, as it does, with social relations and a larger cultural system. Various aspects of social effectiveness have been explored from the

perspectives of speech act theory (6, 22:Ch. 10; 185, 215), the force of text in naturalizing a certain way of perceiving the world (24, 48), and the consequences of text
in power-laden contexts such as formal education (42–44, 153) and medical (38, 39,
135), political, and legal settings (23, 29, 30, 45, 46, 89, 90, 154, 168, 169). At a
more abstract level, attempts to apply linguistic and semiotic notions of creativity to
text accord it the capacity to constitute reality at the levels of an immediate situation
of utterance (191, 195), interacting subjects (190), or a larger discursive formation.
Such creativity, insofar as it makes social reality, is a species of power also. (Contrast
the narrowly linguistic notion of creativity as infinite generativity.)

One major contribution of these lines of research to anthropology is the demonstration that textuality cannot be treated merely as a property of a limited array of
symbolic objects but must be seen instead as an instrument, a product, and a mode
of social action. In other words, the topic cannot be confined to a separate linguistic
sector in the division of anthropological labor, for to take this tack is to impoverish
both linguistics and general anthropology.

Status of Text: Product and Process

What I am calling the status of text breaks down in the literature into at least five parts:
the boundaries of text, the "centering" of text within some interpretive matrix, text as
performance, reception of text, and the construction of synchrony. The last factor
bears on how theories treat the sociocultural present of text, the "now" of production
and reception (as distinct from the temporal developments that may be represented
in the text, which is a problem of narrative rather than the creation of the text itself).
Classical formalism and Saussurian structuralism take as their object a purely synchronous system, for instance, whereas historically grounded approaches to text naturally (if not inevitably) refuse such a view (9, 25). I take up these factors individually, starting with the boundaries of text.

The boundaries of text are what separate it from nontext, the limits without which
it would be impossible to individuate any work from its surround, or separate the textual function of language from everything else that contributes to intelligibility.
Mechanisms of integration operate within text, connecting parts to one another in relations of cohesion (92), cointerpretation (34:190), coordination, mutual adjustment,
and reinforcement (212). These aspects of connectivity produce what Tynianov
(212:36) called the "motivation" of textual units, a notion carried over into Praguean
structuralism in the thesis that poetic works are functional structures in which individual units must be understood relative to the whole work (200:16). On the other
hand, Bakhtin and Medvedev (9) cautioned that the boundaries of all ideological
works are flexible, in that the work is interpenetrated by values proper to the broader
social system beyond it. Instead of clean boundaries, works have ideological horizons
and evaluations. [Compare the phenomenological concept of meaning horizons in
Schutz (184) and Kellner (128:340ff.).] Even linguistic approaches with rigorous
ways of treating textual form and content inevitably confront the fact that under-

standing a text requires situating it in a context (54, 89, 156; and see 205 for a similar recognition in poetics). This means that inference, background knowledge, and extralinguistic features of the communicative situation must be brought to the work in order to make it semantically whole. While formal and functional connectivity can provide a scaffolding for a text's meaning, it is only in union with the sociocultural world outside that it becomes whole.

The unity (or "totalization") of text is contingent, then, on the added increment of information from without. In his phenomenological theory of the literary work, Ingarden (111) took an interesting approach to this dependency. Ingarden starts from what might be called an isolationist view of the work, excluding from it the author, the reader, the process of composition, and the entire world of objects and events that serve as its model or setting (that is, the actual city of Rome is not part of a narrative that "takes place in Rome"). Thus isolated, works consist in four strata: a phonetic formation, units of meaning, schematized aspects, and represented objectivities (111:30). The unity of a work derives from the interaction between strata, making it what Ingarden calls "polyphonous" (111:58). For our purposes, the schematized aspects are most important. No description is ever complete, and no sequence of textual elements is fully interconnected, without interpretive leaps by a receiver.

Ingarden distinguishes two moments in the literary work, the one abstract, schematic and potential, the other concrete, fully specified, and actual. Underlying the former is the premise that all representation is inherently incomplete, full of what Ingarden nicely calls "blank spots" of indeterminacy. These are the points at which details are omitted, connections elided, and background meanings required in order to attain full semantic specificity. It is only through the engagement of a reader/interpreter that the work becomes fully determinate, or what Ingarden called "concretized" (see also 4, 218, 219). One consequence of this view for the status of text is that it is inescapably historicized, since concrete readings always occur in sociohistorical contexts and are subject to interpretive conventions. The idea that the structure of the work is only partially determined also contradicts the formalist-structuralist notion of text as an internally complete functional system.

It is important to appreciate that Ingarden is pointing not only to incompleteness in certain kinds of text, but also to an inescapable condition of all text. As he says,

> This schematic structure of represented objects cannot be removed in any finite literary work, even though in the course of the work, new spots of indeterminacy may continually be filled out and hence removed through the completion of newer, positively projected properties. We can say that, with regard to the determination of the objectivities represented within it, every literary work is in principle incomplete and always in need of further supplementation. In terms of the text, however, this supplementation can never be completed. (111:251)

One can see foreshadowed here the recent concern with schematic structures in discourse theory (34, 38, 97, 137), as well as the constitutive role accorded to literary reception (123) and reader response (206). Ethnographic studies revealing that genres differ in terms of how rigidly they must be repeated, or with what latitude they can be interpreted by performers, also point to the fact that the relation between schematic and concretized moments in text can be subject to social convention (20, 187). Ingarden's insistence that the text can never really be completed also parallels, albeit from a different perspective, the deconstructionist insistence on the basic disunity of text; both reject the notion of text as a finished totality.

A focus on the schematic status of textual works forces one to rethink the idea that the boundaries between what belongs to a text and what does not are fixed. Textual boundaries can be dialectically constituted in the interplay between schematic and concretized moments. The "blank spots" in the schema, like the spaces between portions of a broken line, are a constant reminder that it takes an interpreter to connect the dots and fill in the meaning (even though the blanks themselves are circumscribed by structure). Alternatively one could say that the boundary between intra- and extratextual elements is gradient, showing a range of factors dependent upon combinations of more or less schematic-abstract and concrete-specific features. The latter accords with the linguistic distinctions between literal (schematic) and contextually derived meaning (38, 87, 185); automatically recoverable ellipsis; indexical elements with both schematic features and strictly concretized ones (97, 191); the penumbra of inferences derived from the placement of the text in an interpretive context (88, 89); and finally, conveyed meanings interpretable only on the basis of a relatively deep reading, as opposed to those accessible on the kind of rapid reading one performs on a street sign or the label on a familiar product (34). These two kinds of reading imply potentially different kinds of interpretation, a fact that Vološinov (220:68–69) observed in his distinction between *signs,* which one must understand (through interpretive work) and *signals,* which are intelligible through mere recognition. All of these phenomena have to do with the interpenetration of textual with extratextual factors in understanding, and indicate that the boundaries of text are best conceived as extremely permeable, incomplete, and only momentarily established.

Incomplete owing to indeterminacy, texts in Ingarden's theory are also incomplete in a second sense. They are constantly subject to revision in the successive concretizations that make up their history. By postulating that texts become whole only in the context of an actual interpretation, Ingarden strikes a balance between a totally relativistic approach in which no two instances of a text are the same, and a more static structural one in which situational renditions are determined by the text as a fixed script. Incompleteness at the level of the schema consists in its being partial, whereas the incompleteness of a concretization is due to its being provisory. Thus, what is relatively permanent in a text is necessarily partial, whereas the totality assumed in structural models can never be more than a momentary achievement, a provisory filling in of the blanks. But how does an interpreter/reader proceed in deriving a complete or at least an adequate concretization? This question leads to another aspect of the overall status of text, what I shall call "centering."

Text (as code or work) is centered insofar as it is grounded in a locally defined social context, which functions as the source of information an author and reader draw on to flesh out the interpretation of the textual artifact (itself incomplete). Uncentered text, the residuum of conventional form isolated from any interpretive context, can never have more than a potential meaning (if indeed such an artifact can be isolated at all). It lacks the closure and specificity of fully centered text (cf. 9). Unlike the notion of "text in context," which entails the independence of the two terms and the externality of the latter, "centered text" subsumes the incompleteness discussed above and therefore accords a constitutive function to context within text itself (cf. 48:243ff.; 89). As the Prague School linguists observed (200), language can be evaluated only relative to an end. Given an end, such as the communicative functions posited in structuralism (35, 74a, 115, 171, 200) and ethnography of speaking (107, 187, 191), structure in text can be determined and signification delimited. But ends (socially recognized intentionality) and value orientations are not the sole elements that make up a founding center in text. Other crucial dimensions include production and reception frameworks, indexical grounding, and metalinguistic framing. The textual mechanisms that govern centering (and hence concretization) are an important area for research.

It is one of the postulates of Prague structuralism that language, and therefore text, is made up of many distinguishable functions, each corresponding to the connection between discourse and some aspect of its context. This articulation of form-function-context is a way of locking the schematic structure of text into its concretized realizations. Each complex of functions has two salient properties; functions *regiment* (regulate) the interpretation of text by anchoring it to a center, and, while not isometric with form, are nonetheless *connected to textual form in conventional ways.* Functional regimentations are a modality of centering, then, and at least some functions can be identified by analyzing textual form. Thus, while it is possible to adduce the phenomenon of centering (along with de- and re-centering) as evidence for the final indeterminacy of interpretation and the serendipitous character of structure, this is by no means a necessary conclusion. It is typical of linguistic approaches that they start from the opposite observation that principles of composition (broadly conceived) both reflect and constitute centers. Poetic parallelism (58, 70, 71, 73, 118, 179, 194, 199, 212); rhythmical, metrical, and phonological integration (91, 212, 223); the structure of deictic terms, such as 'this', 'here', 'I', 'you', and 'now' (97, 101, 191); and intertextual reference (124, 178) all help to regulate the centering of text. Thus, even though any strip of text can be multiply interpreted (through alternative centerings), the range of possibilities is never open-ended in the real social world. Rather, it is partly inscribed in textual form, and partly contested by actors (which may be more or less than individuals). Anthropological approaches to text can build productively on this research, while joining it to norms of interpretation (20, 73:165ff.; 84, 85, 160, 162, 200), institutions, and habitual orientations to discourse (111:222ff.), all of which regiment centering in sociohistorically specific ways.

One particularly important instance of functional regimentation is *metalanguage,* which consists of textual elements that refer to, describe, or otherwise characterize text itself, including the very one of which they are a part. Jakobson (117) pointed out the basic role metalanguage plays in human speech, providing speakers with the means to represent, define, and talk about language in ordinary language. Drawing together the logical conception of object language with the Peircean idea that signs translate themselves into other signs, Jakobson, and later Benveniste (21), Weinreich (222), and Silverstein (191), saw the metalingual function as the foundation of semantics. It is important to distinguish between metalanguage, or talk that is directly focused on talk, and *metalingual function,* which is the more general capacity of verbal signs to incorporate meaning components (even backgrounded ones) that signal how the sign is to be interpreted (32). [The same opposition is maintained between poetry and poetic function (cf. 70).] Utterances like "Pragmatics is the study of language use," "This essay will survey recent literature on linguistic anthropology," and "Spoken as an aside, facing away from the audience" (in stage directions to a script) illustrate metalanguage, or metatext in the first sense. On the other hand, the special intonation a speaker uses to offset quoted speech in everyday narrative illustrates the metalingual function in the second. Modern Chinese literature provides excellent examples of both types of metatextuality.

The metalingual function is used extensively by the modern Chinese writer Wang Meng as a resource for signaling "stream of consciousness," interior monologue, and dialogue in narrative. In the story "The Butterfly" (221), for example, subtle changes in descriptive perspective, shifts in pronominal reference, and stylistic indicators of tone and intonation blend together to yield an array of voices including omniscient narration; recalled, fantasized, and embedded speech attributable to one or another character in the story; and interior speech. Inevitably, the interpretation of the text differs according to which of these perspectives the reader adopts. As is evident in Jameson (121:74ff.) and Tay (203), such extensive use of different voicing possibilities has taken on a political charge in modern Chinese criticism, being construed by some critics as a form of Westernization. In one particularly striking passage, entitled "A Judgement" (221:60ff.), the story moves abruptly from third-person description to dialogue in the first and second person, with no specification of who is speaking:

> Shortly after, he learned that Meilan had written a poster completely dissociating herself from him. But this second piece of news affected him not at all.

A Judgement

I ask to be tried.
>   You are innocent.
>   No. That tram's clattering is a dirge for Haiyun. The day she came to my office to see me, her fate was sealed.
>   She sought you out. She loved you. You gave her happiness.
>   I ruined her. . . .

The presence of the label "A Judgement" in this passage indicates to a reader that a major shift of interpretive frame is required in moving from the preceding text to what follows. In what follows, the narrator, apparently inner-speaking to himself, troubles over the death of his wife, Haiyun. The two had met the first time in his office, and this dialogic "judgement" thematically invokes his public disgrace and political downfall, also described in the preceding section of the story. What is important for present purposes is that, on the basis of the page layout, the shifts between first- and second-person pronouns, and the sequencing of the utterances, a reader is able to infer that the passage consists of a series of statement-response pairs in which the central character (the referent of 'I' and 'you') rethinks his relation with his dead wife. With the exception of the section label, however, none of the interpretive framework required to derive these inferences is spelled out, and there are no quotation marks to serve as signposts. Rather, the framework is signaled in the kinds of features just listed, conveyed without ever being commented on. This illustrates the metalinguistic capacity of text to qualify and regiment its own interpretation. We find cues within the text itself that can be read off as instructions on how to read.

Put in more general terms, this fairly complex structure of information is conveyed by contextualization cues (89), indexical-denotational signs (101, 116, 170, 191), signals of footing (76, 141), and pragmatic presuppositions (34, 106, 151, 152, 166, 172, 197). As the papers collected by Lucy (147) indicate, metatext and metatextual functions interact through a variety of mechanisms, including reported speech (cf. 10, 56, 203), performance styles (cf. 18, 20, 213), lexical selection (cf. 92), generic features of format (cf. 97), and syntactic parallelism (cf. 194). Rather than attempting to isolate metalanguage as a kind of text, then, these investigations demonstrate the role of metatextuality in the construction of all coherent discourse.

Metatextual reference and description also contribute in fundamental ways to larger textual works. The Chinese writer Lu Xun provides an appropriate example of this, in the story "A Madman's Diary," in which the unsettling experiences of a madman are reported in the form of a first-person diary. What is most interesting for our purposes is that this autobiographical account is preceded, at the outset of the story, by a brief narrative in which a narrator describes his relation to the "madman" and how he came to recopy the following text. This introductory section embeds the author of the diary (the erstwhile madman) in a second order text, by interposing the narrator-copyist between the reader and the diary. At the same time, it frames the diary as the record of an illness presented "for medical research." As he says, "I took the diary away, and read it through and found that he had suffered from a form of persecution complex. The writing was most confused and incoherent, and he had made many wild statements. . . . I have not altered a single illogicality in the diary. . . . As for the title, it was chosen by the diarist himself after his recovery, and I did not change it" [(146:39); and see (138) for further discussion of Lu Xun's work]. The difference between this example and the one from Wang Meng lies in the direct metalinguistic reference to and description of the diary. This illustrates metatext in the full sense of discourse that is thematically focused on text itself, rather than the backgrounded metatextual functions that aid in most discourse interpretation. The potential interest of both kinds of metatextuality to anthropology is due partly to the fact that the metatextual regulation of language is a matter of social privilege, control, dispute, convention, and ideology. That is, it is a matter of sociocultural histories, as modern Chinese literary debate makes abundantly clear, as well as being an analytic phenomenon typical of all textual traditions.

In addition to the functional regimentations of centering, discourse analysts have identified a number of other devices that codetermine textual interpretation. Of particular note are the various kinds of schematic structures known as frames (64, 75, 76, 101), schemata (24, 38, 101, 211), scripts (27, 34), scenarios, and mental models (34, 125, 126, 137). Also, like Ingarden's "schematic aspects," these fixed data structures are definitionally selective and therefore incomplete. These structures have in common that they are relatively fixed configurations of information corresponding to actional wholes (such as types of events, activities), global scenes, sequential routines, and other extended domains of reference. Given access to such structures, a relatively simple or incomplete text (being schematic in Ingarden's distinct sense) can be concretized on the basis of background information not spelled out but nevertheless accessible to a socially competent interpreter. In linguistic studies, frame semantics holds out the potential of a theory that interpenetrates language and speech context more deeply than earlier paradigms, thereby opening up new research directions for discourse analysis. (To be sure, this potential remains mostly unrealized to date.) It challenges the independence of text, and complements the functional approach to centering by identifying extralinguistic structures.

One difficult problem that arises in connection with centering is what might be called the issue of scope: How "big" a context must one construct in order to make sense of a text (34:58ff.)? How much information, and from what range of sources, must one integrate in order to center it adequately? Some texts require more fleshing out than others, as a result of their elliptical or otherwise context-bound character. The more information required (the less complete the text), the more *global* the interpretation. Conversely, the more determinate (and hence totalized) the literal meaning of the text, the more *local* is its concretization in a given interpretation (cf. 186). Brown and Yule (34:58ff.) suggest this dimension for the purpose of simplifying the interpretive process (for both speaker and linguist). In fact, it incorporates a complex of factors, including: (*a*) the relative automaticity of interpretation—that is, the degree to which it is expectable or routine, and hence locally derivable with little work (104); (*b*) how extensive a contextual frame is required to center the text adequately: even a complex centering, based on a plurality of indexical dimensions, may be relatively automatic; and conversely, even a relatively simple one can be made problematic (deautomatized) by way of paradox or subversion; (*c*) the relative depth of a reading, with deeper, more elaborated readings requiring more global interpretations, and simpler ones being proportionally more local. Texts designed to communicate highly specific propositional information in scientific discourse tend to be self-contained by design, and therefore local in the first sense. The same texts tend simultaneously to require reference to very elaborate philosophical and conceptual systems in order to be understood fully, implying globality in the second and third senses. By contrast, the standard interpretation of a street sign indicating the direction and distance of a landmark is relatively global in the second sense, but local in the first and third. From a theoretical perspective the complexity of localism makes it unsuitable as an explanatory concept, but for the purposes of description it is useful; it can provide a further array of dimensions through which centering can be investigated productively in anthropology.

The recent development of the notion of "public culture" can also be seen as an attempt to take account of the globalization of text and symbolic form in the contemporary world (see 3). While the idea of globalization in this context subsumes internalization and mass media, an agenda distinct from discourse theory in linguistics, the interpretive problems that arise dovetail nicely. How does text that is composed and distributed for an international audience transcend the exclusionary boundaries of ethnic locale (and hence convention-bound locality)? How, by appealing to a large and heterogeneous audience, do such media overdetermine certain kinds of reading and rule out others? What new dimensions of locality in interpretation will be required in order to show the relation between public culture and more traditional(izing) forms? How, for instance, do the postcolonial literatures of Africa, Latin America, and India reflect different local histories of colonialism and still contribute to increasingly internationalized discourse? With these questions we come full circle once again from linguistic approaches to sociological ones. I believe the importance of centering as a topic of investigation lies precisely in its potential to bridge these two orders of study (sometimes called micro- and macro-levels).

Another important approach to the status of text developed out of folklore and the study of verbal performance. Lord's (143) classic work on the oral rendition of traditional narrative, Abrahams's (1) systematization of performance as a paradigm for the study of verbal art, Bauman's (16–18) synthetic development of a "performance mode," Hymes's (108) discovery of performance factors in traditional Native American narrative, and the papers gathered by Bauman and Sherzer (20) are all landmark studies in this approach. The basic shift in performance studies consists in displacing the primary object of textual analysis from linguistic form to the actualization of form in a public display. These studies are all marked by a commitment to close description of performance events, focusing on socially specific criteria for evaluation, the variability of different renditions, the engagement of a socially structured audience, and especially the distinctive responsibility of the performer to perform with mastery. This research posed a fundamental challenge to earlier structuralist accounts of textuality, which privileged textual form over events, by showing that in important ways text itself derives from performance. Rather than defining verbal art, textual form would be itself a product of creative enactments, making it what Vološinov (220) called the "inert [post facto] crust of individual events." Although the analytic framework of performance studies (mainly the ethnography of speaking) has come under criticism in recent years (e.g. 207), this line of research continues to make significant contributions to the anthropology of language (cf. 206a). This is particularly evident in the Americanist literature on native discourse, including Hymes (109) on Native American narrative, Sherzer (187) on repertoires of performance styles among the

Kuna, Tedlock (204) on pause phrasing in Zuñi and Quiché Maya narrative, Hanks (95) on the role of performance in Yucatec Maya shamanic practice, Bauman (19) re-examining the distinction between narrated events and events of narrating, E. Basso (13) and Urban (213) on dialogical performance of South American myths, Wood-bury (224) on Yupik Eskimo traditional narrative, and the papers collected by Sherzer and Woodbury (188). The central issues addressed in this literature are the embodiment of text in posture, breath control, gaze, and other corporeal dimensions of performance; the alternative bases on which text can be phrased (according to different centerings); the involvement and structure of audience in text (internalizing reception into the production process itself, and dialogizing authorship); the place of performed discourse in cultural and linguistic systems; and the kinds of transcription systems required to display this new range of phenomena.

At several points in the discussion so far, the reception of text by reader-addressee-audience has been cited as a constitutive moment in its definition. Surely, Ingarden's (111) theory of concretization, Vodička's approach to literary history (72, 73, 219), Iser's (113) phenomenology of reading, G. Prince's (173) studies of the reader, Jauss's (123) aesthetic of reception, Bakhtin and Medvedev's (9:121ff.) theory of historical actuality, and deconstructionist subversions of interpretation all displace textuality from the level of a formal artifact to the interpretation of the artifact in socially and historically meaningful terms. Text, we might say, is not a kind of language, but a way of reading (or interacting; cf. 5). For an anthropology of text, this research helps to emphasize the sociocultural encounter between text and audience (and therefore author and audience), the institutional and ideological formation of ways of reading, the imposition of interpretations, the lack of closure in text, the dialogical construction of meaning, and the function of reader expectations in centering (48). Even Brown and Yule, who begin by asserting that reader-interpretations are essentially subjective (itself a dubious proposition), nonetheless come to the conclusion that, actually, text is "what hearers and readers treat as text" (34:198ff.). This last factor links textuality back to habitual ways of understanding language, or what we might call a communicative habitus (24, 97). Despite significant differences among them, these approaches all challenge formalism to historicize the notions of text and textuality by analyzing them in relation to their enactment in the reading process. This brings us to the last dimension of the status of text to be discussed here—namely, historicization.

Different ways of defining the status of text imply different synchronies, a fact made explicit in the literature on reception, and in much of the debate surrounding structural models in anthropology. The formalist premise that text is a self-contained system has as one of its corollaries the assumption that this system preexists any instance of its "use." Textual forms are viewed in terms of already constituted types that are infinitely replicated in tokens. When the system does change, it is in accordance with general laws of structural evolution. As Jakobson and Tynianov (118:25) put it, "the history of a system is in turn a system. Pure synchronism now proves to be an illusion: every synchronic system has its past and its future as inseparable structural elements of the system." Note that while this view challenges the notion of a purely synchronic system, it in no way questions the superordinacy of synchrony over diachrony. Rather, it reasserts the encompassment of time within a literary system at a higher level, thereby trivializing the role of human agency and events in creating systems in the first place. Such an account is notoriously partial, leaving out the reworkings of text in the process of reception, the timing and pacing of textual production and distribution, improvisation, the role of overtly traditionalizing rhetoric in formulating tradition, and the ways textual practices and genres emerge from and operate upon sociocultural history (97, 129, 158). Yet these phenomena deserve an important place in textual theory because they help constitute its objects.

In light of such factors, the synchronous present of text ends up looking a good deal more complex than at first appearance. The kind of frame embeddings pointed out by Goffman (75, 76), the phenomenon of reported speech (147), and the indexical grounding of discourse (42, 62, 97, 101, 112, 191, 195) all imply that the "now" of textual production (at whatever point in the process one focuses) is actually a multilayered construct. "Right now" at any point subsumes a past and an anticipated future, along with a narrated space-time that reflexively alters the present of narration. Although sequentiality is a basic feature of language, the intuitively simple idea of linear time, with a clear division between earlier and later, is fundamentally questioned by textual analysis (and was already called into question by Saussure and the Prague School linguists). By progressively fragmenting the textual subject and dismantling the facade of functional equilibrium in text, critical studies have also contributed to a more realistic, and necessarily more complicated, view of social history. In undermining the tidy notion of a well-bounded document, one simultaneously undermines the atemporal givenness of the symbolic system of which it is a part (9).

Voicing

The preceding remarks raise further issues regarding the nature of the subject constructed in discourse, and the kinds of interactive formations in which it is produced. How do different approaches define speakers, authors, agents, and social actors? How do they relate textual forms to their producers? How do they treat the centering of text relative to narrator and narratee (173)? For heuristic purposes, these questions can be lumped under the rubric of *voicing*. Research on participant frameworks, performance, and reported speech all elucidate voicing so defined. There is a difference of focus, however, among these modes of centering and voicing. Consider the contrast between dialogue in the sense of text produced by two or more interactants, and dialogism in the Bakhtinian sense of text whose interpretation entails positing more than one founding center.

The study of dialogue (and multiparty interaction) has contributed to textual analysis important demonstrations of how conversation can produce text bearing the marks of interactive processes. These include the reciprocal orientations of actors (5, 80–83, 99, 101, 182b), joint production of speech acts previously analyzed as one-person acts [contrast (40) with (185) on reference as an interactive achievement; and

contrast (6) with (94) on the typology of speech acts], and the irreducible role of "audience" participation in myth tellings and verbal art (13, 57, 213). Dialogism is subtly distinct from dialogue, in that it does not depend for its definition upon the co-
engagement of speaker-addressee or speaker-audience. Rather, it is the more abstract
notion that text, even when it is produced by a solitary speaker (in the limiting case),
still typically includes language derived from a socially diverse discursive formation.
To borrow Bakhtin's (7) metaphor, words are not semantically stable units with fixed
meanings but rather accumulate the heterogeneous overtones of the situations in
which they are used and of the conflicting ideological horizons out of which they rise.
Dialogism and heteroglossia are in the first instance a property of the discursive formation in which a text is produced, and by extension of the text itself.

   The Bakhtinian approach, which has generated considerable attention in recent literature (13, 19, 96, 97, 159), impinges also on the notion of textual coherence, insofar as it calls into question the familiar notion that a text is oriented by a single coherent viewpoint. Dialogized text, on the contrary, incorporates a variety of
viewpoints that may be artfully played off one another [as in the novel according to
Bakhtin (7)] or may fail to coalesce into a unitary construction at all. This phenomenon also has implications for the constitution of intentionality in text, since the latter is at least partly a function of the relations among an intending actor, socially recognized value orientations, and the capacity of text to refer to and represent mental
states. As discussed by Berman (22), Culler (49), Norris (164), and Silverman (190),
recent critical approaches also undermine the notion of a unitary speaking ego as the
source of text, and so focus on voicing in relation to authorship and interpretation.
By undermining the ideas of a stable textual source and a "speaker" whose identity remains consistent across time (whether one explores time within the narrative, time of
performance, reception history, etc.), these approaches raise issues germane to the anthropology of action. For many of the questions that arise about textual sources in fact
bear on actors in general. This is the case for heteroglossia (7) and ambivalence (96),
both of which undercut the semiotic subject by interposing a plurality of textual
sources (hence decentering the discourse). As Goffman (76) recognized in his treatment of embedding, this semiotic complexity is a consequence of the multiple motivations and identities projected in interaction (cf. 167:144ff.).

Elements of Textual Organization

Despite their differences, the various approaches sketched in preceding sections all
imply certain units and levels of textual organization. Ingarden's work consists of four
main strata, just as Tynianov's constructions are defined by parallelistic series and
rhythmical unities. Brown and Yule's account of discourse analysis incorporates topic,
information, and referential structures, while Culler (49) and Derrida work with alternative centers, and Silverstein (191, 195) demonstrates that alternative functional
hypotheses lead to distinct constituencies in the linguistic analysis of text. Bakhtin
and Medvedev (9) provide one of the clearest and most insightful discussions both of

the units posited by formalist text theory and of their limitations. (Although it appeared in 1928, this work remains incisive as a critique of formalisms today.) On the other hand, Barthes (11) shows the importance of apparently gratuitous details in narrative, in creating what he calls the "reality effect," while Hamon (93) treats semantic "description" as his unit of structure, and Hymes (110) deals with parts, acts, scenes, stanzas, verses, and lines in Native American narrative (see also 187a, b).

Rather than rehearsing the details of these different ways of segmenting units and levels, in this section I briefly illustrate some of the organizations that have emerged in recent literature on text in the Americas. This geographical choice reflects my own interests but is also a productive one for the issue at hand. The problem of defining appropriate units and levels of textual structure has been at the heart of a substantial body of Americanist literature. By way of selective illustration, I sketch here recent work by K. Basso (14, 15) on Apache, Woodbury (224) on Yupik Eskimo, Turner (208–210) on lowland South American mythic texts, and aspects of recent debate over the forms of Maya literary discourse. Although they represent only a fraction of the research in this area over the past ten years, these works illustrate significantly different approaches to structure, with attendant differences in the elements it subsumes.

K. Basso's (14, 15) fascinating studies of Western Apache place names have pushed back the threshold of textual units by showing, in effect, that a single place name can function culturally as an entire text, complete with embedded participant frameworks, reconstructable narratives, and moral implications. Beyond its ethnographic contribution, Basso's work illustrates the vast discrepancy between textual form (in this case, compact descriptions of the social landscape that function as proper names of places) and textual interpretation. In a way that recalls Sapir's observation that Native American words frequently have the linguistic complexity of "word poems" (with all the subtlety of balance and detail that this implies), Western Apache place names function as entire "word texts." With glosses like "whiteness spreads out descending to water," "line of white rocks extends upward and out," "trail extends across a long red ridge with alder trees," "water flows inward underneath a cottonwood tree," and "white rocks lie above in a compact cluster," these place names are used in stereotyped utterances, such as "it happened at _____, at this very place!" (15:105). Properly placed in a conversational exchange, such an utterance invokes a traditional story regarding what occurred at the place, and from this story the moral for current purposes is drawn. This phenomenon provides an excellent illustration of Ingarden's schematic structure, with the "blank spots" consisting in (*a*) the proper viewpoint from which an observer looking upon the place would see the scene described (hence an entire spatial scene complete with observer's perspective); (*b*) the interpretive tradition whereby this place from this perspective stands metonymically for an event (itself the object of a schematic description shared by adult Apache speakers); (*c*) the general moral of the story, again a matter of background knowledge; and (*d*) the application of this moral to the conversational context in which the place name is uttered. All of this information must be reconstructed on the basis of background knowledge, with the ability to do so constituting what might be called the "textual competence" to center the discourse.

Working with traditional narratives from Central Alaskan Yupik Eskimo, Woodbury (223, 224) has elaborated an important new theory of rhetorical structure that demonstrates a range of phenomena nearly inverse to those of the Apache place names. Paying less attention to the cultural background and interpretation of the Yupik texts, and more to the systematicity of the textual artifacts themselves, Woodbury proposes a new formalism for describing text in relation to grammar. The key problem, widely debated in the Americanist literature, is: What kind of discourse units provides the appropriate basis for describing and transcribing traditional texts? Prosodic phrases (152), syntactic constituency (109), pause groups (204), breath groups (95), and periodic recurrence of adverbial particles provide alternative bases on which to segment lines, groups, and other intermediate-sized units of discourse. Woodbury's productive insight was that these alternatives can be combined in a system of systems. Dubbed rhetorical structure, this system would be a component of a larger whole, defined by two principles, modularity and interaction. Modularity denotes the logical independence of the subsystems, and interaction denotes their systematic cooperation. Given this theoretical agenda, Woodbury proceeds to demonstrate the components and mappings that define the Yupik traditional tale. The result is a powerful example of formalist argumentation and descriptive craft that builds on the most recent linguistic theories. One wonders nonetheless whether the determinacy inherent in rhetorical structure can be squared with the widely recognized phenomena of indeterminacy, global centering, and voicing. Concretely, one wonders whether the kind of centering demonstrated in Apache by Basso can shed additional light on the Yupik tales, and conversely, whether formally minimalist texts can be said to have a rhetorical structure.

A distinction emerges in discourse studies between macro-level (209, 214) or "top-down" textual structures like the work, the episode, and the genre, and micro-level, or "bottom-up" ones like anaphora across adjacent sentences and poetic parallelism across lines (34). Units defined at the macro-level may be nonadjacent and yet joined at a superordinate level, the way the beginning and ending of a text are joined in the totality of the work. Local-level units join together too, but are definitionally adjacent and need never coalesce into a work of proportions beyond a single connective unit. In order to study macro-level units, it is necessary to look at entire, culturally meaningful text-works, whereas a great deal can be gleaned about local-level units by studying short strips of text-language. In a series of studies, T. Turner (209, 210) has explored the dependencies and continuities between textual structures at these two levels, arguing in effect that all symbols (and, mutatis mutandis, textual units) be viewed as operational structures produced by transformations that operate both intra- and inter-symbolically. Like the modern linguistic notion that the internal semantic structure of a word can be of the same order of configurational complexity as a sentence (222), Turner's claim is that the internal structure of a symbol is homologous with the structure of the relations between symbols. In present terms, textual semantics, rhetorical structure, and modes of centering must be understood as "radically inseparable" (208:53) realizations of a larger cultural logic. From this theoretical perspective, Turner has explored Kayapó myths (209) as well as theories of metaphor (210). While Basso's work epitomizes textual centering, and Woodbury's develops a formalism for relating micro- and macro-level connectivity in the textual form itself, Turner's synthesizes structural with Marxist approaches to thematic meaning in text. One wonders from this perspective whether the semantic structure of Apache place names might not be recapitulated in the patterns of inference by which they are interpreted, or similarly, whether the modularity and interaction of Yupik rhetorical structure might point to deep-seated cultural orientations. It would be productive in turn to investigate the rhetorical structure and centering of the Kayapó myths in relation to their symbolic organizations.

Middle Americanists have been intensely interested in text structure, building productively on Garibay's (74) studies of Nahuatl verse. Mayanists in particular have debated over alternative phrasings of traditional narrative and ritual discourse (60, 61, 69, 84, 85, 95, 98, 100, 103, 163, 204, 204a), as well as over the role of parallelism in everyday conversation (33), in the differentiation of genres, in colonial documents (96, 97), and in pre-Columbian hieroglyphic texts (69, 105, 127, 144, 145). Linguistically oriented studies of discourse have revealed significant patterns in information structure and its relation to sentential syntax (55), and drawing on general theories of genre and intertextuality, have attempted to contribute to a practice-based theory of genre (96–98, 100).

Text and Power

Anthropologists have explored various aspects of the relation between textual productions and social power. Starting with the relatively abstract notion of pragmatic creativity (191), text production and reception can change social reality by altering understandings and relations. This capacity to take effect and to generate consequences is grounded in the general effectiveness of speech as a form of action (6, 140, 185). However, not only does text have locutionary, illocutionary, and perlocutionary force potential, but it is also a powerful mode of naturalizing social reality (24, 25, 48, 97) and socializing natural reality (as in the Apache place names described by K. Basso). In the former case, asymmetries, ideological skewings, perceptual limitations, and values accruing to social relations take on the appearance of natural, inevitable conditions. By being embedded in forms of textual production, aesthetic orientation, and modes of reception, historically specific social facts become invisible and unquestionable. This is a tangible form of influence over the routine awareness and orientation of actors, distinct from but complementary to the consequentiality of speech acts (cf. also 111:276ff. on the influence of schematic structure over its own concretization).

Less abstract are the kinds of power transacted through textual processes in particular institutional settings. The role of verbal discourse in social reproduction through education (24, 31, 42–44, 153), in control of specialized knowledge in medical settings (38, 39), in courtroom and bureaucratic settings (90:Ch. 9, 10;154), in workplace interviews (89:Ch. 8), and in ethnographic interviews (32) have all been opened up as areas for further research. Widely held ideologies of equal opportunity and differential natural ability in school, for instance, mask processes through which social asymmetries in the pedagogical context are projected into the objects of instruction. Textual competence reproduces social and economic asymmetries, becoming a form of symbolic capital controlled, amassed, and distributed hierarchically. In legal settings the consequences of textual forms, such as testimony and inference, can be tangible, just as they can in other arenas of social dispute, responsibility, and asymmetry (7:342ff.; 29; 46; 90:Ch. 10; 104a; 148; 222a,b). Alongside these trends, anthropologists have maintained an active interest in the textual forms of political rhetoric and persuasive language (23, 28, 30, 36a, 45, 169). Text, then, can be viewed as a form of cultural capital, as a realization of speech act force, as a mode of naturalizing and familiarizing social realities, as an instrument of authority, and as the medium (and the measure) of political debate. In all of these areas, a linguistically and critically grounded understanding of textual analysis can make substantial contributions to social research.

BROADER IMPLICATIONS OF TEXTUAL ANALYSIS

By way of concluding this essay I briefly consider the implications of textual analysis for social theory and interpretation. A variety of contemporary approaches concur in rejecting the isolation of the textual object from its social context, and this rejection entails rejecting the objectivist premise that the analyst herself stands apart from the social world and observes texts from a privileged, value-free vantage point. Textual studies have shown that the analytic enterprise is itself a species of textual practice and therefore must be evaluated accordingly. As the papers collected by Rabinow and Sullivan (175) show with force, the hermeneutic approach to text has significantly influenced ways of viewing social experience in general, and this influence must inevitably lead to a reflexive critique on the part of analysts. Rieger's (177) exploration of literary and semantic structures in philosophical texts, Lee and Postone's (137a) on narrative structure in the writings of Karl Marx, and Green's (86) provocative application of literary methods to the sociological writings of Weber and Simmel indicate an important area for future analysis. The focus of such study will be the textual processes and rhetorical systems that form our own evaluation metrics in academic discourse, thus realizing what is perhaps the most basic contribution of text analysis to social science, the challenging of its own discursive formations. In my opinion this challenge will not be met by adopting the solipsism whereby everything is text and all meaning is subjectively created, including the analytic discourse of anthropology. Nor can one afford the opposed and anachronistic assumption that formal structure determines textual production. The study of textuality has oscillated between these two poles in the past. It must ultimately transcend them if it is to realize its potential of transforming scholarly discourse while contributing to a deeper understanding of the world beyond the academy.

ACKNOWLEDGMENTS

This paper was researched and written with the support of a grant from the National Endowment for the Humanities (RO21374-86). I gratefully acknowledge this assistance, as well as the suggestions and critical comments of James Collins and especially Terence Turner. I have also benefited greatly from discussions with the members of an ongoing seminar on Literary Theory and Social Theory sponsored by the Center for Psychosocial Studies in Chicago. For their occasional observations and generous participation I wish to thank the members of the seminar, and especially John Brenkman, Vincent Crapanzano, Steve Gable, Loren Kreuger, Ben Lee, Leo Lee, Larry Lipkin, Gary Saul Morson, Greg Urban, and Michael Warner. To Lynn MacLeod, my research assistant, editor, and production team, I owe special thanks. In addition to editing the entire manuscript including references, she printed, proofed, and copied it, never losing her sense of humor. I am solely responsible for remaining errors and vagueness of exposition.

REFERENCES

1. Abrahams, R. 1970. A performance centered approach to gossip. *Man* 5:290–301

2. Ahmad, A. 1987. Jameson's rhetoric of otherness and the "national allegory." *Soc. Text* 15:65–88

3. Appadurai, A., Breckenridge, C. A. 1988. Why public culture? *Public Cult. Bull.* 1(1):5–9

4. Arakawa, Gins, M. H. 1979. *The Mechanism of Meaning.* New York: Harry N. Abrams, Inc.

5. Atkinson, J. M., Heritage, J., eds. 1984. *Structures of Social Action: Studies in Conversation Analysis.* Cambridge: Cambridge Univ. Press

6. Austin, J. 1962. *How to Do Things with Words.* Oxford: Oxford Univ. Press

7. Bakhtin, M. M. 1981. *The Dialogic Imagination: Four Essays.* Transl. M. Holquist, C. Emerson; ed. M. Holquist. Austin: Univ. Texas Press

8. Bakhtin, M. M. 1986. *Speech Genres and Other Late Essays.* Transl. V. W. McGee: ed. C. Emerson, M. Holquist, Austin: Univ. Texas Press

9. Bakhtin, M. M., Medvedev, P. M. 1985. *The Formal Method in Literary Scholarship: A Critical Introduction to Sociological Poetics.* Transl. A. J. Wehrle. Cambridge, Mass.: Harvard Univ. Press

10. Banfield, A. 1982. *Unspeakable Sentences: Narration and Representation in the Language of Fiction.* Boston: Routledge & Kegan Paul

11. Barthes, R. (1968). 1982. The reality effect. See Ref. 205, pp. 11–17

12. Basso, E. 1985. *A Musical View of the Universe: Kalapalo Myth and Ritual Performances.* Philadelphia: Univ. Pa. Press

13. Basso, E. 1986. Quoted dialogues in Kalapalo narrative discourse. In *Native South American Discourse,* ed. J. Sherzer, G. Urban, pp. 122–77. The Hague: Mouton

14. Basso, K. H. 1983. "Stalking with stories": names, places and moral narrative among the Western Apache. In *Text, Play and Story: The Construction and Reconstruction of Self and Society,* ed. S. Plattner, pp. 19–55. Washington, D.C.: Am. Ethnol. Soc.

15. Basso, K. H. 1988. "Speaking with names": language and landscape among the Western Apache. *Cult. Anthropol.* 3(2):99–130

16. Bauman, R. 1975. Verbal art as performance. *Am. Anthropol.* 77:290–311

17. Bauman, R. 1977. Linguistics, anthropology and verbal art: toward a unified perspective. See Ref. 182a, pp. 13–36

18. Bauman, R. 1977. *Verbal Art as Performance.* Prospect Heights, Ill.: Waveland Press

19. Bauman, R. 1986. *Story, Performance and Event: Contextual Studies of Oral Narrative.* Cambridge: Cambridge Univ. Press

20. Bauman, R., Sherzer, J., eds. 1974. *Explorations in the Ethnography of Speaking.* Cambridge: Cambridge Univ. Press

21. Benveniste, E. 1974. Sémiologie de la langue. In *Problèmes de Linguistique Générale,* Vol. 2, pp. 43–66. Paris: Editions Gallimard

22. Berman, A. 1988. *From the New Criticism to Deconstruction: The Reception of Structuralism and Post-Structuralism.* Urbana: Univ. Ill. Press

23. Bloch, M., ed. 1975. *Political Language and Oratory in Traditional Society.* London/New York: Academic

24. Bourdieu, P. 1977. *Outline of a Theory of Practice.* Transl. R. Nice. Cambridge: Cambridge Univ. Press

25. Bourdieu, P. 1982. *Ce que Parler Veut Dire.* Paris: Éditions de Minuit

26. Bourdieu, P. 1983. The field of cultural production, or: the economic world reversed. *Poetics* 12:311–56

27. Bower, G. H., Black, J. B., Turner, T. J. 1979. Scripts in memory for text. *Cognit. Psychol.* 11:177–220

28. Brenneis, D. 1984. Grog and gossip in Bhatagaon: style and substance in Fiji Indian conversation. *Am. Ethnol.* 11(3):487–506

29. Brenneis, D. 1989. Language and disputing. *Annu. Rev. Anthropol.* 17:221–38

30. Brenneis, D., Myers, F., eds. 1984. *Dangerous Words: Language and Politics in the Pacific.* New York: New York Univ. Press

31. Briggs, C. 1985. Treasure tales and pedagogical discourse in Mexicano New Mexico. *J. Am Folklore* 98(389):287–314

32. Briggs, C. 1986. *Learning How to Ask: A Sociolinguistic Appraisal of the Role of the Interview in Social Science Research.* Cambridge: Cambridge Univ. Press

33. Brody, J. 1986. Repetition as a rhetorical and conversational device in Tojolabal (Mayan). *Int. J. Am Linguist.* 52:255–74

34. Brown, G., Yule, G. 1983. *Discourse Analysis.* Cambridge: Cambridge Univ. Press

35. Bühler, K. 1934. *Sprachtheorie.* Jena: Gustav Fischer

36. Caton, S. 1987. Contributions of Roman Jakobson. *Annu. Rev. Anthropol.* 16:223–60

36a. Caton, S. 1987. Power, persuasion and language: a critique of the segmentary lineage model in the Middle East. *Int. J. Middle East Stud.* 19:77–102

37. Chafe, W. 1976. Givenness, contrastiveness, definiteness, subjects, topics and point of view. See Ref. 142, pp. 25–55

38. Cicourel, A. 1985. Text and discourse. *Annu. Rev. Anthropol.* 14:159–85

39. Cicourel, A. 1986. The reproduction of objective knowledge: Common sense reasoning in medical decision making. In *The Knowledge Society,* ed. G. Böhme, N. Stehr, pp. 87–122. Dordrecht: Reidel

40. Clark, H. H., Wilkes-Gibbs, D. 1986. Referring as a collaborative process. *Cognition* 22:1–39

41. Clifford, J., Marcus, G., eds. 1986. *Writing Culture: The Poetics and Politics of Ethnography.* Berkeley: Univ. Calif. Press

42. Collins, J. 1985. *Conversation and knowledge in bureaucratic settings.* Presented at Ann. Meet. Am. Anthropol. Assoc., 84th, Washington, D.C.

43. Collins, J. 1986. Differential treatment in reading instruction. See Ref. 47, pp. 117–37.

44. Collins, J. 1987. *Hegemonic practice: literacy and standard language in public education.* Presented at Ann. Meet. Am. Anthropol. Assoc., 86th, Chicago

45. Comaroff, J. L. 1975. Talking politics: oratory and authority in a Tswana chiefdom. See Ref. 23, pp. 141–63

46. Comaroff, J. L., Roberts, S. 1981. *Rules and Processes: The Cultural Logic of Dispute in an African Context.* Chicago: Univ. Chicago Press

47. Cook-Gumperz, J., ed. 1986. *The Social Construction of Literacy.* Cambridge: Cambridge Univ. Press

48. Culler, J. 1975. *Structural Poetics: Structuralism, Linguistics and the Study of Literature.* Ithaca, N.Y.: Cornell Univ. Press

49. Culler, J. 1981. *The Pursuit of Signs: Semiotics, Literature and Deconstruction.* Ithaca, N.Y.: Cornell Univ. Press

50. Daneš, F. 1964. A three-level approach to syntax. In *Travaux Linguistiques de Prague,* Vol. 1, pp. 225–40. Prague: Éditions l'Académie Tchécoslovaque Sciences

51. Daneš, F., ed. 1974. *Papers on Functional Sentence Perspective.* Prague: Academia

52. de Man, P. 1971. *Blindness and Insight: Essays in the Rhetoric of Contemporary Criticism.* New York: Oxford Univ. Press

53. Derrida, J. 1978. *Writing and Difference.* Transl. A. Bass. London: Routledge & Kegan Paul

53a. De Saussure, F. 1972. *Cours de Linguistique Générale.* Édition critique préparée par T. de Mauro. Paris: Payot

54. Dillon, G. L., Coleman, L., Fahnestock, J., Agar, M. 1985. Review of Brown and Yule, *Discourse Analysis;* Leech, *Principles of Pragmatics;* and Levinson, *Pragmatics. Language* 61(2):446–60

55. DuBois, J. W. 1987. The discourse basis of ergativity. *Language* 63(4):805–55

56. Ducrot, O. 1984. *Le Dire et le Dit.* Paris: Les Éditions de Minuit

56a. Duranti, A. 1984. Lauga and talanoaga: two speech genres in a Samoan political event. See Ref. 30, pp. 217–42

57. Duranti, A., Brenneis, D., eds. 1986. The audience as co-author. *Text* 6(3):Spec. Issue

58. Eagle, H. J. 1981. Verse as a semiotic system: Tynjanov, Jakobson, Mukařovsky. *Slav. East Eur. J.* 25(4):47–61

59. Eco, U. 1984. *Semiotics and the Philosophy of Language.* Bloomington: Indiana Univ. Press

60. Edmonson, M. 1970. Metáfora Maya en literatura y en arte. In *Verh. 37th Int. Amerikanistenkongr,* Munich, pp. 37–50

61. Edmonson, M. S., ed. 1985. *Supplement to the Handbook of Middle American Indians,* Vol. 3: *Literatures.* Austin: Univ. Texas Press

62. Errington, J. J. 1988. *Structure and Style in Javanese: A Semiotic View of Linguistic Etiquette.* Philadelphia: Univ. Pa. Press

63. Feld, S. 1982. *Sound and Sentiment: Birds, Weeping, Poetics and Song in Kaluli Expression.* Philadelphia: Univ. Pa. Press

63a. Feld, S., Schieffelin, B. B. 1982. Hard talk: a functional basis for Kaluli discourse. See Ref. 202, pp. 350–70

64. Fillmore, C. 1985. Frames and semantics of understanding. *Quad. Semant.* 5(2): 222–54

65. Firbas, J. 1964. On defining the theme in functional sentence perspective. In *Travaux Linguistiques de Prague,* Vol. 1, pp. 267–80. Prague: Editions l'Académie Tchécoslovaque Sciences

66. Firbas, J. 1974. Some aspects of the Czechoslovak approach to problems of functional sentence perspective. See Ref. 51, pp. 11–37

67. Foley, W. A., Van Valin, R. D. Jr. 1984. *Functional Syntax and Universal Grammar.* Cambridge: Cambridge Univ. Press

68. Foucault, M. 1972. *The Archeology of Knowledge.* Transl. A. M. Sheridan Smith. New York: Pantheon

69. Fought, J. 1985. Cyclic patterns in Chorti (Mayan) literature. See Ref. 61, pp. 147–70

70. Friedrich, P. 1979. *Language, Context and the Imagination.* Selected and introduced by A. S. Dil. Stanford: Stanford Univ. Press

71. Friedrich, P. 1986. *The Language Parallax: Linguistic Relativism and Poetic Indeterminacy.* Austin: Univ. Texas Press

72. Galan, F. W. 1978. Toward a structural literary history: the contribution of Felix Vodička. See Ref. 150, pp. 456–76

73. Galan, F. W. 1985. *Historic Structures: The Prague School Project, 1928–1946.* Austin: Univ. Texas Press

74. Garibay, A. M. 1953. *Historia de la Literatura Nahuatl,* Vols. 1, 2. Mexico City: Porrua

74a. Garvin, P., ed. and transl. 1964. *A Prague School Reader on Esthetics, Literary Structure and Style.* Washington, DC: Georgetown Univ. Press

74b. Geertz, C. 1987. Deep play: notes on the Balinese cockfight. See Ref. 175, pp. 195–240

75. Goffman, E. 1974. *Frame Analysis: An Essay on the Organization of Experience.* New York: Harper Colophon Books

76. Goffman, E. 1981. *Forms of Talk.* Philadelphia: Univ. Pa. Press

77. Goodman, N. 1976. *Languages of Art.* Indianapolis: Hackett

78. Goody, J., ed. 1968. *Literacy in Traditional Societies.* Cambridge: Cambridge Univ. Press

79. Goody, J., Watt, I. P. 1963. The consequences of literacy. *Comp. Stud. Hist. Soc.* 5:304–45

80. Goodwin, C. 1981. *Conversational Organization: Interaction Between Speakers and Hearers.* New York: Academic

81. Goodwin, C. 1984. Notes on story structure and the organization of participation. See Ref. 5, pp. 225–46

82. Goodwin, M. H. 1982. "Instigating": storytelling as social process. *Am. Ethnol.* 9:799–819

83. Goodwin, M. H. 1988. *Retellings, pretellings and hypothetical stories.* Presented at Ann. Meet. Am. Anthropol. Assoc., 87th, Phoenix

84. Gossen, G. 1974. *Chamulas in the World of the Sun.* Cambridge: Harvard Univ. Press

85. Gossen, G. H. 1985. Tzotzil literature. See Ref. 61, pp. 65–106

86. Green, B. S. 1988. *Literary Methods and Sociological Theory: Case Studies of Simmel and Weber.* Chicago/London: Univ. Chicago Press

87. Grice, H. P. 1975. Logic and conversation. In *Syntax and Semantics 3: Speech Acts,* ed. P. Cole, J. Morgan, pp. 41–58. New York: Academic

88. Gumperz, J. 1977. Sociocultural knowledge in conversational inference. See Ref. 182a, pp. 191–212

89. Gumperz, J. 1982. *Discourse Strategies.* Cambridge: Cambridge Univ. Press

90. Gumperz, J., ed. 1982. *Language and Social Identity.* Cambridge: Cambridge Univ. Press

91. Halliday, M. A. K. 1985. *An Introduction to Functional Grammar.* London: Edward Arnold Publishers Ltd.

92. Halliday, M. A. K., Hasan, R. 1976. *Cohesion in English.* London: Longman Group Ltd.

93. Hamon, P. (1972). 1982. What is a description? See Ref. 205, pp. 147–78

94. Hancher, M. 1979. The classification of cooperative illocutionary acts. *Lang. Soc.* 8:1–14

95. Hanks, W. F. 1984. Sanctification, structure and experience in a Yucatec Maya ritual event. *J. Am. Folklore* 97(384):131–66

96. Hanks, W. F. 1986. Authenticity and ambivalence in the text: a colonial Maya case. *Am. Ethnol.* 13(4):721–44

97. Hanks, W. F. 1987. Discourse genres in a theory of practice. *Am. Ethnol.* 14(4): 668–92

98. Hanks, W. F. 1988. Grammar, style and meaning in a Maya manuscript. *Int. J. Am. Linguist.* 54(3):331–64

99. Hanks, W. F. 1988. *The interactive basis of indexical reference.* Presented at Month. Meet. Chicago Linguist. Soc., December, 1988

100. Hanks, W. F. 1989. Elements of Maya style. See Ref. 102

101. Hanks, W. F. 1989. Metalanguage and pragmatics of deixis. See Ref. 147

102. Hanks, W. F., Rice, D. S., eds. 1989. *Word and Image in Mayan Culture: Essays on Language and Iconography.* Salt Lake City: Univ. Utah Press

103. Haviland, J. 1986. Con buenos chiles: talk, targets and teasing in Zinacantan. *Text* 6:249–82

104. Havránek, B. 1964. The functional differentiation of the standard language. See Ref. 74a, pp. 3–16

104a. Hill, J., Irvine, J. 1989. *Responsibility and Evidence in Oral Discourse.* Cambridge: Cambridge Univ. Press

105. Hofling, C. A. 1989. The morphosyntactic basis of discourse structure in glyphic text in the Dresden Codex. See Ref. 102

106. Horn, L. R. 1988. Pragmatic theory. In *Linguistic Theory: Foundations.* Linguistics: The Cambridge Ser., ed. F. J. Newmeyer, 1:113–45. Cambridge: Cambridge Univ. Press

106a. Hrushovski, B. 1980. The meaning of sound patterns in poetry: an interaction theory. *Poetics Today* (Spec. Issue, Roman Jakobson: Language and Literature) 2(1a):39–56

107. Hymes, D. 1974. *Foundations in Sociolinguistics.* Philadelphia: Univ. Pa. Press

108. Hymes, D. 1977. Discovering oral performance and measured verse in American Indian narrative. *New Lit. Hist.* 8(3):431–57

109. Hymes, D. 1981. *"In Vain I Tried to Tell You": Essays in Native American Ethnopoetics.* Philadelphia: Univ. Pa. Press

110. Hymes, D. 1987. Tonkawa poetics: John Rush Buffalo's "Coyote and Eagle's daughter." See Ref. 188, pp. 17–61

111. Ingarden, R. 1973. *The Literary Work of Art: An Investigation on the Borderlines of Ontology, Logic and Theory of Literature.* Transl. G. Grabowicz. Evanston: Northwestern Univ. Press (From German)

112. Irvine, J. 1985. Status and style in language. *Annu. Rev. Anthropol.* 14:557–81

113. Iser, W. 1980. The reading process: a phenomenological aproach. See Ref. 206, pp. 50–69

114. Jacobsen, W. H. Jr. 1967. Switch-reference in Hokan-Coahuiltecan. In *Studies in Southwestern Ethnolinguistics,* ed. D. Hymes, W. Bittle, pp. 238–63. The Hague: Mouton

115. Jakobson, R. 1960. Concluding statement: linguistics and poetics. In *Style in Language,* ed. T. A. Sebeok, pp. 350–77. Cambridge, Mass.: MIT Press

116. Jakobson, R. 1971. Shifters, verbal categories and the Russian verb. In *Selected Writings of Roman Jakobson,* Vol. 2: *Word and Language,* pp. 130–47. The Hague: Mouton

117. Jakobson, R. 1980. Metalanguage as a linguistic problem. In *The Framework of Language by Roman Jakobson.* Michigan Stud. Humanities, pp. 81–92. Ann Arbor: Univ. Mich. Press

118. Jakobson, R. 1985. *Verbal Art, Verbal Sign, Verbal Time,* ed. K. Pomorska, S. Rudy. Minneapolis: Univ. Minn. Press

119. Jameson, F. 1972. *The Prison-House of Language.* Princeton, N.J.: Princeton Univ. Press

120. Jameson, F. 1981. *The Political Unconscious.* Ithaca, N.Y.: Cornell Univ. Press

121. Jameson, F. 1984. Literary innovation and modes of production: a commentary. *Mod. Clin. Lit.* 1(1):67–77

122. Jameson, F. 1986. Third-World literature in the era of multinational capitalism. *Soc. Text* 15:65–87

123. Jauss, H. R. 1982. *Toward an Aesthetic of Reception: Theory and History of Literature.* Vol. 2. Transl. T. Bahti. Minneapolis: Univ. Minn. Press (From German)

124. Jenny, L. (1976). 1982. The strategy of form. See Ref. 205, pp. 34–63

125. Johnson, M. 1987. *The Body in the Mind: The Bodily Basis of Meaning, Imagination and Reason.* Chicago: Univ. Chicago Press

126. Johnson-Laird, P. N. 1983. *Mental Models.* Cambridge: Cambridge Univ. Press

127. Josserand, K. J. 1987. *The discourse structure of Maya hieroglyphic texts.* Presented at the Ann. Meet. Am. Anthropol. Assoc., 86th, Chicago

127a. Justeson, J., Campbell, L., eds. 1984. *Phoneticism in Mayan Hieroglyphic Writing.* Publ. 9. Albany, N.Y.: Inst. Mesoamerican Stud., State Univ. N.Y. Albany

128. Kellner, H. 1978. On the cognitive significance of the system of language in communication. In *Phenomenology and Sociology,* ed. T. Luckmann, pp. 324–42. New York: Penguin Books

129. Kittay, J., Godzich, W. 1987. *The Emergence of Prose: An Essay in Prosaics.* Minneapolis: Univ. Minn. Press

130. Kristeva, J. 1969. *Semiotikè.* Paris: Seuil

131. Kristeva, J. 1974. *La Révolution du Langage Poétique.* Paris: Seuil

132. Kučera, H., Cowper, E. 1978. Functional sentence perspective revisited. See Ref. 150, pp. 191–230

133. Kuno, S. 1978. Three perspectives in the functional approach to syntax. See Ref. 150, pp. 119–90

134. Labov, W. 1972. *Sociolinguistic Patterns.* Philadelphia: Univ. Pa. Press

135. Labov, W., Fanshel, D. 1977. *Therapeutic Discourse.* New York: Academic

136. Laclau, E., Mouffe, C. 1983. Beyond the positivity of the social: antagonism and hegemony. In *Hegemony and Socialist Strategy: Towards a Radical Democratic Politics,* Ch. 3:93–148. London: Verso

137. Lakoff, G. 1987. *Women, Fire and Dangerous Things: What Categories Reveal About the Mind.* Chicago: Univ. Chicago Press

137a. Lee, B., Postone, M. 1987. Narrative structure and the reading of Marx. *Work. Pap. Proc. Cent. Psychosoc. Stud. 12.* Chicago: Cent. Psychosoc. Stud.

138. Lee, L. 1987. *Voices from the Iron House: A Study of Lu Xun.* Bloomington: Indiana Univ. Press

139. Lessing, G. E. 1969. *Laocoon: An Essay Upon the Limits of Poetry and Painting.* Transl. E. Frothingham. New York: Farrar, Strauss & Giroux

140. Levinson, S. C. 1983. *Pragmatics.* Cambridge: Cambridge Univ. Press

141. Levinson, S. C. 1988. Putting linguistics on a proper footing: explorations in Goffman's concepts of participation. In *Erving Goffman,* ed. P. Drew, A. Woolton, pp. 161–293. Cambridge: Polity Press

142. Li, C., ed. 1976. *Subject and Topic.* New York: Academic

143. Lord, A. 1960. *The Singer of Tales.* Cambridge: Harvard Univ. Press

144. Lounsbury, F. G. 1980. Some problems in the interpretation of the mythological portion of the hieroglyphic text of the Temple of the Cross at Palenque. In *Third Palenque Round Table, 1978,* Part 2, ed. M. G. Robertson, pp. 99–115. Austin: Univ. Texas Press

145. Lounsbury, F. G. 1989. The names of a king: hieroglyphic variants as a key to decipherment. See Ref. 102

146. Lu, X. 1980. *Selected Works.* Vol. 1. Transl. X, Yang, G. Yang. Beijing: Foreign Languages Press. 2nd ed.

147. Lucy, J., ed. 1989. *Reflexive Language: Reported Speech and Metapragmatics.* Cambridge: Cambridge Univ. Press

148. Luong, H. 1988. Discursive practices and power structure: person referring forms and sociopolitical struggles in colonial Vietnam. *Am. Ethnol.* 15(2):239–53

149. Lyons, J. 1977. *Semantics,* Vols. 1, 2. Cambridge: Cambridge Univ. Press

150. Matejka, L., ed. 1978. *Sound, Sign and Meaning: Quinquagenary of the Prague Linguistic Circle.* Mich. Slavic Contrib. 6. Ann Arbor: Univ. Michigan Press

151. McLendon, S. 1977. Cultural presupposition and discourse analysis: Patterns of presupposition and assertion of information in Eastern Pomo and Russian narrative. See Ref. 182a, pp. 153–90

152. McLendon, S. 1982. Meaning, rhetorical structure and discourse organization in myth. See Ref. 202, pp. 284–305

153. Mehan, H. 1979. *Learning Lessons: Social Organization in the Classroom.* Cambridge: Cambridge Univ. Press

154. Mertz, E. 1987. "Realist" models of judicial decision-making. *Work. Pap. Proc. Cent. Psychosoc. Stud. 15.* Chicago: Cent. Psychosoc. Stud.

155. Mitchell, W. J. T. 1986. *Iconology: Image, Text, Ideology.* Chicago/London: Univ. Chicago Press

156. Morgan, J. L. 1982. Discourse theory and the independence of sentence grammar. See Ref. 202, pp. 196–204

157. Morris, C. 1971. *Writings on the General Theory of Signs.* The Hague: Mouton

158. Morson, G. S. 1981. *The Boundaries of Genre: Dostoevsky's Diary of a Writer and the Traditions of Literary Utopia.* Austin: Univ. Texas Press

159. Morson, G. S., ed. 1981. *Bakhtin: Essays and Dialogues on His Work.* Chicago: Univ. Chicago Press

160. Mukařovsky, J. 1964. The esthetics of language. See Ref. 74a, pp. 31–70

161. Mukařovsky, J. 1977. *The Word and Verbal Art: Selected Essays by Jan Mukařovsky.* Transl., ed. J. Burbank, P. Steiner. New Haven/London: Yale Univ. Press

162. Mukařovsky, J. (1941). 1982. Structuralism in esthetics and in literary studies. See Ref. 200, pp. 65–82

163. Norman, W. 1980. Grammatical parallelism in Quiché ritual language. *Proc. Annu. Meet. Berkeley Linguist. Soc.* 6:387–99

164. Norris, C. 1982. *Deconstruction: Theory and Practice.* London/New York: Metheun

165. Ochs, E., Schieffelin, B. B. 1983. *Acquiring Conversational Competence.* London: Routledge & Kegan Paul

166. Oh, C. K., Dineen, D. A., eds. 1979. *Syntax and Semantics,* Vol. 11: *Presupposition.* New York: Academic

167. Ortner, S. 1984. Theory in anthropology since the sixties. *Comp. Stud. Soc. Hist.* 26:126–66

168. Parmentier, R. 1987. Naturalization of convention. *Work. Pap. Proc. Cent. Psychosoc. Stud. 17.* Chicago: Cent. Psychosoc. Stud.

169. Parmentier, R. 1989. The political function of reported speech: a Belauan example. See Ref. 147

170. Peirce, C. S. 1955. Logic as semiotic: the theory of signs. In *Philosophical Writings of Peirce,* ed. J. Buchler, pp. 98–119. New York: Dover

171. Prague Lingusitic Circle. (1929). 1982. Thesis presented to the First Congress of Slavic Philologists in Prague, 1929. See Ref. 200, pp. 3–31

172. Prince, E. F. 1981. Toward a taxonomy of given-new information. In *Radical Pragmatics,* ed. P. Cole, pp. 223–56. New York: Academic

173. Prince, G. 1980. Introduction to the study of the narative. See Ref. 206, pp. 7–25

174. Propp, V. 1958. *Morphology of the Folktale.* Transl. S. Pirkova-Jakobson. Bloomington: Indiana Res. Cent. Anthropol.

175. Rabinow, P., Sullivan, W. M., eds. 1987. *Interpretive Social Science: A Second Look.* Berkeley: Univ. Calif. Press

176. Ricoeur, P. 1971. The model of the text: meaningful action considered as a text. *Soc. Res.* 38(3):529–62

177. Rieger, L. (1941). 1982. The semantic analysis of philosophical texts. See Ref. 200, pp. 83–102

178. Riffaterre, M. (1971). 1982. Models of the literary sentence. See Ref. 205, pp. 18–33

178a. Rosengrant, S. 1980. The theoretical criticism of Jurij Tynjanov. *Comp. Lit.* 32(4):355–89

179. Ruwet, N. (1975). 1982. Parallelism and deviation in poetry. See Ref. 205, pp. 92–124

180. Said, E. 1975. *Beginnings: Intention and Method.* Baltimore/London: Johns Hopkins Univ. Press

181. Said, E. 1985. An ideology of difference. *Crit. Inq.* 12(1):38–58

182. Sanchez, M., Blount B. G., eds. 1975. *Sociocultural Dimensions of Language Use.* New York: Academic

182a. Saville-Troike, M., ed. 1977. *Linguistics and Anthropology.* Proc. Georgetown Univ. Round Table on Lang. & Linguist., 1977. Washington, D.C.: Georgetown Univ. Press

182b. Schegloff, E. A. 1982. Discourse as an interactional achievement: some uses of 'Uh huh' and other things that come between sentences. See Ref. 202, pp. 71–93

183. Schegloff, E., Sacks, H. 1973. Opening up closings. *Semiotica* 8:289–327

184. Schutz, A. 1973. *Collected Papers I: The Problem of Social Reality,* ed. M. Natanson. The Hague: Martinus Nijhoff

185. Searle, J. 1976. *Speech Acts: An Essay in the Philosophy of Language.* Cambridge: Cambridge Univ. Press

186. Searle, J. 1979. Literal meaning. In *Expression and Meaning: Studies in the Theory of Speech Acts,* pp. 117–36. Cambridge: Cambridge Univ. Press

187. Sherzer, J. 1983. *Kuna Ways of Speaking: An Ethnographic Perspective.* Austin: Univ. Texas Press

187a. Sherzer, J. 1987. Poetic structuring of Kuna discourse: the line. See Ref. 188, pp. 103–39

187b. Sherzer, J., Woodbury, A. C., eds. 1987. Introduction. See Ref. 188, pp. 1–17

188. Sherzer, J., Woodbury, A. C., eds. 1987. *Native American Discourse: Poetics and Rhetoric.* Cambridge: Cambridge Univ. Press

189. Silverman, D., Torode, B. 1980. *The Material Word: Some Theories of Language and Its Limits.* London: Routledge & Kegan Paul

190. Silverman, K. 1983. *The Subject of Semiotics.* New York: Oxford Univ. Press

191. Silverstein, M. 1976. Shifters, linguistic categories and cultural description. In *Meaning in Anthropology,* ed. K. H. Basso, H. A. Selby, pp. 11–55. Albuquerque: Univ. New Mexico Press

192. Silverstein, M. 1985. The culture of language in Chinookan narrative texts; or, On saying that . . . in Chinook. In *Grammar Inside and Outside the Clause,* ed. J. Nichols, A. C. Woodbury, pp. 132–71. Cambridge: Cambridge Univ. Press

193. Silverstein, M. 1985. The functional stratification of language and ontogenesis. In *Culture, Communication and Cognition: Vygotskian Perspectives,* ed. J. V. Wertsch, pp. 205–35. Cambridge: Cambridge Univ. Press

194. Silverstein, M. 1985. On the pragmatic "poetry" of prose: parallelism, repetition and cohesive structure in the time course of dyadic conversation. In *Meaning, Form and Use in Context: Linguistic Applications,* ed. D. Schiffrin. Proc. Georgetown Univ. Round Table on Lang. & Linguist., 1984, pp. 189–99. Washington, D.C.: Georgetown Univ. Press

195. Silverstein, M. 1987. The three faces of "function:" preliminaries to a psychology of language. In *Social and Functional Approaches to Language and Thought.* ed. M. Hickmann, pp. 17–38. Orlando: Academic

196. Spivak, G. C. 1985. Three women's texts and a critique of imperialism. *Crit. Inq.* 12(1):243–61

197. Stalnaker, R. 1974. Pragmatic presuppositions. In *Semantics and Philosophy,* ed. M. Munitz, P. Unger, pp. 197–214. New York: New York Univ. Press

198. Stalpers, J. 1988. The maturity of discourse analysis (review article). *Lang. Soc.* 17(1):87–98

199. Steiner, P. 1982. The roots of structuralist esthetics. See Ref. 200, pp. 174–219

200. Steiner, P., ed. 1982. *The Prague School, Selected Writings, 1929–1946.* Transl. J. Burbank, O. Hasty, M. Jacobson, B. Kochis, W. Steiner. Austin: Univ. Texas Press

201. Steiner, W., ed. 1981. *The Sign in Music and Literature.* Austin: Univ. Texas Press

202. Tannen, D., ed. 1982. *Analyzing Discourse: Text and Talk.* Proc. Georgetown Univ. Round Table on Lang. & Linguist., 1981. Washington, D.C.: Georgetown Univ. Press

203. Tay, W. 1984. Wang Meng, stream-of-consciousness and the controversy over modernism. *Mod. Chin. Lit.* 1(1):7–24

204. Tedlock, D. 1983. *The Spoken Word and the Work of Interpretation.* Philadelphia: Univ. Pa. Press

204a. Tedlock, D. 1987. Hearing a voice in an ancient text: Quiché Maya poetics in performance. See Ref. 188, pp. 140–75

205. Todorov, T., ed. 1982. *French Literary Theory Today.* Cambridge/Paris: Cambridge Univ. Press and Editions de la Maison des Sciences de l' Homme

206. Tompkins, J. P., ed. 1980. *Reader Response Criticism: From Formalism to Post-Structuralism.* Baltimore: Johns Hopkins Univ. Press

206a. Tsitsipis, L. 1988. Language shift and narrative performance: on the structure and function of Arvanítika narratives. *Lang. Soc.* 17(1):61–87

207. Turner, K. 1987. Bringing it all back: Joel Sherzer and the San Blas Kuna. *Int. J. Am. Linguist.* 53(1):86–102

208. Turner, T. 1977. Narrative structure and mythopoeisis: a critique and reformulation of structuralist approaches to myth and poetics. *Arethusa* 10(1):103–63

209. Turner, T. 1985. Animal symbolism, totemism and the structure of myth. In *Animal Myths and Metaphors in South America,* ed. G. Urton, pp. 49–106. Salt Lake City: Univ. Utah Press

210. Turner, T. 1988. *"We become araras": operational structures and the play of tropes in Gê and Bororo ritual and culture.* Presented at Annu. Meet. Am. Anthropol. Assoc., 87th, Phoenix

211. Tyler, S. 1978. *The Said and the Unsaid: Mind, Meaning and Culture.* New York: Academic

212. Tynianov, Y. (1924). 1981. *The Problem of Verse Language.* Transl., ed. M. Sosa, B. Harvey. Ann Arbor, Mich.: Ardis

213. Urban, G. 1986. Ceremonial dialogues in South America. *Am. Anthropol.* 88(2):371–86

214. Urban, G. 1986. Semiotic functions of macro-parallelism in Shoklain origin myths. In *Native South American Discourse,* ed. J. Sherzer, G. Urban. The Hague: Mouton

215. van Dijk, T. A. 1977. *Text and Context.* London: Longman

216. van Dijk, T. A. 1982. Episodes as units of discourse analysis. See Ref. 202, pp. 177–95

217. van Dijk, T. A., ed. 1985. *Handbook of Discourse Analysis,* Vols. 1, 2, 3, 4. New York: Academic

218. Vodička, F. 1964. The history of the echo of literary works. See Ref. 74a, pp. 71–82

219. Vodička, F. (1941). 1982. The concretization of the literary work: problems of the reception of Neruda's works. See Ref. 200, pp. 103–34

220. Vološinov, V. N. 1986. *Marxism and the Philosophy of Language.* Transl. L. Matejka, I. R. Titunik. Cambridge, Mass.: Harvard Univ. Press

221. Wang, M. 1983. *The Butterfly and Other Stories.* Beijing: Panda Books

222. Weinreich, U. 1980. *On Semantics,* ed. W. Labov. Philadelphia: Univ. Pa. Press

222a. Wertsch, J. V. 1987. Modes of discourse in the nuclear arms debate. *Work. Pap. Proc. Cent. Psychosoc. Stud. 8.* Chicago: Cent. Psychosoc. Stud.

222b. Wertsch, J. V. 1988. Voices of the mind. *Work. Pap. Proc. Cent. Psychosoc. Stud. 19.* Chicago: Cent. Psychosoc. Stud.

223. Woodbury, A. C. 1985. Functions of rhetorical structure: a study of Central Alaskan Yupik Eskimo discourse. *Lang. Soc.* 14:150–93

224. Woodbury, A. C. 1987. Rhetorical structure in a Central Alaskan Yupik Eskimo traditional narrative. See Ref. 188, pp. 176–239

7

The Five Gourds of Memory

THE MEMORY IN THE PRESENT

$\mathbf{F}$austo Bolon in Yotholin arrived at Don Séeb's home at about four in the afternoon January 21, 1990. He was complaining of intestinal cramps and sleepless nights. He came requesting that Don Séeb, a well-known *hmèen* 'shaman' (lit. 'do-er'), diagnose and treat him. He was accompanied by his wife and young child, as is typical for such afternoon visits. The long sun barely glimpsed through the packed earth walls of Don Séeb's house. That night it would be cold again, and Don Séeb, committed to poverty, would sleep by the altar. He would shiver in the dampness. It reminded him of sleeping in the forest, where you feel the cold most.

Fausto and his wife sit behind the altar as Don Séeb steps forward and sits facing the *sàantos* 'saints (images)'. Reaching out with his right hand, he takes down the *lùuč* 'gourd bowl' in which he keeps his seven crystals, soaking in the holy water they require to cool their fire. (Crystals are burning hot and if left unattended, they risk cracking from their own heat.) The candle is lit. He begins his prayer:

(1)   *Pór la señal de la sàanta krùus*
              del nuestro enemìigo lìibrenos
                    señor dyòos pàadre
          En el nòombre del pàadre
              del ʔìiho
                    de los espiritu sàanto → ##

          ↑_ _↑
          Pádre mio saás in síʔipi
          ʔuúč inkuta tučùun amèesa
                    inmaánsih kwèenta ti a dyòosil
                    impresentartik teč bʼin šan
          bʼeʔ òora tuyoóʔl amèesa
                    ↓_ _↓
                    le sùuhuy kristal → ##

197

> By the sign of the sacred Cross
> from our enemies free us
> Lord God the Father
> In the name of the Father
> of the Son
> of the Holy Spirits. ##
> Father of mine forgive my sin
> of sitting at the base of your altar
> to pass the word to your gods
> to present to you too
> now atop your altar
> the blessed crystals. ##

[## indicates point at which Don Séeb draws a breath.] (AV.03.47.40)

These are the first breaths of the opening prayer of the ritual genre called *tiič'k'áak'* 'illumination', a kind of divination practiced by many Maya shamans, including Don Séeb.[1] The term means literally 'hold out fire in hand', as one does with a torch on a dark path (and it is commonly used in this everyday sense). It involves the use of marble-like crystals to literally see events and states of affairs not actually present. In some cases, the shaman looks into the body of the patient, seeing an illness or misplaced wind. In others, he looks into the earth of the patient's home or productive land, seeing otherwise invisible malevolent winds. In both cases, the evil thing appears in the crystal as a wisp of smoke, which sometimes has the outline form of the intruding wind itself.[2] The crystals are called *kristal* 'crystal(s)' or *sáastun* 'light rocks', a term that reflects the pervasive focus on vision in this ritual genre.

The overall dynamic of *tiič'k'áak'* 'illumination' involves a mutual orientation between spirits and humans. Don Séeb addresses the *yuneilô'ob* 'lords' in prayer, asking them to turn their gaze upon the matter at hand. They in turn provide an image in the glass, which Don Séeb can interpret and convey to the patient. Gazing intently into the crystals for 2 minutes 57 seconds, he sees what is wrong with Fausto: he has been struck by a *'ìik'* 'wind', a low grade wind that lives beneath the surface of the earth and wanders at about waist level above the ground, causing illness in those with whom it collides (AV.03.52.18). Fausto was naturally concerned with the circumstances of this encounter, and Don Séeb told him that it had taken place in the Puuc hills just south of Yotholin, where he lives, and Oxkutzcab, where they were at the time. He had evidently walked past the mouth of a cave or an old *sahkab* 'limestone pit' (lit. 'white earth') at the wrong moment, for its air had struck him squarely in the gut.

The treatment would be straightforward, mostly. For Fausto's present symptoms he should bathe in a mixture of rubbing alcohol and a sachet of powders that Don Séeb gave him. This would fortify the superficial *b'ak'el* 'flesh' in the places it had been struck. Each day he would also drink an infusion of another powder in warm water, to relax and flush out the inner organs. There were four more sachets of powders, which Don Séeb numbered 1–4. They were to be drunk one per day (AV.04.17.13). The most important step Fausto would have to take, though, was to make an offering out in his yard, near the foothills of the Puuc. Five gourds of *sakab'*, a milky corn gruel that Maya people offer with prayers when petitioning the divine. Don Séeb asked about the *sakab'* at the outset of his diagnosis: *Kaʼ 'iik wá uăan sakaʼil apiʼuk?* 'Do you give the little *sacab'* of your Puuc?', he asked, meaning more or less 'do you make gruel offerings for the benefit of the Puuc hills near your home?' Fausto responded:

(2)	FB	*Máʼ ač*	Not really,
	DS	*Hŋŋ* ↑	Huh?
	FB	*Hmʼ* ↓	Nope.
	DS	*Máʼ umpuliʼ iʼ*	Never?
	FB	*Mpuliʼ*	Nope.
	DS	*Máʼ sùuk teč iʼ*	You're not used to it.
	FB	*ĉeén impàadres [...]*	Just my parents, [...]
		tóʼ oneʼ máač k hač bin	We don't really go [to do it] [...]
		kàasi [...]	
	DS	*Pwes yahi beyoʼ* ↓ *[...] lelaʼ*	Well that's too bad [...] This one's
		kuk'aátik	asking for it.

[FB = Fausto Bolon; DS = Don Séeb]   (AV.03.52.18)

The guardians of the land were asking for five gourds of *sakab'*, and Fausto's distress was their sign. His wife interjected that they did not even know the prayers that had to be said when you make an offering (AV.03.57.45).

Virtually any adult Maya person would know that to give *sakab'* is to make a ritual offering in both word and action. Fausto and his wife had seen his father do it, but did not know the words. They did not know the actions either, and Don Séeb had to explain that they were to offer five gourds in their own yard, probably right outside the house. The woman quipped that she only owned four gourds, and would have to buy another. Don Séeb made it clear that the crucial number is five (AV.04.22.00). Meanwhile, he recommended a *saántiguar* 'sanctification', a basic blessing that lasts about ten minutes. Fausto sat facing the *santos* on the altar as Don Séeb chanted the blessing, standing behind him to his right, brushing his body lightly with the fresh flowers in his right hand, occasionally touching his back with the fingertips of his left. He seemed to feel better afterward, and they took their leave with a new lightness.

Later that day, Don Séeb described the conditions under which he had first acquired his vocation as a shaman. Among the Yucatec, as is common in cultures in which shamanism is practiced, the charismatic experiences of an initiate are often shaped into a narrative, a story or set of stories which are then told, in part or in whole, for pedagogical purposes. It is of course an emblem of the real shaman that he (or rarely she) have direct encounters with spirits, whom the local people call variously *yunĉilóʼ ob* 'lords', *ʼìik'óʼ ob* 'winds', and *(ʼúuĉben) máakóʼ ob* '(old) people'. Yet the selective display of the story instructs the patient or audience at the same time that it legitimates the teller. One of the key roles that shamans play is as teachers. On this particular afternoon, Don Séeb would tell his story in nearly full form before a Hi 8 video camera, as his daughter-in-law, three grandsons, his off-key apprentice, and a filmmaker watched on. He would tell how he got lost in the woods that night many years ago, how he was unconscious for seven days and finally came to his senses, awakened by the wind and the singing of birds; all the things he saw when he returned, all the spirits he encountered and tests he endured; how he fell to his knees and thanked God upon awakening; how he offered five gourds and *sakab'* each day for nine days running after that; how the visions continued during dreams and noctural encounters in a wakened state. The only thing lacking in this telling, according to our plan, would be the names and locations of his spirits. This he chose to withhold, since it would allow other people to address and move them.[3]

Don Séeb and I had talked for several years about making a film of his practice. We had first met thirteen years earlier when he performed a *č'áa čáak* rain ceremony at an agricultural cooperative where I was working. Unable to speak Maya at the time, I had had to wait until three years later when we would meet again, by chance, and our work together would begin in earnest. With time, Don Séeb began to talk about making a film, so that people all around Yucatán could see his religion. He recognized that my writings on the topic could never achieve this end. After all, how many people in rural Yucatán can read English, and even if they could, how would they get books from North America? In the face of evangelical Protestantism, rural medicine and the pressures of government agencies, he felt, the old religion was being forgotten in contemporary Yucatán—*tub'in utuú'sá'al* 'it is being forgotten'. The tragedy, as he sees it, is that this religion is really autochthonous, genuine, and true. It is *maya* 'Maya', *indio* 'Indian', *hač wayil e'* 'really from here', consubstantial with the past in which the great pyramids were fully inhabited, and the Maya conversed (*čikbal*) fluently with birds and animals. In his everyday life and practice, he lives this ancient way, occupies its spaces and times, talks with its enchanted inhabitants, weaving them constantly into the present. What he hopes to achieve with a film is to *k'aáhsik* 'remind' people of this history, so that it will be *k'ahá'an* 'remembered'.

This paper is about forgetting and remembering, past and present. It is about the five gourds. It is guided by the aim of understanding how Don Séeb, as a *hmèen* 'shaman', conceives of tradition and sustains it in his very way of life. None of the terms in the discussion is innocent, but I will purposely proceed without lengthy definitions. The first step is to get a sense of how Don Séeb talks about remembering and forgetting, and the central role these things have in his shamanic practice. We begin with the story he told that afternoon in front of the camera, all about his first encounters with spirits.

THE MAKING OF A SHAMANIC CONSCIOUSNESS

As Don Séeb told it, it was nearly forty years ago when he was taken away by the *yunčiló'ob* 'lords'. He was about thirty-three at the time, working in the southern forest in a place called Pol Wacax (lit. 'head [of] cow'). He was tending his own small *milpa* '(unirrigated) corn field', living with his recently married second wife, in a small house in a clearing in the woods. Nearby was a great *ʔaákʼal čeʔ* 'wetland' covered with old forest that belonged to a wealthy *cʼùul* 'non-Maya person'. This person had decided to make a great *milpa* of his own, and had hired thirty men from the town of Mani to clear the forest with ax and machete. They were living together in a large *galerón* 'plank house' through the woods from Don Séeb's solitary homestead (AV.04.25.ff). As a gesture of friendship, the men invited Don Séeb to come hear *cikbal* 'conversation' at their house that night, and he went. One of them told a story called *Espejo de virtud* 'Mirror of virtue', a long and vivid narrative of events in a town, called Eč Balam 'Black Jaguar'. Don Séeb still tells the story often, but passed over it without any comment this time. He was more concerned with recalling what happened after he left the *galerón* at about 11:00 P.M.

He was returning home by the path he always took, when he suddenly lost his senses. As he put it:

(3) When I took my leave, I went to sleep. But when I left the plank house to go out on the path, I don't know how I got lost, my *ʔìikʼ* 'wind, animacy' was lost. My *tùukul* 'thought' was lost. I never arrived home. I forgot about it. I went somewhere else. I entered the woods. Surely, that's how people get lost. But my path wasn't gone, my *ʔìikʼ* was just forgotten. I was lost. My *náʔat* 'understanding' was lost, taken away. And I was taken away, my body was taken away. My *ʔìikʼ* did not awaken. I don't know how many days I disappeared from among the people, from my family. I didn't know anything at that time, because everything was lost, everything was forgotten to me (AV.04.24.51).

Don Séeb never made it home that night. He was taken away by the spirits for what later turned out to be seven days and nights. It is unclear what happened during this time. On other occasions, he has hinted at spirit encounters, but this time he passes over the week in the forest as though it were a void. Instead, what he underscores is that while he was unconscious, the thirty-odd local men were unable to find him, even using hunting dogs, including his own seven. It was as if, bereft of consciousness, the body became invisible as well.

Speaking from the viewpoint of those searching for him, Don Séeb says that *desaparecernahen* 'I disappeared' (F.33.B.6:38). What he means by this is that he became imperceptible to the search party, vanishing from their olfactory, auditory, visual, and tactual fields. The most dramatic evidence of this is that his own dogs were unable to track him. But this imperceptibility was only the outer view on what was an even more dramatic set of changes going on within. Table 7.1 summarizes the ones expressed in (3), assuming that the moment of his loss of consciousness marks the line between before and after.

For Don Séeb, being taken away apparently entailed total memory loss. As he stayed in the woods those seven days without food or water, he was severed from his own body and its sensory modalities, made into a sort of *tabula rasa*. The term *ʔìikʼ* can be paraphrased roughly as one's animacy, mobility, and overall 'wide awakeness' in the phenomenological sense of knowing where one is. It is significant that this same

TABLE **7.1** A Turning Point

BEFORE	AFTER
in plank house	on path homeward
in a group	alone
awake	asleep
with *ʔiik'*	*ʔiik'* lost
with *tùukul*	*tùukul* lost
homeward bound	home forgotten
oriented	lost in woods
with *ʔiik'*	*ʔiik'* forgotten
with understanding	understanding taken away
in control of body	body taken away
	all is forgotten

term is used to designate the winds that blow upon the earth, the spirits who are embodied in the wind, the breath each person draws, and the force that makes the blood circulate in the veins. Nor is this a matter of metaphorical extension from a single literal meaning. For Maya shamans, all of these referents are literally the same thing under different aspects.

To be awake, in one's senses, is described in Maya as being aware of, or 'remembering', one's wind, *k'aáh inwìik'* 'my wind is recalled (to me)'. A person who is unconscious is described as *tú'ub' uyìik'* 'his wind is forgotten (to him)', and to tell someone to 'get with it, pay attention!' one says *k'aáh awìik'* 'recall your wind!' This relation of remembering with being awake and forgetting with being asleep comes up repeatedly in Don Séeb's talk. We can see it in (3) where his first description of losing consciousness on the path refers to sleep. Under normal circumstances, when people sleep, their thought and understanding are freed from the confines of the body to wander the earth and experience through dreaming. Normally one loses one's *ʔiik'* 'breath, wind' only at death, but Don Séeb's was a special case. It was what we would call 'ecstasy', following Eliade (1968). Even so, it became clear that this ecstasy, although never labeled death, was for Don Séeb a kind of death (or at least a form of *má' kušá'an* 'not alive').[4]

When he came to in the forest Don Séeb found his senses little by little, leaning against a great tree. In his words, he was awakened by an *ʔiik'* 'wind', and regained his senses in a rapid sequence: first his vision, then his awareness of his own body (the sense of his own posture and ability to alter it), next his thought, then speech, and finally his hearing. With the latter sense comes the ability to return home, because it was the baying of his seven dogs that he finally heard and used to locate the path home.

(4) I awakened, then, my understanding, my thought, just like that. Just like you awaken when you sleep. I awakened. When I awakened there in the forest beneath a standing tree, my eyes looked up. I looked at the tree. It was huge and beautiful. But it was as if I were crucified, because my arms were outstretched (*siná'an*) like this [showing arms reaching to sides, cruciform]. I awakened, I awakened. I was leaning against the tree when I awakened and my thought returned. And an *ʔiik'* came to me to awaken me. So, instead of

moving my legs there at the foot of the tree, I knelt down and made a gesture upwards and raised my eyes, like this [showing gaze and prayerful posture]. And then I said to Hàa-hal Dios 'True God', God of all earth:

"My Lord, I don't know what happened to me, my thought was lost, but thank you, for you have awakened me. Now I have awakened. I feel that my ears have been opened. My thought has been opened. Thank you very much. *Dios Padre, Jesu Cristo, Espiritu Santu.* Pardon me for speaking to you from here where I am standing. I don't know what happened to me. Pardon me. Awaken my thought more. Help me to find my home because, my thought is not really open to my home."

So I waited awhile, and then I heard the barking of my dogs (AV.04.30.42).

The posture that Don Séeb found himself in is a familiar one in Maya history (Bricker 1981; Redfield and Villa Rojas [1934] 1962; Sullivan 1989). Since the early colonial period, the Maya have taken over the Christian cross as the central symbol of Almighty God. Despite appearances, it is considered an authentically Mayan image by most Yucatec Maya people, including Don Séeb. Arms outstretched in the manner of Jesus Christ, he literally embodied the Cross. This, along with the ecstatic quality of his loss and awakening, led him to experience the ecstasy as a hierophany, a direct encounter with the divine. He drops to his knees (in the Catholic manner) and thanks God.

It is interesting that Don Séeb does not mention whether, at the moment of awakening, he could remember anything he had experienced while out of his senses. It is as if he were blank and the time spent unconscious was void. Having thanked God then, he hears the sound of his dogs and returns home. It was early morning. His wife, frightened by his absence and furious with him for not telling her he planned to be away for seven days, criticizes him severely when he returns home. She tells him of the search parties, and how the other men thought he must have died. The other people *k'eyah* 'bawled him out' also. In response, he tells them nothing. Instead he absorbs their criticism, avowing a total lack of knowledge of what they were saying, and claiming that he did not go anywhere. Once alone, he goes out to his yard, about ten mecates from the house, and lashes a small altar. He cuts a small cross from a *šyáaš nik'* tree. He figures, "they had brought me away and so I thought I must feed them with a bit of *ʔuk'ul* 'drink'" (AV.04.35.00). He instructs his wife to prepare *sakab* 'corn gruel', and he takes the five gourds in which he will offer it.

Like Fausto Bolon, Don Séeb didn't know how to pray properly to offer the *sakab'*, but unlike him, he did not let this stop him from doing it. Standing in front of the five gourds, he said much the same thing he had told Fausto to say earlier that day, over thirty years later. Say this to God:

(5) I have faith, but I don't know how to say it. I have faith that the *ʔìik'* 'winds, spirits' of the Lord exist. The *ʔah káahkabóʔob* 'land guardians' exist. The *ah kaánanóʔob* 'guardians' exist. I just believe in them. I don't know how to speak to them.

But the Our Father, that I knew. I said it every day since I was a kid. So, then I said, there above the *ʔuk'ul* 'drink':

"Good, Lord, forgive my sins. This sacred ʾ*uk'ul* 'drink' and the things that happen to me, may you know that here we are on earth. You are the Lord of Heaven. I am speaking to you. God the Father, Jesus Christ, Holy Spirits."
So I said it (AV.04.39.00).

Don Séeb continued offering *sakab'* in his yard each evening for nine evenings in a row, each time praying the Our Father and asking forgiveness. Each time saying he had faith and wanted to learn how to pray, but did not know how. On the ninth night he went home to sleep and was awakened at about 11:00. His name was being spoken through the roof of the house, as though someone were calling to him from about three meters up in a tree outside. First on one side then on the other, he heard his name "Séeb! Come out here, we're talking to you!" So he went out full of happiness, with no fear, and followed the voice as it receded into the woods behind the house. It was pitch black out and he had to scramble on all fours to make his way through the trees. Finally he reached the source, voices coming from up in the branches of a *ramón* 'tropical oak' tree. They told him that he was now going to hear *ɛikbal* 'conversation'. He had been chosen to feed them, to feed the earth, and to care for other creatures. They were going to give him a religion. Just then, he heard prayer rising up from the tree, not just by a single voice, but five of them all chanting together (AV.04.48.18). It was the song that would become his own, and that he still sings when offering *sakab'*. Overcome by the beauty of it, he knelt down in the dry leaves. Taking a handful of earth in each hand, he told God that he wanted to remember the prayer he was hearing, saying:

(6) Father of mine, forgive my sins, I have been named to present this sacred earth. Herewith I manifest to you that I, too, am earth. I show myself to you, so that you bless me. What has been said to me, let it stay in my head. Let it stay in my heart. Let it stay in my hearing also. Because I like very much the talk that is happening to me. I want to learn it (AV.04.50.06).

This encounter marked the beginning of a new phase in the education of Don Séeb. He had been blank for a week, awakened, prayed, found his way home, offered the five gourds of *sakab'* for nine nights in a row. All this was done without any memory of *yunɛilóʾob* 'lords', nor any instruction in prayer by them. Now he would begin to experience direct conversations with the *yunɛilóʾob*, always alone, at night, voices coming from the trees above his head. Little by little he learned the prayers that he still performs. The spirits introduced themselves to him individually, giving their proper names for prayer address, but never showing themselves to him. He met the five *yunɛil baálanóʾob* 'jaguar lords' this way. They stand guard over the earth at its four corner points and in the center. He even met another two jaguar lords, bringing the total up to seven, and learned the names of others.

When things quieted down up in the tree, Don Séeb went home and slept peacefully. Each time he slept after an encounter, he was taken away again in his sleep. Like the initial ecstasy, these sleep state experiences occurred when Don Séeb was not awake. Unlike the world of ecstasy, the world of sleep yielded richly saturated portraits of individual spirits, places, evil beings and their practices. Once asleep, the *yunꞓilóʔob* 'lords' would arrive and tell him they had come to take him out. They took the form of very tall men wearing large brimmed hats, and they told him they were going to show him the world as it is, so that he could see it. This was a phase in which Don Séeb acquired a vast body of knowledge and began to routinize certain practices. He had already made nine offerings with the five gourds, and now he began to pray more often in other contexts, learning the special forms of *resar* 'prayer' and *kʼay* 'song'. He underwent numerous tests of his faith, lost in unfamiliar places, under assault by evil in the form of *maákóʔob* 'people' seeking to kill him. These people were the squadrons of the devil, the *kʼàasi báʔal* 'evil thing', which arose of its own force in the material world, during the seven days of creation.

 The story gets long at this point, because Don Séeb learned so many things and has such richly developed memories of them. He took great pains to remember upon awakening, and this is when he developed his own writing system as a mnemonic. He was actually illiterate, and it pleased him that he was the only one who could read the notes. During the encounters, the lords repeatedly admonished him to remember everything, reinforcing his desire to forget nothing. In fact, during these encounters Don Séeb was experiencing things for the express purpose of remembering them. Some situations, like the diagnosis of Fausto Bolon, seem to be built on retrospection, so that the present is constructed out of revisions of the past. This is the force of Don Séeb's vision of what had befallen Fausto a week earlier, and also the import of Fausto's statement that his father used to offer *sakabʼ* but they never did it any more. Just as people become accustomed to certain practices, so too land can become *sùuk* 'accustomed, habituated' to being nourished by offerings. The past produces the future.

 In the case of pedagogical encounters with spirits, the logic is different, because these happen in order to be remembered later. It was only late in his apprenticeship to the lords that Don Séeb began to experience things as having already occurred once before. For the most part, each dream encounter was a first-time experience, something to be recalled or reenacted later. The present radiated a future of remembering in which it would reappear under new circumstances. This was true of both kinds of nocturnal encounter that he had, both asleep and awake under the trees. So much occurred in this phase that we can barely scratch the surface of it here. I want to show just two features. First, how the spirits admonished him to remember what he was seeing. And second, how they instructed him to continue offering *sakabʼ*. If the exercise of memory is central to shamanic practice, then the offering of *sakabʼ* is the quintessential mnemonic.

 In recounting his story before the camera, Don Séeb emphasizes how the spirits instructed him to remember them. The message was clear: we are your salvation and if you forget us you will perish. The first of five warnings occurred outside the church where Don Séeb had just been brought by four *maákóʔob* 'people' (spirits in the form of men, dressed as bullfighters). Under siege by the evil ones, he had been saved by these four and brought into the church to confess his sins. After that, he looked up toward heaven and saw a round opening in the roof of the church. Through it *sakabʼ* fell down upon his head and shoulders, like a baptismal shower of offeratory corn gruel. Once outside the church he was led by the four to an abandoned plaza in the town. They said to him:

(7) 'OK, we've brought you here. Do you remember us from when we talked to you, when you were still alive (*laáyli kušá'aneče'*)? Do you remember when we talked to you out there in the forest? [DS gestures with left hand.] When we first engaged you?
    Yes, I remember, I said to them.
    Well, that was us.
    It was you.
    Yes, it was us [gestures with left hand].
    So then you must know that there are others following you. You are about to be taken from us. You will be killed' (AV.05.14.12).

And with that, another group of *máakó'ob* 'people', from the squadron of evil, arrived. They claimed Don Séeb for themselves and wanted to show him their power. There was a great tree before them in the plaza and these other men began praying before it, casting their arms in its direction. The tree withered before Don Séeb's eyes. And then the four lords told him that there was one more to come. And a fifth *yuncil* 'lord' arrived and they told him "We are now complete . . . the day you forget it, you will be seized" (AV.05.16.00). And they began to pray and the tree, dead and desiccated, began to bud before his eyes. Buds and then leaves burst forth from the tree and Don Séeb was again enchanted and joined in their prayer. At this point all five lords introduced themselves to him, taking care first that he had chosen their path and not that of the evil people.

(8) I am so and so. This one is so and so. The other one is so and so. Five of us, looking over you. Do you remember when you addressed us with five gourds of *'uk'ul?* That's why we're coming after you. We are what they call nature (AV.05.19.16).

At this point in the story, Don Séeb was careful not to mention the names of the five spirits on film, introducing them only as *hulano* 'so and so'. They continued talking to him, telling him to give himself over to True God and serve them. "Help us with a bit of *sakab*'" they said. And later, *"Má' atúu'skó'on, k'áahó'on teč"*: 'Do not forget us. Remember us.' 'Because if you do not remember us—even just think of us and we will be with you—you will die' (AV.05.22.00). Don Séeb left then, taking the road toward his home and out of the dominion of Good. Once out on the road, he was again attacked by evil. In the throes of death, he again had to remember.

(9) And I could feel that I was dying. And as I was dying, and I heard myself addressed again: 'Remember the grass called *sip če'*. I was given a bunch of *sip če'* to wipe across my body. And when I had it I did so. [Imitating *sáantiguaar* gestures on his own body] . . . And I came back to my senses (*k'áah'inwìik*). Eehh! I came back to life!' (AV.05.36.36).

It is interesting that in this case, Don Séeb is told to 'remember' a plant that was being introduced to him by the spirits for the first time. He surely knew going into the dream that *sip če'* leaves are medicinal and especially associated with ritual. This much is common sense. In this episode, he was being taught something else. Given to man by the *yunҫilṓ'ob* 'lords', the leaves of this plant activate their protective power, which can in effect save a person from impending death by evil. Just as Don Séeb continues to offer five gourds, and instructs his patients to do the same, so too he continues to cure with *sip če'* leaves.

And so it continued through successive crises in which Don Séeb was on the verge of annihilation and had to be saved by the spirits. The key was to remember them, or something that they told him to remember, in the nick of time. He did it, and this repeated act of remembering became his path to salvation. The vivid detail with which he told his story before the camera is the best indicator that he still does remember, he is still reproducing it, now thirty years hence. His continued practice of offering five gourds of *sakab'* is the embodiment of this memory for the spirits to whom it is directed.

But there are twists and blank spots in Don Séeb's memory. What does it mean to say that he remembers today what occurred while he was asleep so long ago? He is surely producing his memories, and they have without doubt changed in form over the intervening time. How can we talk about this change? The story Don Séeb tells of his early learning suggests a range of different modes in which he experienced: (i) fully awake, routine commonsense awareness; (ii) fully vacated blank unconsciousness (ecstatic); (iii) nocturnal waking state (on the path, under the trees); and (iv) nocturnal sleep state (dream travels). The first provides a horizon against which charismatic experiences are defined, and to which Don Séeb returned after charisma. It is evidently the state in which he offered the five gourds out in his yard. It rarely occupies the foreground today in his stories of spiritual activity, and was only minimally developed in this telling before the camera. The second appears to be hermetically sealed. His memories go to the onset and awakening from ecstasy, but do not penetrate it directly. What happened out in the woods for those seven days remains a zone of imperception, as it was for his neighbors and dogs in Pol Wacax, and for himself at the time. He certainly remembers that it happened, but what transpired remains opaque. It is the nocturnal activities that followed ecstasy, which were to be the most productive source of memory, and which provide much of the memorial knowledge that he relies on in his practice today. During this time he was introduced to good and evil, instructed in choosing between alternatives, and his faith was tested repeatedly. He met the *yunҫil baálanó'ob* 'jaguar lords' who would later become his regular interlocutors, and who provide the images he now reads in his crystals.

Today, Don Séeb's contact with spirits is by far the most direct when he is actually performing *resar* 'prayer' or *k'ay* 'song'. This is when his discourse gives the fullest picture of the world to which it speaks. Scores and scores of spirits are named by their proper address forms, in the proper order, actually moved for well-defined purposes. The delivery style is deeply worked. He has beautified it continuously ever since he first heard the spirits singing in the trees. Where his initial prayers were simplified Our Father and Hail Mary forms, awkwardly spoken in Spanish, his prayer today is in Maya (much of it archaic), chanted in long, controlled breath groups, with regular prosodic contours. Its thematic and symbolic content is virtually encyclopedic. It embodies the total logic of good over evil, the spiritual history of Yucatán since before the conquest, parts of the Bible and the Book of Chilam Balam, the entire biography of encounters he has lived. He regularly performs *č'áa čaák* rain ceremonies, *heč luʔum* 'earth cleansing', *wàahil kòol* 'breads of the field,' and other major productions in which he directs the collective efforts of dozens of people over a period of days (Hanks 1984a, 1990a). Without entering into a description of this range of practices, which would be far beyond our current purposes, it can be fairly said that prayer performance, alongside storytelling, has become a basic form of memory. Where it was once simple Spanish formulas, it has now developed into a Mayan art form, with the kind of symbolic and aesthetic density one would expect. It is the only place where the names of his spirits and their precise relations are inscribed.

Along with this dramatic development of prayer was a change in the status of the memories it encoded. When prayer was just a way of telling God that you were sorry and loved goodness, it was easy to think about it and paraphrase it in everyday talk. Don Séeb can easily tell Fausto to say "Here it is God. I don't know how to pray, but this *sakab'* is for you." And after he makes the offering, Fausto can easily turn around and repeat more or less accurately what he said at the altar. The reason is that at this level of skill in praying, there is almost no difference between *resar* 'prayer' and *čikbal* 'converse, talk to'. Not so for a master like Don Séeb in 1990. His prayer has split off radically from everyday *čikbal* in its content, grammatical structure, prosody and the bodily postures in which it is performed. And curiously, as it has incorporated more and more memorial knowledge, Don Séeb's *resar* has become harder and harder for him to talk about after the fact. He performs *resar* every day of his life, usually many times per day, but cannot discuss the specific meaning of it. Over the eleven years that we have worked together, I have recorded over 200 hours of audio and video tape with him, and I have found him often unable to remember spirits' names or the proper order of their mention in prayer. Talking together, reviewing a transcription, he expresses mild surprise at what he says while praying, or is only vaguely aware of it. *Resar* is studded with special discourse particles, but he appears to be unaware of them, and unable to say why they are there. The level of detail in his accessible memory of his own prayer is so gross as to indicate a real break in his consciousness. It is as if *resar* has become a blank spot, or at least a zone of vagueness in the everyday present, as ecstasy was in the everyday past.

I first encountered this blank during the initial conversation in which Don Séeb and I got acquainted. I did not recognize it at the time. With no prior knowledge of Don Séeb or Maya shamanism, I was too preoccupied with trying to understand him to speculate about what he was failing to mention. It was late at night on Friday, August 21, 1980, and Don Séeb and I were sitting on a couple of rocks beside the altar at which he was performing a *č'áa čaák* rain ceremony. I had heard that the ceremony was to be held, but did not really know what it was about. We had met briefly three years before. Arriving there around 9:00 P.M., I found him arranging things at the altar on the edge of the woods. As I recall, I did not recognize him. A small group of men were sitting under a covering about twenty meters behind the altar, laughing and talking, listening to music, and playing cards by candlelight. They were wrapped up in their game and seemed unaware of Don Séeb's activities at the altar. He was beginning a ceremony that would last until dusk the following day, making the initial offering, mentioning most of the spirits whom he would address again over the next hours, stating the basic request for rain. He laid out the gourds of ʔ*uk'ul* 'drink', stood at the foot of the altar, and began to pray.[5]

By now his *resar* 'prayer' had matured and what he produced was full-blown, beautified *payal čiʔ t'àan* 'summons mouth speech'. When he began to pray I recognized him; it was the same enchantment I had felt upon hearing him the first time. Whereas the term *resar* may be used to refer to prayer in Spanish or Maya, everything from the Our Father to a rain ceremony, *payal čiʔ t'àan* is usually used in reference to *resar* in the Maya genres.[6] These include, roughly, all the agricultural ceremonies, exorcism of individuals, and inhabited land, most of the curing discourse, divination, and some other miscellaneous categories. It does not include, in my experience, the Catholic prayers or sacraments. The offering of *sakab'* as performed by a first-time initiate or nonshaman is also a case of *resar* but not a *payal čiʔ t'àan*. What Fausto Bolon was to do for his Puuc and Don Séeb did in his yard were too rudimentary and vague to do anything beyond nourishing the spirits. It does not mobilize them for specific ends. The difference is that in the main Maya genres, shamans literally move spirits from their places in the cosmos and summon them to the altar according to a precise logic. Hence the name of the category.

What Don Séeb did at the altar that night was to summon the spirits, to lower them one by one around himself, so that they could drink the ʔ*uk'ul*. He prepared them for the main offerings the next day, when he would *k'ubik* 'deliver' *noh wáah* 'great breads', *b'ak'el, hóʔočeʔe* 'meat', *k'òol* 'gravy', *balčeʔ* 'mead', and *sakab'*, along with incense, flowers, and the full altar setting. This night he prayed for just under seventeen minutes, lowering the spirits. I recorded the prayer on audio tape. Afterward, sitting off to the side of the altar, we talked. I was unaware that we were in the midst of spirits who had been lowered from the highest reaches of the heavens, and who were feasting on the ʔ*uk'ul* laid out for them. And yet there were signs I have come to recognize.

SHAMAN AS TEACHER

As he began his *resar* Don Séeb's pace had been deliberate and even.[7] The breath groups were of normal length and contour. As he continued praying, his delivery style became increasingly intense. The speed of articulation picked up so that there were more words and consequently more spirits addressed, or more elaborate forms of address, per breath group. The breath groups got longer. After eleven minutes of this, the frogs were bellowing in the background, overpowering the insistent hum of crickets and other insects. At just under thirteen minutes it began to rain, individual drops hitting the mic on the altar, making little explosions in the recording of his voice. A minute later it was rain-ing quite hard and his prayer was even more *peká'an* 'moved, fast' in style (this is his description of the style, cf. Hanks 1984a). At fifteen minutes and twenty-six seconds into the prayer the mic was getting drenched and I had to stop recording. Cut to silence.

When the recording picks up again Don Séeb and I are sitting off to the side of the altar. The frogs are making a din and you can hear the men's radio playing cumbia music in the background. This was the first time Don Séeb spoke to me about his practice. As I recall, I had told him of how I learned Maya, and had come to be working in the area. He reciprocated with a story about a Maya *campesino* 'peasant farmer' who learned to address the guardian spirits of his milpa '(unirrigated) corn field', but only after offering five gourds of *sakab*. At first the man saw several venomous snakes while working his field and he asked God that they be removed. In response, he was whistled to, which he took to be a sign.

(10)   DS   *'Entóns ká'anhih tún tu pensamièentó tuún e'* ↑ *'ue'iik* →
             leti' e sìinko lùuč'u'uk'ul o' →
             So then the thought occurred to him that he give those five gourds of drink.
        WH   *Hàah* →
             Yeah.
        DS   *Hàah* → *sìinko lùuč u sakáab o'* →
             Yeah. Five gourds of its *sakab*.
        WH   *Hàah* →
             Yeah.

Although this was the first time in my life I had heard of the five gourds, Don Séeb's first utterance unambiguously treats it as something we both already know about. The farmer would make his offering and after that he would meet up with spirits singly and in groups. They would tell him their names and how to address them. He would go along gathering spirits this way through successive encounters.

I did not know at the time that it was his own history that Don Séeb was memorializing on the story, any more than I knew that the spirits the farmer came to address were really with us as we talked. He knew these things, though, and he started to give hints about ten minutes into the story, when he made a side comment to the effect that he could not remember the name of one of the farmer's familiar spirits, even though he had just said the name while praying.

(11)   DS   *Béey inwoó syèete tukaštá'* → *tú'ubu ten e'* → *lel o'* ↓ *'inwá'ala*
             I think he found seven [spirits]. I forget [the name]. That one, I said it
             té''ič e resar o' → *pero má tu permitirik wal*
             right there in the prayer. But he probably doesn't permit
             ká ink'á'as e'e' →
             me to remember it.
        WH   *Hàah*
             Yeah.

DC   *Má'a [unintel] (tu)tǔ'ubu ↓ hm' biínih' k binih →*
        It doesn't —It's forgotten. Nope. It's gone. K- It's gone.
        Hàah kutàa pero → púuƈu bey o' →
        Yeah. It comes but gets away like that (too).   (F.33.A.27:29)

In retrospect, this little forgetting was the trace of a world-making remembrance. I was to see scores of such cases over the next ten years, but I had no idea of this at the time. Had I noticed the blank and understood, it would have changed the situation I found myself in. For Don Séeb was doing something surprising: insofar as he could recall, he was telling me in the narrative the very names and attributes of the spirits whom he cites in prayer. It is this information that he has steadfastly omitted from the film project. Sitting in the dark that night, he could safely assume that I would be incapable of remembering, or even of understanding what was going on. Yet he knew I was recording and approved.

And so the farmer went along, learning more and more from the lords. He kept noticing that when he delivered up his blessed work to the blessed spirits, it would start to rain. The rain would come to make his corn grow—"like you just saw," he said to me (F.33.A.33:23). Coming to the end of the spirits whom the farmer learned to address, Don Séeb made another foray into the present. This time it was the characters in the story who became figures in the present. He said that the spirits named in the story are the ones "left to *tó'on way a'* 'us right here'." His pronoun choice is unspecified as to who, other than himself, belongs to the 'we', but the spatial reference picks out the current space in which we were talking. He repeated this attribution to 'us' three times, and when I asked for clarification, suggesting that it was *his own work* that he was describing, he responded:

(12)   DS *Teč e ↑ wá a suèerte mèen tata dyòos →* [pause]
                You, if it's your fate, by God the Father, [pause]
                déestinàadóeč utí'áal e' →
                [if] you are destined for it,
                čeén kén awúuy a ťá'anah → 'eéspiritual 'anih →
                you'll just hear yourself being addressed. It's spiritual.

        WH *Háah*
                Yeah.

        DC *Taná'atik ↑ 'éspiritual 'anih ↓ 'ìik''anih beyo' ↓*
                Do you understand it? It's spiritual. It's wind, spirit like I said.

        WH *'Ahah →*
                Ahah.

DC   *Má tán awile ↓ hàah kàadá e⁷ → kut'àankeč →*
You don't see them. Yeah, every once in a while they address you.
Kàadá e⁷ kut'àankeč → ká ⁷anak a féeh →
Every once in a while they address you. So that you have faith.
Ká hoók'eč a kašteh
So that you go out looking for them [repeats this several times].

WH   *Hàah*
Yeah.

DC   *Wá má ⁷e⁷ ↑ yàan ut'àaŋ → yàan ubiskeč →*
If not, they'll speak—they'll take you away.   (F.33.A.38:18)

At this point I was mildly confused since he was unequivocally including me in the story. He shifted immediately into another story, but this one was about himself, for real. He had been taken away, he said. For seven days he had disappeared in the woods before *k'aáh inwìik'* 'I came to my senses'. He can't remember anything from the time he was out, but when he came to, cruciform against a tree, he thanked God and returned home. That night he heard a voice through the roof of his house:

(13)   *⁷U á la nòoče túun → e⁷ ká tinwú⁷uyah yá⁷ala ten e⁷ →*
So that night I heard myself told:
č'àa sakaⁱ o⁷ → č'áa sìinko lùuč i saka⁷ →
Give the *sakab*. Give five gourds of *sakab*.   (F.33.B.9:54)

Making the offering of five gourds, he went home, slept, and was taken away to a town called Eč Balam 'Black Jaguar'. And so forth.

We continued talking for another hour that night, and I went to bed. I can vaguely recall being interested in what he was telling me, but my field notes are blank on the topic. We agreed to talk again. I would visit him at his house in the afternoon some day. At the time, I was working closely with three other people on unrelated topics, and I had little inkling that this conversation in the rain would alter my fieldwork as it did.

It was a couple of weeks before I went to visit Don Séeb. He was living in the same house he lives in today, the same one in which Fausto Bolon had come for a cure and in which we were filming. Sitting by his altar while Fausto and his wife gazed into the crystals and took instructions on how to offer five gourds of *sakab'*, I remembered. We would talk for hours almost each day, recording, getting purposely 'lost' in the woods, reviewing *payal či⁷ t'àan*. He became interested in my dreams and would go through them at length. We traveled to perform major ceremonies, him performing and me helping on the periphery. An off-key apprentice, I learned a lot about public performance, but never stood up to do it. I forgot about our first conversations and for some reason never listened to the recording until recently. The beginning was a blank.

THE FIVE GOURDS OF MEMORY

Most of the questions about memory raised in this account are too hard to answer, and there are too many holes in the story. What, in cultural terms, are the precise relations between a Maya shaman's experiences when awake, ecstatic, asleep, dreaming, sitting in the woods at night, and praying? How far does the grounding of everyday common sense go toward making charismatic experiences intelligible? Should we look at the shamanic growth process as one in which a progression of life worlds are passed through, starting with the void of ecstasy and ending with the blank space of prayer? Are these alternative worlds or merely alternative ways of occupying a single world? The question is partly empirical. For Don Séeb there is only one world, and it is exhaustively contained within the globe-shaped universe in which East is at the top, a familiar vision to Mayanists (compare Gossen 1974). But the question also has a theoretical edge to it, because how we think of memory depends upon how we think of experience in the present.

This raises the thorny issue of how many kinds of present one wants to distinguish. How long or short, continuous or spotty, thick or narrow, full or empty is "now"? There is good linguistic and ethnographic evidence that the quality of the present in Mayan prayer is different from that in everyday interaction. This suggests a range of different kinds of now in which Don Séeb's experiences, including his memories, have taken shape. What is true in one kind of present cannot be true in another. The *yunɛ̓iló⁹ob* 'lords' cannot be seen by anyone who is awake, but they can very well be seen and addressed in sleep. When Don Séeb returned from this ecstasy his wife accused him of having left the area and he responded that he had gone nowhere. Which statement was true? By the normal rules of evidence his wife was surely right and the dogs offered convincing proof. But from within the world of ecstatic hierophany, Don Séeb was closer to the mark. Ironically, instead of going away himself, he was abandoned by his consciousness, left behind in the woods. That he became imperceptible when this happened marks the depth of his remaking. To borrow Goodman's (1978) terms, he was entering into a process in which aspects of his earlier world were decomposed, to be then recomposed, reordered, reformed, and supplemented. Things like sleep took on a whole new weight. Particularly in the case of a shaman, it seems inevitable that we recognize multiple realities in which different things can be true.

Memory connects different realities, and the conditions on remembering differ according to which kind of present one occupies. This seems to be the upshot of Don Séeb's inability to recall prayer or ecstasy when not actually in the state. And to be *in* prayer or ecstasy is not really the same as to *remember* prayer or ecstasy. Praying, Don Séeb is in a posture that he calls *čičan* 'tiny', so small that he is nowhere, ontologically reduced to a point, which has no end points: *'miná⁹an inšùul'*, 'I have no end', he says, meaning that he is too small to have borders, *'mišbá⁹alen'*, 'I am nothing'. Through this point the force of the spirits is channeled; he sometimes calls it *fluido* 'current' and likens it to electricity (and his divining crystals to the telephone). It is in this state of tininess that the spirits—the same ones he addresses—give *payal či⁹ t'àan* to Don Séeb. They give it to him each time anew. Therefore, he does not "have" prayer at all; he just voices what comes to him from without. It would not occur to us to ask whether the divining crystals "remember" the repertoire of signs that they show, and yet they channel an image in a way parallel to how Don Séeb channels speech. The memory of prayer is not an abstract representation that endures in the accessible thought of a shaman. It is the ability to adopt a posture in practice, and the fact of doing so. The conditions under which this is done are constrained more and more elaborately as the shaman grows. With this, the prayer discourse itself becomes more elaborate, because prayer is just the voice of the divine, and the more one practices the more current passes through.

This helps make sense of why Don Séeb has a spotty memory of prayer when he is not performing. But there is another thing. He has never described himself to me as having been tiny during the early learning process, or when conversing with spirits. But the *resar* 'prayer' and *k'ay* 'song', which the *yunęilóʾob* voice through him today, is *the same prayer* they taught him out in the woods. It has become more elaborate as he beautifies it, but it has not changed in the basics, nor in source. When he was learning, Don Séeb joined in and prayed along with the praying *yunęilóʾob* on more than one occasion. When he prays today he is doing the same thing, joining them, both memorializing the initial communion, and living it again for the first time every time. If he really could remember prayer, if he did have a stable mental representation of it somewhere, it would make sense that he would deny it.[8]

This brings us to the use of prayer in the offering of *sakab'.* Why is this the central act of devotion in the early training of a shaman, and why does he prescribe it for his patients today? There are obvious parallels to be made between the restorative power of offering *sakab'* in the aftermath of ecstasy, and the curative power of it in the aftermath of being struck by a wind. Fausto would go off and do the same thing that afternoon as Don Séeb had done many years before, as the faithful peasant did in the story, and as the spirits tell humans to do. But this functional rationale leaves too much unsaid to be satisfying. How is memory embodied in the five gourds of *sakab'*? We can only point in the direction of an answer.

Unlike other kinds of offeratory ritual, in which food and drink are delivered to the *yunęilóʾob* 'lords', the five gourds of *sakab'* are offered in solitude. It is basically a personal prayer. This is one reason that Don Séeb never does it for any of his patients, whereas he performs almost all other ritual treatments himself. Other Maya men whom I know well also perform the offering for their own purposes, but none has ever allowed me to listen to it. Given the nature of our relations, this is noteworthy (for examples, see Hanks, 1990a, 362ff.). According to all reports, including Don Séeb's stories and his instructions to patients, the thematic content of the prayer varies according to its particular purpose. As an initiate, Don Séeb expressed thanks and the hope of greater learning. The faithful peasant asks for protection from snakes, and Fausto Bolon would ask for protection from the winds in the Puuc. It is also performed as a *primisia* ceremony in the agricultural cycle (ibid. 370ff). It requests divine protection at each stage in the preparation of the *milpa* '(unirrigated) cornfield', and also serves as a promissory note for a large scale thanksgiving ceremony such as the *wàahil kòol* 'breads of the milpa', to come after the harvest is in. In all of these contexts however, in spite of the great variation in people's ability to pray, the prayer seems always to include a sort of Credo. The supplicant expresses his dependence upon God and belief in the existence of the invisible. This is the first step and the grounds for making further ritual gestures. In Don Séeb's case, it was his first step toward becoming the *yùumil* 'owner, responsible agent' of the feeding of the jaguar lords. Moreover, as his narratives make clear, the spirits remember such offerings, and request them if not provided spontaneously. Fausto Bolon's father had habituated the Puuc lords to something he had failed to continue with, and his illness was the sign.

Why *sakab'* instead of *balče* 'mead' or some other offering? And why five gourds? Maya speakers, including Don Séeb, often use the term *gràasya* 'grace' to refer to what we would call corn, meaning primarily the living plant and its edible fruit. The cultural relation between corn and life is too well known among students of Mesoamerica to need emphasis here. However, it is worth underscoring that by offering corn gruel, a person is presenting to the spirits the central substance with which he sustains his own life. It is not the economic preponderance of corn farming that motivates this. The Oxkutzcab region is the major citrus producer for the Yucatán peninsula, but there will never be a five gourd ceremony in which orange juice is offered. Rather, it is the link of consubstantiality and the enormous historical depth of corn growing in this area. Unirrigated fields are dramatically vulnerable, as well, and illustrate the constant dependence of human life on the natural forces. Then too, a better description of *sakab'* would examine how it is prepared by women, and consumed in the family group after offerings. These topics have been unfortunately ignored in this paper but would speak to the issue at hand.

The significance of the number five can be inferred with some certainty. It is common sense among Maya speakers that any productive or inhabited space has five parts, corresponding to the four corners plus center. Together these make up the perimeter of the space. This has a pervasive impact on how people describe and understand the form of yards, fields, altars, even the world as a whole. When I was discussing the *saántiguar* prayer with Don Séeb early on in our work, I asked him how many parts he thought the prayer had. He said five, because it is whole (Hanks 1984a). When the jaguar lords spoke to him from the tree, they were in a group of five. When they restored to life the tree that had been withered by evil, they did so as a group of five. It was five packets of medicine that Don Séeb gave to Fausto Bolon. A cycle of five *saántiguar* blessings performed one per day makes up a *hó' oče' e* 'main offering' and is routinely prescribed for patients in a grave state. While wholes are built up on sets of three, seven, nine, and twelve for other purposes, five is the minimal totality of human space, and the instrument of well-being. It corresponds to the number of directional spirits who stand upon the earth as guardians, and the sectors of the world over which they watch. Any Maya campesino knows about five, its general significance being no more esoteric than the knowledge required to tell God you believe in what you cannot see. The memory and awakening embodied in the five gourds of *sakab'* is as basic and universal as milpa agriculture itself. At the same time, as Don Séeb's story reminds us, it is the first step toward a deeper, more specialized remembering, and the greater forget that comes with it.

NOTES

1. Film footage on which parts of this paper are based gathered by Peter H. Thompson filmmaker, in a collaborative project entitled "The Shaman of Oxkintok." This project has been made possible by grants from the Rockefeller Foundation and from the Lichtstern Fund, Department of Anthropology, the University of Chicago, whose support I gratefully acknowledge.

2. Don Séeb went on to show Fausto the image in his crystals, which he described to him as a hunchbacked form (*p'usukbal* 'in a hunched position'). This is unsurprising, since the ancient *generación* 'generation' of beings to whom earth winds belong are usually thought of today as hunchbacked midgets.

3. The idea being that you move spirits by citing their names in the proper order, corresponding to their locations in the cosmos. Interestingly, in the illumination ceremony, Don Séeb always asks the patient his or her name and place of residence, this information being necessary to direct the spirits to the right place.

4. There is also a symbolic relation of partial identity between sleeping and death. Don Séeb has commented on this explicitly, and there is a commonly heard expression in everyday Maya which describes deep sleep as *yiíȼ'in kiímil* 'the younger sibling of death'.

5. My field notes are inadequate to tell me what Don Séeb was offering exactly, since the term 'drink' covers both *sakab'* and *balče'*, the latter a fermented honey and bark drink that is considered intoxicating. The text of the prayer states only that it is *'uk'ul*. While praying, Don Séeb stands at the "foot" of the altar, and the "front" is the far side, toward which the altar faces (see Hanks 1990a for analysis of the spatial orientation of altars).

6. This is at variance with Villa Rojas's ([1945] 1978) observations on the use of the term in Quintana Roo.

7. These remarks are impressionistic and I have not yet done the necessary transcription and measurement to substantiate them.

8. I believe this is related also to Don Séeb's vocational commitment to poverty. Despite a very considerable practice, he makes little money and retains even less. He prefers to awaken each morning unsure of where his next meal will come from. That way his dependency on the spirits is all the more clear.

REFERENCES

Bricker, Victoria R.
    1981   *The Indian Christ, the Indian King.* The historical substrate of Maya myth and ritual
        (Austin, University of Texas Press).
Eliade, Mircea
    1968   *Le chamanisme et les techniques archaïques de l'extase* (Paris, Payot).
Goodman, N.

1978   *Ways of Worldmaking* (Cambridge, Hackett Publishing Co.).
Gossen, Gary, H.
1974   *Chamulas in the World of the Sun.* Time and space in a Maya oral tradition (Cambridge, Harvard University Press).
Hanks, William F.
1984a   Sanctification, structure and experience in a Yucatec Maya ritual event, *Journal of American Folklore,* 97 (384), 131–66.
1984b   "The interactive basis of Maya divination," paper presented at the Eighty-Third Annual Meeting of the American Anthropological Association (Denver, Colorado).
1990a   *Referential Practice.* Language and Lived Space among the Maya (Chicago, University of Chicago Press).
1990b   "Temporal orientations in Maya shamanic performance," paper presented at workshop De palabra y obra en el Nuevo Mundo (Trujillo, Spain).
1992   Intertextualité de l'espace au Yucatán, *L'Homme,* 122, 123, 124 (avril–décembre), XXXII (2, 3, 4), 55–76.
1992   Metalanguage and pragmatics of deixis, in J. A. Lucy, ed., *Reflexive Language.* Reported speech and metapragmatics (Cambridge/New York, Cambridge University Press), 127–57.
Redfield, R. and A. Villa Rojas
1962   [1934] *Chan Kom, a Maya Village* (Chicago, University of Chicago Press).
Sullivan, Paul
1989   *Unfinished Conversations.* Maya and foreigners between two wars (New York, Alfred A. Knopf).
Villa, Rojas, A.
1978   [1945] *Los elegidos de dios.* Etnografía de los Mayas de Quintana Roo (Mexico, INI) [Série de Antropología social, 56].

Part III

Meaning in History

8

Copresence and Alterity in Maya Ritual Practice

There is a saying in contemporary Yucatec Maya that every person is a different world, *cada untuúl maák eᵒ, yàana mùundo,* meaning that each one has motivations and experiences that are only partly knowable by others.[1] The idea is that people's words and actions are never transparent and rarely to be taken at face value. This commonsense maxim, a maxim of difference, operates on two levels at once, differentiating people from one another, and also differentiating a person's inner experiences from his or her outer expressions. The two distinctions are widely assumed to be both obvious and important. For the people with whom I have done fieldwork in southern Yucatan, only a child or simpleton would assume that human action is as it appears.[2] Furthermore, the divide between inside feelings and outer expressions is part of a much more elaborate sense of individual body space and its relation to experience. For much of routine practice, these ideas have the status of tacit assumptions, widely taken for granted and often unnoticed. Taken together, they divide people and locate their individual experiences in the silent, invisible world of the unsaid and unseen.

Differences are not always divisive, of course, and contemporary Yucatec common sense unites people in certain ways even as it separates them in others.[3] The common differences between *campesinos* 'peasants' and *ingenieros* 'engineers', between siblings and parents, coresidents and neighbors, patients and a doctor, all provide fields of equivalence, as well as its opposite. Widely held values such as *legalidad* 'legality, propriety, decency,' *cortiedad* 'courtesy,' and *cariño* 'affection' also contribute to the sense of sharedness among people. Shared engagement in organized religions, such as Catholic and any of the various Protestant sects, underscore and actively promote solidarity, as do organizations like Alcoholics Anonymous and the ejidal system of land distribution do which *socios* belong. People assume that their differences are intertwined with commonalities as well.

These tacit assumptions about difference and sharedness produce a great deal of ambiguity, irony, and ambivalence in social relations. Maya people appear particularly sensitive to these things, making them skeptical of appearances and often thin-skinned by Angloamerican standards. The kinds of *enredos* 'gossip' and *envidio* 'envy' that have been widely documented in contemporary indigenous communities are also prevalent in rural Yucatan. A compadre of mine in Oxkutzcab was saving money for home improvements and decided to sell his stereo for the cash. He expressed concern that the neighbors would resent his project as a way of holding himself above the others. Another compadre explained to me that I, as a North American and his compadre, could remain in his home after he left for work during the day, whereas he would never permit his own brother to do so. The reason was that, were he left alone with the wife, his brother would surely attempt to seduce her. It's not that the brother was a bad person he explained, but just that he is a Yucatecan man who lives in the same household. No man could be trusted under those circumstances. This rationale overlaps with other aspects of interaction among coresidents too. As I have documented elsewhere (Hanks 1990:Chapters 3, 7), verbal interactions among coresidents of Maya homesteads are governed by strict rules of avoidance, whose effect is to insulate a married woman from all of the male consanguines of her husband.[4] One rationalization for this that I have heard repeatedly is that one cannot know anyone's intentions, even a brother. While there is clearly more going on in avoidance than this, these patterns are consistent with the basic assumptions of interpersonal difference and nontransparent expression.

Some kinds of ambiguity are the product of another, related assumption, namely that the world is made up of dynamic interactions between polar opposites. Weather, body states, emotions, food, personalities, human relationships are all characterized by the interplay between opposite values like good/bad, wet/dry, hot/cold, mobile/static. The fact that every human being is considered to be both good and evil at the same time means that one must not expect totally unequivocal intentions or behaviors from others. This becomes especially salient in the almost manicheistic logic of Don Seéb, a Maya shaman with whom I have worked for a number of years. For him, the interactions of opposing values are pervasive in the material and spiritual world (which he distinguishes), and provide the dynamic framework within which he practices. For example, as a ritual specialist, he does battle with evil forces, spirits with proper names, who were present at the creation of the world and will be party to its ultimate destruction. The devil, as the embodiment of evil, really exists and is the ring leader of squadrons of evil forces, many of which play important roles in the normal functioning of the world. Pressed on the point, he considers evil to be coordinate with good, and foresees no ultimate triumph of one over the other. The relation of ambivalence to shamanism is further evident in the commonsense assumption, made by virtually any Maya person who would seek a shaman's services, that real shamans actually do practice both good and evil. The ability to kill by sorcery (*hechizo*) appears to be the measure of one's ability to cure, bring rain, and do the other good deeds of a shaman. Curing is not a matter of rendering a patient pure or sterile of evil, but of redressing the balance between evil and goodness. Like other shamans, Don Seéb knows that many people come to him ostensibly seeking care but actually looking to test him by deceiving him. A patient arrives complaining of some problem and requesting a diagnosis, during which (s)he attempts to lead the shaman on to a false interpretation. The shaman for his part must discover the deception, at the risk of being mocked and revealed as a charlatan. Thus, there is a baseline of significant ambivalence on the part of both shamans and their patients. This ambivalence is a key part of the background against which ritual practice must be understood.

In this paper we examine some of the relations between Don Seéb, his patients, and the spirits whom he summons in ritual practice. The three kinds of participant have different backgrounds and different roles in the actuality of performance. In a real sense, they have different histories, and their interactions at the altar embody a complex historical process: as the ritual present emerges in practice, the potentially infinite differences among participants, objects, and events are organized into a controlled (and controlling) framework. The opacities of motive and outcome are never fully transcended, but Maya ritual is designed to achieve transparency and realignment according to regular patterns. Taussig (1987) and others are right to underscore the fragmentary quality of some shamanic practice, but curing rituals among Maya people are marked by a profound regularity of structure. And they are meant to order the life of the patient. This is evident in everything from the bodily postures adopted by participants, to the altar, the language of prayer, the time and place of performance, and the production and consumption of medicinal substances. Order itself functions in Maya shamanic discourse as the basis of well-being; illness and calamity are explicitly treated as disorder in need of redress. During performance, disorder exists as a lived reality in the suffering of the patient, and as potential outcome of the procedure, should it fail. In cases of witchcraft (*hechizo*) and certain forms of exorcism, the potential for disorder is acute and special precautions must be taken from the outset. Here as elsewhere, a value is actualized in close association with its contraries. The question then arises, How is difference constructed and made meaningful in the ritual present? How do Maya shamanic genres produce social fields in which sheer difference is transformed into more subtle and meaningful relations of alterity, and states of illness into states of well-being?

I

We will take "difference" to be a neutral term designating the mere fact of nonsameness among two or more people, objects, or events. To say that two people are different in this sense does not presuppose that they are comparable or identical in any ways. Shamans and nonshamans are different in many respects, for instance. They take different things for granted when thinking about wind, rain, and body aches and have recourse to different help when trying to solve a problem. Some Maya shamans, but not all, tend to be eccentric in ways that a lay person would find difficult to sustain. People know as common sense that the vast majority of a shaman's practice is hidden from them, and guarded as secret, and yet the same common sense says that some shamans really do have direct experiences with spiritual forces, or at least the great ones in the past did. Shamans are uncanny and surrounded with an aura of potential that is never revealed but always present as the possibility of strange feats. An altar or ritual space is different from a nonritual space in terms of its directional orientation and function. Time seems to pass differently in the two contexts as well, with ritual time characterized by certain forms of reversal and transposition atypical of nonritual. These points of contrast amplify the commonsense assumptions about difference from which we began, but they do not in themselves reveal much about Maya shamanism or patient-shaman relations.

The divide between shamans and others becomes distinctive in contexts of ritual performance. Not only do specialists and nonspecialists coparticipate in events such as divination, curing, and rain making, but they both interact with spirits in these contexts, too. Maya shamanic practices nearly all involve groups of spirits, who in turn differ meaningfully from one another. In performance, mere differences among actors undergo a subtle shift and become something more loaded. When a shaman and a patient are interacting in front of an altar, the differences between them in terms of background knowledge are brought together in a single manifold. They sustain an interactive relation in which they are alternately speaker, addressee, questioner, respondent, patient in treatment, shaman care-giver, supplicant, beneficiary. They in turn bear fundamentally distinct relations to the spirit agents who are enlisted in performance. Under such circumstances, differences that are usually backgrounded become sites of irreversible social asymmetry. Differential background knowledge provides the shaman with the ability to uncover aspects of the life of the patient, for instance, whereas the patient cannot reciprocate by gazing into the life of the shaman. Similarly, the shaman's relation to his tutelary spirits has little or no relevance to the patient's everyday experience. Except when they jointly engage in a diagnosis or cure, in which case it becomes the means by which the patient's experience is revealed or altered. In the same performance process, the shaman's subordinate relation to the spirits inverts, and he exercises power over them. He moves them from their resting places in the cosmos, literally lowers them to the altar. This practice is called *ʔéensik* '(to) lower (them)'. Whereas the spirits ordinarily oversee human affairs from their perches in the heavens, in ritual they step in and change things in the world.

Maya ritual discourse always engages actual people under actual circumstances and nearly always anticipates some outcome as the effect of proper performance. The shaman (*hmèen* lit. 'do-er'), patient or beneficiary, witnesses, the state of well-being or prosperity sought after, even the socioculturally defined place in which the performance occurs—all serve to anchor it in a local history. While the synchronic present of speech is rarely a matter of sheer simultaneity, its immediate horizons are proximal, and the social individuals (people and objects) who occupy it are, by definition, copresent. It is in this temporal frame that fleeting interactions between shaman and patient emerge from one moment to the next. The differences between them, and their differing relations to the spirits, are realigned precisely according to the practice in which they are coengaged. For divination, this involves shaman and patient interacting in question-answer pairs and in more extended talk. For *saántiguar* blessings, the patient remains a mute, third-person object on which the shaman causes the spirits to act. But even here the patient's physical aspect is engaged in precise ways with the altar, the spirits, and the shaman. Moreover, (s)he is enjoined to concentrate on well-being and the *santos,* that is, to keep the proceedings in his or her intentional focus. As they occur, ritual processes produce and transform relations among the participants. Some of the preexisting differences between them are invested with the value of distinction, others are effaced, and new ones are created.

Beyond the actual present, shamanic performances articulate with a midrange historical frame. This brings into play another order of relations among the principals. It encompasses such factors as the prior familiarity and patterns of shaman-patient interaction, any prior treatment for a current condition, including diagnostic rituals whose purpose was to identify the condition and prescribe treatment. It also includes the history of encounters and memories binding a ritual specialist to his familiar spirits and to those humans from whom he has learned. For it is only over a period of years that a Maya man can become a true *hmèen* 'shaman,' that his vocation can mature and that his *reésar* 'prayer' speech can become beautiful. There are more than a dozen genres of shamanic discourse in Yucatec Maya, some of them with subtypes and specialized forms, along with scores of spirits whose individual proper names, locations, and agentive capacities must be learned in order to perform properly. To this must be added the exacting interactive skills required in order to perform diagnosis using the *saástuún* 'divining crystals', which themselves must be acquired under charismatic circumstances. All this knowledge and prior experience is part of the actuality of performance, but it is present as past. It has the status of the pregiven, that which has happened and cannot be changed retrospectively.[5] It is *contemporary,* but not current, and it defines a field of relative *familiarity,* not of immediate copresence. When projected into subsequent experiences, this frame pertains to anticipations less immediate than the nearly actual ones of the local frame. A blessing performed on one day is often part of a series in which it is prospectively oriented toward subsequent reenactments, and ultimately toward a cure. This prospect is inscribed in the performance itself.

Some aspects of the ritual present derive from a more distant horizon. This applies to factors such as the cosmological framework within which spirits have certain axiomatic characteristics inherent in their identity. For instance, individual spirits known by names such as *lak'in ʔiik'* 'east wind', *ht'uúp balan ʔiik'* 'youngest brother jaguar wind' and *ʔah k'ìin koba* 'priest Coba' are held to have been created *before* other spirits, such as the Catholic derived saints. This fact never changes according to local circumstances, but is part of the background presupposed in any performance. Similarly, most spirits, especially the oldest ones by this definition, are endowed with fixed spatial coordinates that define their proper place in the cosmos. The five jaguar spirits stand in the sky between earth and the clouds, in the first of seven atmospheres ascending from the ground of humanity to heaven and the source of divinity. The East Wind and other purely directional spirits are higher and do not guard over inhabited spaces as do the jaguars. In any class of spirits that includes one called *ht'uúp* 'youngest brother', this individual stands in the middle of horizontal space, and the other members of the group are distributed by direction according to the familiar schema East, North, West, South, (Center) (Gossen 1974; Hanks 1984b; Redfield and Villa Rojas

1934; Tozzer 1941; Villa Rojas 1945). These and many more facts like them belong to a different order of history, neither copresent nor contemporary, but rather memorial. While features of memorial time are present in performance, they are present as originating in a distant past. At this range, the differences between spirits, and between humans and spirits are fixed according to original creations, mythic events whose consequences define the present, and cosmological eras whose properties are immutable.

While a shaman's knowledge and ability to make effective use of memorial history change greatly over his lifetime, this history is always present as having originated in the past. It is pregiven, the prefigurement of present and future. At this level, the shaman and patient exist only as human beings with different kinds of roles in the world, not as actual individuals with specific identities. One sign of this in performance is the shaman's presentation of himself as merely "a sinner," "a sun person," and of the patient as merely "the angel" (if prepubescent), "your daughter" (if female), "your son" (if male), and so forth. No specific identifying names or descriptions are used for human participants in either *saántiguar* 'sanctification' or *paʔ ʔiik* 'exorcism', the two most common genres of curing. These genres involve a memorial frame in which such factors are irrelevant. Shaman and patient engage as elemental humans, not as so and so.

Change occurs in all three zones of the phenomenal present, but it does so at different rates and with different consequences. The emerging actuality of ritual is subject to rapid, unforeseen change. No matter how choreographed by convention, its contours are interactively realized, and this leaves them open to improvisation on the spot. Consequences at this level include immediate effects, as when a distraught patient experiences sudden catharsis and visible improvement during performance, or the images in the divining crystals finally appear, after repeated attempts to call them up. At this level the relations among the interactants are similarly subject to rapid realignments, and mere differences can become suddenly distinctive. An otherwise irrelevant detail of the patient's background is cast into the light of scrutiny in divination, or the patient is informed that the minor aches and pains that led her to seek shamanic care in fact reflect a grave underlying condition. This appears indeed to be an area of true mastery in shamans, who are typically subtle observers capable of integrating whole clusters of unnoticed physical and mental attributes into a unifying diagnosis. Out of the patient-shaman relation emerges a new state of being in the patient.

Over the clinical history of an illness treated repeatedly for days, weeks, or even months, points of change may be equally sharp, but are subject to a process of sedimentation, and in some cases, routinization. This is especially so in a shaman's history of encounters with spirits, which may occur over decades. Each individual encounter has the status of a fact and a sign of greater factuality in the spiritual world. Recalling an encounter from long ago, a shaman may revise his appreciation of what really went on, and what it means for his vocation, but this does not alter the factuality of the encounter. Similarly, patients commonly learn from a shaman that they have been accidently struck by a nocive wind, whose unperceived blow to them triggers a chain of reactions and distress eventuating in full-blown illness. The illness then presents itself in the ritual present as a set of symptoms and signs from the spirits. Although it becomes actual in this moment, it is present as rooted in an etiology. This is typical of cases in which patients suffering from mild fever, nocturnal sweating, and unexplained hypertension turn out in diagnosis to have been in the path of a malicious wind. In all these contexts, events occur and take effect only over a period of time, during which their deleterious consequences unfold slowly. At the moment of their revelation, these facts emerge as constitutive of the patient's state of being and relation to the shaman.

Changes at the level of memorial history are much slower and more difficult to pinpoint, but they are nonetheless at work. One clear example of this is the incorporation of the conquest and early colonial period historical events into Maya cosmology. The memorial history of contemporary shamanic practice belongs to the age of biblical creation, that is, a Europeanized world. Most contemporary Yucatecans consider shamanism to be indigenous, but it is a post-conquest indiginiety. The spirit *Ah Kin Coba* has the status of a fixed coordinate from the perspective of the present, a spirit who occupies one of the four temples just below *Gloria* 'heaven'. But even this evidently native fact has been constituted through the mediating history of the Spanish colony. According to the Chilam Balam of Mani, the individual so named was a Maya leader in Mani province on the eve of the Spanish conquest (Solis Acala 1949:173). Indeed, when one discusses shamanic practice with a specialist, it becomes clear that many aspects of the memorial cosmology, which is today considered an icon of a pure Indian past, are in fact colonial products. The point here is not only that memorial history changes, albeit at a rate very different from the more local histories of the contemporary and actual world. Equally important is that this order of history can be brought into the present in such a way as to change the relations among present parties and thus realign differences to create certain distinctions and erase others.

The purpose of distinguishing these fields of the present is not to suggest that they are isolated from one another, or that one can sort out elements of ritual performance neatly into three piles. The aim is to understand how rapidly emerging features of action combine and interact with more slowly changing schematic and memorial ones, and how this process produces the relations of alterity that bind coparticipants. Once brought into play, an aspect of memorial history, such as the cosmology of cardinal directions, or the partial equivalence of human flesh with earth, is *made actual*. Two "phase changes" take place in the process of actualizing cosmology. The first is that apparently timeless features are temporalized. In the activity of *reésar* 'prayer, praying', the performing shaman transposes structures into the diachronic stream of performance (see sec. III below). This always involves synchronizing them with other similarly transposed elements. In this process the relations among elements are altered. This is not merely a logical abstraction, but one of the most important foci of Maya shamanic performance. Shamans follow strict conventions that govern the order in which spirits must be cited in prayer, and if they are cited out of order, the effectiveness of performance may be lessened as a result. Moreover, any competent Yucatec shaman knows that spirits are cited according to the purposes at hand; one simply does not lower down the *čaák* 'rain spirits' onto a patient in order to cure distress, just as one never mentions in a *čaá čaák* rain ceremony earth spirits who play a key role in *pa*ʾ *ʾiík* 'exorcism'. In curing rituals, even the speed of verbal articulation and the bodily rhythm of the shaman's gestures are varied according to the age and strength of the patient. Strong people can be treated in *peká*ʾ*an* 'fast' style, whereas weaker or more vulnerable ones require slower, more gentle prayer. All of these factors indicate that when memorial history is actualized in performance, it necessarily changes "phase" and acquires the temporal contours of the present. Rhythm, timing, and selectivity make a difference in performance.

The second phase change that arises when cosmology is actualized is that it is tied into highly local, idiosyncratic aspects of the present. The spirits of the cardinal directions and the *čaák* 'rain spirits' may themselves be timelessly ancient, but when they are invoked in a specific rain ceremony performed for the *socios* 'members' of a certain agricultural unit, they join the company of humans in local time. They enter the field of relevant distinctions. This joining has a spatial ground in the Maya belief that spirits are actually summoned from the heavens in prayer and brought to the altar, where they commune with each other in physical copresence with the shaman and beneficiaries. Maya offeratory altars are constructed according to precise principles of layout that diagram the positions occupied by different spirits once summoned. This copresence must be properly managed or the performance will be flawed. The articulation of cosmology with the local situation of performance is further reflected in the elaborate indexical structures that typify prayer. Prayer makes specialized use of pronouns, demonstrative elements, and other linguistic forms that delicately signal features of local context (Hanks 1984a, b).

One of the best examples of this is the dialogue that takes place between shaman and spirits in divination. Having cited and hence lowered to his altar the relevant spirits, the shaman holds a divining crystal in his right hand and gazes at it while asking the spirits to show him what is wrong with the patient.

(1)   wá tumèen k'ohá'ani šan   And if an illness too
       ti ulú'umi šan   in the earth too
       le kwèerpo síih šan   of the body was born too
       tulú'umi šan e kwèerpóo ↑   in the earth of that body
       'é'esé'ešten   (then) show it to me
       té' tasàanto kristalé'eš   right there in your holy crystals!
                                        (breath group 9; F.126.A.032)

While spirits do not speak human language under these circumstances (they do during charismatic encounters with the shaman, usually in the forest), they respond to the shaman's questions by showing him signs in the spherical looking glass of his crystal. The canonical sign of illness is a wisp of smoke, whose location in the crystal is taken to indicate the location of the illness in the person's body. The logic of this exchange may be roughly summarized as follows: the shaman brings the guardian spirits to his altar by way of prayer, and then asks them to gaze upon the patient, knowing that they can see evil or illness even far away or inside the body. The spirits do this and deliver their diagnosis to the shaman through the medium of smoke visible in his crystal. The crystal stands for the human body, such that the location of the smoke on one side or another indicates the location of the illness in one body part or another. To adequately explain how this process works out in individual cases would require a separate paper. For our purposes, the essential point is that spirits whose identity is fixed in memorial history become part of the immediate present in prayer. This means they enter the world of human experience, where they become interlocutors addressed in the second person and capable of acting on behalf of specific individuals with their individual concerns.

If the macrohistory of cosmology is transposed into the lived present of ritual performance, the inverse happens as well. Fleeting idiosyncrasies of human affairs are subsumed into the enduring universals of cosmology. Socorro Xiu and her sister-in-law from Akil came on the morning of July 17, 1984, to the home of Don Seéb, a well-known shaman in Oxkutzcab, in order to find out why their children were constantly sick, their domestic fowl dying off, and their nights plagued by strange noises coming from out in the yard (names are fictitious, but the case was witnessed and recorded by author, F.125.090ff). The two were concerned and wanted to determine whether these things were signs of some greater danger, and whether they could remedy it with the shaman's help. His first move was to go to his altar and open dialogue with the guardian spirits using the divining crystals. I adjusted my tape recorder and remained silent near the altar. It turned out after prolonged consultation that the *soólar* 'yard' inhabited by the women was polluted by the presence of the evil spirit named *ščakk'aɁ teɁ Ɂiik'*. This spirit, which has no place in domestic space, was nested in the southeast corner of the yard, a fact that Don Seéb learned by the location of the smoke in his crystal. Furthermore, the spirit was causing damage in the homestead by moving along a diagonal axis from its nest at the corner to the front door of the house. Any time spirits move freely through lived space they are susceptible of striking humans and animals, thereby causing illness. It would be necessary to perform a *heɁ lúɁum* 'fix earth' ceremony to get it out of there and cleanse the space, Don Seéb told the two women.

What ensued was a brilliant interaction between Don Seéb and the women, as he continued to hold and intermittently study the crystals. The issue at this point was to determine what materials the women would have to gather for the performance, and how much he would charge them for doing it. Price varies according to the case, and he learns the proper rate from his crystals as well (this one would cost the women 700 pesos, although the same performance today might cost 70,000, due to inflation). By the end of the episode, the women left knowing that the odd occurrences around their homestead were caused by the above-named spirit, who would be swept out of the yard by Don Seéb in a 'fix earth' ceremony that would take place in the near future, according to proper procedures. In other words, the fragments of their own experiences had been articulated through the terms of shamanic cosmology, in which they made sense and could be acted upon.

The upshot of these ethnographic observations is that the lived present of ritual performance is never a simple simultaneity. Rather, it is an internally complex process produced by the interactions of elements rooted in distinct temporal fields. In the foregoing remarks we have signaled only a portion of this complex, and a more thorough discussion would be needed to examine the differences of perspective, memory, and anticipation that distinguish shaman from patient, along with the patient's subsequent behavior and prior relation with the illness at hand. In the process of performance, actors adopt highly constrained perspectives and postures as their momentary 'now'. This in turn affects or even produces the relations between them, defining difference and identity according to a changing phenomenal present. The shaman, as a specialist, enjoys much more scope on this point than do nonspecialists, for he is continuously aware of the memorial sources of his spirits, the macrohistory of their existence both before and after his own lifetime, and what is going on as he chants their names. Patients typically have no access to this, all of which is esoteric. One important plane of difference between the participants then is their unequal access to the different historical sectors of the present.

As a further illustration of this, Don Seéb once told me of his experiences in the archaeological site known as Labna, in the Puuc region of Yucatan. We were visiting the site together, when he told me that he often came here and walked the grounds. The difference was that when he came, it was still densely populated with Maya nobles and there was a great bustling marketplace in the center. The Labna that I knew well was an archeological monument, partly in ruin and surely not inhabited by anyone other than the INAH guard and his family. Walking side-by-side, we were nonetheless inhabiting different temporal frameworks. The vast asymmetries in knowledge and understanding that separate shamans from their patients and friends result in similar discrepancies, since the former occupy a temporal framework that reaches from memorial history to the emerging situation of performance and henceforth, whereas the latter have only diffuse access to the memorial histories in which shamanism is rooted.

II

When one shifts attention from historical frameworks to the relations between frameworks and social actors, a subtle change takes place. The main issue is no longer the different historical fields combined in practice. Rather, the key issue becomes how actors locate themselves within these fields, how they construe their lived present and its relation to other nonactual time frames. This is another matter of basic difference between shamans and nonshamans. A shaman may be aware of cosmic structures of *longue durée*, but he also realizes that his own present as a *hk'iinil wiínik* 'sun person' engaged in prayer is more narrow than this. The patient is typically not aware of the particular memorial structures to which the shaman is responding, yet he or she knows they exist 'out there' and may well project a sense of the great Maya history to which this divination on this Friday afternoon is linked. The history of illness leading up to a clinical episode is not merely a diachronic frame of mid-range. It is a stream of experience that the patient inhabits, and that the shaman, from his distance, must come to know (however imperfectly). This all involves differential attention on the part of ritual participants to portions of the phenomenal present, to their own placement in it, and to the placements of their interlocutors. While all participants may anticipate well-being as the intended outcome of proper performance, the meaning and valence of this typically differs from person to person. A *pa' 'iik'* 'break spirit, wind' exorcism has for a seasoned shaman like Don Seéb a typicality that makes it familiar, repeatable, and predictable, to a degree. The very same performance may be terrifying for a patient, and I have witnessed patients weep and swoon during ritual treatment. The shaman anticipates in detail the symptoms likely to emerge from a current condition, while the patient may be at odds to even describe the current state of affairs, and at a loss as to its likely trajectory. Insofar as their participant roles differ basically in the performance itself, shaman and patient necessarily situate themselves differently to what is going on, and assume different degrees of responsibility for different aspects of the overall event. All of these factors contribute to the modes of participant involvement in ritual performance. I will summarize such factors under the rubric of "orientation." There are various kinds of orientations, and coparticipants in ritual events sustain different ones according to their distinct ways of inhabiting the framework of ritual performance.

The actions described here always involve the engagement of one or more social actor in an intentional project, that is, pursuing what Alfred Schutz called an "in order to motive." This goal-directedness by no means exhausts the sociocultural meaning of shamanic performance, nor need it even be neatly delimited. Patients for instance enter into ritual contexts with many diverse motivations, as shamans know well and I have witnessed. The effects of ritual action may also outstrip the intentions of those who undertake them. A good example of this arose when Don Seéb described how he had performed a rain ceremony for members of an agricultural cooperative in the Puuc region. There had been little rainfall before the ceremony, but by its end, a torrential downpour had started, eventually flooding and causing extensive damage to the area. It is also clear that participants co-engaged in ritual action need not all share the same intentions. It is a matter of common sense among Maya people that patients go to shamans with various motives, sometimes to test or dupe them, and that some shamans themselves pursue strategies of self-enrichment or chicanery at odds with the apparent purposes of performance. These factors are consistent with the maxim of difference. They all go beyond any simple equation between one intention and one act, yet they do not alter the basic premise that ritual actions do entail intentional projections. Much of routine social action is also habitual and guided by ingrained patterns of which actors may not even be aware and which they need not represent in intentional terms. Finally, it is quite possible to speak of agency, events, and actions in the context of social collectivities to which terms like "intention" and "motive" do not apply in any simple way.

These numerous qualifications serve to delimit the scope of intentionality in ritual action, without effacing it completely. There are ethnographic factors that reinforce its role. The first is that Maya shamans rarely discuss or practice *reésar* 'prayer' outside the context of actual performance. In conducting research on the therapeutic ritual known as *saántiguar* 'sanctification', a prayer that lasts anywhere from about eight to twelve minutes, I found that Don Seéb was unable to discuss it in detail. Despite his active practice of performing the ritual dozens of times every week over the past thirty years, he was unable to remember the names of the spirits he routinely cited and could discuss it only in general terms. Working from tape recordings I was able to determine a good deal of systematic covariation between the form of the prayer and the characteristics of patients (Hanks 1984b). Yet when I pointed this out to him, he responded that he cannot recall the prayer because he has never memorized it. Rather, when starting a performance, the key is to be what he calls *hač čičan* 'tiny', namely focused entirely on the situation and on the well-being that one wishes to bring about. Given the requisite state of intention and volition—a proper orientation and posture—the spirits do the rest by speaking through him. The discourse of prayer is itself marked by frequent use of conventional expressions describing what the performer is doing, such as begging, requesting, and cleansing, and these formulae all index intentional states.

(2)   ʔinkʼaátik   'I request'
         ʔintʼanlaántikéʔeš   'I address you all'
         ʔinȼikbatik téʔeš   'I recount to you (pl)'
         ʔinwokʼohʼoóltik   'I beg (lit., 'weep-will')'

The patient, for his or her part, is enjoined to concentrate on the saints and on the sought-after well-being in order to help the shaman secure results. In other words, the engagement of coparticipants is culturally proscribed. This orientation is part of what it means to occupy a position in the ritual context.

A related feature of performance is that it is always accompanied by some paraphernalia, which may be as simple as a saint's image, a flower, and a lit candle, or as elaborate as a multipart altar construction. In all cases, the prayer takes place in the physical copresence of these elements. This spatial proximity is also inscribed in the discourse in a series of conventional expressions, including the following, all of which recur in all genres of prayer.

(3)   kuliken tučùun amesa   'I am seated at the foot of your altar'
         waliken tučùun amesa   'I am standing at the foot of your altar'
         apaktikóʔ on téʔ tulúʔ umi   'You gaze on us there on the earth
                         kʼeban   of sin'

Thus an important part of occupying the ritual frame is to be corporeally located within it. For all curing performances, as far as I know, the patient must actually be present with the shaman before the altar, and there are numerous constraints on how people position themselves relative to it.[6] Altars canonically face East-Southeast, with the shaman standing to the West facing in the same direction as the altar. Any *santos* on the altar are understood to be icons of spirits actually located in their cardinal places. Thus, a cross stands for Christ who himself is located in the East, but faces toward humanity in the West. The cross reproduces this orientation, placed on the front (East) side of the altar and facing the shaman to the West. Depending upon the genre of performance, a patient-beneficiary may be placed between the shaman and the altar, or behind the shaman. In both cases (s)he faces the altar, adopting the same visual alignment as the shaman. Visual imagery is pervasive in Maya prayer itself, with the spirits requested to "turn your gaze and look upon us," to "give a sign," to *saásikuúntik* 'enlighten' and *čikbesik* 'make manifest'. The candles placed on the altar are there so as to lead the spirits by their light. All of these corporal alignments and gaze vectors are basic, rule-governed parts of performance. They reinforce the grounding of ritual in the corporeal present, and they provide the critical pathways by which the spirits engage with their human others.

Apart from the relation of participants to the altar and the spirits whom it embodies, the relation between shaman and patient further extends the corporeal grounding of performance. In curing ceremonies, shaman and patient are within immediate reach of one another, and the shaman touches the patient continually as he prays. In *saántiguar* 'sanctification' and *pa⁷ ⁷iík'* 'break spirit, wind' ceremonies, he brushes the patient with fresh flowers or *sipče⁷* boughs as he prays, basically sweeping the body while he begs the spirits to cleanse it of illness. The patient canonically remains immobile, sitting or standing in front of the altar, gazing on the *santos*. A Maya shaman's breathing is rigidly constrained during performance also, since prayer is canted in breath groups with highly regular prosodic contour (Hanks 1984b). The unit of one breath is considered by Don Seéb to constitute a single whole within which a meaningful group of spirits is cited, an interval whose contents are synchronous. To break the breath group in mid-utterance is to risk losing the thread of the performance (*t'ó⁷ok'ol u ⁷iilo*). The regularity of voice, breathing, and touching create a sonorous and tactual field around the patient, which Don Seéb considers essential to curing.

These aspects of intentional and corporeal engagement provide an actional ground in performance. In terms of the temporal frameworks described in the preceding section, they happen in the actuality of ongoing experience. The rhythm of breathing, touching, gazing, and experiencing anchors the phenomenal present of performance in the local copresence of participants. One layer of the ritual "now" is equivalent therefore to the emerging corporeal present. While there are important asymmetries in between them, shaman and patient share this corporeality as a mutual ground for their interaction. Borrowing a term from Goffman (1974) and students of interaction, we can say that coparticipants in ritual find a common "footing" in their bodily copresence before the altar. This fact gives a certain priority to what we called the local temporal frame, for it is here that copresence is defined.

It is important to see that action takes place on more than one level, and the ritual now is not coextensive with participants' body time. The easiest way to see this is to consider that, while copresent at the altar, shamans and patients describe events from the past, eventualities in the future, and places distant from their current here-now. The *saástuún* 'divining crystals' provide a technical means for shamans to gaze upon events and states of affairs that may not even be visible under normal circumstances, and if so, may be separated from the present performance by arbitrarily great distances in time and space. A plot of land like the one described above may be unsafe for humans not because an external evil force has come to occupy it, but because it is *sùuk* 'habituated' to receiving ritual cleansing, which the current owners have failed to undertake. Land is always inhabited by spirits, and spirits have memory. A plot in which *heč lú°um* 'fix earth' ceremonies are periodically held, say every few years, may become unsafe if a current owner fails to maintain it properly. Autochthonous winds that would normally be held in check by jaguar spirits suddenly roam freely causing havoc, because the jaguar spirits have not been properly cared for. It is natural that in arriving at a diagnosis, a shaman discusses with a patient events that occurred in the past, and much of the divination may be focused on reconstructing the past occurrences that have led the patient to seek the shaman's services in the first place. It is an interesting fact of Maya practice that people rarely inform a shaman of why they have come, asking instead that he diagnose them himself. Instead of telling him what ails them, patients usually start with statements to the effect of "I just came to see if you would illuminate me Don Seéb." It is only in the course of the ensuing divination that the motives of their visit will emerge clearly. While this interaction occurs on the "home field" of the corporeal present, it also concerns nonpresent matter, extending outward to distant space and time.

Ritual enactments mediate between local, emerging time and midrange schematic time. The historical scope of performance extends even farther by way of the spirits to whom the shaman addresses his prayer, for as we said, these agents embody memorial history that is in some cases as old as creation. The following example is the sixth breath group in a *tiíč'k'aák'* divination performed for a young woman who turned out to have a simple nervous condition.

(4)	lèetyo *yun sàanto šp'iris tuún balam*	Those ones Lord Holy Stone Jaguar
	kint'ano bakan	I address them evidently
	tuk'aàba *kristo* b'èey šan	in the name of Christ so too
	ikil in maánsik kwèenta bakaán	whereby I pass the story evidently
	ti° *sak papa° tuún*	to White Pelting Stone
	ikil in maánsik kwèenta	whereby I pass the story
	tio bakan *yùun°ah k'in čaán*	to them evidently Lord Priest Chan
	°ah k'ìin koba° šan ↓	Priest Coba too
	°ah k'ìin kolon te° č'iíb' ↓ ##	Priest Colonte Write. (F.47.A.323ff)

Each of the italicized spirit names refers to an individual familiar to Don Seéb as a shaman and engaged routinely in his practice. He can describe their origins in memorial space and time and their role in the present, whereas few nonshamans would even know their names, aside from Christ, and virtually no one without specialized training would be able to state their attributes. The first is a member of the jaguar spirits who have guarded over the earth since its creation. They are located at the four corners of the heavens just above the earth's atmosphere. *Sak Papa Tun* is a high-ranking rain spirit of the Chac class, located high above the jaguar lords, but below the *Ah K'iines*, whose temples are just below the entrance to *Gloria* 'Heaven'. The name *Sak Papa Tun* is probably derived from the preconquest class of Maya Pauatun spirits described by Thompson (1970). In his study of Yucatec prayer, Gutiérrez Estévez (1988:77) remarks that Chacs are associated with the *arkanheles* 'archangels' from Catholic cosmology and suggests that this link may be motivated in part by phonetic similarity between the Spanish term and the classical Maya term *canhel*. The latter was used to designate a symbol associated with rain deities. In Don Seéb's practice, the associations are interesting and vary according to ritual genre. *Sak Papa Tun* does work with Michael the Archangel in *č'áa čáak* rain making, but in *tiič'k'áak'* divination, he works with other classes of spirits. They collectively produce visible signs of the patient's state of being in the crystals. In other words, the spirits are ancient, but the relations among them, and the ways in which they can alter human affairs, are different according to the genre of practice in which they are actualized.

The last three are particularly interesting from a historical perspective. All *ah k'iin* 'sun man (priest)' spirits are considered very ancient by Don Seéb and are located in three temples, at the top of the East, North, and South sectors of the heavens, respectively. There is a fourth *ah k'iin*, named *ah k'iin tùus* (lit. 'Deception priest') who resides in a temple in the West, but he plays no role in divination and is therefore not cited. Were he to enter into a divination, according to Don Seéb, he would likely deceive the shaman and ruin the diagnosis. Of the three who are cited, two of them appear to be identifiable in the Codex Peres. This book consists of Maya manuscripts taken from the archives of Mani, Yucatan, by fray Juan Pio Peres in the mid-nineteenth century. An erudite scholar of Maya, Pio Peres hand-copied the documents together in what has come to be known as the "codex" named after him. Among the documents were transcripts of the prophecies and pronouncements of Maya priests, as well as contact-period lists of Maya chiefs and priests located around the Mani area, which included Oxkutzcab. Don Seéb was raised in Mani and practices in Oxkutzcab today; so it is unsurprising that common features relate his ritual discourse to the documents copied by Perez. The second part of Codex Perez starts with quotations from seven *ah k'iin* priests in Mani, the fifth of whom is named *Ah Natzin Yuban Chan, ah kìin,* or what could today be called simply *ah k'iin chan.*

Shortly after this, the Codex continues with a series of historical descriptions (possibly prophecies) arranged by *katun* periods (a calendrical unit of twenty years), each with the name and line drawing of the *ah k'iin* priest who *hedz* 'fixed, erected' the *katun* (Solis Acala 1949:172). This series includes one *Ah Kin Chi,* also known as *Kinchil Coba,* who 'fixed' the *katun* named Oxlahun Ahau 'Thirteen Ahau'. As it turns out, Don Seéb also cites an *Ah Kin Chi* in other rituals, and I believe that this may be an alternate name for the same historical character (on the existence of alternate names in the hieroglyphic corpus, see Lounsbury 1989). Immediately after this in the Codex there is a list of Maya nobles from the Mani region, and *Ah Kin Chi* is listed as the "teniente" of Tutul Xiu, the *halač uinic* 'true man', or highest ranking noble of the entire province. What these details indicate is that the spirits in question have a dual existence: in the emerging present of performance, they are spirits who occupy high temples in the heavens and can be addressed through prayer. In the distant past of memorial history, these same individuals were once human and served as priests and prognosticators in native society. Don Seéb is actually aware of this discrepancy and considers these and many other spirits to be Maya humans who became *encantado* 'enchanted' during the Spanish conquest and who exist now and forever more as spirits.

There is a strong parallel between Don Seéb's identity as shaman engaged in divination and the colonial identity of *ah k'ìin* priests as prognosticators. The position of *ah k'ìin* 'sun man, priest' is a well known one in the colonial history, and the Spanish routinely described these men as 'sacerdotes'. Among their functions was to consult spirit forces who descended to them through the roof of a house and whose words they would in turn interpret for nonpriests (for whom they would be unintelligible without the mediation of the *ah k'ìin*). Today, Maya shamans, including Don Seéb, are often described as *k'ìini wíinik* 'sun person', because of the pervasive importance of the Sun in Maya cosmology. This descriptor is a near equivalent semantically to the older one. Joined together, these facts suggest a substantive link between modern divination and ancient prognostication, modern shamans, and ancient *ah k'ìin* priests. They also suggest a powerful continuity between conquest-period Mani and contemporary Mani, embodied in the persistence of named agents. In effect, when these spirits deliver a diagnosis to Don Seéb in his crystals, they are continuing to do what they did when they were humans on earth, namely, deliver esoterically acquired knowledge to a human collaborator. When Don Seéb in turn explains the diagnosis to a patient, he is doing the same thing the ancient Ah Kin priests did, interpreting esoteric signals in the light of current affairs. Thus, it is unsurprising that Don Seéb anticipates that he too will become enchanted upon death and continue to frequent the same Mani of his lived experience, forever.

When we say that shamanic ritual mediates between local and memorial historical frames, it is this movement back and forth that we underscore, along with the homologies that sustain it. It is equally important however to bear in mind that the joining of these fields through reference and historical description is not a neutral fact pertaining to the "system design" of Maya ritual practice. It is a necessary condition of effective performance, an objective that shamans seek to attain with greater and greater surety. Don Seéb's relation to the Ah Kin spirits is not a matter of symbolism or similarity, but direct copresence, which he brings about through the technical skill of *reésar* 'prayer'. Nearly seventy years old, he has spent half a lifetime learning and beautifying his discourse in order more effectively to work with the spirits. His frame of reference emerged slowly over a long apprenticeship to spirits, during which he was taken away by them and instructed in their modes of speaking.

This brings us to the next major point, namely, that the borderzone between the local emerging present and the global memorial past can be crossed in both directions.

Participants in ritual (as in other kinds of interaction), are not fixed permanently in their corporeal field, but can take up a footing in other frames, just as they can bring objects from other frames into their corporeal field through speech. Thus, according to lengthy explanations by Don Seéb, a shaman projects himself out into the cosmos through prayer, in effect traveling from spirit to spirit along a path leading from the altar to the heavens. In divination, the "earth" (elemental physical being) of the patient is brought before the spirits so that they can examine it. In both of these cases, participants in the performance are transposed from the immediate spatiotemporal field into the distant reaches of the cosmos. Instead of remaining anchored in the bodily origo of speech and describing distant places in distant terms, they project themselves through prayer to those places, temporarily leaving the bodily origo. The inverse process also takes place routinely in prayer, when spirits are lowered from their respective places down to the altar. The lowering is an explicit technique, described as *'eénsik yunc il* 'lowering lords' and it is governed by conventions that shamans, and to a lesser degree many nonspecialist Maya people as well, can articulate. This indicates that the divisions between local and memorial histories are permeable to the orientations of actors. Not only can Don Seéb refer to things "out there," but through prayer he can refer to things *from the perspective of someone who actually is out there,* and he can bring the "out there" into his current "here." Each one of these realignments entails a recasting of the relations between shaman and other copresent humans.

Among the transpositions that take place in ritual performance, we can distinguish two gross kinds, which I shall call centripetal and centrifugal. The former involves drawing historically distant individuals and events into the immediate present, in effect making actual what existed long ago or far away. As esoteric as it may sound, this trope is common even in European discourse, but tends to be associated with storytellers who "vividly" describe events from long ago, as in "Imagine this happening right here. This table is the field of battle, . . ." Such effects are usually considered "figurative" or "imaginative" ways of bringing the past into the present. A similar transposition is also at play in Catholic liturgy when the body and blood of Christ are actualized in the sacrament of Communion.[7] In Maya shamanic practice, this actualization is not figurative, but rather invested with factual reality. It motivates much of the spatial arrangement of the scene. The altar becomes the place to which spirits are lowered, so as to co-occupy the present with shaman and patient. In all cases involving movements of dangerous spirits, powerful guardian spirits are first posted around the shaman to protect him from being struck. Called *liík'sik k'aák'* 'raising up fire', the spirits make a defensive ring through which evil cannot pass. In major rain and thanksgiving ceremonies, offerings are laid out on the altar in a pattern that diagrams the locations of the spirits to whom they are presented, and these spirits are actually lowered to the offerings and allowed to dwell there during a key, communionlike portion of the event (Hanks and Rice 1990: Chapter 8). Even in the smaller therapeutic rituals of *saántiguar* 'sanctification' and *pa' 'iík'* 'break spirit, wind' exorcism, spirits are summoned to the altar to brush over and in some cases actually enter the body of the patient. Insofar as these spirits have known historical coefficients, which they do, by lowering them, the shaman performs both spatial and temporal transposition. The process is centripetal in the sense of projecting elements from the memorial horizon into the immediate focus of performance. The historical and ontological differences between spirits and humans provide pathways along which the former come into direct contact with the latter. Agents in memorial history become agents in the emerging present.

Centrifugal transposition plays less of a role in Maya shamanism, because it is a specialized feature of only some genres and not a generalized feature of all *reésar* 'prayer'. It plays a particularly important role during the apprenticeship of a shaman, when spirits may take him away with them in order to teach him, leaving his physical body unconscious or disoriented, yet taking his consciousness on a pedagogic journey. These "out of body" experiences are crucial in the learning process and constitute a specialized case of centrifugal transposition. It is in direct contact with spiritual others that the shaman acquires his specialized knowledge. Within divination performances, the divining crystals serve as an instrument of centrifugal transposition also. The shaman's field of visual perception is dilated to such an extent that he can witness events in distant space and time. The so-called "prophetic" discourse of the conquest-period Ah Kin priests, which so obsessed and fascinated Spanish commentators, appears to rely on another form of transposition. According to the descriptions in the Books of Chilam Balam, the Ah Kin would receive knowledge from spirits that he would then interpret in the form of assertions regarding events in the future. Where the modern shaman uses the *saástuún* 'divining crystals' as his instrument of projection, the classic priests evidently relied on an esoteric discourse of history and prognostication, involving astrological and calendrical units. While Maya prophecy is too poorly understood to make secure statements, it would be fruitful to compare it with modern divination.[8]

We have seen that the temporal field of shamanic performance is internally complex. At one extreme, it encompasses the instantaneous, emerging present, in which the corporeal engagements of participants take place. At the other, it encompasses spatially and temporally distant individuals and events who are present as originating in the past. The two poles are not coordinate, in the sense that the former can be known and experienced by way of routine perceptual and actional capacities, whereas the latter is accessible only through memory, anticipation, or highly technical skills of projection. The "phenomenal present," that is, the meaningful, lived present, may include any subportion of the total historical manifold of performance. The lived present is not only a temporal field, but a field occupied by social actors, just as a communicative event is not only a configuration of roles, but a configuration occupied by actual interactants. Occupancy involves orientation, for there are many ways of occupying the present, and performing shamans do it differently than patients.

There are two key points here: (i) orientation always involves two factors, a home base that serves as ground or origo for the actor, and a broader field in which the home base is located. An emerging present on the one hand, and a memorial time frame (such as a calendar) or spatial map on the other. Both elements are necessary if one is to speak of an "orientation." (ii) The home base of an actor is usually, by default, the corporeal present, but this can easily be changed. Two changes have concerned us, (a) the centrifugal transpositions through which the ritual here-now is displaced from the corporeal field to some spatiotemporally distant zone in the cosmos; (b) centripetal transpositions through which spirits and distant events are drawn into the now of performance, made present to the participants.

In the next section we examine in more detail the process of moving spirits to and from the altar of performance. This involves both kinds of transposition, centripetal and centrifugal, and is governed by highly systematic rules of discourse. Two cultural premises make spirit movement an exacting art. On the one hand, spirits exist in determinate places in space and time, just as they have proper names and perform determinate functions in the cosmos. According to the literature and my own field work, Maya shamans attend to a detailed memorial calendar and map of the cosmos (there may well be variation, but there appear to be powerful commonalities). In order to move a spirit from its place and bring it into the world, it is sufficient to pronounce its name, but in order to do so properly, it is necessary to speak the name under just the right conditions. On the other hand, spirits improperly moved are inherently dangerous. Even benevolent forces cause havoc when wrongly handled. The earth of a homestead may become uninhabitable, with domestic animals dying off and human inhabitants becoming chronically ill. A patient may be overcome or perish from exposure to uncontrolled forces, or the shaman himself may be struck down while performing. Transposition involves direct contact between human and spiritual agents, and the resulting field of alterity is inherently volatile.

III

The first step in understanding how Maya shamans move spirits is to situate the altar as a space of performance. There are different kinds of altars, according to the ritual context in which they are used, but all are quadrilateral with a leg at each corner.[9] The domestic altar, of both shamans and nonspecialists, is canonically placed in the east side of the house, in the *moy* 'end' area. It is usually a wooden table on which are kept the family *saàntos* 'saints, images,' fresh flowers, and a burning candle, in addition to the shaman's divining crystals and other paraphernalia.[10] As we said above, altars are always endowed with a front side, which is the edge closest to the (inter)cardinal direction to which the shaman faces. They also have a back side called *tučùun* 'at the foot of' where the shaman stands, a right and a left. Just as the human body has front-back, lateral and vertical axes, so too does an altar. Atop the altar are *sàantos* and in some cases arcs that represent the spirits and the heavens they occupy. Endowed with directionality, the altar may be seen as the center point from which vectors radiate indefinitely far, along specific axes. This is why the shaman and patient face East. If the participants fail to mirror the orientation of the altar in these terms, then the performance may be infelicitous. A shaman who faced away from the altar while praying would almost surely be suspected of witchcraft or incompetence, and a patient who refused to position him- or herself properly would thereby violate the proper conditions of the act.

Apart from the body-centric orientation of altars is the memorial structure of cosmic space to which they face. Like most mesoamerican cosmologies, Yucatec Maya incorporates a fundamental schema of cardinal directions, arrayed in a vertical hierarchy of *tàasil* 'layers'. Holding aside disputes as to whether the basic spatial configuration is quadripartite or five-part, and whether intercardinal points are basic or derived, it can be said that North, South, East, and West play a basic role in Yucatec shamanic practice. In the context of performance, the cardinal points are defined as regions containing specific, named places. *ʔiikʔóʔob* 'winds, spirits' are described as brothers and *maákóʔob* 'people' who originate from these places, and their qualities depend partly upon their provenance.[11] Ritual discourse creates a point-by-point path or 'road', as the shaman proceeds from place to place. The altar and the true cardinal locations are separated by great distance in time and space, and the role of transpositions is to mediate this. The cardinal locations are described as *tukantíʔ ie il káʔan, tukantíʔ ie il lǔʔum* 'at the four corners of (the) sky, at the four corners of the earth', the 'center, middle'. Some spirits originate in the *čuúmuk* 'center' and are usually described as the smallest or youngest of the brothers, yet the most powerful.

In most socially significant spaces, including towns, homesteads, plazas, and traditional cornfields, the four corners plus the center define the space as a whole. For instance, in the creation of a cornfield, the corner and center markers are laid down in the forest, and offerings made in the center before the remaining *šúʔuk* 'boundary markers' are laid out and before any trees are felled. Similarly, in the *hee lúʔum* 'fix earth' ceremony, which purifies the land within a single bounded *soólar*, the altar is always placed in the *čuúmuk* 'middle' of the yard, and offerings are buried there and at

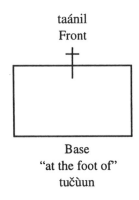

taánil
Front

Base
"at the foot of"
tučùun

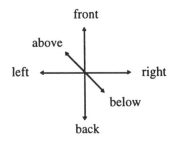

Fig. 8.1 Centered Orientation of the Altar

the four corners. The 'middle' of town is often defined by the location of a great *yáašče°* 'ceiba' or *laáwrel* 'laurel' tree.[12] Whether it is a relatively small domestic space, a municipal one, the top of an altar, a cornfield or the entire world, its four corners-plus-center define its schematic totality. The corners are connected not by perpendicular lines radiating from the middle, but by a perimeter, connecting the outer points.[13] It is this perimetal configuration that defines the limits of space and therefore the difference between inside and outside. In most cases of illness caused by the pollution of inhabited space, the problem is due to a breached perimeter: *°iik°* 'spirits, winds' that should be immobile or kept outside find their way inside and roam freely. But *miná° an u derečo* 'they do not have the right' to do this, as Don Seéb puts it, and his task is to corner such a spirit and expel it from the space. In this way, his practice presupposes a logic of perimetal division based on the cardinal places. Note the contrast between this, shown in Figure 8.2, and the directional schema in Figure 8.1.

Ritual precisely relates the distant, memorial structures of cosmology to the emergent, centered structures of the corporeal field. We can see this in the way the two orientations, centered-local and cardinal-global, are combined. The key to this combination is to move spirits from the cardinal places down to the altar, positioning them within a space endowed with right/left, front/back, and above/below, with the altar itself serving as center point. The first step is to properly arrange the corporeal field of the altar and the participants relative to the cardinal points. This precludes things like an altar facing West, a shaman performing while sitting under or standing atop the altar, a patient standing in front of the altar instead of at its foot, and so forth. When lowered to receive the offerings in the *heéč lú°um* 'fix earth' and *č'aá čaák* 'get rain' ceremonies, spirits arrive at the 'front' of the altar, and no one except the *b'ó°ol* 'shaman's assistant' is

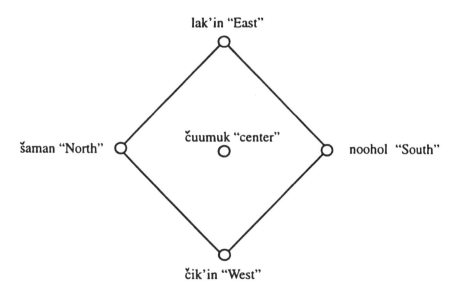

Fig. 8.2. Cardinal Places

allowed to pass there during the entire event. The memorial and emergent spaces must
be properly aligned at the outset. Recall also that these spaces correspond to different
temporal fields of the ritual present, a memorial past, and a momentary actuality.

Thus there is a dual orientation in the corporeal field of performance, with the altar serving as pivot: to the East facing West are the spirit addressees, in front of whom
stands the *sàanto* image on the East edge of the altar, also facing West. To the West of
the altar surface facing East is the shaman in prayer, with the audience to his back.
The audience canonically faces East, recapitulating the shaman's orientation, although
there is more flexibility for audience members to sustain other postures and engagements than there is for the shaman or patient to do so (see Figure 8.3).

Assuming a properly aligned corporeal field, the next step is to lower the spirits in
some principled order, so that the five-point schema of their origin places is transposed
into the altar space in the right way. This amounts to uniting the ontologically and
temporally distinct zones of the ritual present. It is at this point that the static schema
of spatial positions is temporalized, transformed from a structure into a progression
with sequence and duration. The spirits are summoned step-by-step, not all at once,
and enter into the actuality of utterance production, in which the present is a constantly emerging center point from which before/after, and other centered relations, radiate. The cardinal schema, by contrast, is a synchronic unity in which the present is a
timeless quadrilateral perimeter, inside of which the world exists and outside of which
is nothing. In Yucatec shamanic practice, the lived present is the product of combining the two spatiotemporal fields into a single whole, a dynamic field in which relations of alterity are produced and transformed. How does this happen? Let us first consider the centripetal cycles by which spirits are made present at the altar.

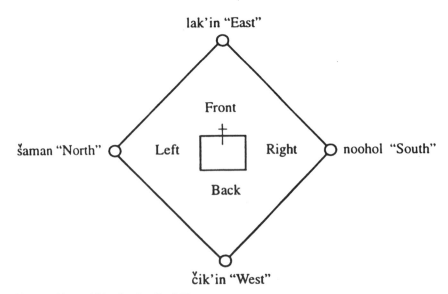

Fig. 8.3 Altar within the Cardinal Places

In the traditional genres of shamanic practice in Maya, the basic dynamic of prayer is the same:[14] spirits, who are located in cardinal places throughout the vertical and horizontal universe, are *ʔeénsáʔal* 'lowered' to the place of performance, actually *peéksáʔal* 'moved' from their appointed places and brought down to an encounter with the shaman, and those he presents in the performance space. The space of the altar, referred to in performance as *téʔ tulúʔumil kʼebʼan* 'there on the earth of sin', and *tučùun ʔumèesa X* 'at the base of X's altar (where X is a spirit name)', is reconstituted in an absolutely orderly process. Spirits are lowered in the order of their locations of origin. There are differences among types of performance, but in major ceremonies, the opening phases of the ritual, in which spirits are lowered, proceed in the counterclockwise order E > N > W > S > C, whereas the closing phases, in which the shaman *sutikóʔobʼ* 'returns them', the preferred order is clockwise, E > S > W > N > C (Hanks 1984b:138–41). The first phase is called *heʔik bèel* 'opening the road', or *kʼašik mèesa* 'binding (the) altar', and the second is called *wačik mèesa* 'untie (the) altar'.

The binding of the altar in ritual discourse is the opening of a 'road' between the immediate present and the memorial cosmology, and between the agents that occupy these different fields. Roads and paths are spoken of in everyday Maya as leading 'up' to their destinations, and travelers as walking 'over' and 'in front of' them (since 'off the path' in Maya is *pàačil* 'behind' it). It is common in routine interaction for roads to be named by their destination, as in *ubʼèel akʼil* 'the road (to) Akil'. The day, state of being and destiny of the individual are also said to be *ʔu bèel* 'his road'. Work which has gotten under way, into full swing, is said to have *čʼik beh* 'taken road'. Don Seéb describes his shamanic vocation as his *bèel* 'road', and has an elaborate philosophy according to which his economic poverty is the *ʔekʼ beh* 'small path' that the spirits taught him to choose during his apprenticeship to them (doubtless a biblical reference). These various realizations of the path have in common that they are *directional*. Whether one considers it as an emerging stream of experience whose finality is unknown, as a life course, or as a vector from an origo to an end point, paths according to the Maya lead somewhere. When a shaman opens the road to the spirits, he follows a succession whose order and end points were fixed in the memorial past. Yet his engagement takes place in the emerging present of performance, in which the corporeal field defines a moving center with a before and after. Instead of being placed directly *opposite* to the West, East comes *before* and *in front of* it, and is always separated from it by an intervening corner. During the centripetal opening phase, when spirits are lowered to the altar, North comes between East and West, whereas South interventes during the centrifugal closing phase, when they are sent back. Given the cosmological premise that the earth is lower than the spirits mobilized in prayer, centripetal transpositions always move from high to low, and centrifugal ones from low to high.[15]

Why privilege the altar as an origin point? It is possible to conceive the inverse case, in which the spatiotemporal locations from which spirits are lowered are the real origins, and the altar is a momentary end point. This would amount to taking the perspective of the spirits rather than the shaman, and it would reverse the reference point, so that the distant memorial frame of the cosmology becomes the true *center*, and the corporeal field of the performance becomes a destination. From this perspective, the temporal structure described in section I of this essay also shifts: the space-time occupied by spirits in their places of origin defines a synchronic present of cosmic proportions, in which the temporal extent of a ritual performance adds up to little more than a volumeless point.

When a shaman is engaged in moving spirits, as opposed to other aspects of his practice, it is the altar that serves as center, and the local, corporeal present that defines the ritual now. Spatial evidence for this lies in the fact that the two sequences, counterclockwise for opening and clockwise for closing, are also described by the terms *šč'iik* 'leftward' and *šnó'oh* 'rightward' respectively. Notice that in order for "leftward" to designate the opening sequence E > N > W, and "rightward" to designate E > S > W for closing, one must face the East, as do the altar and human participants. From the perspective of a divinity in the East looking toward the altar in the West, the right-left orientation would be inverse. Thus the altar is the center, and centripetal transpositions come into it, while centrifugal ones go away. The temporal priority of the momentary present of utterance is less clear-cut, but suggested by the way altars are "bound" and "untied" through successive steps. It is crucial that certain steps happen *before* other ones, and that the lowering of spirits be coordinated with the breathing and movements of participants. During divination sessions, shaman and patient periodically exchange information that can affect both the shaman's choice of prayer form and his diagnosis, on a moment's notice. Finally, in all ritual, there is a sense that things should somehow be different after performance than they were before it. These factors are based on the local time frame in which human action unfolds, and not the memorial one in which spirits occupy the heavens forever.

IV

Cyclic time, as it is sometimes called, plays its strongest role in contemporary Maya shamanic practice right at the moment at which memorial history (cosmology rooted in the deep past) joins the momentary present of ritual performance as it happens. The memorial frame is a spatiotemporal field of great extent, reaching all the way from the current creation, one in a series, to its predicted destruction. It contains cycles in the sense of recurrent intervals like the *k'iin* 'day', *uinal* 'month' (twenty days) and *há'ab* 'year' (360 days). In this field, identity and difference among humans and spirits are fixed by immutable principles. The planets move through the heavens, the seasons change, and the years accrue in a succession that encompasses many repeating cycles. But on this point, the same could be said of European cultures, in which planetary movements combine with historical origin points, such as the birth of Christ, to yield a calendar of repeating units, like the day, week, month, and year. In order for this kind of cyclicity to become a powerful force in action, other factors must be added to it.

One such factor would be the premise that repeating calendrical units, or conjunctures of them, are not mere quantities, but are qualitatively endowed. This would mean that each occurrence of a certain month or day would determine something of the quality of human experience during that phase. It would therefore allow for prospective statements about the character of things to come and retrospective statements that identify aspects of the present as re-occurrences of the past. There are some indications that the Yucatec Maya tradition of "prophecy" worked like this, and that calendrically based augury played an important role in Maya writing, although the practice of prophecy remains obscure. In any such system, the kind of temporal field that we described in section I, with an emergent present, a midrange past, and a memorial post, would be heavily weighted toward the memorial structures of cosmology. The corporeal present would be clearly subordinated to the logic of the past and to the almost timeless present of cosmology. The line between emergence and reproduction would blur in the successive repetitions of preestablished series. This kind of cyclicity precludes human agency, it seems to me, and it is fundamentally ahistoric in the sense of unchanging. Given what we know of Yucatan on the eve of the Spanish conquest, and of the historical content of glyphic inscriptions, it seems unlikely that such a vision ever determined Maya practices completely. In the contemporary material under discussion, this is only one moment in a more complex, and interesting, process.

It is more likely that this kind of cyclic recurrence interacted with the emerging present of human affairs, as it does in modern shamanic ritual. Here we find cyclic recurrence in a very powerful and central role, mediating between the memorial structures of the cosmos and the corporeal present of performance. All those factors of the emerging present that leave it open to sudden change and human agency remain in play, such as individuals' intentional engagements, bodily postures and processes, biographic idiosyncrasies, the particular purpose and place of a given performance. The field of the present is quick with potential differences not yet transformed into distinctions, dichotomies, or divisions. Rather than determining these as a reoccurrence of the past, cyclic principles mediate between the present and the memorial past. It is not an identity between past and present that cycles achieve, but a transposition. The "home field" of corporeal actuality serves as the human center that shaman and patient inhabit, and into which the memorial distances of cosmic space and time are transposed. This process combines the vertical and cardinal directional logic of cosmology with the front-back, right-left, over-under logic of the altar and the ritual participants. Based on a parallel combination of spatiotemporal structure and successive movement, the cyclic order of ritual prayer is an ideal medium in which to transpose elements between the corporeal and the cosmological levels.

As strong as it is, however, cyclicity in shamanic performance can be overridden by events. Performances can fail to secure the desired outcomes. Maya people are critical about success, and most do not accord any surefire magic to a shaman's prayer. The desired results may be secured, and then again they may not, if conditions are unfavorable. In reading the descriptions of prophecies during the early colonial period, in the Books of Chilam Balam and in accounts of regional resistance to the Spanish (Jones 1989), one gets the strong impression that prophecies were open to dispute in those days, as well. Unfortunately we know relatively little about the rhetoric with which native "prophets" convinced their audiences of the accuracy of their interpretations. In modern shamanism, virtuosity of performance and a reputation for getting results are key resources for shamans, without which they may be shunned by patients. Both factors pertain to the local present inhabited by shaman and patients.

Another way in which cyclic principles may be overridden is when special circumstances require that the canonical forms of practice be violated. When counteracting witchcraft, in particular, Don Seéb occasionally scrambles the proscribed order of spirit citation for the express purpose of confusing any *hechicero* 'witch (evil shaman)' who may be attempting to neutralize the patient's defense, or who may wish to assault Don Seéb himself. On one occasion I witnessed a *pa' 'iík* 'break spirit, wind' exorcism in which the patient, a single woman of about eighteen, became distressed and Don Seéb was forced to stop the ceremony abruptly in midstream. Over the decade that we have worked together, this is the only time I have seen such an occurrence. Startled, I asked him after the patient left what had happened, and whether the performance would be effective in its fragmentary form. Yes, it would be effective, he said. What happened was that the ritual prayer had had the effect of dislodging a malevolent wind that was in the patient's abdomen, causing it to shoot upward toward her heart. At the time he stopped, she was gasping for breath and swinging her head side to side, sweating and groaning in pain. Synchronous with her distress, Don Seéb felt the identical pain shooting upward toward his own heart, and he knew that he was in mortal danger, too. The ritual process creates a lived present in which the shaman co-occupies the bodily experiences of the patient. The division between them is temporarily suspended. When he was a younger man, he said, he could have sustained the attack and finished the treatment, but at his age he was too weak.

Examples like these show that in the combination of memorial history and cosmology with ongoing experience, experience retains a relative independence. Even in routine practice, spirit forces whose origins lie in a memorial cosmology engage in human affairs, but they do not determine them. The conjunction of historical frames in the ritual present alters social relations and experience, without resolving all the ambiguities or contradictions. Maya people are generally sophisticated about this, and rarely expect automatic solutions from shamans (or anyone else). Like the *Ah K'ìin* priests of the colonial period, whom they enlist in prayer, shamans' actions are open to challenge. Ritual practices build up a dynamic field in which the infinitely many potential differences between things are recast into meaningful oppositions. Nonidentity becomes alterity, and alterity the method of change. More the road to difference than the rule of timeless identity, cyclic principles are a pathway into and out of the present.

NOTES

Translations from the Mayan are in single quotes.

1. This paper is a revised version of an earlier one presented at the seminar De Palabra y Obra en el Nuevo Mundo, Trujillo, Spain, October 1990. I wish to express my gratitude to the organizers and participants in this seminar, and in particular to Manuel Gutiérrez Estévez, Gary Gossen, Jorge Klor de Alva, Miguel Leon-Portilla, Richard Price, Sally Price, and Don Jaime de Salas. Yucatec Maya examples are cited in the standard orthography used by Mayanists: ' is glottal stop; ¢ is /ts/, č is /tsh/, š is /sh/, C' is glottalized consonant, acute accent is high tone and grave accent low tone. For further explanation, see Hanks (1990).

2. Actually, the term 'simpleton' in English has a somewhat different loading than the standard Maya expressions for such people: *¢iímin* 'horse,' *coño* 'jerk', *č ičupòol* 'hardheaded, dense, thick'.

3. I use the term Yucatec here rather than "Maya" because there are difficult questions regarding the relations between Maya and non-Maya elements of life in modern Yucatan, as elsewhere in postcolonial contexts. Although the research reported on here was conducted entirely with Maya speakers in the municipio of Oxkutzcab, many of my introductory remarks seem to apply more widely to Yucatecans across ethnic and cultural backgrounds.

4. This is complemented outside the residential unit by men's avoidance of their friends' spouses. In my experience among younger men, a friend's wife is never addressed or even acknowledged when the three happen to be in the same place at the same time.

5. An important distinction must be drawn here: one's understanding of prior experiences is constantly subject to revision. For instance, a shaman can decide upon reflection that a stranger encountered in the woods was actually a spirit in human form. But he cannot willfully effect a revision of the past such that the encounter never took place at all. Shamans can do many things to alter the world, but they cannot operate on the past as a way of changing the present. Patients routinely ask shamans to alleviate current conditions by counteracting their cause, but they do not ask them to erase the cause from their past. Shamans can make things go away, but they cannot create a world in which they never happened.

6. Shamans make house calls for gravely ill people and when they do, they use the *santos,* flowers, and candles of the household. Patients unable to sit up are treated in their hammock, with altar parts placed near them.

7. Manuel Gutiérrez Estévez pointed out that much of what I am saying about Maya ritual practice applies as well to Catholic practice. This is indeed true and is worthy of close investigation, but cannot be addressed in this paper.

8. The difficulties are severalfold. On the one hand, virtually all of the sources on prophecy are either Spanish-authored (Cogolludo, Lizana, Landa, Perez, Sanchez de Aguillar), produced in response to Spanish (idolatry trials, Chi's Relación), or embodied in relatively opaque Maya texts (such as the Books of Chilam Balam). The translations of the Maya texts are far from secure, in my opinion, and the contemporaneous Spanish sources are tainted in various ways. For one thing, it is abundantly clear that the Franciscans and other early colonial authorities seized on the idea of Maya prophecy and attempted to use it as evidence that the Maya would inevitably succumb to their efforts at colonization. Whatever these so-called prophecies were prior to such intrusions, they would have been unquestionably altered by them. For further discussion see Sullivan (1989), Jones (1989), Farriss (1984), Edmonson (1982), Hanks (1988:344–48)).

9. Except the temporary lashed structures wedged among tree branches for some private offerings. These may have a linear form if the offering consists only of five gourds of *saka'* 'offertory gruel', arranged in a side-by-side pattern (cf. Hanks 1990).

10. Altars for major ceremonies in the domestic and agricultural cycles such as *heéɬ lú'um* 'fix earth', *č'áačaák* 'get rain', and *wàahil kòol* 'breads of the milpa', are temporary, out-of-door constructions. The building process is described as 'binding' the altar, done by lashing freshcut branches with *'anikab* vine or wire. My field notes indicate that these altars tend to face southeast, so that the four corners, rather than the front edge, are aligned to the cardinal locations (F.79–80; F.82.B), or south (F.115.A).

11. The following three paragraphs appeared in slightly different form in Hanks (1990: Chapter 7).

12. Nash (1970:3–10) describes the importance of the 'center' in Tzeltal (Tzo'ontahal).

13. Gossen (1974: chapter 1) discusses comparable configurations in Tzotzil and Nash (1970:292–96) shows the pervasive presence of the square, four corners, and four sides in Tzeltal.

14. The following four paragraphs are condensed from Hanks (1990:336–39).

15. Exceptions to this arise in the relatively rare cases when Don Seéb cites earth spirits whose

origin points lies beneath the earth. The rarity of these cases is due to the fact that such spirits are lesser and more prone to malevolence than those in the heavens. This moral ground is consistent with other aspects of the cosmology that cannot be taken up here (see Hanks 1984b, 1990).

REFERENCES

Edmonson, Munro, trans. and ed. 1982. *The Future of the Itza, the Book of Chilam Balam of Tizimin.* Austin: University of Texas Press.
Farriss, Nancy M. 1984. *Maya Society Under Colonial Rule: The Collective Enterprise of Survival.* Princeton, N.J.: Princeton University Press.
Goffman, E. 1974. *Frame Analysis.* New York: Harper and Row.
Gossen, G. H. 1974. *Chamulas in the World of the Sun: Time and Space in a Maya Oral Tradition.* Cambridge, Mass.: Harvard University Press.
Gutiérez Estévez, M. 1988. La oración en la canida yucateca. In Gutiérrez Estévez, M. ed., *Alimentación Iberoamericana, simbolos y significados.* Trujillo, Spain: Fundacion Xavier de Salas, Instituto Indigenista Interamericano. 61–88.
Hanks, W. F. 1984a. The interactive basis of Maya divination. Paper presented at the Eighty-Third Annual Meeting of the American Anthropological Association, Denver, Colorado.
———. 1984b. Santification, structure and experience in a Yucatec Maya ritual event. *Journal of American Folklore* 97(384):131–66.
———. 1988. Grammar, style and meaning in a Maya manuscript. *Int. J. Am. Linguist* 13(3):331–364.
———. 1990. *Referential Practice: Language and Lived Space among the Maya.* Chicago: University of Chicago Press.
——— and Don S. Rice, eds., 1989. *Word and Image in Maya Culture: Explorations in Language, Writing and Representation.* Salt Lake City: University of Utah Press.
Jones, G. D. 1989. *Maya Resistance to Spanish Rule: Time and History on a Colonial Frontier.* Albuquerque: University of New Mexico Press.
Lounsbury, F. G. 1989. The names of a king: Hieroglyphic variants as a key to decipherment. In Hanks and Rice 1989.
Nash, J. 1975 (1971). *Bajo la mirada de los antepasados: Creencias y comportamiento en una comunidad maya.* Mexico: Instituto Indigenista Interamericano.
Redfield, R. and A. Villa Rojas. 1962 [1934]. *Chan Kom, a Maya Village.* Chicago: University of Chicago Press.
Solis Acala, E. 1949. *Códice Pérez.* Mérida: Liga de Acción Social.
Sullivan, Paul. 1989. *Unfinished Conversations: Maya and Foreigners between Two Wars.* New York: Alfred A. Knopf.
Taussig, M. 1987. *Shamanism, Colonialism and the Wild Man: A Study in Terror and Healing.* Chicago: University of Chicago Press.
Thompson, E. S. 1974 [1970]. *Maya History and Religion.* Norman: University of Oklahoma Press [Spanish translation].
Tozzer, A. M. trans. and ed. 1941. *Relacion de las Cosas de Yucatan,* by Fray Diego de Landa. Cambridge: Peabody Museum of American Archeology and Ethnology, Harvard University.
Villa Rojas, A. 1978 [1945]. Los Elegidos de Dios: Etnografía de los Mayas de Quintana Roo. Série de Antropología Social, 56. Mexico: INI.

9

Intertextuality of Space in Yucatán

This essay explores the intertextual variation between a map and two land surveys from sixteenth-century Yucatán, Mexico. The central problem is to characterize variant descriptions of a single place in terms of the different perspectives they embody, and the different relations that articulate them in an intertextual series. The Mapa de Mani, a drawing of the boundary and internal divisions of Mani province, is briefly contrasted with two contemporaneous surveys of Yaxkukul, Ceh Pech province. Comparison reveals that the two surveys are produced by overlapping groups of patrilineal kinsmen, and record overlapping but distinct geopolitical boundaries, using different rhetorical styles. It is concluded that colonial Maya genres of mapmaking and surveying embody the social and political relations among their producers.

During the first century of colonial society in Yucatán, native writers produced a significant corpus of official and semi-official documents, describing their contacts with the Spaniards, their own histories, their customs, and the limits of their territories. They addressed the King of Spain in order to complain and request his mercy. They addressed their local communities in order to document their actions and their identities, to document new events, and to express their interpretations, often critical, of the foreigners. Having been taught to write in European forms by Franciscans, they produced documents in Maya language that bear many European features, some as obvious as scribal style and page layout, and others as subtle as the evaluative attitude of a narrator to the story he tells. Throughout the discourse of colonial Maya, there is a core of ambivalence and ambiguity that poses real challenges to historical description and to theories of culture as well.

Much of colonial Maya discourse is also characterized by a special type of intertextuality, which consists in the existence of multiple versions of what appears at first to be a single text. We have, for example, two almost identical letters that were written in 1567, one of them copied seven times, the other six times, all thirteen copies being signed by a number of Maya nobles (the lists of whom overlap). This odd fact was interpreted by Gates (1937), Tozzer (1941), and other researchers as a sign of inauthenticity (Hanks (1986). Among the official documents of the community of Sotuta, we find a series of what appear to be complementary agreements on the same subject (the limits of the region), separated by several days and several details (Roys 1939:421–30). Even in the case of apparently indigenous literature, a similar multiplicity is evident: for instance, the Books of Chilam Balam appear to contain one story told differently according to regional perspectives. This similarity was so strong that Barrera Vasquez and Rendón (1974) were able to bring them together in a single "Book of the Books of Chilam Balam," and Edmonson (1982) was able to reorder the "chapters" of one of these Books, in order to better reflect what he took to be their common historical basis. The problem of multiple versions is even more general, of course. Faced with a series of texts that describe or formalize what appears to be a single matter, we are often tempted to reduce the variation to a single text that constitutes the basis for the others. But this does not eliminate the alternative interpretations, and what initially appears as a wealth of evidence rapidly becomes an absence of certainty.

For what is a version? How can we evaluate the relative truth of two descriptions, and at what level of divergence, or by what criterion of nonequivalence, must one recognize that two texts simply treat different subjects and not a single one? According to what criteria are they versions of a single text and not simply texts that happen to be similar, but are actually distinct? These questions, it seems to me, pertain to textual, and consequently, historiographic, analysis in general, and not only to Yucatán in particular.

A typical approach to textual analysis is based on a judgment of truth: we calculate the relation among a series of texts by comparing them to an independent common reality, in order to sort out the true from the false. The part that is false can be called myth, lies, or mistakes, depending on the case, but what concerns us here is the inaugural division between the true and the nontrue. The tendency to interpolate this distinction is only strengthened by the fact that texts in official Maya claim to be true and assert their own accuracy as descriptions. It is thus according to the criterion of truth that they anticipate being judged. In an analytical perspective, however, it is important to realize from the outset that truth judgments incorporate limiting assumptions. To focus on the truth of a document is already to assume a dichotomy between text and reality. Once this is done, it becomes possible to compare the text with the real world in order to judge the correspondence between the two. Thus, either different descriptions of the same thing must be reducible to a single version that corresponds to reality, or else they are contradictory and, therefore, they cannot be equally true. Critical analysis becomes a kind of decipherment of truth behind appearances, and textual interpretation a kind of detective story.

Without denying the importance of searching for the truth, we have to realize that there are other factors that such a search can obscure. The descriptive function of texts constitutes only a part of their overall communicative force. Official documents often have a performative effect in their own social context. To the degree that the goal or the effect of a discourse is to establish or to change a social relation, the descriptive truth of what it affirms can very well be secondary or even irrelevant. Official discourse produces social objectivity as often as it represents it. The interactions between prefabricated and emergent aspects (between representative and constitutive moments) is lost in any approach that equates sense, truth value, and correspondence to the extra-discursive world. Understanding the relation between two documents by juxtaposing them to a third term, the Real, is at best an oblique, and at worst a misleading, method. The kinds of objectivism and realism that favor such an approach slip easily into a naive or nostalgic belief in the transparency of expression. Once we realize that our knowledge of a social world is inevitably mediated by the perspectives of the people we observe, and by our own, this transparency evaporates. Rather than positing a truth beyond perspective, we do better to study the perspective itself, its cultural formation, its incorporation in the discourse, and the effects of its application to society. It is important to realize that this move deeply relativizes our reading of any work of discourse, but it does *not* mean that there are no facts. On the contrary, it implies that the facts of meaning, action, and agency are relational, and their interdependence is more basic than is assumed by the isolation of symbol from the world.

These questions can be restated in a concrete case. What is the relation between the two extant texts that describe the limits of the village of Yaxkukul in the region called Ceh Pech in the northern part of Yucatán during the 1540s? Often called *Crónicas,* these two texts narrate the process of inspection of boundaries around Yaxkukul (Martinez Hernandez 1926; Barrera Vasquez 1984).[1] They have different dates, separated by eight days, and each comprises a list of locations that delineate the boundaries between Yaxkukul and the neighboring places, each location being marked by a symbolic marker. The lists overlap, but they are not identical. Also, the lists of participants in the survey, as well as the ones responsible for the texts, are partially overlapping. We know that at the time, the Spaniards were concentrating the Maya population under the policy of *congregación* and *reducción,* and that they demanded of the natives declarations of municipal limits. Both texts make reference to that policy, which motivated both the production of a survey and the official aspect of the document that reported it.

In spite of what they share, the two *Crónicas* of Yaxkukul present different images of their apparent place of origin. One is signed by Alonso Pech, dated April 30, 1544. The other, by Pedro Pech, or Ah Macan Pech in Maya, father of Alonso, is dated May 8 of the same year. Given these dates (the validity of which is questionable; cf. Barrera Vasquez 1984; Restall 1991), we will call the former "Yaxkukul document number 1" (YD1) and the latter "Yaxkukul document number 2" (YD2). Given the problems inherent in dating these documents, these labels are heuristic. The two differ in terms of style. In YD1, descriptions are in the first-person singular of the present tense, which imparts a sense of immediacy to the prose, making it similar to a dramatic text or to the transcription of a guided tour. Conversely, YD2 is almost entirely written in the past tense, in the third person, which gives an impression of distance to the text. The first mentions seven place-names and dozens of names of persons absent in the second. YD2 in turn refers to five place-names that are missing in YD1 (Barrera Vasquez 1984:101). Moreover, the two assert different distributions of boundary markers along the limits of villages. They both make reference to what they call *pictunob* 'numerous markers', *multunob* 'stone heap markers', *tiitz* 'corners', *cruzob* 'crosses', and *behob* 'roads, paths'. Hence, they have an identical inventory of types of markers.

Inventory marker types in the Yaxkukul land surveys

pictun	'8000 stones'	19 cited in YD1, 13 in YD2
multun	'stone mound'	12 in YD1, 1 in YD2
Cruz	'cross'	5 in YD1, 9 in YD2
tiitz	'corner'	4 in YD1, 6 in YD2
behob	'roads'	4 in YD1, 5 in YD2

However, they locate the markers differently in relation to the named places. The two distributions may even be contradictory, but we do not know, and perhaps never will. This set of differences casts us back on the general question of the criteria by which to evaluate the relation between these two texts.

In this essay, I adopt an approach of the kind that Nelson Goodman (1978: Preface) called "irrealist." I do not concentrate on the correspondence between the texts taken as propositional structures and reality taken as an independent variable. Instead, I explore the correspondences between the texts themselves. This approach allows us to engage in intertextual research without prejudging questions that can only be the outcome of study, not its point of departure. It also allows us to investigate alternative ways of reading the texts, instead of fixing them as objectivist description. To assume a criterion of truth as correspondence is to ignore the fact that modes of reading and criteria for truth (or "goodness of fit," as Goodman proposes to call it) always depend on the genre of discourse. The colonial genres in Yucatán were changing dramatically during the sixteenth-century (Hanks 1987). If we look at intertextuality itself, we can explore the relations between texts and images, built space, and other elements of social practice(s), without presupposing intersemiotic limits. Goodman (1978:7–17) proposed five dimensions for comparing versions (the order is mine): (i) elimination and supplementation, (ii) deformation, (iii) relative weighting, (iv) composition and decomposition, and (v) order. These dimensions have the advantage of being applicable to alternate versions without projecting a unitary world of self-same objects. We turn now to the intertext of Yaxkukul.

ONE SPACE, TWO REGIONS: MAPS AND DISCOURSES

The two documents of Yaxkukul mention the existence of a map that was supposed to go along with them. Unfortunately, no map has been found, and we can only guess what it would have been like. YD1 mentions the map many times and relates it to the general instructions given by Don Tomas Lopez (Medel) concerning maps of indigenous communities (Barrera Vasquez 1984:39; 1.353). It designates itself as *hunpel ynformacio yokol hunpel mapa* 'a report on a map' (ibid.: 1.364). After having individually referred to the neighbors that live around Yaxkukul, and thus share its borders, this text makes known that all of them have their own maps.

(1)   *lay lakoob*   These companions (kinsmen)
             tu hool luumoob   at the head(s) of (their) land(s),
         yanix u Mapaob   They also have maps
             tu tzucentzucilob cahob   from town to town.
                                                        (ibid.: 1.382)

Similarly, we know that other regional collections of texts contain contemporary maps, as, for instance, the Xiu family papers, which include 145 documents from the colonial period; the first of these is a map dated 1557 (see also Morely and Brainerd 1983:220–22).

The existence of one (or many) maps of Yaxkukul raises interesting questions about the two written versions. It indicates from the outset that Maya nobles had access to a range of symbolic resources that included graphic design as well as writing. The map combines the writing and graphic design insofar as it shows place names, lines indicating roads and borders, churches, and crosses (cf. fig. 9.1). On the other hand, it appears that many written texts did not include any drawings.[2] What is the relation between the information readable on a map like the Mani map, and the information conveyed by a linguistic description?

The map of Mani clearly shows a round perimeter that forms a circle in the middle of which is found the church of Mani. We can see seven (perhaps eight) routes beginning from the center and leading to neighboring places, each one of them with its own church with a cross on top of it. In the interior of the double border are written the names of several dozen locations, evidently found outside the region defined by Mani. Each of these places is marked with a cross atop a standard square shape. Outside the perimeter there is a legend indicating other places (encircled above) and identifying the document as a copy of an earlier map of Mani (below). Notice that this identification puts the drawing both in an intertextual series and in a relation of derivation from an earlier original.[3] Lacking clear temporal structure, the map provides no criterion of succession that could lead the reader from a beginning to an end. Certainly, the center functions as a natural point of departure in a geometrical sense, and the routes indicate an order of distance beginning from the center. But one can just as well begin "reading" the map from the place called Yotholin or Pustunich on the lower right, as from Mani, in the center. In fact, beginning from any point on the map whatsoever, one can continue in any direction, without having to follow a preestablished trajectory. Lacking a scale indicator, we do not know the length of the routes, nor the distance between the places (although the sequence probably indicates relative contiguity).

A principle of selectivity apparently excludes all types of markers except for routes, churches, and crosses, and we do not know from the map whether there are *pictuns* or *multuns* in Mani like the ones found in the documents of Yaxkukul. Without special reading instructions, nothing indicates the relative size of the places. Perhaps the most remarkable absence is the total lack of mention of the native participants or the survey itself, both necessary preconditions to the elaboration of a map. Just like the texts, the

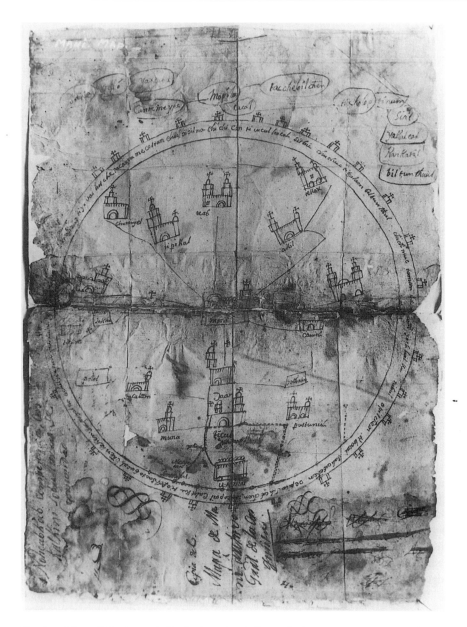

Fig. 9.1. Map of Mani, 1554. (Latin American Library, Tulane University, New Orleans, Louisiana)

map totalizes information that has been collected by someone, probably by way of an official tour of the appointed locations. This agent, probably a group of delegated individuals, is never identified except for the name of the copyist, who is an intermediary and not a source. (The linguistic analog would be quoted speech in which the quoter is identified, but the quoted is not.) Nor is there any indication of the authorities in charge of the neighboring places, who must have shared borders with the territory of Mani. If anyone really made a tour of the region, we know neither where it began nor where it ended. It would be a reasonable guess that the convent of Mani was either the point of departure or the destination of the tour (or perhaps both), but we still do not know the route that was taken. Most of this information is cited in the two Yaxkukul documents. At the same time, the drawing provides "gratuitous" details that are absent from the Yaxkukul texts, such as, for instance, the difference between the churches with one entrance (like Akil) and the ones with two (like the church of Tekax), the shape of the cross, and the curious crook in the road between Mani and Akil. If we wanted to describe the style of the map, we would have to include the forms of conventional symbols (including orthography), topology, vertical orientation, absence of relief, the inclusive circular perimeter, and the treatment of space inside the perimeter. Although the linguistic texts include much similar information, the question of style is fundamentally different, and this difference will help us compare the two documents of Yaxkukul.

Both Yaxkukul texts indicate a perimeter that delimits the region of the village. They also mention routes that lead to neighboring villages. But while the map of Mani places a convent in the center and at the point of origin of all traced routes, the Yaxkukul texts provide no details regarding the interior of the perimeter. We can infer that the church mentioned in the texts determines a sort of center, but we cannot place it relative to other locations (except for the interior ones). Moreover, because the descriptions of Yaxkukul leave the interior empty, we do not know if the roads actually crossed each other, if they converged in the center, or if they were totally disjoint. The lists of places around Yaxkukul constitute a border, so to speak, and the descriptions of direction indicate a passage, but the circular idealization that is evident on the map is entirely missing in the written texts. Instead, we can infer an irregular but, more or less, quadrilateral perimeter from these texts (Barrera Vasquez 1984:102). Crosses and other markers are mentioned, but unfortunately, we have no idea of their form. Just like the writing outside the graphic map, both texts are followed by guarantees of their own authenticity, origin, and basis in consent among the authorities. There is no indication of scale or of relief in the texts, and the relations of succession among the locations must be inferred by a diagrammatic reading of the text: we have to assume that the order indicated by the text corresponds to the order of distribution in space. The "gratuitous" details referred to above are also missing in the texts, but there are others. For example, one frequently finds boundary markers paired with landmarks such as trees, wells, and other aspects of the cultural landscape. It is possible that these landmarks are not part of the boundary proper, but that they functioned as auxiliary markers, specifying the landscape according to the perceptual habits of its inhabitants.

Thus, starting from a superficial comparison, we see that the two documents of Yaxkukul share certain features that distinguish them from the map, that link them to one another, and connect them both to an inspection tour undertaken by local authorities. At the same time, we find intertextual differences along the lines proposed by Goodman (1978) for the comparison of world versions. The play of elimination and supplementation is clear in the two lists of places, as well as in the names of the people who participated in producing the texts. The boundary of Yaxkukul is deformed, that is, differently formed, and there are important contrasts in the placement of markers. The two texts are also distinguished by the metalinguistic identifications that they bear, their respective authors, the asymmetrical distribution of markers, and by overall narrative style.

YD1 AND YD2: A COMPARISON

Generic Identities

Analysis of other Maya language documents of the sixteenth century indicates that there was a generic category that I call "official Maya." Written by authorities trained in alphabetic writing by the Franciscans, the texts belonging to this general category share certain distinctive, genre-specific traits that separate them nicely from more "traditional" discourse genres like the Books of Chilam Balam on the one hand, and other European discourse genres like maps and documents in Spanish on the other.[4] These features include: the use of Maya language in a way that shows clear influence of Spanish (mostly Franciscan) discourse fused with literary forms that apparently go back to pre-Columbian practices. Just like official documents in Spanish, but in striking contrast to the Maya discursive tradition, these texts affirm their own authenticity and locate themselves in both time and space. That is to say, they refer to their authors by name, and they mention the date and place of their production. These features undoubtedly reflect the Spanish notarial conventions, and they have a major impact on the discourse. A comparison of texts of this genre to others belonging to more traditional genres and to hieroglyphic inscriptions indicates the emergence of a new discursive voice through official Maya. For it is during this era and within that generic category that the first person "I" and "we" first appear, as well as adverbs for "now" and "here." The absence of these indications in the Books of Chilam Balam poses serious problems of interpretation, because we never know from where the narrative voice proceeds (Hanks 1988). Similarly, the hieroglyphic corpus evidently lacks indexical elements for referring to immediate (extralinguistic) conditions of speech— no "I," "we," "you (pl.)," "here," "there," "now," "this," "that" (Bricker 1986, ch. 5). These pre-Columbian texts seem to be located outside the history that they recount; their truth is guaranteed by means of a mode of objectivism that pretends to record pure history unsullied by the individual perspective of an author. But colonial official discourse is intermingled with the local histories that it describes, and hence it must repeatedly affirm its own truth. The Yaxkukul documents share this concern.

The category of official Maya includes a range of more specific genres such as *cartas* 'letters' addressed to the king of Spain to request his favors, *informes* 'reports' describing one or the other situation, *acuerdos* ' legal documents' formalizing local agreements, and *deslindes* 'land surveys' such as the two Yaxkukul documents (Hanks 1987:672). In these terms, the two documents in question are identified in different ways. The first presents itself as an *informacio derecho* 'report of rights' (Barrera Vasquez 1984:16, 1, 17) and afterward as *forma derecho de froceso* 'legal procedure form' (ibid.: 19, 1, 59), while the second identifies itself as *u hahil u tituloil kax* 'the true title on the forest' of Yaxkukul (ibid.: 96). Does this difference correspond to different ends of the two texts, different kinds of surveys, both or neither?

The notion of genre applies here on two levels. Beyond the question of the genre of the text, we must also consider the genre of practice which it describes.[5] As we have already observed, these descriptions presuppose the inspection of the region prior to the production of the document in which the results are reported. As we said, the two documents describe the inspection in different terms. The map of Mani by contrast makes no mention of a joint inspection. Document YD1 describes the actions of the authorities as *upislahal luumob* '(for) the terrains to be measured' (Barrera Vasquez 1984:18, 1.52 and cf. 1.315). During the narration of the visit, the text simply describes the act of going from marker to marker, as illustrated in the following excerpt:

(2)   *noholtan yn binel*   Southward I go along
        tzol pictun   counting out stone markers
                                   (ibid.: 25, 1.154).

In the end of this part of the narrative, the survey is described as *u ximbaltabal u pach luumob* 'the visiting of the limits of the lands', hence my use of the term "visit" to describe the original event of which the document is the report.

Text YD2 uses similar, but not identical terms. In the beginning, it states *Catun ppizah hun-hun-ppizib tu sut pach Santa Yglesia lae* 'Then one measure at a time, we measured all around this Blessed Church' (ibid.:91). But shortly later we read that the *encomendero* Don Julian Doncel had given the order that:

(3)   *utial ca xicob u dzabob*   In order that they go place
        u chicul kax u lum on   the forest markers of their lands
        . . . yoklal tan u ppi-sitab   for the measuring is ongoing
        u chi kaxob xaman,   of the mouth of the forest to the North,
        ti likin Cupul,   to the East among the Cupul,
        baix chikin xan   and so to the West too.
                                        (ibid.).

What is important here is the implication that this visit was not a simple routine inspection of borders, but rather a question of *setting the borders*. A few lines later a parallel phrase is used, *utial u binbalob u dzabob u ppictunilob u pach u cahalob* 'So that they go out placing the stone markers of the borders of their town' (ibid.: 92).

During the rest of the narrative, the text affirms many times that the visit was under-taken in order to place boundary markers in the region, and not in order to verify al-ready existing ones. In the end, we read *cu nuptamba uxotol u pach ca cahal he tux hopi lae* 'The cutting of the border of our town completed here where it started' (ibid.:96), a phrasing that only reinforces the interpretation that the visit in question was done in order to *set* limits that would be, from then on, official.

These details can thus help us understand the reason for the visit described in the two documents of Yaxkukul, and thus the status of these texts themselves. The activ-ity of *tzol* 'count' is well known among Mayanists, because it also designates the Maya calendar, called *tzol kin* (*kin* 'time, day, sun'), as well as the pre-Columbian ritual pro-cessions designated *tzol peten* (*peten* 'region') in the Books of Chilam Balam (Hanks 1987:675; 1988). These processions, too, fixed the boundaries between the geopolit-ical regions of Yucatán, just as the calendar is an instrument that fixes temporal units. As far as the activity of *ppiz* 'measuring' is concerned, we know that it was part of *tzol* events in the Books of Chilam Balam, and that it is still practiced today by Maya agri-culturists when they measure their land (Redfield and Villa Rojas 1934; Hanks 1990). Despite the fact that the visits of Yaxkukul were undertaken in response to the re-quirements of the colonial government then, they were evidently composed in a na-tive framework. Seen as a kind of symbolic practice, the act of *tzol* is thus a term in an intertextual relation of which the production of written documents would be an-other term. Consequently, we know that the two documents are part of a series the source of which lies in the same (family of) spatial practice(s).[6] It is remarkable, in that respect, that the two texts are described in Spanish generic terms, whereas they portray the visit of the frontier as a native genre of practice.

Participants

Who were the agents who produced this discourse of spatial and textual practices? We know that at the time in question Maya elites were struggling to secure their own po-sitions in the new colonial order, and that it was Crown policy to accord a privileged status to the native nobility (Chamberlain 1948; Farriss 1984; Hanks 1986). At the same time, pressure on Maya communities from the Spanish *encomenderos* was con-siderable. It is significant in this regard that the two Yaxkukul texts cite two different *encomenderos:* YD1 refers to Gonzalo Mendes (Barrera Vasquez 1984:1.7, 333) whereas YD2 refers to a certain Julian Doncel (ibid.: 82, 91, 96, 97, 98). According to Barrera Vasquez (ibid.: 82, n. 333), neither of these two in fact held title to the *en-comienda* of Yaxkukul. Rather, it was part of the land retained by *Adelantado* Fran-cisco de Montejo. Both of them participated in the *cabildo* ('municipal council') of Merida and are frequently cited in the lists of witnesses in official documents (Scholes and Adams 1938). It is possible that one of the relevant factors for the production of these texts was precisely the effort on the part of the Maya to satisfy the requirements of both so-called *encomenderos.* Whereas YD1 was transcribed by the scribe Juan Matu, YD2 does not mention any scribe.

In the local governments called *Republicas de Indios,* the native nobles played the role of intermediaries between the autochthonous communities and Spanish church and bureaucracy. Local authorities had to address themselves to two sectors of the social field, an interior and an exterior, and this fact motivates much of the ambiguity of the discourse that they produced. Because the documents of this period incorporate first-person and deictic elements identifying authors and contexts of production, the social ambiguity of the context is more or less directly inscribed in the textual form. The result is a double-edged rhetoric of identification. On the one hand, the discursive agents had to reinforce their indigenous noble status, by using an elegant language, interspersed with allusions to tradition and indications of their knowledge. On the other hand, they had to display their status as authorities in the colony by giving evidence that they obey the king, the Christian God, and the power of the Spaniards. By way of an example, let us briefly consider the identification of the authors of the two texts of Yaxkukul texts. First, text YD1.

(4)	*yoklal u halil*	Because truly
	licil ca dzaic ca firmail	we give our signature
	con justisiail	we *Justicias*
	helel tu lahun cakal u kinil	today, the 10th-for-two times 20 day
	u yuil de Abril	of the month of April
	de mil quinientos y quarenta	of one thousand five hundred and forty
	y quatro años/	and four years/
	Dn Alonso Pech/gor./	Don Alonso Pech, Gobernador
	Grabier tun alcaldes/	Grabier Tun, Alcalde
	Pº Canul regidor/ [...]	Pedro Canul, Regidor, [...]
	testigos yn mehenob/	witnesses, my descendants
	Dn Lucas Pech/	Don Lucas Pech
	Dn Miguel Pech/	Don Miguel Pech
	Dn Gregorio Pech/	Don Gregorio Pech,
	lay hidalgos	who are *hidalgos*
		(Barrera Vasquez 1984:19, 1. 61–78)

We can see in the excerpt in (4) a typical combination of indigenous and Spanish elements. As we have already seen, the presence of names identifying the individuals in charge, date and official titles, unambiguously index the Spanish sector to which the document is addressed. This relation would be unequivocal even if the text did not contain a single word of Spanish. Use of the underlined Spanish terms only reinforces and renders explicit this inference. At the same time, the Maya aspect of the language, and more specifically, an elite variant of Maya, is evident in the syntax, in the use of the formula for apposition in order to apply the title *Justicias* to the ones responsible, in the vigesimal shape of the date ('two times twenty minus ten' to denote '30') and in the names of the families of Pech, Tun, and Canul.

By comparison, consider now the identifying expressions in YD2.

(5)   *Lay u hahil in firma,*   This is my true signature
      hele, en 8 de mayoil 1544   today, the 8th of May 1544
      Dn. Pedro Pech,   Don Pedro Pech,
      ti Dn. Alonso Pech   to Don Alonso Pech
      yetel Dn. Miguel Pech,   and Don Miguel Pech
      yetel Dn. Francisco Pech,   and Don Francisco Pech
      yetel Yxkil Itzam Pech,   and Yxkil Itzam Pech
      yetel Ah-Tunal Pech,   and Ah-Tunal Pech
      yetel Ah Dzulub Pech,   and Ah Dzulub Pech
      yetel tulacal mac cahob   and all the inhabitants
      uay tu pach lay kilacabob lae.   here around these lineages
                                       (Barrera Vasquez 1984:91)

Here we have a hybrid, comparable to the preceding one, of indigenous elements in
syntax, the family names and the reference to witnesses that live in the region. The
phrase in which the date is given conforms more closely to Spanish rules, but names
of authorities are given in Maya form.[7] Moreover, the reference to Mayan lineages
contrasts with the list of names given in YD1. It also invokes the historical legitimacy
of the inhabitants and suggests that the region was organized around a predominant
descent group, whereas YD1 puts the church in the center.

However, there is another more subtle aspect of the identification of the parties responsible for producing these documents. This relates to the order in which their
names are mentioned. It is evident in excerpt (4) that the *gobernador* is mentioned before the *alcaldes,* who precede the *regidores,* who are followed by witnesses without office. That is to say, the order of mention reproduces the political hierarchy of the government of the *Republica de Indios.* On the contrary, in (5), we have no indication of
titles of the individuals involved, or of the principle that governs the order of their
mention. In order to get to that we have to look elsewhere in the sources, and in fact,
thanks to the excellent research of Ralph Roys (1943, 1957), Günther Zimmermann
(1970), and Nancy Farriss (1984), we can identify (at least provisionally) the individuals in the two lists. Figures 9.2 and 9.3 show the named principals for YD1 and
YD2 respectively.

These two figures represent the individuals from the Pech patriline who are cited
in the two documents. The blackened symbol indicates the person that plays the role
of narrator in the document, i.e., the "I," and the number assigned to each corresponds to the order of mention in the text. Thus, figure 9.2 indicates that Don
Alonso Pech is the first named in YD1, where he occupies the role of first-person narrator, Don Lucas figures second, Don Miguel third, and so forth. The names of
Nachan, Diego, Ixkil Itzam, Martin and Ah Macan (all of them members of the Pech
family) are not cited in the preamble of the document presented in example (4), but
they are introduced during the narrative of the tour that follows. Figure 9.3 shows
that Don Pedro Pech plays the role of the first person who narrates in YD2, Alonso
is then introduced, then Miguel, and so on up to Ah Dzulub. At this point, two questions arise, namely, what is the relation between the two groups of principals in the

two versions, and what were the principles of succession that governed the order of their mention in each text?

With respect to the first question, the sources indicate that the authors of the two documents were father (YD2) and son (YD1) respectively, both of them baptized; also, that the son had rights to the title of *gobernador,* whereas the father probably did not (at least, not at this given time). The *cabildo* of Yaxkukul, members of which are mentioned in excerpt (4) of YD1, included people who were not members of the Pech family line (according to what we infer from their names).

The predominant family lines in the Maya towns evidently did not hold a monopoly on positions of authority in the *cabildos.* We can see, finally, that the two lists of names have some forms in common, i.e., Alonso and Ixkil Itzam Pech. I believe that there are other individuals denoted in both texts, but that this fact is obscured by variable use of Christian and Maya names. Other sources indicate that the individual called Don Pedro Pech was the same individual as the one named Ah Macan Pech, and that Nachan Pech in YD1 was probably the individual called Miguel or Francisco in YD2. Whatever the case, there seem to exist a number of persons mentioned in

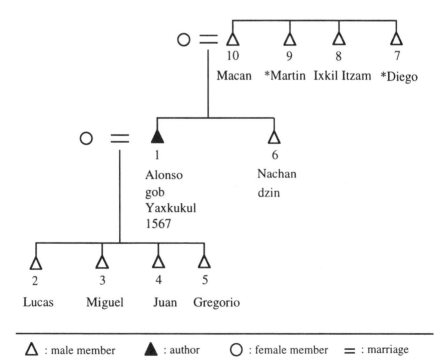

Δ : male member   ▲ : author   ○ : female member   = : marriage

* Position in the Pech family lineage uncertain. Titles and town names added.

Fig. 9.2. Members of the Pech Family Named in the Yaxkukul Document 1 (YD1)

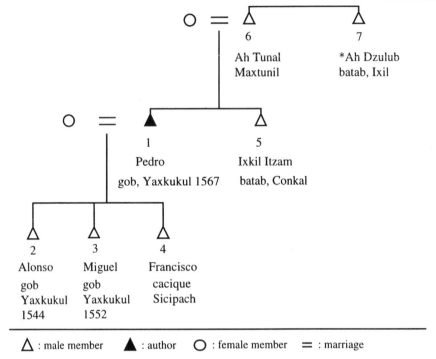

Fig. 9.3. Members of the Pech Family Named in the Yaxkukul Document 2 (YD2)

both documents, and who were, in all likelihood, members of a group of interest and influence in the region.

Regarding the second question, the order of naming, the schemas in Figures 9.2 and 9.3 clearly show two principles of citation.[8] First, each of the two documents represents three generations of the Pech line, with the authorial 'I' defining generation <0>, his children generation <−1>, and his parents generation <+1>. This corresponds to a relatively local kin group, and we can only wonder what would have been the relations of coresidence, alliance, and inheritance that would have cross-cut the groups named in the two documents. The second principle is more subtle and seems more arbitrary in the classical sense of the word (that of Saussure 1972). It governs succession of mention according to the rule $0 > -1 > 0 > +1$ ('x > y' = 'x precedes y'). That is to say, we begin with the narrator, who defines the generational basis (0), move next to his descendants (−1), then to his siblings (0), finally to the generation of his father (+1). It is remarkable that beneath their differences, the two texts follow this same principle of succession. This detail supports the hypothesis that the documents are the products of the same discourse logic.[9] Also, it can provide a clue to the analysis of other intertextual series in the colonial Yucatec documents, which are numerous and pose difficult problems of interpretation. This is summarized in the following table.

Rule of succession in participant reference

$$0 > -1 > 0 > +1$$

where 0 indicates generation of authorial 'I', -1 indicates first descending generation, and $+1$ indicates first ascending generation; $0 > 1$ is read "0 is denoted before 1 is denoted"

Referential Specificity and Treatment of the Perimeter

There are further important differences between the two documents in terms of their relative specificity of reference. Immediately after the excerpt in (4), document YD1 presents a list of thirty-one witnesses generally called *nucil uinicob* and *noxibtacob* 'great men' (Barrera Vasquez 1984, lines 79–110). These people were individually named (none of them being from the Pech family line), and they were the ones *before whom* the document was certified.[10] They are introduced by the formula *tutanil* 'before/in front of'. In contrast to this, the authorities related to the Spanish Crown are introduced from the very beginning of the document by way of the formula *tukaba* 'in the name of'. In this text a systematic relation is established between the three groups of agents. First is the narrator and the principals who are said to have directly participated in the visit and in the production of the text. These agents occupy the role of the first person I and We. Second is the King of Spain and the authorities that represented him. These are the ones to whom the document was addressed and who were introduced by the formula 'in the name of'. These agents occupied the role of addressee (although there is no overt second person). Third are the witnesses and local Maya chiefs—neither authors, nor addressees—who were introduced by the formula 'before/in front of'. As we saw in excerpt (5), document YD2 does not provide any list of the authorities of the *cabildo* of Yaxkukul. Nor does it give any list of witnesses, but instead the simple clause at the end of example (5) "with all the inhabitants here around these lineages", which is equivalent to an *etcetera* clause. Finally, YD2 does not maintain the linguistic distinction between the ones *in the name of whom* and the ones *before whom* the text was produced. Taken together, these facts indicate a striking difference between the two texts in terms of the relative specificity of their participant references. Document YD2, narrated by Pedro Pech, the father, seems to presuppose the more precise information provided in document YD1, narrated by Alonso Pech, his son. These facts suggest a "generational" reading of the texts. Document YD1, by far the more specific, presents a "modernizing" and inclusive version: it is based on a new form of government, placing the son in charge of the *cabildo* and it mentions the thirty-one great men that are not of the Pech family line. Document YD2 is exclusive (noninclusive) and oriented toward the past: it puts the father in charge of the region and suppresses any reference to the *cabildo* and to the representatives of other family lineages/different descent.

The two texts have roughly the same organization: a preliminary part that introduces the authors and the addressees, followed by a narrative of the inspection tour, i.e. the visit to the borders and the inventory of border markers. Finally a conclusion affirms the authenticity and the truth of the document. As soon as we compare the narratives of the border inspection, we realize that even here there are significant differences between the two versions. The first point of contrast concerns the participants that visited the borders, for YD1 enumerates the important people who accompanied Don Alonso Pech during the visit, whereas YD2 does not cite any of them. If Don Pedro Pech actually did visit the borders of Yaxkukul, this document implicates by omission that he did so alone.

On the contrary, Don Alonso Pech cites the names of the contiguous neighbors of Yaxkukul, who accompanied him during his visit around their common border. So he begins at a landmark called *ch'en chac nicte* 'Red water lily well' accompanied by a noble that he calls *yn dzin nachan pech* 'my younger sibling Nachan Pech'. They continue along the border together for a succession of five border markers, and they separate at a place called *chun catzin* 'Catzim trunk (a kind of tree)'. Don Alonso, at that point, is joined by *yn yum don Diego Pech yetel u kuchteel* 'my (fore)father Don Diego Pech with his deputies' who accompany him during the brief interval of one border marker. At *mul ac* 'Turtle Mound' he leaves Don Diego and is joined by *yn yum Ixkil Itzam Pech yetel u kuchteel* 'my (fore)father Ixkil Itzam Pech with his deputies' who accompany him as far as *halal actun* 'Halal cavern' where he leaves Ixkil Itzam and is joined by Ah Namon Pech with his deputies. The tour continues like this for two more intervals, during which Don Alonso is accompanied by other groups of important people, each of them with their own deputies. The text makes clear that these principals lived in the villages neighboring with Yaxkukul, and that they consequently shared a segment of its border. In all, Don Alonso completes the tour with six groups of nobles, each of them with their deputies. There is no overlap among these groups, and the only agent who traverses more than one interval is Don Alonso himself. The story is narrated in the first-person singular, as in example (6).

(6)   *noholtan yn binel tzol pictun*   Southward I go counting stone markers
        tulacal u binel latulah kuchul   it goes all the way until it arrives
      tu chun mul ac   at the foot of Mul Ac
        yan u pictunil—   There's a marker there.
      ti cin ppatic ah cumkali   There I leave off the Cumkal people.
        tiix cin chaic in yum   there too I join my (fore)father
      yxkil ytzam pech ah sicpach   Yxkil Ytzam Pech of Sicipach
        y u kuchteelob   with his deputies.
      Cacathil yn binel yetelob   Pairwise I go along with them.
                                             (Barrera Vasquez 1984:25–26, 1.
                                             154–62)

The idea we get from this excerpt is that there is a "central" noble, Don Alonso, who has undertaken a visit of his frontier, joined by his neighbors from one interval to the next. In using the first-person singular in conjunction with the names of the ones who have visited the perimeter with him, this text maintains a very tight relation to the visit of the perimeter of which it constitutes an account. The contrast with YD2 in this respect is so striking that it is legitimate to ask whether the two texts in fact deal with the same perimeter. Not only does YD2 not mention any neighbor that had accompanied Don Pedro during his visit, but also this visit is narrated entirely in the third person, and it refers to different places than the ones mentioned in YD1.

(7)	*Binbal noholtan,*	Going Southward,
	tan u tzolol u yam ppictunil	the intervals between markers are counted out
	latulah u manel Pacabtun.	until it passes (by) Pacabtun.
	Layli ubinel u tzolol	The counting out goes along still
	u ppictunil noholtan	of the stone markers Southward
	u chucic Kom-Sahcab.	it arrives at Kom-Sahcab.
		(Barrera Vasquez 1984:93)

This passage is from the part of the narrative immediately following the one in which the place Chun Catzim is mentioned, a place common to both documents. It corresponds because of its position to the part transcribed in (6). However, instead of citing Chun Mul Ac, it mentions a different place, Pacabtun, which is never mentioned in YD1. We can also see a striking difference in style: the use of verbal participles, coupled with the third-person singular of the passive voice, introduces a distance of perspective between YD2 and the visit that it describes, something that is entirely absent from YD1. One could also say that the first document is more or less directly superposed on the visit, and, in a sense, that it allows the readers to engage in the visit themselves, whereas the second is distanced from the visit and it assumes a detached point of view. YD2 is more like a map such as the Mani map, whereas YD1 is more scriptlike. Maintaining a more "impersonal" perspective, YD2 could also be considered closer to the style of hieroglyphic codices. Conversely, YD1 is similar to a guided tour that the reader follows from one step to the next.

We have barely scratched the surface of a comparison between the two documents of Yaxkukul, both of them evidently produced in the 1550s. In a more complete analysis one would have to examine the distribution and classification of boundary markers, because this raises other interesting contrasts. The two documents mention the following types of borders: *pictun* '(lit.) eight thousand stones', which are numerous and, evidently, the least important among the markers (nineteen in YD1; thirteen in YD2); *multun* '(lit.) pile of stones', less numerous but still of minor importance (twelve in YD1; one in YD2); *Cruz* 'cross' (five in YD1; nine in YD2); *tiitz* 'corners' (four in YD1; six in YD2) and *behob* 'routes' that run across the frontier of Yaxkukul (four in YD1; five in YD2). Within each text, there are regular correlations among these markers, such that one can predict by the presence of a marker of a given class the presence or the absence of a marker of some other class. It is not my purpose to investigate these relations here, but it is clear that the two documents use the same inventory of the marker types, but do not distribute them in the same fashion. We know that the two texts refer to the same space because they share a majority of place names, and they cite them in the same order. What differentiates between the two is the type of marker assigned to each location, but not the locations themselves (with a few exceptions).

This fact raises an interesting question for future research, namely, whether the typology and the distribution of the markers reflect political alliances among the regions, rather than geographical divisions among places. Because if we assume the border between two places to be a material division, then it becomes difficult to establish correspondences between the two documents. Either one is true and the other is false, or they describe two different places. On the contrary, if we consider the boundaries to be the concretizations of social relations, then it becomes possible to hypothesize that the geographic space of Yaxkukul was in reality the seat of two regions: the one corresponding to the network of Don Pedro Pech (father) and the other to that of Don Alonso Pech (son). The duality in turn articulates the two *encomenderos* and the deep-seated differences in style. There are at least two ways of understanding this duality. We can posit two sectors of alliances: the two individuals represent different but overlapping alliances with their neighbors, and hence they describe in their respective documents two regions that overlap partially. Alternatively, we can posit two sectors of discourse, figure, and ground. The document of the son, YD1, focuses on the *cabildo* and the allies that participated in the tour and the text, leaving the traditional authority of the Pech lineage in the background. The document of the father, YD2, focuses on the authority of the Pech family and the support that it enjoyed in the region, leaving in the background its participation in the *cabildo* and the new order that it represents. These two solutions, duality of regions, as defined by social relations, and duality of discourse as defined by verbal style, are surely not mutually exclusive. In any case, a comparison of the versions shows that the place called Yaxkukul comprised two regions, and this fact, it seems to me, merits further research.

CONCLUSION

It is probable that any study of the social world, inasmuch as it attempts to encompass the self-descriptions of agents, must include the study of versions and variants. These self-descriptions are essential to comprehend a society, to the degree that they constitute the interpretive context in which values are established. In everyday life, agents describe themselves and produce images of their world. These descriptions, which are reflexive and oriented by their particular perspectives, are an integral part of social reality, as Charles Taylor (1985) pointed out. This has two important corollaries. On the one hand, language, like images, belongs to the world and not to a domain of representations that remains apart from it. On the other hand, an agent producing an utterance is thereby engaged in the world that (s)he describes. Models of discourse based on the truth of correspondence between text and world overlook this double engagement. It happens that agents occupy the world in different ways, and this inevitably produces a heterogeneous discourse, a play of perspectives across versions. The study of variation was of course basic to formalism and classical structuralism, but it was too often done without attention to the agents' perspectives that are the sources of the versions.

Intertextuality among variants always implies a tension between two tendencies, the one centripetal and the other centrifugal. The former tends to constitute individual texts according to a generic model that provides principles of selection and combination. This totalizes the text, giving it an internal logic and clear boundaries. Thus, the two documents of Yaxkukul are both complete texts, with the requisite parts, coherent narratives, witnesses, and authors. On the basis of comparison with a graphic map, it is easy to establish that YD1 is a complete composition with its own structure and style. YD2 is probably a fragment, because it lacks certain parts that are present in YD1, but it is still complete in terms of the main elements and the description of the boundaries of Yaxkukul. On this level, the series implies four genres of practice, the *forma derecho* 'form of rights' of YD1 and the *tzol pictun* 'border count' visit that it describes; the *titulo* 'title' of YD2 and the *ppiz luum* 'land measure' that it describes. The documents suggest that these four productions correspond to four different groups of participants, and, perhaps, four different structures of participation.

But these distinctions reflect only half of the story. Intertextuality always inserts texts in one or more series, and this is what relates them centrifugally to a network of transtextual relations. If the first tendency renders the text complete and irreducible, the second renders it incomplete and purely relational. In this perspective, we see that the four events of Yaxkukul overlap to such an extent that one wonders whether the two texts were not in fact part of a single orchestrated textual production, and also whether the two inspections of the boundaries of Yaxkukul were not in fact a single event described from two different perspectives—or perhaps two tours, the sum of which added up to a "visit" in the full sense. Similarly, the groups of participants appear to be different but they are related as four generations of the Pech family. The upshot of these observations is that the two individual texts may well be two fragments of a single whole.

Of course these relations are independent, which means that the two texts could be independent and the two visits identical, or vice versa. Moreover, identity is only one intertextual relation among others. All these equations could be recast focusing on relations of sequence, elaboration, and simplification (YD1 of the document elaborates the group of participants in the tour that it describes); transposition (an element *x* is transposed from YD1 to YD2); presupposition (YD2 presupposes what is made explicit in YD1); rhetorical complementarity (YD1 adopts more of a Spanish official voice, in certain respects, than does YD2); relative weighting, and so on (see Jenny 1982; Goodman 1978). The important point is to realize that intertextuality displaces the object of study from individual texts to transtextual relations. Such a displacement seems to be called for by the facts of the colonial discourse of Yucatán.

It remains to be emphasized that these relations do not simply bear on symbolic discourse but also on space itself. In the end, we do not know what the limits of

Yaxkukul were in 1544, because we do not know how to interpret the various markers. It seems inevitable that the observed distinctions did reflect a difference, if only because they are so systematic and apparently uncontradictory. We have phrased this difference in terms of regions in the same space, adopting a dichotomy suggested by de Certeau (1984). This way of talking about things may prove wrong, but it has the temporary advantage of underscoring that space is socially constituted just as profoundly as is discourse and its agents. According to archeologists, the Maya monuments were built upon one another from period to period, like architectural palimpsests. Traditional discourse like the Books of Chilam Balam range in intertextual series as well, and colonial documentation in "official Maya" is typified by an insistence on multiple versions. The documents of Yaxkukul illustrate this more general phenomenon. They are the residue of social processes in which objectivity is produced. This production is always realized under a horizon of perspectives.

NOTES

Translations from the Mayan are in single quotes.

1. A third text exists that treats the same border and mentions a number of the same facts, namely, the *Crónica de Chac Xulub Chen* (Brinton 1969:193ff.). This third version will not be analyzed here.

2. The documents of Sotuta reproduce crosses in verbal description; see Roys, 1939; Hanks 1989.

3. Notice that the legend, written in Spanish outside the map's border, is oriented on the page in such a manner that the north pole is at the top. By contrast, the writing of Maya names and the drawings of churches inside the border are oriented with the east at the top. Intermediate between these two extremes, the writing in the border itself follows the circle and hence has no fixed orientation, apart from having its base in the interior, not the exterior, line.

4. I am summarizing research presented in a series of articles: Hanks 1986, 1987, 1988, 1989, 1990.

5. This way of asking the question assumes that the notion of genre applies to social practices and not only to linguistic manifestations of discourse.

6. It is possible that one of the distinctive traits of *tzol* was exactly that, in this genre, the action anticipates a written record.

7. A Spanish surname indicates that its bearer was baptized and thus presents himself as an adherent of Catholicism. The use of a Maya surname indicates either that the person has not been baptized, or is aligning with pre-Christian tradition. In this case we know, thanks to other sources, that the individuals mentioned in YD2 also had Christian surnames, which indicates that here they chose to underline their Maya side.

8. It is possible that some individuals, shown in the generations above and below Ego, in fact belonged to a more distant generation. The problem is related to the kinship terms: *mehen* 'child' can refer to biological son, son of a brother or grandson (Martinez Hernández 1929: 623, ref. 303), and *yum* to father, grandfather, regional chief called *halach uinic,* monks, governor by his subordinates, and still other uses. Hence it could be that my diagrams combine,

in three generations, groups that in reality make up four or five. They are consistent with the interpretations of Roys (1939), Zimmermann (1970), (1984) and Farriss (1984).

9. Note that this logic does not concern the tour of the boundaries that should precede the making of the documents, since it governs the order of linguistic reference and not necessarily the order of the described action. This common feature is important because it indicates that the two documents form a closely articulated intertextual series.

10. It is likely that the text was read in public, in order to verify that all witnesses agreed on its content, but nothing in the document confirms this inference.

REFERENCES

Barrera Vasquez, Alfredo
  1984 Documento Numero 1 del deslinde de tierras en Yaxkukul, Yucatán. Mexico, Instituto Nacional de Antropología e Historia (Collección científica: "Linguística" 125).
Barrera Vasquez, Alfredo (with Sylvia Rendón)
  1974 *El libro de los libros de Chilam Balam.* Mexico City: Fondo de Cultura Económica (1st ed. 1948).
Bricker, Victoria R.
  1986 *A Grammar of Mayan Hieroglyphs.* New Orleans: Tulane University ("Middle American Research Institute Publication" 56).
Brinton, Daniel G., ed.
  1969 *The Maya Chronicles.* New York: AMS Press (1st ed. 1882).
Certeau, Michel de
  1984 *The Practice of Everyday Life.* Translated by Steven Rendall. Berkeley: University of California Press.
Chamberlain, Robert S.
  1948 *The Conquest and Colonization of Yucatán, 1517–1550.* Washington, DC: Carnegie Institution (Publication 582).
Edmonson, Munro S.
  1982 *The Ancient Future of the Itza: The Book of Chilam Balam of Tizimin.* Austin, TX: University of Texas Press.
Farriss, Nancy
  1984 *Maya Society under Colonial Rule. The Collective Enterprise of Survival.* Princeton: Princeton University Press.
Gates, William
  1937 *Yucatán Before and After the Conquest by Friar Diego de Landa with Other Related Documents, Maps and Illustrations.* Baltimore, MD: The Maya Society ("Maya Society Publication" 20).
Goodman, N.
  1978 *Ways of Worldmaking.* Cambridge: Hackett Publishing Co.
Hanks, William F.
  1986 "Authenticity and Ambivalence in the Text: A Colonial Maya Case," *American Ethnologist* 13(4):721–44.
  1987 "Discourse Genres in a Theory of Practice," *American Ethnologist* 14(4):64–88.
  1988 "Grammar, Style and Meaning in a Maya Manuscript," *International Journal of American Linguistics* 54(3):331–64.

1989   "Elements of Maya Style," in William F. Hanks & Don S. Rice, eds., *Word and Image in Mayan Culture: Explorations in Language, History and Representation.* Salt Lake City: University of Utah Press.
1990   *Referential Practice: Language and Lived Space among the Maya.* Chicago: University of Chicago Press.
Jenny, Laurent
1982   "The Strategy of Form," in Tzvetan Todorov, ed., *French Literary Theory: A Reader.* Cambridge: Cambridge University Press: 34–63.
Martinez Hernández, Juan
1926   *Crónicas Maya. Crónica de Yaxkukul.* Mérida: Yucatán.
1929   *Diccionario de Motul, Maya-Español Atribuido a Fray Antonio de Ciudad Real.* Mérida: Talleres de la Compañía Tipográfica Yucateca, S.A.
Morley S. G. and G. W. Brainerd
1983   *The Ancient Maya.* 4th ed., rev. by Robert J. Sharer. Stanford: Stanford University Press.
Redfield, Robert and Alfonso Villa Rojas
1934   *Chan Kom: A Maya Village.* Washington, DC: The Carnegie Institution.
Roys, Ralph L.
1943   *The Indian Background of Colonial Yucatán.* Washington DC: The Carnegie Institution (Publication 548).
1957   *The Political Geography of the Yucatán Maya.* Washington DC: The Carnegie Institution (Publication 613).
Roys, Ralph L., ed.
1939   *The Titles of Ebtun.* Washington DC: The Carnegie Institution.
Scholes, Frances V. and Eleanor B. Adams, eds.
1938   Don Diego Quijada, alcade mayor de Yucatán, 1561–1565; documentos sacados de los archivos de España y publicados por Frances V. Scholes y Eleanor B. Adams (Bibliotecha hitórica mexicana de obras inéditas, 14–15). México, Antigua librería Robredo, de J. Porrúa e hijos.
Scholes, Frances V. and Ralph L. Roys
1968   *The Maya Chontal Indians of Acalan-Tixchel: A Contribution to the History and Ethnography of the Yucatán Peninsula.* 2nd ed. Norman: University of Oklahoma Press (1st ed. 1948).
Saussure, Ferdinand De
1972   *Cours de linguistique générale.* Édition critique préparée par Tullio de Mauro. Paris, Payot.
Taylor, Charles
1985   *Philosophical Papers. 2: Philosophy and the Human Sciences.* Cambridge: Cambridge University Press (Chap. 4, "Understanding and Ethnocentricity": 116–33).
Tozzer, Alfred M., trans. and ed.
1941   *Relacion de las cosas de Yucatán, by Fray Diego de Landa.* Cambridge: Harvard University, Peabody Museum of American Archeology and Ethnology.
Zimmermann, Günther
1970   *Briefe der indianischen Nobilität aus Neuspanien an Karl V und Philip II um die Mitte des 16. Jahrhunderts.* München: Kommissionsverlag Klaus Renner.

10

Language and Discourse
in Colonial Yucatán

INTRODUCTION

Recent developments in Mayanist research have led to significant revisions in our understanding of pre-Columbian Maya culture and history. Epigraphers have made real progress toward understanding the Mayan hieroglyphic texts.[1] At the same time new interpretations have emerged of the iconography that typically accompanies glyphic texts, and adorns pre-Columbian Maya material arts.[2] Archeologists, collaborating with ethnohistorians,[3] have made similar advances in the understanding of Maya public space,[4] regional political systems, and ideologies.[5] These developments have led to an increasingly complex view of the Maya and their systems of representation, in which hieroglyphic inscriptions once thought to be strictly ritual in reference are now understood to recount the historical exploits of named individual rulers, acting within regional political configurations. Viewed as a system of objective reference, glyphic discourse projects a social world that we can learn about by reading the inscriptions. Much of the iconography serves the same referential function of projecting a world, such as the gathering and interaction of nobles portrayed on the walls of Bonampak. It is noteworthy that the referentialist hypothesis subsumes two quite separate ideas, the one bearing on the functional properties of glyphs and other symbolic forms, and the other bearing on the historical factuality of the world that the forms portray.

Alongside the realization that the glyphs record "historical" facts, epigraphers have demonstrated that they have a syntactic structure closely linked to that of spoken Mayan languages (especially Cholan and Yucatecan). In particular, the once dubious notion that the glyphs correspond to speech sounds has been shown to be true beyond reasonable doubt, and phoneticism is now a staple of Mayan epigraphy. Moreover, phonetic correspondences are only the beginning of what is proving to be a powerful set of linguistic parallels between the formal structure of glyphs and the syntax and discourse organization of spoken Mayan languages. These twin breakthroughs, referential function and language-based form, have helped lead to quantum changes in the way scholars think about pre-Columbian Maya society. For those of us who study the colonial society and discourse, in which indigenous and European worlds collide, this research serves as a reminder that the Maya sector is no less complex and dynamic than the Spanish.

Less dramatic but equally significant changes are taking place in the study of post-conquest Mayan cultures as well. Particularly in the areas of colonial history,[6] literary studies,[7] native resistance[8] and contemporary ethnography,[9] an increasingly complex view of Mayan peoples is emerging as well. Since the fall of Mayapan confederate rule in northern Yucatán in the mid-1400s, and probably long before, Yucatán was subdivided into some sixteen political geographic regions. Called *cacicazgos* in the European scholarly literature, these regional units differed significantly in their internal structure and external relations (Farriss 1984; Roys 1957). There were well-known enmities among regions, such as that between Mani and Sotuta provinces, and differences of production, as in the salt beds of Chikinchel, Chakan, and coastal Ceh Pech provinces, and the honey and cacao production of Chetumal (Roys 1957:54). According to Edmonson's (1982, 1986) inferences, there was a significant boundary running north-south and separating the eastern region of the peninsula, under the influence of the Itza lineage, from the western region, under the influence of the Xiu. Jones's (1989) studies of the southern frontier zone establish the role of the Sierra province of Mani as a source both of fugitive Indians who went on to populate the Ix Pimienta area, and of pro-Spanish Indian militia who helped Europeans round up and defeat these fugitives. Regional diversity, political division, and stratification were facts of life in colonial Yucatán, as they had been long before then.

Starting in the early colonial period, Maya resistance was aimed at gaining access to power within the emerging social and cultural fields of the colony. It does not appear to have been aimed, at least in the main, at overthrowing the new order imposed by the Spanish so as to return to an erstwhile pristine pre-Hispanic past. I have seen evidence of such a longing among some contemporary Yucatec Maya men, but the colonial sources point in the opposite direction. As Bricker (1981), Farriss (1984), and Jones (1989) show persuasively, the Yucatec Maya sought to secure for themselves a position in the colonial society. This appears to be true even when pursuing the strategies of flight (Farriss 1978; Jones 1989), millenarian appeals to a purely Indian future (see Bricker 1981 and Sullivan 1989), and indeed consolidating regions of resistance from which Spaniards were physically excluded (Jones 1989; Sullivan 1989). The principals leading these movements were usually people who had had extensive contact with the Spanish, were bilingual and bicultural to a degree, and went on to create social contexts in which Spanish and Maya practices were fused rather than isolated (see Miller and Farriss [1979] for an early example of religious fusion, and Hanks [1989a] for textual examples). This point is of particular importance in attempting to evaluate the local responses to Spanish rule, and the impoverished blends of cultural forms that they gave rise to. For the goal was evidently not to banish the Europeans and their god from the local world, but to secure some of the privileges of membership.

The Franciscans had a profound impact on Maya moral, religious, and literary practices. By learning the native language early and well, the friars engaged with the

Indian nobility as of the sixteenth century and trained their children in Christian doctrine, Latin, Spanish, and alphabetic writing. These strategies of conversion contributed to the emergence of culturally ambivalent actors, many of whom would occupy the influential posts in the local town councils, and serve as advisers to the Spanish authorities, as well (cf. Collins 1977; Farriss 1984; Hanks 1986; Ricard 1947; Todorov 1984). These same actors were in many cases practitioners of "pagan" rituals that combined Catholic and Maya elements, and were among the principal instigators of resistance to the Spanish. Religious practice and instruction were therefore crucibles for cultural hybridization from the earliest years of the colony.

Throughout the colonial period and as late as the Caste Wars in nineteenth-century Yucatán, Maya resistance to Spanish rule has been organized around religious symbols (such as the cross), and led in part by ritual specialists (native priests, diviners, shamans). To a degree, this is a corollary of the influence of the monastics, for the symbols of Christianity were among the first inculcated in the native population of Yucatán, as well as the valley of Mexico and elsewhere in Spanish America. At the same time, ritual specialists in the indigenous society controlled the modes of symbolic production in which space and time were ritually constituted. They have been and remain the main repository of calendric and historical knowledge among the Maya, and have evidently always had a political function. These facts suggest that the broad effectiveness of the European religious in reshaping the imaginary and self-image of the Indians (Gruzinski 1988) was complemented by an effective and highly influential indigenous priesthood. It may well be this priesthood who were among the most active in engaging with the Europeans, meeting them head-on in front of the altar, as it were. At the upper levels of institutionalized priesthood among the Maya were the chilan prophets who advised chiefs and the ritual specialists who directed major events such as the processions described in the *Books of Chilam Balam*. This sector appears to have been an early target of the Spanish, and it is unclear to what extent such roles continued to function in the Maya sector into the colonial period. It is clear however that lesser experts continued to engage in curing human illness, interpreting dreams, and performing local agricultural rituals (Sánchez de Aguilar 1900 [1613]). And, as the idolatry trials indicate, private and small-scale worship involving pre-Columbian deities persisted (as it does to this day).

Although Yucatecan society obviously continued to change throughout the colonial period, the first century and a half of colonial rule appears to have had a formative impact on the development of hybrid cultural practices that have persisted to this day. Many basic patterns took shape as early as the sixteenth and seventeenth centuries. The policies set forth in the *Ordenanzas* of Tomás López Medel, the establishment of the *encomienda,* and strategies of conversion set in motion processes still ongoing in Yucatán. Some of the best examples of this are linguistic. Maya scribes produced a wealth of semiofficial texts that show the emergence of significant novel features, many of them traceable to Spanish and in particular, Franciscan discourse practices. They include the first-person narrator (conspicuously absent from hieroglyphic and more "traditional" Maya genres such as the *Books of Chilam Balam*); forms of address based on relations between authors, principals, witnesses and absent, royal addressees; the use of the sign of the cross as a discourse boundary marker; and the self-deprecating, affectively charged supplication typical of some parts of Catholic worship. These are among the distinctive features shared by early colonial and modern shamanic discourse (Hanks 1987). They are not mere details of linguistic form, as they might appear. Rather, they are the symbolic traces of modes of agency and forms of action that took shape in the colonial period and remain operative today.

Discourse analysis can contribute significantly to historical methods. Texts incorporate metaphors that can serve as keys to understanding, and the evolution of a textual tradition is both a history itself and a way into a broader history in which the metaphors are grounded (a position taken by Edmonson 1970, 1973). Similarly, as Borah (1984) discusses in relation to Nahuatl in Central Mexico, the use of often opaque native language terms in colonial documents can pose formidable problems for historians (something well attested in the corpus under study). Beyond metaphor, it has become increasingly clear that the genre systems, rhetorical structures, intertextual relations, and conditions of discourse production and reception all contribute crucially to the meaning of documents. This is one area in which there is extensive overlap in the descriptive problems faced by historians and linguists, and collaborations between them can be the most fruitful.

THE EMERGENCE OF COLONIAL GENRES

In earlier phases of Mayanist research, there was considerable emphasis placed on the intricacy and aesthetic refinement of Maya representational canons. The fascination with native histories, art forms, songs and literary texts rested on twin urges widely felt among European(-extracted) researchers. The first was the desire to come face to face with an untainted, purely Maya world, which could be reconstructed by painstaking research. The second was the urge to find in that world artistic, literary, and "intellectual" achievements commensurate with those of the classical traditions in the west. These are worthy commitments and they have served the field well in the past. They have also obscured a great deal. In the Yucatecan context, one expression of them has been the classicizing focus on real "native literature." This focus usually rests on two ontological commitments: that there was a real native voice to be found out there, and that there was a meaningful category of "literature" in which to find it. Given this, it follows naturally that we should look to texts such as the *Books of Chilam Balam,* the artistic and ritual forms to recover the authentic Maya voice. The problem is that this project tends to essentialize the chosen texts, making them icons of ethnic essence, when in fact they are all tainted, colonial productions. Moreover, it invites one to ignore or undervalue the letters, wills, petitions, land surveys, doctrinal materials, and other nonliterary discourse produced in Maya language throughout the colonial period. If there have been advances in colonial history in Mesoamerica, and I believe there have, they have been due in part to a broadening of investigation to include, and even make central, such para-canonical forms. "Literature" can no longer be taken for granted as a viable object for historical study.

One consequence of this broadening of the field of study has been to make opaque many things that seemed transparent in the earlier paradigm. Despite their familiar labels, such as *carta* 'letter', *crónica* 'chronicle', and *acuerdo* 'accord', colonial Maya documents are basically unfamiliar. The reason for this is that the Spanish genres were adapted and altered in very significant ways in Maya language documents, becoming in effect what Morson (1981) called "boundary genres." Most of the existing translations and analyses of these documents have been undertaken by scholars immersed in the vocabulary of Maya language, but not attentive to grammatical structure, nor to the conventions of idiomatic usage in Maya (noteworthy exceptions being Barrera Vásquez 1984 and Bricker 1981). Similarly, although many of the texts in question exist in both Spanish and Maya versions, there are typically significant differences between the two, and a history based solely on the European language sources risks overlooking a great deal. The consequences of such oversight can indeed be debilitating because different readings of texts result from critical analysis of the native language versions (Hanks 1986, 1988, 1989a). More importantly, to work exclusively with European or indigenous language sources invites the assumption that the two are substitutable, that translation really is based on transparent equivalences between languages. A letter is a letter regardless of the language it is written in, just as a land survey and a sworn affidavit can be rendered in Spanish as well as Maya. What is missed in such a view is the fact that equivalence is always partial and guided by criteria that are open to debate. Translation is a discourse practice subject to all the political and social crosscurrents that impact on other practices. Upon close examination, for instance, letters and land surveys in Maya turn out to contain passages in verse, recurrent signs of the cross, and ritual-like tropes that resonate with both the broader system of Maya genres and apparently unrelated Spanish ones, such as prayer and doctrinal forms. They also express communicative aims unlike the ones usually associated with the corresponding Spanish genres. Land surveys in Maya, like the ones in Yaxkukul in the mid-sixteenth century (Barrera Vásquez 1984; Martínez Hernández 1926), resemble ritual scripts more than objective descriptions. This is due in part to poetic aspects of the language that are lost in translation. Such texts document the emergence of a novel system of genres out of the fusion of Spanish and indigenous systems (Hanks 1987, 1989a, 1992). More than any super-category of art or literature, this process of blending cultures promises to reveal dynamics of Mesoamerican histories and cultures that will help us to understand the present.

The discourse genre provides a level of textual analysis that encompasses individual texts without effacing the differences between them. The importance of this stems from the fact that texts cannot be properly analyzed or even read, in isolation, but must be placed within the larger discursive formations of which they are a part. Looking only at individual documents without exploring their intertextual ties can actually obscure significant features. A practical example of this is provided by letters sent to the Crown by Maya nobles in the mid-sixteenth century. Tozzer (1941), Gates

(1937), and others have observed that several Maya-language letters, all praising the Franciscans, were sent to Philip II in the 1560s. The two main versions of the letters were each sent in multiple copies from several provinces (reproduced in Zimmermann 1974). Given the knowledge that the Franciscans were under investigation at the time for having used excessive force in their attempts to extirpate idolatry, the content of the letters appeared suspect. How could the Maya praise the friars after having been tortured and punished severely by them? Moreover, real letters express the views of their authors and the fact that all thirteen copies of the letters say the same thing indicates that they must have been produced from a single template. Tozzer and Gates drew the inference that the letters were inauthentic fabrications by the Franciscans to improve their image with the Crown. However, placed in the context of other Maya genres, this inference becomes questionable. The regional differentiation from which we began makes it clear that there was no single "Maya" perspective that the letters could fail to express, and in fact the signatories were from towns outside the areas in which Franciscan excesses were most flagrant. Also, the existence of multiple copies may well be motivated by the widely attested convention in Maya discourse of producing serial instances of a single text. This applies to the repeating portions of the *Books of Chilam Balam,* to other colonial documents in Maya, and to modern shamanic performance as well. Rather than prove the inauthenticity of the letters as letters, the serial versions suggest their authenticity as discourse designed to convince the Crown and alter social realities. Once again, the intertextual features of genres affect the ways individual texts can be read.

Although my focus in this paper is colonial discourse and current understandings of it, it is worth pointing out that these issues have a direct impact on how we understand modern Maya society in Mexico today. The genres of shamanic discourse in modern Yucatán, for instance, carry forth many of these discourse features and raise similar problems of description. There have been studies of selected shamanic forms (Villa Rojas 1945; Sosa 1986; Love 1984, 1986, 1989), but these have not explored the roots of modern practices in the colonial period. Traditionally viewed as a repository of pre-Columbian cosmology, the elements of shamanism deriving from Catholic forms of worship have tended to be underplayed, or mentioned without comment, even though they reflect a cultural ambivalence deeply connected to that of colonial boundary genres. Among other shared features, one finds signs of the cross used as discourse boundary markers and supplications to a personal fatherly God over the world of sin, both indicative of Catholic practices. Among the different shamanic genres, most of those aimed at securing divine intervention in human affairs are performed in series of five or nine, according to the genre and intensity of the request. Perhaps most noteworthy are the robust cyclic patterns in shamanic discourse structure, for these bear striking relations to forms of cyclicity that occur in land surveys such as the Yaxkukul document of 1554 (cf. Barrera Vásquez 1984; Fought 1985; Gossen 1974). Shamanic performance is a discourse system that carries within itself forms of (inter)textuality related logically and substantively to those that emerged in the colonial period.

DIMENSIONS OF GENRE SYSTEMS

How can we go beyond presumptive categories such as "Literature" to achieve a clearer and more provocative sense of the colonial Maya? In this section I outline a set of questions that grow out of work mentioned in the preceding sections, but, hopefully, point beyond it. Contemporary shamanism in Yucatán will continue to serve as a counterpoint to the colonial materials.

An initial question is simply, What types of discourse are we dealing with, and what kinds of indigenous (that is, colonial) expressions designate them? In somewhat more technical terms, What kinds of metatextual categories emerged in the discourse formation of colonial Yucatán? What were the metadiscursive expressions used by native authors and speakers to designate their own actions? In modern ritual performance, shamans use a set of highly regular linguistic expressions that state what it is that they are doing in performing, as in "I beg weeping," "I speak the name of spirit," and other (semi-)performative expressions (Austin 1962; Levinson 1983; Searle 1976). They also describe, as they pray, their own location at the foot of the altar, their bodily posture, the purpose of the performance. Under certain circumstances, they use standard labels for the ritual genres, like *pa꞉ ꞏi꞉ik꞉* 'sweep wind (exorcism)' and *heč lúꞏum* 'fix earth (cleansing of inhabited space)', in order to precisely state what it is they are currently engaged in. All of these verbal resources describe aspects of discourse, and it is for this reason that they are called "metadiscursive" or simply "metalanguage."

The colonial documents also show a range of metalanguage, including (semi)performative expressions such as "we wish to recount to your ear, Ruler" and "in the name of the power of the Governor," standard labels of genre categories like *carta* 'letter' and *ppiz luum* 'land survey' (lit. 'measure earth') and other explicit descriptions of the documents themselves, the actions in which they are produced, and the outcomes they are aimed at. The use of metalanguage provides invaluable evidence of how native authors classify their own communicative engagements. It also links texts into a set of genres that organize such factors as author intention, proper circumstances of production, how literal or figurative, general or specific description should be understood. Metalinguistic devices help govern the text-to-context mappings, which in turn guide readers and hearers in the proper understandings of texts. Given the focus of cultural and historical research on contextualizing forms and practices over time, metalanguage is a significant resource.

One of the most important foci in Maya textuality is the discourse expression of the immediate context in which a text is produced, and to which it is addressed. This holds equally for written and spoken discourse, verbal and image-based modes. In distinction to "content-based" analyses, which focus on what texts describe, this statement focuses on reference to authors, addressees, and other participants, on the discursive "We-here-now" in which the text arises. The question is: are there precise commonalities in the text-to-context relations across the various colonial genres under study? Stated more precisely, are the indexical categories in Maya colonial and shamanic discourse configured in constant, or at least consistent, patterns? In the colonial documents, how are participants and places of production referred to (including pronouns, descriptive epithets and vocatives, spatial and temporal deictics, place names, locative descriptions, dates)? In the modern shamanic materials, the performing shaman, patient, spirit addressees, location of performance, and cosmological time frame are encoded in distinctive patterns (Hanks 1990). That is, the ritual present has an organization different from other kinds of present, and intimately related to the formal structure of shamanic speech. How consistent is it with the kinds of present constituted in colonial discourse?

Part of the present is the participant framework of discourse production, the personnel involved in creating a document or verbally mediated act. In the colonial documents, this relates primarily to the authors, witnesses in front of whom a text is authenticated, and authorities in whose name it is produced. The first question on this point relates to the selection of those whose names appear in documents, as opposed to those who do not. In the case of official land surveys and agreements, the structure of *cabildo* government in the Indian republics can serve as a framework in which to motivate who gets named, but in other genres of text, such as letters or petitions, the motivations for citing one set of principals but not another remain opaque. In the series of letters sent to the Crown in the 1560s for instance (see Zimmermann 1974; Hanks 1986), each letter is signed by a different group of local nobles. In other documents from the same period, many of the same people (apparently) are named, but the groupings differ. This raises the likelihood that the practice of signing, or being named as witness in a document, was a meaningful act subject to strategic decision and not merely determined by structural factors such as place of residence or age. Another dimension of naming is the use of Spanish as opposed to Maya first names, a point on which the two land documents from Yaxkukul differ. As Tozzer (1941) and others have recognized, the introduction in baptism of European first names actually created a significant amount of ambiguity in person reference, since one comes across numerous instances of names like "Juan Cocom" or "Pedro Pech" in the texts, without being able to determine how many different individuals are being referred to. A related issue is the use or nonuse of titles and honorific epithets such as *batab* 'chief', *gobernador* 'governor' (of *cabildo*), *nucteil* 'elder (lit. great tree)', *nohxib* 'elder' (lit. great man), *principales* 'local authority' (official Spanish title given to important men in the wards of the Indian republics), and so forth. On this point there is the recurrent issue of whether a title is used at all, and if so which language it is in, as an index of which sector the agent is identified with. But there are also very interesting and regular patterns in the poetic structure of the more elaborate titles used in reference to the Crown. The king is referred to in a wide range of expressions ranging from *Rey* or *su majestad* all the way through *ca noh ahau rey ah tepal de su majestad* "Our great lord king majesty of his majesty." Preliminary research indicates strongly that one of the conditioning factors in determining which epithet occurs in a given context is the poetic and rhetorical structure: epithets are integrated into the stylistic context, and their form is sensitive to local factors such as rhyme and meter.

In those documents in which a long list of individuals is named, including all the texts produced by the town councils, the order in which the names appear is significant. Sometimes the order follows directly from the political hierarchy of the *cabildo,* with *gobernador* first, followed by *regidores, alguaciles,* and so forth through the collection of *principales.* In such cases, the order is title-based rather than actor-based. At other times, order of reference to participants cannot be explained on the basis of the hierarchy to which the titles correspond, and we must look elsewhere for clues. In each of the two land documents from Yaxkukul, for example, a group of Maya nobles from the Pech patriline is named. They are said to have taken part in the boundary survey and, by implication, to ratify its results. Naming in this context is a way of expressing collective consent, something that Maya authors underscore repeatedly. Because both Maya and Spanish name forms are used in the Yaxkukul surveys, and because the two documents name distinct but overlapping groups of people, it is difficult to establish precisely who was involved in each version of the survey. Based on the research of Barrera Vásquez, Roys, Tozzer, Farriss, and others, it is nonetheless possible to infer (if not establish) the identity of the individuals and the relations they bore to each other.

At this level of detail a fascinating pattern emerges. Despite important differences between the two texts, they appear to follow precisely the same principle of naming, according to which the primary author ("I") is named first, followed by his descendants, followed then by his siblings, and finally by his predecessors. Schematically, the generational order of succession in reference is $0 > -1 > 0 > +1$, that is, first the primary author, then his descendants, then his siblings, then his father's generation (see Hanks 1992 for details). This intriguing pattern can only be discerned on the basis of identifying the individuals named and is not revealed in the titles or descriptions provided in the text itself. If corroborated in other documents, such a principle would provide a key to one of the discourse practices in which local Maya communities engaged. Given that these documents were, according to the reports of scribes, read aloud to the gathered public, the order of naming would have become a public and noteworthy factor among the Maya. Yet no Spanish commentators, to my knowledge, have made mention of such a practice. It is tempting to speculate that this, like many other discourse practices, was part of the Maya sector of the colonial field, but never entered into the awareness of the Spanish to whom the texts were nominally addressed. This is analogous to the poetic effects that one finds in the Maya versions of documents that are entirely absent from their Spanish translations. While the Spanish and Maya versions of a document are at some level "the same text" and say the same thing, their different forms are actually the trace of two distinct publics, and therefore two distinct receptions. The meaning structures corresponding to the two publics differ accordingly.[10]

This raises a further question regarding the overall production context of colonial documents, namely the public(s) by which they were received. While we can make various hypotheses regarding the public on the basis of what is actually stated in a document, this is only part of the story. The specified addressee of a letter of petition or the immediate receiver of a land survey document are only the most proximal in what is a differentiated series of publics. This is a point on which linguistic approaches to the microdetails of form lead outward to much broader questions regarding the scope and development of discourse formations over time. For those of us trained in the tradition of virtuoso readings of texts, it is important to recognize that the public cannot be defined on the basis of textual form. A letter addressed to the king by a group of nobles in a place like Mani or Yaxkukul would have traveled through channels from the local context to the regional capital (Mérida), perhaps to central authorities in Mexico, through the Council of Indies, before the royal court. That is, the official "public" is actually a trajectory through a hierarchical context. Unfortunately, little is known about such trajectories in the Maya sector, or the hierarchies through which they may have led, although the European sector has been described in depth.[11] In the case of land surveys, like the Yaxkukul or Sotuta documents, or land sales, the notion of a public is stretched through time. These documents become the basis for claims over property and land rights that may occur hundreds of years after the original text is produced. Obviously, the original text need not be formulated in such a way as to reflect subsequent publics to which it will be addressed, nor need these publics be in any sense continuous. In appropriating an ancient text for the purpose of legitimating a claim to land, identity or any other value in the present, one defines oneself as a public of a certain kind. Independent of textual form, this process is an ongoing one that ultimately includes academic appropriations like the ones in this paper (where I cite a text to prove a point). The challenge from the perspective of current research is to understand how the formal details of textual structure interact with the social and historical formation of publics. It is this interaction that fixes meaning, if only temporarily.

Two more productive dimensions of discourse analysis for which the genre is an appropriate unit revolve around intertextuality. "Intertextuality," as used here, is merely the relation between two or more texts, however this relation is established. Common authorship, provenience from a single town, petition-response, common theme, original-translation, possibly even commonality of scribe are all forms of intertextuality routinely encountered in the colonial discourse. Obviously not all relations that fit this loose definition of intertextuality are equally interesting or important. Sameness of ink color, scribal style, paper, or date are intertextual relations that are trivial under many circumstances, and gain significance only for certain purposes. Genre categories establish intertextual relations by defining the framework within which two or more texts can be identified as the same. This identification can of course be blunt and unrevealing, or it can be based on subtle clues whose cumulative effect is to really alter the way the document is understood. If I am right, the linguistic style of letters from the Maya nobles to the Crown in the 1560s index their common identity as a rhetorically charged genre whose meanings go far beyond the apparent "semantic content" of the texts as glossed in Spanish translations. Similarly, the two Yaxkukul land surveys bear many intricate relations to one another (Barrera Vásquez 1984; Hanks 1992).

Colonial Yucatec documents, like ones from elsewhere in the Americas, make use of both written text and images of various kinds. This raises another large area in which Americanist research reveals challenging diversity. Maps on which place names and various other information are written are obvious cases of word-image intertextuality, but this is just the beginning. The frontispieces in books, insignias on letters, the likeness of people in the *Books of Chilam Balam* (e.g., Edmonson 1986), synoptic diagrams of the indigenous calendar and other artifacts, the numerous forms and uses of the graphic cross, and perhaps even signatures (which are often halfway between writing and an arbitrary graphic sign) illustrate a formidable range of text-image relations. There have been important studies of the encounter between European and indigenous cultures using mixed media documents from central Mexico, such as the native codices (Burkhart 1989; Gruzinski 1992) and colonial period pictographic manuscripts, but less has been done on this topic in the Maya region. Recent work in "iconology" (Mitchell 1986), building upon the writings of Panofsky (1976) and Goodman (1976, 1978), could contribute significantly to this research by providing an analytic framework in which to systematically study the relations between image and text. Too often, work in the Mesoamerican region has been aimed at revealing the "meaning" or cultural symbolism of texts, while overlooking systematic aspects of form. Once again, I think the genre as a unit of analysis provides an appropriate framework within which to address this issue because word-image relations clearly do vary across genres. This variation can provide a key to motivating the attested forms. The need for systematic study of this topic is all the more pointed in that the pre-Columbian traditions combined glyphic text with iconography in ways that have been studied by art historians and those working with hieroglyphic materials.

CHANGE IN DISCOURSE

Colonial discourse is characterized by change: first-time combinations, transformations, syntheses of European with indigenous forms to produce a social world different from both of its sources. The most obvious instances result from introduction of new elements, including European words, phrases, ways of describing the world, genres, page layout, and so forth. If a linguistic element can be readily identified and is unambiguously absent from pre-contact forms, then its occurrence is an innovation. The word *Dios* for instance occurs frequently in sixteenth- and seventeenth-century Maya texts, but is obviously absent from all discourse prior to the arrival of the Spanish.[12] More interesting from a linguistic perspective are novel patterns of usage in which indigenous discourse forms are used according to European conventions. This is the case with the use of pronouns and demonstrative forms in colonial Maya texts. *Ten* 'I', *toon* 'we', *tech* 'you', *uaye* 'here'. The words are all Maya and a mechanical search of the texts would not identify them as innovations caused by the colonial experience. However, such expressions are conspicuously absent from pre-conquest hieroglyphic texts and extremely rare in other, evidently ancient discourse genres, even when written in Spanish script.[13] The motivation appears to be that the Spanish used writing in ways that the Maya did not, and their standards for authenticity and accountability required that texts of certain genres bear unequivocal marks of their producers. The linguistic details of pronouns and other shifters are the reflex of new communicative practices such as letter writing, signing and dating documents, and addressing an individual addressee.

A second class of innovations in colonial Maya discourse turns on shifts in the reference of pre-existing Maya expressions when used in address to a Spanish participant. For example, the range of reference of the term *ahau* 'ruler' was limited to the king in colonial texts, in contrast to its broader usage to designate regional rulers in texts directed to indigenous audiences (pre-Columbian and native-addressed sources). An inverse case is provided by the expanded use of the term *yum* 'lord, father' for reference to Spanish friars and authorities in the colonial documents. By contrast, in indigenous sources, it is restricted to kinsmen in ascending generations. The implication of such examples is that the hybrid colonial language served as a plane of mediation between the two major sectors of the discourse field. One and the same textual element follows two distinct patterns according to which sector of the colonial field it is directed. These cases are more difficult to determine than the first kind, since they can only be defined at the level of the entire field. Correspondingly, the expertise required of a colonial actor capable of recognizing and manipulating such ambivalent patterns would be relatively high.

Some of the most subtle but pervasive changes that occurred during the colonial period consist in the extra foregrounding and consequent semantic shifts in native elements that already existed prior to Spanish contact but took on novel associations following it. One of the clearest examples of this is the symbol of the cross, which is reported to have been in use among the Maya before Spanish contact, but acquired a new salience and range of associations once linked to the omnipotent Christian deity. Another is the concern with authenticating personal identity on the basis of descent and history of residence. A similar concern surely inscribed in the hieroglyphic accounts of lineage and rule, yet the Spanish emphasis on recognizing the native nobility appears to have given rise to a significant discourse displaying and authenticating the true autochthony of native authors. Such changes are difficult to analyze, since they must be inferred from usage. Still, they are of basic importance insofar as they go to the heart of the expressive habits and routine assumptions of those who produced the texts. Analogous examples can be seen at the level of realignment in the political relations among the different regions of the Yucatán. The well-known contradiction between the 1562 letters to the Crown signed by Maya nobles of Ceh Pech, Ah Kin Chel, and Chikinchel provinces, and the denunciation of these by Xiu and Pacab nobles of Mani (Zimmermann 1970) is a case in point. All the evidence suggests that Yucatán, after the fall of Mayapán in the thirteenth century, was divided, and relations among the provinces were often strained. Yet the intrusion of the Spanish and their differential dealings with the provinces shifted and highlighted differences in a way that inevitably produced new relations among the Maya themselves.

Some cases of innovation appear to be improvisations. That is, they involve novel forms attested only in a single context, in which the form contributes directly to the overall aim of the discourse. The persuasive rhetoric of the 1562 letters reproduced in Zimmermann (1970) appears to be a case of this. There are verse forms in these letters unlike any others I have encountered, and they are most striking precisely at points of heightened rhetoric in the letter. One objective of future research will be to compare widespread with apparently idiosyncratic features, in order to locate clear cases of improvisation. For any discourse feature, how broadly distributed is it across exemplars of its genre, across related genre types, and through time? Widely distributed features are likely candidates for the status of system conventions, whereas specialized ones may define single generic types of innovations.

There is sufficient documentation of colonial Maya discourse, and it is distributed across the provinces in such a way that it may be possible eventually to define regional styles reflecting improvisation and asymmetries in the discursive field. On the basis of unsystematic comparison, it is quite possible that the Ceh Pech zone to the north, the Mani-Sierra zone to the south, and the Campeche zone to the far south represent stylistic regions. This hunch is based on readily apparent differences in style and phrasing across documents from the three areas. In a narrowly textual sense, a grasp of regional variation would almost certainly clarify some of the many opaque portions of the literary discourse in the *Books of Chilam Balam* and elsewhere. If we assume that shared style is reflective of common position in a discursive field, then such facts would also lead to hypotheses regarding the social relations among different regions in the Maya sector of the colony, which would in turn lead beyond the Spanish-dominated historiography to date.

Intertextuality of the Cross

In order to illustrate some of the factors sketched in the preceding section, I will briefly describe the range of uses and appropriations that the Christian cross entered into in some of the colonial genres under discussion. At this point, I am not concerned with the questions of whether the Maya really had a "cross" before the European arrival, or whether they understood the European cross in terms of an indigenous prototype. Rather my aim is to trace the incidence of this central symbol across a series of discourse genres in order to show the scope of appropriation and innovation involved. It becomes immediately evident that the cross is in fact a complex family of symbolic practices, including the material form, the graphic signs, the inscription on the body through making the sign of the cross, crucifixion and the wearing of talismans, the verbal formula, the spatial marker inscribed on the landscape at points of threshold, and the textual boundary marker inscribed on verbal discourse at points of beginning or ending. The meanings of the symbol change according to which context it occurs in, and which genres frame its use. In fact, one wonders in the end whether all the things designated as *cruz* in the European discourse belong to the same family at all. A second point is that the intertextual trajectories of a form like the cross are partly guided by the social field and partly by the arbitrary properties of representational systems (language, iconography, architecture). Thus, one reason that the cruciform shows up in nonreligious contexts such as letters and chronicles is that the agents who produced these were among the same people who were trained by the Franciscans.

There is much in the secular Maya discourse that resembles the language of doctrine and prayer, because the speaker/authors were drilled in doctrine and they were the same monastics who trained the translators and wrote the bilingual dictionaries. Other cases appear to follow a more arbitrary, almost Saussurian logic. Some Maya priests are reported to have experimented with crucifixion as a mode of sacrifice to bring rain for the fields (see below). When so, the crosses on which victims were presented were themselves thrown into the cenotes in the manner of Maya offerings. Thus, once incorporated into the practices of the Maya, the symbol was transformed and treated according to a logic distinct from that of the Spanish.[14]

Acquaintance by Violence

The cross was one of the first arrivals in the new world, and it embodied the violent confrontation between Christianity and the indigenous religions. This initial confrontation was clearest in Cortes's dramatic practice of smashing idols and replacing them with the cross (Diaz 1963:62, 83). As Diaz reports, Cortes followed the practice of placing a cross and an image of Our Lady in the places from which he removed idols. The banner that accompanied the wooden cross showed a red cross with blue and white flames emanating from it, and the logo, in Latin, "Brothers, let us follow the cross, and if we have faith we will conquer" (Tozzer 1941: 14–15). While it is highly unlikely that anyone understood this logo in most places where it was installed, the cross is widely associated with the arrival of Christians, even in evidently Maya sources.

Tozzer (42, n. 211) cites the report from the *Relación de Mérida* according to which a Maya prophet, a Chilam Balam from the town of Mani, is said to have prophesied the arrival of white bearded people from the East well before they first arrived. Sánchez de Aguilar (1900 [1613]:95) recounts what seems to be the same story. The passage they refer to appears to be the following one, taken from the *Chilam Balam of Chumayel* (Edmonson 1986:73; lines 501–7).[15]

ualac uil ytza	Let the Itza stand up
ualac uil tan cah e	let stand up in town,
Yum e	Father,
u chicul hunab ku canal	The sign of Hunab Ku in heaven
hulom uaom che	the erect wood (cross) must arrive
Etçahan ti bal cah e	It is placed in the world
uchebal u sashal yokol cab e	so that it illuminate the earth
Yume e	Father.

Attributed to the prophet Chilam Balam, this passage is difficult to understand precisely because it could be read in various ways. On the reading reflected in the gloss, the Itza are warned that they must erect a sign of Hunab Ku in their midst. The standing wood cross of the Christians is sure to arrive: *hul-om* is a kind of assurative future tense, according to Coronel (1620: folio 28), that means the event described in the clause *ha de suceder sin falta.* The expression *uaom che* can be parsed literally as *ua(l)-h-om,* 'will stand erect' + *che* 'wood'. It is a standard expression used by the Franciscans to designate the cross in Maya—although it is interesting that it is never used in the doctrinal materials, where the Spanish terms *Cruz* or *Xcilich Cruz* ('blessed cross') are retained. It is unclear whether the same expression was used by Maya speakers in reference to a staff or other vertical pole distinct from the cross. The reference to standing erect may be due to the inherent vertical orientation of the Christian cross, which has a head, two arms, and a front just as does the human body, or it may be motivated by the practice of elevating the cross above the sight line of humans. Both in churches and when carried on an elevated pole in procession, the cross itself is usually higher than the human sight line, requiring that one gaze up at it, and never down.

The *Books of Chilam Balam* contain several more passages that report the arrival of the Spanish, including the following from the Tizimin book.[16]

Ti likin utal	They came from the East
Ca uliob uaye	when they arrived here
Ah mexob	The bearded ones
Ah pulob	The [?] ones
Ti chicul ku sac	At the sign of the white god
Uahom che canal	the cross on high
	(Edmonson 1986: lines 1177–83)

In this passage the arrival of the Spanish is correlated with the arrival of the erect cross of the white god. This description recalls Cortes's presentations of the cross and banner bearing the cruciform. The same association with the cross is also at play in the *Chilam Balam of Chumayel* (Edmonson 1986:108).

Y oklal lay katun yan	For this katun period was the one
ca uli tz'ulob	when the foreigners arrived
Ti u talelob ti likin	It was from the East they came,
ca uliob e	when they arrived
✠ *Ti ix hop'i cristianoil xan i*	That was when Christianity began also.

What is most interesting in this example for our purposes is that the line in which the word *cristianoil* occurs is flanked in the left column by a graphic cross, in the Maltese style. This is the same style of cross as appears in the *Doctrinas* of Coronel (1620) and Beltrán de Santa Rosa (1746). It is also the same shape cross as the one that adorns the crowns of all the Maya chiefs shown in graphics in the *Chilam Balam of Chumayel* (Edmonson 1986) (Fig. 10.1).

In summary then, the association between the arrival of the Spanish, their physical presence in Yucatán and their claim on the place, and the cruciform was reinforced by the Spanish themselves, and appears to have been established in the consciousness of Maya authors also.

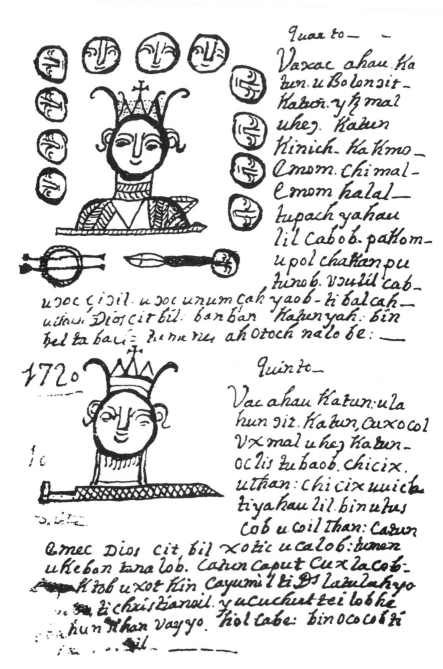

Fig. 10.1. From the *Katun Count, Book of Chilam Balam of Chumayel* (n.d.).

Catholic Space, Christian Doctrine

Of course the supplanting of Mayan idols by Spanish cruciforms is only an initial context for the cross, and it does not exhaust the meanings of the form. The core locus in which these meanings were elaborated were the conversion efforts and religious practices of the Franciscans. While I have just begun to investigate this topic, it is obvious that altars within church structures had crosses atop them. This locates the form within the imposing architectural spaces of the churches and cathedrals, some of which were built using the stone material taken from smashed temples and other Maya structures. Mass, the central sacrament performed in this space, was performed facing the cross. The bodily gestures of genuflecting, as a sign of reverence, and the sign of the cross, as a blessing, both inscribe the cross onto the human body. This is in turn reinforced in the small crosses carried or worn on the body, and attached to the rosary beads used in prayer. The vestments, chalices, and other liturgical objects would probably have been adorned with crosses as well. While it will require much research to fill out these sketchy observations, it is fair to say that the cross was both encompassed within built space, becoming the sacred object within the sanctuary, and placed or performed directly on the human body. In addition to the investing of the cross with the passion of Christ and the mystery of resurrection, Catholic practices invested it with spatial values that had to do with its positioning and the postures taken in front of it.

The missionization of the indigenous people of Mexico included the production of a vast corpus of doctrinal materials in native languages, including prayer texts, sermons, pedagogical tracts designed to explain points of practice and belief, and the doctrinal dialogues that Indians were forced to memorize and perform for the *padres* to prove their advancement on the road to Catholicism. This literature, and the pedagogical activities in that it was used, further amplified the values of the cross.

Writing in the mid-seventeenth century, the Franciscan historian Cogolludo lamented the lack of reverence among Maya people for Christian religion. Of Cacalchen, where he resided, he said that people only went to doctrine classes because they were counted and punished for absence. Not one person was accustomed to taking communion (Cogolludo 1971: 252). In order to counteract this tendency to spiritual absenteeism, there were well-defined mechanisms. *Pueblos* were divided into *barrios,* each with a saint's name, and each under the responsibility of an Indian *principal. Principales,* who where summoned by the *batab* for any significant event, and who figure prominently as witnesses in most written documents from the *pueblos,* were responsible to make certain that everyone in their respective *barrios* attended church. Attendance was taken after Mass, either by the *doctrinero* cross-checking all those present against a list of the *vecindad,* or, in larger places, by the *principal* himself (Cogolludo 1971: 291). After the service, all those at Mass exited into the courtyard, where they were separated according to their barrio of residence. According to Cogolludo the *principal* was required to account for any missing persons, and if not was given a public flogging by the *gobernador.*

The inculcation of *doctrina* went beyond the Mass to include forced instruction. On feast days the catechism and dialogues were performed in a dialogic song, with the *doctrinero* asking questions of faith and practice, and the Indians answering according to doctrine. Men and women were separated during these sessions, at which attendance was very high, and virtually universal among the Indian officials (Cogolludo 1971: 293). Adults were examined on the *doctrina* at the time of marriage, and at the annual obligatory confession. In the case of children, the regime was even more rigorous, as boys under fourteen and girls under twelve were gathered daily and brought in procession to the church, where they practiced *doctrina* (Cogolludo 1971:294).

These introductory remarks indicate three facts regarding doctrinal literature in early colonial Yucatán. The first is that the *doctrina* was inculcated in the Maya population from an early age and with systematic enforcement. Although we cannot know how many people actually learned the teaching, or how they might have used it in their everyday practices, it is clear that efforts were undertaken to maximize the scope and depth of exposure.[17] The second fact is that there were institutionalized links between the *cabildo* government in Indian republics and the enforcement of Catholicism. Through their obligatory attendance at services and responsibility for the attendance of their constituents, the *gobernadores, regidores, alguaciles,* and *principales* played a dual role mediating between ecclesiastic and municipal fields. The third fact is that doctrine was associated with the regimentation of space: it was practiced by adults on church grounds, with people divided according to gender and residence. Children were inculcated in the rite of procession from their homes to the centralizing church, where they practiced their doctrine. Each of these three points reinforces the centrality of doctrinal practices as a source of discourse production. As we will see, its tie to local government gave to doctrinal language a channel through which it proliferated into a range of secular genres, while its tie to space prepared the ground for the reconfiguration of space in the image of religion.

Coronel's *Doctrina Cristiana* (1620) is the earliest extant doctrine in Maya, although it is based on earlier, now lost versions. The frontispiece has the Maltese-style cross atop a shield of flames with an egg-shaped central area from which rays and flames (?) radiate. Initials IPIS. The first entry in the *Doctrina,* as in Beltrán's after him, is the sign of the cross.

EL PERSIGNARSE

Tumen uchicil, cilich cruz,
tocon ti cahualob,
yumile, caDiose,
tuKaba Dios citbi
yetel Dios mehenbil,
yetel Dios Spiritusancto
Amen Jesus.

This sign establishes a key link between the graphic and material shape of the cross and the naming of the three aspects of God, the Father, the Son, and the Holy Ghost. Inscribed on the body, this triad is associated with the forehead, the heart, and the shoulders in the gesture accompanying its utterance.

Beltrán de Santa Rosa's *Doctrina* was written over 100 years later, but addresses itself directly to Coronel.[18] Beltrán was a native of Yucatán, and his knowledge of Maya language was evidently far deeper than that of his predecessor. Like Coronel, Beltrán begins his *Doctrina* with a frontispiece showing the cross, this time in the equilateral simplified Latin style, from which rays emanate. The verbal sign of the cross is the first entry in the doctrine proper and retains most of Coronel's wording (fig. 10.2).[19]

PERSIGNARSE.

TUMEN u chicul cilich cruz	By the sign of the blessed cross
tocen ti kanalob	protect me from evil
yumbil hahal Dios,	Father true God
tukabá Dios yumbil	in the name of God the Father
yetel Dios mehenbil	and God the Son
yetel Dios Espiritu Santo.	and God Holy Spirit
Amen	Amen

It is interesting that neither Coronel nor Beltrán describes the hand gestures that are synchronized with speech in making the sign of the cross. The use of the right hand, touching forehead (on 'Father'), center of chest (on 'Son'), left shoulder then right shoulder (on 'Holy Spirit') must evidently have been supplied by the priests as they taught the doctrine.

The power of the cross is explained in the *Doctrina* in terms of its tie to the passion of Christ and the mystery of his incarnation in human space. Coronel imparts this in one of nine articles of faith, which he subtitles *HE UNAH VCILICH VINICIL LAE,* roughly "This is what is necessary for a beautiful life." The third entry in the list is,

Vyoxppel yocçabal tiol	The third faith:
numci tiya vchebal vlohicon	[He] suffered in order to save us,
çijnijx tiCruz	and he was crucified on the Cross,
cimi	died
caix muci	and was buried

Both Coronel and Beltrán treat the cross in the dialogic sections of their respective *Doctrinas*. It is here that the cross as sign, the passion of Christ, and the power to protect are all woven together into the proper conduct of a Christian. In Coronel's dialogic exposition, he introduces the cross in the following exchanges.

Kat. Cenx ú chicul Christiano?
  Ask. 'What is the sign of a Christian?'

Kam. Lay cilich Cruz la ✠
  Receive 'This sacred Cross here: ✠

Kat. Balx ú chun?
  Ask 'Why?'

DECLARACION

DE LA

Doctrina Cristiana

—EN EL—

IDIOMA YUCATECO

POR EL

R. P. FRAY PEDRO

BELTRAN DE SANTA ROSA.

MERIDA.-YUCATAN.
IMPRENTA DE LA LOTERIA DEL ESTADO.

CALLE 61, NUMERO 492.
1912.

Fig. 10.2. Title page from *Beltran de Santa Rosa's Doctrina Cristina*.

> *Kam. Yoklal ú uayazba Cristo*
> *çinan ti Cruz ú lohion.*
> 'Because Christ transfigured himself,
>   was crucified on the Cross to save us.'

It is interesting in this passage that Coronel integrates the Maltese-style cross into the grammatical structure of the question-answer pair, equating this specifically graphic version of the cross with the wooden cruciform on which the crucifixion took place. The two of course differ in shape, with the material cross conforming to the proportion of the human body, with arms high up on the vertical, whereas the maltese version has the horizontal axis bisecting the vertical in the middle. Looking at this passage in context with the earlier ones, there is a three-way relation established among the crosses: the *Cruz* (wooden) is the instrument of Christ's passion; the *cilich Cruz* (Maltese) is the sign of a Christian; and the *cilich Cruz* (verbal) is the sign of the *Cruz* (wooden). In terms of the system of Christianity, the original, material cross is the core of this series, with the two other versions standing as signs of it. Notice that only the wooden cross is properly described as *uahom che* 'erect wood'. It is not presented as a sign of anything other than itself, nor is it qualified by the adjective *cilich* 'beautiful, sacred'. It is the real thing, of which the others are signs. Assuming that the Maya expression was semantically transparent, and not an idiom, it would make no sense to describe any of the other crosses as an 'erect wood'. This may explain why we find only the Spanish term *Cruz* in the *Doctrina:* the priests needed to tie together what was in fact a whole range of semantic values clustered around the cross, and to do this, it was more efficient to retain a single term. It is also possible that the Maya expression was associated with a tree or other indigenous symbol from which the Franciscans wanted to insulate the cross, at least in these contexts.

Part of the value of the cross was said to be its actual ability to protect persons from evil. This power accrued to the entire family of cross forms, and not only to one or another version. Beltrán (1900:35) asserts the power in his dialogic section.

> *Kat. Heix Cruze yan ua yuchucil uchebal ú tocicoon*
> *ti cah[ua]lobe?*
> Ask. And the Cross, does it have the power to protect us
>   from our enemies?

> *Nuc. La ika, yoklal u Coyahob*
> *ca Yumil ti Jesu-Cristo ti ú cimilie.*
> Answer. Yes, because they vanquished
>   our Lord in Jesus-Christ to his death there.

In other words, the fact of Christ's having died on the cross is presented as the source of its power. In discourse like this one, it is critical that the referent of the word *cruz* be understood to designate the form in general, and not the unique wooden object on which Christ is said to have died. As a symbol, the cruciform is replicable infinitely with no loss in authenticity. Part of the replication process is the transposing of the form across different symbolic media, construction, graphic illustration, speech or writing, inscription on the body. How did the Maya addressees pick up on this range of forms and meanings?

Integrations of the cross in Maya ritual practices

The presence in indigenous Maya culture of a symbol formally similar to the Christian cross is a well-known theme in Mayanist research. Cortes's party encountered crosslike symbols at Cozumel and Campeche, and there has been speculation that the Maya reception of the Europeans was strongly influenced by their reaction to the cross they brought. As Roys put it, the European cross "so startlingly resembled one of the most sacred Maya symbols" that it must have impressed the Indians (1943:15, 77). Fascination with pre-existing commonalities is attested in the Spanish discourse of the period; Landa, Cogolludo, Lizana, and Sánchez de Aguilar all addressed the question of whether Christianity had somehow preceded the Church to the New World, and commented on such things as an autochthonous form of baptism. The evidence regarding Maya reactions is less clear, since there is no indigenous discourse in which the European culture is likened to that of the Maya. In fact, most of what is known regarding the Maya reception of the European cross is found in reports addressed to Europeans, such as the testimony brought out in the infamous idolatry trials of the latter half of the sixteenth century.

It is difficult to make sense of these reports both because they vary in content, and because they are of questionable status. Based almost entirely on testimony extracted from natives under the inquisitional rigors of the Franciscans, or on reports by the Franciscans themselves, texts describing Maya practices are undoubtedly inaccurate in ways we cannot measure. Mayanist scholars, like the Spanish before them, have long debated the "idolatry question," and there is a significant corpus of literature bearing on this aspect of our problem.[20] It is not my purpose here to reengage these debates, but to illustrate a range of forms under which the cross entered the imaginary of the colony, both European and indigenous sectors. We cannot know whether people like Lorenzo Cocom colluded in crucifixion for their own ends, as he was said to have done in testimony extracted by Franciscans, just as we cannot really know who "Lorenzo Cocom" was (a problem noted by Tozzer 1941:44, n. 216). These gaps in truth and reference preclude any attempt to read the reports as straightforward factual descriptions. But this is only one way of reading documents, and there are other dimensions of truth and factuality that can be gotten at through intertextual analysis. Regardless of whether the things reported really happened, or how often they occurred, it is evident that the cross served as a powerful instrument for producing multiple meanings.

The Maya cruciform appears to have been associated with water and perhaps a stylized version of the *yaxche* tree (Roys 1943:75; cf. Burkhart 1989:70 for Nahuatl analogue). The latter was the *axis mundi* of Maya cosmology, standing in the middle of the world and rising to heaven. In the cosmology, four other trees are arrayed, one per cardinal corner, the five being called *imix che* 'trees of abundance'. If the potential association between the cross and the trees of abundance is correct, then it may have reinforced the use of the cross to mark certain landmarks on maps (a topic addressed in the next section). That is, the cross becomes a device for organizing space in its cardinal aspect.

The next passage, from the same manuscript, refers to the arrival of the cross in the Maya towns, a sign of the "unified god" of the Christians, whose gift to the Indians would be enlightenment. Although this passage attributes the prophecy of the arrival of the cross to the native prophet Chilam Balam, the language belongs in part to the Franciscans. The underscored portions refer to the sign of the 'erect wood' cross using the Maya expression adopted by monastics, and appealing to the monastic metaphor of enlightenment through conversion.[21]

U profesia Chilam Balam	The prophecy of Chilam Balam
Tix kayom Cabal Chen Mani	it will be sung in the well of Mani
Oxlahun Ahau uhetz' iuil katun	Thirteen Ahau [was] the seating of the katun
Ualac uil Ytza	Let the Itza stand up
Ualac uil tan cah e	Let it be erected in the middle of town,
Yum	Father,
uchicul hunab ku canal	the sign of the unified God on high
ulom uaom che	The cross [lit. erect wood] shall arrive
Etsahom ti cah e	they shall place it in town,
Uchebal u sashal yokol cabe	in order that the world be enlightened
Yum	Father (Edmonson 1982: lines 3951–65)

The tie between cruciforms and Maya ritual practice is attested in the scant (and doubtless skewed) descriptions of Maya "idolatry" that emerged from the testimony taken by the Franciscans during the idolatry trials. One Augustin Che reported for instance that Juan and Lorenzo Cocom had been present at the crucifixion of a boy and girl, which was carried out in front of a clay cross (Sánchez de Aguilar 1900 [1613]: 76; cf. Tozzer 1941:44). In another incident reported from the town of Homun, Maya people are said to have made food and drink offerings to the cross inside the Catholic church, in memory of their idols. The purpose of the rite was evidently to request rain for the *milpa* (Tozzer 1941:162).

In a number of cases, like the Cocom one just cited, the Maya appropriation of the cross was more radical than merely defining the space in which an offering was made. There were reports of actual crucifixions, which predictably scandalized the Franciscans. Evidently, these usually involved the sacrificing of children, whose hands were nailed or lashed to the cross with vines, and whose hearts were extracted either while the cross was still standing, or after it was taken down. In some cases the name "Jesus Christ" was written on the body of the victim. This inscription upon the body is further echoed in testimony given by Juan Couoh of Yaxcaba, who reported a human sacrifice in which a man was sacrificed inside the church, his heart taken out, two cruciforms incised on the freshly extracted heart, which was then placed within the mouth of a large idol, identified with the Maya god Itzamna (Tozzer 1941:118 n. 541). There appears to be an association in some of these cases with water (rain), as the victims were thrown, still attached to the cross, into a cenote. According to Tozzer (1941:116), Francisco Hernández, one of the first missionaries to Yucatán, reported that the Maya venerated the cross as a "god" of water or rain.

In other cases the tie to rain is missing and the central logic of sacrifice is one of substitution. In testimony taken from Antonio Pech, Juan and Lorenzo Cocom, probably the same individuals cited above, are said to have participated in the crucifixion of two young girls. The pair of Maya nobles were themselves dying and the purpose of the offering was to exchange their lives for those of the sacrificial victims. The *Ah Kin* is reported to have said "Let these girls die crucified as did Jesus Christ, he who they say was our Lord, but we do not know if this is so" (Tozzer 1941:116). In this quote, the parallel between Jesus Christ and the young girls suggests that the concept of self-sacrifice by a savior was transposed into the Maya practice along with the cruciform death. This appears to differ subtly from the offerings of blood for rain that are well known among the Maya, although the precise nuances are difficult to pin down.

A third variation on the sacrificial cross is provided by reports of animal offerings in which pigs were crucified, as in testimony from Sahcaba in 1562 (Tozzer 1941: 163 n. 853). It is difficult to tell how this practice related to animal sacrifice in front of the cross, as mentioned in the testimony of Francisco Tuz. Tuz reported that at the cenote of Chichen there was a "church of demons" in which a cross was erected and dogs and other animals were sacrificed (Tozzer 1941:183 n. 955). In both of these reports, crosses were said to have been burned as part of the offering. This raises the interesting possibility that the cross served both as central embodiment of the divinity to which offerings were made, and as itself an offertory object. The fire that consumed the cross, or crosses, was itself extinguished with the blood of the animal sacrificed.

In all of the variants sketched above, the role of mediating between the human body, the space of action, and the divine seems to be basic to the meaning of the cross. The verticality inherent in the Maya gloss of the word "cross" plays upon the orientation of the body and the position one adopts when facing the altar in prayer. Although the phrasing was set by the Franciscans, it was adopted, at least in some contexts, by the Maya. Crucifixion and the incision of a cruciform on the heart represent embodiment in its most dramatic sense. Of course, the crucifixion of Jesus Christ, the mystery of the incarnation, and the partaking of the body of God in the eucharist all turn on corporality as the pivot between the divine and the human. But the Maya cases hint at a broader understanding of the spatial consequence of the cross beyond the flesh. The placement of crosses on roads, the centrality of churches in the towns, the latent association between crosses and rain, and the directionality of the Maya "trees of abundance" can all be understood to anchor the meaning of the cross in a broader lived space.

Cross as a spatial operator

Commenting on the ubiquity and veneration of the cross in the Maya sector of colonial Yucatán, Farriss (1984: 315) notes that crosses were "placed at the four pathways entering each town, atop boundary markers, [and] on the doorways of houses." This distribution, which is consistent with the Maya land surveys that I have seen, suggests that the core spatial value of the cross was to mark thresholds. In the two Yaxkukul land surveys, crosses are reported at a total of ten points along the boundary of the town by that name. The two surveys, dated only days apart and signed by different but overlapping groups of nobles, differ in basic respects (explored in Hanks 1992). The earlier one cites five crosses, of which one is unmentioned in the later version, and the later version cites nine crosses, of which five are unmentioned in the early version of the survey. Although the two distributions of crosses are not identical, they are consistent in terms of the distribution of crosses in relation to roads and other landmarks along the boundary. The surveys mention several roads into the town of Yaxkukul, and both cite crosses at the points at which the roads intersect the perimeter.[22] In addition, they both cite at least one cross at a corner point where there is no road (*noh tiitz luum* 'great corner [of the] land' in the Maya), making these 'corners' the second most likely locus for a cross. There are no crosses mentioned in either version of the survey at a point that is neither a threshold on the road nor a *noh tiitz luum.* This is a powerful regularity binding together what are otherwise divergent versions of the survey. Other known surveys, such as those from the towns of Sotuta and Mani appear to follow these or similar principles, although I have yet to examine them sufficiently closely to tell.

Within towns there were many crosses as well, and these suggest a function slightly different from threshold marking. Inside churches, the cross is closer to the center, as Farriss suggests, than it is to the threshold. Here the verticality of the raised crucifix becomes significant: one gazes up at the cross and genuflects in front of it, whereas there is no evidence, to my knowledge, that boundary crosses are experienced as "above" or "in front of" the threshold they index. Recall from the reports of idolatry that sacrifices were often made at the foot of an altar, and that in some cases of crucifixion, the entire cross with the offertory victim was thrown down into the cenote. The latter form of delivering the offering is surely a Maya factor and not a Spanish one, but in other respects the Maya appear to have taken over a similar posture toward the ritual space of the cross as did the Spanish.

There is further evidence that churches were conceived as defining the middle of town space, and this suggests that the cross may have stood for interiority in municipal space, as well as boundary-establishment. This is suggested by the placement of convents in the main plaza area of towns, and also the description of the church in the land surveys. The church in Yaxkukul is mentioned as a starting or ending point in both surveys, as that point around which the perimeter runs. In the well-known, contemporaneous map of Mani, the convent is shown in the center of a clearly bounded circular region (reproduced in Morley 1983). The border of Mani is depicted as a double line inside of which are small square shapes, each with a cross atop it. This is once again consistent with the hypothesis that crosses defined boundary points as well as interiors of municipal space.[23]

We cannot know exactly how the boundaries between colonial Yucatecan towns were marked on the ground—beyond written and graphic portrayals in documents. Extant material remains are insufficient to determine where markers were on the sixteenth-century landscape, or what they looked like. Still, it is critical to distinguish the two planes analytically: how space was portrayed in documentary genres, versus how it was constituted in other cultural forms.[24] Once we make this distinction, it becomes possible to examine the documents as defining a space in themselves. Thus, the paper on which the first and more complete Yaxkukul survey was written was itself marked by an oval-shaped seal with a Maltese-style cross atop it. The mention of the word *Cruz* in the surveys is itself significant. Of all the objects that populated the boundaries between towns, including significant natural features, why were crosses singled out as belonging to the larger class of boundary markers, while other things were not? The reason is likely to lie in Spanish practices of placing crosses on the landscape, although I leave this question for future research. It is noteworthy that none of the boundary crosses is ever designated as a *uahom che* 'erect wood [cross]', the term sometimes used for the ritual cross. Even though they probably stood erect, crosses marking boundaries were probably accorded a slightly different status than those that occurred in sacred spaces. It is unlikely for instance that boundary crosses were experienced as having a head and arms, as were the ritual crosses, and even less likely that they had anything akin to the sequential structure of the sign of the cross as made on one's body (forehead > chest > left shoulder > right shoulder, done with the right hand). In each context, the meaning of the cross, and the conceptual organization it implies, is slightly different. A further factor may have been the rhetorical aim of the surveyors to convince the Spanish that the landscape around Yaxkukul had been appropriately "converted," as marked by the laying out of crosses. For this purpose, using the Spanish term itself is clearly more forceful.

All of these spatial uses recall the placement of the cross inside churches, atop the altar, and upon the body. The effectiveness of the symbol in marking a spatial division is distinct from the more focally ritual uses, and yet it derives from them. In a sense, the incarnation, crucifixion, redemption, replication of crosses, and all the ritual practices in which they are maintained have to do with the production of spatial divisions; between heaven and earth, spirit and flesh, divine referent and human symbols. A final instance of the cross as a landmark in social space is in the place names given Indian towns by the Spanish, and often used in official documents. The full name of Yaxkukul, as cited in both surveys, is "Santa Cruz de Mayo Yaxkukul."[25] Most if not all towns had such long names, which were used in some contexts, but not others. To my knowledge there has been no systematic study of when they occur, as opposed to the simplified names.

Cross as a discourse operator

With the use of crosses in written documents, both as drawn and as designated verbally, we move a step away from the material forms in the landscape and the embodiment of the crucifixion. Another class of instances are the crosses that punctuate official and semiofficial documents of various genres. These have the discourse function of indicating the opening or closing of segments in discourse, much as the sign of the cross is performed at the end of the Catholic Mass. Thus, for instance, in the first Yaxkukul survey, the local priest is said to be blessing the participants after the survey report has been completed. It says,

tan u dzaic u bendisio ca yum/	"our father is giving his blessing
Padre franco hernandes Clerigo	Father Francisco Hernández, Cleric
yokol tulacal uinicob/	upon all people
Uay ti cah lae	here in this town
tu kaba Dios yumbil	In the name of God the Father
Dios mehenbil	God the Son
Dios esptu S.to	God the Holy Spirit"
	(Barrera Vásquez 1984:41–42)

The implication of this passage is that the document reports an actual enactment in which people gathered and a final blessing was performed in order to bring the event to a close. This fits very well with the rest of the linguistic style of the survey, which is marked by first-person, present-tense description.[26] This reinforces the inference that the sign of the cross was a closure device performed in the boundary inspection.

In the collection of documents entitled *Documentos de Cacalchen en lengua Maya,* a set of texts from the town of Cacalchen and its neighbors, there are numerous wills.[27] An initial perusal of these indicates that many of them have in common an opening formula in which the verbal sign of the cross is used in a way we would expect: it is a boundary key indicating that the testament immediately following it is sworn truth. It says,

Tukaba dios uchuc tumen tuçinil	In the name of god the maker of all things
citbil	eternal
mehenbi	[and of the] son
.y. espiritu santo	and [of the] holy spirit
oxtul personas tuhunali hahal dios	Three persons in one true god
Tukabaix bolon pixan cacilich colebil	And in the name of nine spirits our holy lady
ti çuhuy Santa Ma	in blessed virgin Mary
yohel tob tulacal uinicob	Let all men know
bin ylic yunil intestamento	they shall see the paper of my testament
intakyah than	my final testament
cen ah cimil ti franco kuk	I, dying person, Francisco Kuk

Dated July 28, 1647, this testament starts with an almost verbatim quote of the sign of the cross presented by Coronel (1620) and discussd by Beltrán de Santa Rosa (1912).[28]

There are other instances of the graphic and verbal signs of the cross in Maya language documentation of the period, although I have not yet sufficiently examined them to comment on the variants. There appear to be two main functions served by such uses of the cross: (i) to mark some kind of a division in section, or theme, or at the very opening or closing of the text, so that what follows the cross is differently keyed; and (ii) to invoke the power associated with the cross as a talisman and as that in whose name actions can be undertaken as sanctioned by God. The first function is a direct transposition of the cross as index of a threshold; the second recalls the didactic explanations of the power of the cross in the dialogues included in Christian doctrine. In future research it will be fruitful to explore the ways in which occurrences of the signs of the cross in apparently nonreligious discourse actually indicate intertextual series in which the religious texts are merely one endpoint, and thematically distant or unrelated genres are the other. This open-endedness is one basic feature of the intertextuality of the cross.

Another is the variability in which the cruciform is put in play. In the Sotuta land documents, graphic signs of the cross are integrated into the verbal text to stand for boundary markers, along the lines of the boundary crosses at Yaxkukul, but with a different discourse representation (Roys 1939:425; cf. Hanks 1987:675). In other cases, like the Cacalchen wills, it is the verbal formula that is taken up and perhaps altered to fit a new discourse context. In still others, the verbal sign of the cross, with its formulaic "in the name of" appears to have been integrated into the participant structure of those who produced documents. Rather than naming the Father, Son, and Holy Spirit, the three parties in whose name an act is undertaken are the king, the *encomendero,* and the governor, all cited in the three-part structure "in the name of x, and y, and z" (see Hanks 1987:682ff.). What we see here is the progressive shifting of the sign of the cross away from the focally religious discourse of prayer, into more secular discourse uses, in which the schema of acting "in the name of" an authority serves to invoke the power of the authority itself.

Cross as background feature of colonial linguistics

The final set of genres I will illustrate are the linguistic materials prepared by friars, including dictionaries and grammars. In these contexts the cross also plays a role, but it is strictly in the background. That is, the focal objective of the discourse is to translate or explain a point of language structure, and the cross, under one of its various guises, serves as an accidental feature of the example. For instance, example sentences offered to illustrate a certain grammatical construction may happen to describe the cross, or the cross will be mentioned in explaining some other concept. An illustration of this is found in Beltrán's *Arte* (1746: section 261), when he explains how the progressive aspect is formed in the Maya verb. The section is entitled, *Tiempos de siendo y habiendo,* and among the examples he presents is the following:

numcina ti yaa ca ah Lohil, ena ma ahkebani
"no siendo pecador, nuestro Redentor padeció"

Here the reference to the Redeemer and the passion indirectly refers to the cross on which the crucifixion occurred, without mentioning it. The important point is that Beltrán is explaining the grammatical structure (Verb1-*na, ena* Verb2), and the doctrinal content of the example is secondary to this expository goal. To be sure, the grammatical descriptions are peppered with such examples, which reflects the overall purpose of the text to help in teaching the language to those who would preach and educate in it. Still, the doctrinal discourse has the status of background, available discourse which can be called on to illustrate points of grammar. Such uses are peripheral to the semantics of doctrinal language, because it is "mentioned" rather than actually expressed. Just as mention in language is a metalinguistic mode in which the normal meanings and presuppositions of a term are suspended, so doctrinal discourse has linguistic forms that can be commented on. It is important to realize that such uses are nonetheless equally significant as the other, more direct ones. For they tell us about the horizon of assumptions and the aims of the authors and projected audience, even though they say nothing about how the objects designated by *Redentor, pecador,* or *padeció* are used, or where they are located.

I have just begun to investigate the appearance of the cross and other features of doctrinal language in the colonial metalinguistic texts. I am most concerned with the relation between the *Doctrina* and *Arte* produced by Coronel, and later revised by Beltrán. The Motul and San Francisco dictionaries, also being the products of the friars, show a similar pattern in which doctrinal language is the stuff of many of the example sentences and explanations of Maya language. In these cases, the intertextual relation between doctrinal genres and metalinguistic ones is motivated mainly by the fact that the same agents— the Franciscans—produced them, as part of a single program of conquest. This raises a number of important questions, but cannot be pursued here because further research is required.

CONCLUSION

By way of concluding, let me summarize the variants of the cross that we have adduced. Table 10.1 shows eleven variants according to their standard linguistic designations, the overall form, the material of which they are fashioned, and the "actional context" in which the variant occurs. This is clearly a preliminary summary that only points toward an analysis not yet done. One of the first questions that arises is how many crosses this cluster of forms represents. At one extreme, it could be claimed that everything in Table 10.1 is a single symbolic form that happens to be realized under different forms according to the context in which it occurs. There is no issue as to whether all these things really are the same thing, because the essential sameness is what defines them all. The implication of such a view is that all of the eleven entries in the table are equally basic, and their differences are arbitrary. But this is at odds with the theological system that defines the form and at least some of the practices in which it was used. The sign of the cross and the threshold cross are just that; they are signs of the original passion and death of Christ. It makes no sense to say that the original crucifixion was a sign of the boundary marker or graphic Maltese cross. In other words, even if one asserts that all variants point to some other unitary symbol, still they do so from different degrees of remove. Moreover, if they are all ultimately equivalent, what explains the proliferation of contextual variants?

If we come from the perspective of the issues outlined in the first parts of this paper, a slightly different question arises. What were the intertextual vectors along which the cruciform, and other aspects of doctrine, spread in the discourse genres of Yucatec Maya? The initial presentations of the cross were made by the *conquistadores,* the Franciscans shortly thereafter, the church-based worship in which human relations to the cross were fixed, and the doctrinal instruction in which an explanatory catechism was developed in which the meanings of the cross were amplified and further rooted in local discourse. The cross as a bodily or architectural adornment follows from these other, more basic contexts. The original crucifixion, as defined by church practices, establishes the origin point of this series, with the practice of the sacraments at the altar, and the doctrinal instruction referring back to the core crucifixion. The shift from these contexts into the ritual performances of Maya priests, in the crucifixions and cross offerings (by fire and water) which they performed, was to link the two fields of Catholic and Maya ritual practices. Both of these were defined by their practitioners as distinct from everyday speech and action, and both involved structured performances based on codified traditions. The intertextual reproduction of crosses among the Maya seems in this case to be based on the homologous position of *payal či⁾ t'àan* 'prayer' in the two sectors.

Other instances appear to follow more from common agency than common generic positioning. The very Maya nobles who were trained in European languages and writings, by the Franciscans went on to produce the maps, chronicles, letters, and official documents from the Maya towns. The fact that doctrinal language proliferates into these nonreligious genres is motivated by the commonality of author-producers. Similarly within the Spanish sector, the grammars and dictionaries produced by friars were not in themselves doctrinal texts, but being produced by the same authors of Maya-language doctrine, they show the signs of doctrinal speech. Although we have barely scratched the surface of this topic here, the metalinguistic texts show that the language of doctrine and conversion was uppermost on the minds of the friar-linguists, and that it served as a backdrop that could be called upon to provide expressions, statements, descriptive perspectives, and the other semantic/discursive elements needed to illustrate a grammar or dictionary. The spatial uses of the cross to mark thresholds as well as the inner sanctum of built space (home and church) are partly implicit in the penumbra of spatial corollaries of the incarnation, resurrection, and locus of the crucifixion at Mount Calvary, and partly due to European practices of displaying the cross in the landscape. It is still too early to determine to what extent and in what ways the boundary crosses were

TABLE 10.1 *Variants of the Cross*

DESIGNATION	FORM	MATERIAL	ACTIONAL CONTEXT
cruz	sinan posture, affixed to wooden cross	corporeal, passion and death	crucifixion, original crucifixion, reenacted offering by dropping in well
cruz	anthropomorphic	mixed media	on altar, Eucharist, genuflect
u chicul cruz	head>heart>left>right with right hand	corporeal, motion	enacting sign on head and torso
u chicul cruz	3 part naming	corporeal, speech	sequential uttering of formulac "In the name of"
cruz*	sinan posture: erect with arms outstretched to side	corporeal, posture	prayer offering, payalči'ʔt'àan
cruz	etched, probably crude intersecting lines	corporeal, on heart	offering in church in mouth idol
cruz	unknown	wood, miniature	offering by immolation
cruz*	anthropomorphic miniature	corporeal, talisman	dressing the body, for everyday ritual
{(cilich) uahom che, (cilich) cruz}	anthropomorphic	wood, stone, metal	marking landscape threshold
(cilich) cruz	Maltese	ink on paper	legitimating discourse seal; at front of work
(cilich) cruz	words	ink on paper	linguistic presentation of sign Doctrinal definition of sign graphic illustration of a referent

(* Indicates that I have not yet attested this form in reports of colonial crosses, but infer its likely existence.)

doubly interpretable for the Maya, indexing the endurance of an indigenous tradition even as it changed to encompass, and be encompassed by, Europeans. Rather than focusing on the status of different practices as Maya or European, or indigenous colonial, the research needed to address this question will bear centrally on the intertextual trajectories along which the two traditions interpenetrated each other, and the blended genres of practice to which they gave rise.

NOTES

Translations from the Mayan are in single quotes.

The research on which this paper is based was supported by a grant from the National Endowment for the Humanities (RO-22303-91), which I gratefully acknowledge. My principal collaborator in this project, Nancy Farriss, has made substantial contributions to the conceptual and empirical dimensions of the work. Her help is and has been invaluable. To Serge Gruzinski, Nathan Wachtel, and other members of CERMACA I wish to express my thanks for having made it possible for me to attend the Colloquium and for my stay as a visiting professor at the Ecole des Hautes Etudes en Sciences Sociales. Commentaries by Roger Chartier and Jean-Claude Schmitt, and discussions with Serge Gruzinski, Antoinette Molinié, and Aurore Becquelin Monod have also helped me greatly to appreciate both the limits and the possibilities of the themes addressed in this paper. I remain grateful to them and to the other participants in the colloquium.

 1. Bricker 1986, Coggins 1980, Hopkins 1987, Josserand 1987, Justeson and Cambell 1984, Kelley 1976, Lounsbury 1980, 1984, 1989, Marcus 1976, Mathews 1984, Schele 1982, Stuart 1985.

 2. Freidel and Schele 1989, Schele and Miller 1986, Hanks and Rice 1989, Miller 1989.

 3. Hammond and Willey 1979, Jones 1977, 1989, Jones, Rice and Rice 1981.

 4. Ashmore 1981, 1989, Sharer 1983.

 5. Marcus 1976, Scholes and Roys 1948.

 6. Bricker 1981, Carmack 1981, Dürr 1987, Farriss 1978, 1984, 1987, Gosner 1989a, b, Hawkins 1984, Jones 1989, Miller and Farriss 1979.

 7. Edmonson and Bricker 1985, Gossen 1974, Hanks 1986, 1987, 1988, 1989a, b, c, Tedlock 1983.

 8. Bricker 1981, Farriss 1984, Jones 1989, Sullivan 1989.

 9. Adams 1970, Collier 1975, Hanks 1990a, Nash 1975, Warren 1978, Watanabe 1983, 1984.

 10. Another example of this, which will not be explored here, is the spatial coordinates corresponding to the people. It is obvious from multiple sources both pre- and post-conquest that Maya peoples defined space in terms of schemata like the four cardinal points plus center familiar from the cosmology. The question then arises in land surveys why the surveyors chose to proceed in the order they did, and whether there are cosmological motivations for the forms of spatial reference in the document. Given that all of the principal agents engaged in the surveys and in the documentation themselves occupy social space, the order of their mention could be covertly spatial, as well as a generational or rank order.

 11. See for instance the major study by Vicenta Cortés Alonso [1984] "La escritura y lo escrito, España y América en los siglos XVI y XVII." Manuscript distributed at 1984 Summer Institute, Newberry Library.

12. To a modern reader, this is self-evident, and perhaps trivial. But sixteenth-century Spaniards debated at length over the possibility that Christianity had actually preceded them to the New World, a debate triggered by the apparent similarity of native forms to the cross, baptism, and other aspects of Catholicism. The incidence of some Spanish words in Maya, such as *Don, Dios, santo, espíritu, Cristiano, cruz,* and official titles in municipal government is unsurprising on the assumption that they designate brand-new concepts that can be understood only in reference to European traditions. Actually, this is usually false and, in any case, translations could be produced for virtually any Spanish expression. Some terms resist translation because the translators chose not to use a potential equivalent from the target language.

13. The first person pronoun does indeed appear in the *Books of Chilam Balam,* and in the *Rituals of the Bacabs,* but evidently in quoted speech only. The point of this observation is that in colonial texts, the first-person singular is used to identify the author of the text, and not only the quoted sources of some stretch of reported speech.

14. The connection between rain and cenotes is direct for the Maya, whose traditional cosmology establishes a cycle of water between underground rivers, cenote-type wells, rain clouds and rainfall. There is further suggestion in the documents that Maya ritual uses of the cross involved sacrificing the cross itself, that is, including the cross within the offering, as opposed to Catholic practice, in which it stands for the divinity to whom prayer offerings are made but is not itself offered up.

15. Edmonson's presentation of the Maya text is highly readable and will serve as our point of reference. However, the translations that he proposes are in many cases open to debate, and I therefore present the examples with my own translations. For an extended review of the problems in translating these texts, see Hanks 1988.

16. This is not an instance of prophecy, but of past-tense report.

17. In Sanchez de Aguilar's *Informe contra Idólatras,* dated 1613, he reinforced the impression that Maya people had been thoroughly indoctrinated, stating flatly that they all either knew doctrine well, or their lack of knowledge was a sin (Sanchez de Aguilar 1900 [1613]:99). In his complex and fascinating portrait of the Indians, he argued that by the date of his writing the Maya had demonstrated uncommon achievement and intelligence in learning the ways of Spaniards; he even compared them favorably to the Moors for having so adeptly taken on Spanish ways. This apparent praise then provides the rhetorical foundation upon which he condemned their continued practice of the "vomit" and "sodomy" of idolatry as fully punishable and within their own responsibility. They would be exonerated of idolatry neither for lack of instructors nor for lack of sophistication about the nature of their blasphemy.

18. Beltrán de Santa Rosa, RP Fray Pedro. 1912 [1757, 1740]. *Declaración de la Doctrina Cristiana en el idioma yucateco.* Mérida, Yucatán: Imprenta de la Lotería del Estado.

19. The differences are defended point by point by Beltrán in his doctrine, in which he presents a reasoned and fascinating critique of Coronel's word choices in the Maya.

20. Tozzer 1941, Farriss 1984, Clendinnen 1987.

21. Notice that this passage is nearly identical (but not quite) to the earlier one presented as the prophecy of *Chilam Balam.* The earlier example was taken from *Chilam Balam of Chumayel* and this one is from the *Chilam Balam of Tizimin.* Although we cannot enter into close comparison of the two in this context, it would be worthwhile. For the Maya expression *uahom che* see Martinez Hernandez (1929: 887).

22. With one exception: both surveys mention the road between Yaxkukul and Tixkumcheil, and neither one mentions any cross at this road.

23. Even within the church and when placed atop a ritual altar, the cross could be said to

mark a threshold, the threshold between the human and the divine. This description would fit contemporary practices of Maya shamans (Hanks 1990a, b).

24. In drawing this distinction I am not privileging either the documentary or the other modes as more "real" or the measure of truth. We need simply to recognize that space is multiply defined, and here we have to deal with a difference of dimensions in a larger social world.

25. The second survey precedes this name by the adjective *yax* meaning 'first', 'green.'

26. The second survey, which reports the facts of the boundary from a third-person, past-tense remove, lacks the sign of the cross (cf. Hanks 1992).

27. The volume is number Yucatec 21 in the Ayers collection of American Indian Documents, which I consulted at the Newberry Library, Chicago, IL.

28. The term *citbil* in particular was in the early version of the sign of the cross, but Beltrán de Santa Rosa pointed out a serious infelicity with the translation: it is true, he said, that *citbil* means eternal, but unfortunately it is the term also used for an indigenous deity whom the Maya still worshiped in the eighteenth century (Beltrán de Santa Rosa 1912: 8–9). This revision of Coronel on the basis of secondary associations of the Maya term is typical of Beltrán's *Doctrina*. Beltrán's work is distinguished by an extraordinarily deep knowledge of Maya language and a commitment to formulating the *Doctrina* in discourse that was both referentially precise and readily intelligible to a mid-eighteenth-century Maya speaker. In my experience, it is Beltrán's revised form, *Dios yumbil,* which remains in use today.

REFERENCES

Adams, Richard N. 1970. *Crucifixion by Power, Essays on Guatemalan National Social Structure,* 1944–1966. Austin: University of Texas Press.

Alberro, Solange. 1992. *Les Espagnols dans le Mexique Colonial, Histoire d'une Acculturation.* Cahiers des Annales. Paris: Armand Colin.

Anderson, Arthur J. O., Frances Berdan and James Lockhart eds., 1976. *Beyond the Codices, the Nahua View of Colonial Mexico.* Berkeley and Los Angeles: University of California Press.

Ashmore, W. 1981. Some issues of method and theory in lowland Maya settlement archeology. In *Lowland Maya Settlement Patterns,* ed. W. Ashmore. Albuquerque: University of New Mexico Press. 37–69.

——— 1989. Construction and cosmology: Politics and ideology in lowland Maya settlement patterns. In Hanks and Rice, eds. 272–86.

Austin, John L. 1962. *How to do Things with Words.* Cambridge: Harvard University Press.

Bakhtin, M. M. 1981. *The dialogic imagination.* Cambridge: Harvard University Press.

——— 1986. The problem of speech genres. In *Speech genres and other essays,* trans. Vern McGee, ed. Michael Holquist and Caryl Emerson. Austin: University of Texas Press. 60–102.

Bakhtin, M. M. and P. M. Medvedev. 1985 [1928]. *The formal method in literary scholarship, a critical introduction to sociological poetics.* trans. Alberte J. Wehrle. Cambridge: Harvard University Press.

Barrera Vasquez, Alfredo. 1957. *Codice de Calkini.* Biblioteca Campechana, 4. Campeche.

——— 1980. La lengua Maya. *Diccionario Maya Cordemex.* Merida: Ediciones Cordemex. 39a–53a.

——— 1984. Documento Numero 1 del deslinde de tierras en Yaxkukul, Yucatan. *Coleccion cientifica, Linguistica* 125. Mexico: Instituto Nacional de Antropologia e Historia.

Barrera Vasquez, Alfredo (with Sylvia Rendón). 1974 [1948]. *El libro de los libros de Chilam Balam.* Mexico City: Fondo de Cultura Económica.

Barrera Vasquez, Alfredo, Juan Ramon Bastarrachea Manzano and William Brito Sansores. 1980. *Diccionario Maya Cordemex.* Mérida: Ediciones Cordemex.

Basso, Keith. 1990. *Western Apache language and culture, Essays in linguistic anthropology.* Tucson: University of Arizona Press.

Bauman, Richard. 1977. *Verbal art as performance.* Prospect Heights, IL: Waveland Press.

Becquelin Monod, Aurore. 1979. Examin de quelques paires sémantiques dans les dialogues rituels des Tzeltal Bachajon (langue Maya du Chiapas). *Journal de la Société des Américanistes* 66: 235–263.

———1981. Des Pieds et des mains. Analyse sémantique des concepts en tzeltal (Maya du Chiapas). Centre National de Recherche Scientifique, Paris. *La Linguistique* 17(2): 99–118.

Beltran, de Santa Rosa María. 1740. Novena de Christo crucificado con otras oraciones en lengua Maya. Mexico (Copy in Berendt Linguistic Collection, no. 21).

———1746. Arte de el idioma Maya reducido a succintas reglas y semi-lexicon Yucateco. Mexico (Gates reproduction).

———1816. Declaración de la Doctrina Christiana en el idioma Yucateco. Merida (Gates reproduction).

Beltran de Santa Rosa Maria, R. P. Fray Pedro. 1912 [1757]. *Declaracion de la doctrina cristiana en el idioma yucateco.* Merida, Yucatan: Imprenta de la Loteria del Estado.

Berendt, Carl Hermann. 1868. Coleccion de platicas, doctrinales y sermones en lengua Maya por diferentes autores. (Berendt Linguistic Collection, number 46–47).

Borah, Woodrow. 1984. Some problems of sources. In Harvey and Prem, eds. 23–41.

Bricker, Victoria R. 1974. The ethnographic context of some traditional Mayan speech genres. In *Explorations in the ethnography of speaking,* eds. Richard Bauman and Joel Sherzer. London: Cambridge University Press. 368–88.

———1981. *The Indian Christ, the Indian King, the historical substrate of Maya myth and ritual.* Austin: University of Texas Press.

———1986. *A grammar of Mayan hieroglyphs.* Middle American Research Institute, Publication 56. New Orleans: Tulane University.

———1989. The last gasp of Maya hieroglyphic writing in the Books of Chilam Balam of Chumayel and Chan Kan. In Hanks and Rice, eds.

Brinton, Daniel G., ed. 1969 [1882]). *The Maya Chronicles.* New York: AMS Press.

Brody, Jill. 1986. Repetition as a rhetorical and conversational device in Tojolabal (Mayan). *IJAL* 52 (3): 255–74.

Brown, G. and Yule, G. 1983. *Discourse Analysis.* Cambridge: Cambridge University Press.

Burkhart, Louise M. 1988. Doctrinal aspects of Sahagún's Colloquios. In Klor de Alva et. al., eds.

———1989. *The Slippery Earth, Nahua-Christian Moral Dialogue in Sixteenth-Century Mexico.* Tucson: University of Arizona Press.

Carmack, Robert. 1981. *The Quiché Mayas of Utatlan.* Norman: University of Oklahoma Press.

Certeau, Michel de. 1984. *The practice of everyday life,* trans. Steven Rendall. Berkeley: University of California Press.

Chamberlain, Robert S. 1948. *The conquest and colonization of Yucatan, 1517–1550.* Washington DC: Carnegie Institution (Publication 582).

Chi, Gaspar Antonio. 1941 [1582]. Relacion, reproduced in Appendix C, Tozzer 1941.

Clendinnen, Inga. 1987. *Ambivalent Conquests, Maya and Spaniard in Yucatan, 1517–1570.* Cambridge: Cambridge University Press.

Cline, Howard, ed. 1975. Guide to ethnohistorical sources, part 4. *Handbook of Middle American Indians,* Vol. 15. Austin: University of Texas Press.

Cline, S. L. 1981. Culhuacan, 1579–1599: An investigation through Mexican Indian testaments. Ph.D. dissertation, University of California, Los Angeles.

1984. Land tenure and land inheritance in late sixteenth-century Culhuacan. In Harvey and Prem, eds., 277–310.

Coggins, C. 1980. The shape of time: some political implcations of a four-part figure. *American Antiquity* 45: 727–39.

Cogolludo, Fray Diego López de. 1971 [1656]. *Historia de Yucathan.* Graz, Austria: Akademische Druck.

Collier, G. 1975. *Fields of the Tzotzil: The Ecological Basis of Tradition in Highland Chiapas.* Austin: University of Texas Press.

Collins, Anne. 1977. The Maestros Cantores in Yucatan. In Jones, ed. 233–47.

Coronel, Fray Juan. [1620] 1929. Arte en lengua Maya. In Juan Martinex Hernandez ed., Diccionario Maya Motul. Merida: Talleres de la Compañia Tipografica Yucateca, S.A. 3–55.

[1620a]. Doctrina Christiana en lengua Maya. Mexico (Gates reproduction).

[1620b] . Discursos predicables, con otras diversas materias espirituales, con la Doctrina Christiana, y los articulos de la Fe, recoplidaoos y enmendados [en lengua Yucateca]. Mexico (Gates reproduction).

Davis, Natalie. 1987. *Fiction in the archives: Pardon tales and their tellers in 16th-century France.* Stanford: Stanford University Press.

Diaz del Castillo, Bernal. 1963. *The Conquest of New Spain.* Translated with an introduction by J. M. Cohen. Harmondsworth: Penguin.

Dibble, C. 1974. The Nahuatlization of Christianity. In *Sixteenth-century Mexico: The Work of Sahagún,* ed. M. Edmonson. Albuquerque: University of New Mexico Press.

1988. Sahagún's appendices: There is no reason to be suspicious of the ancient practices. In Klor de Alva et. al., eds.

Diccionario de San Francisco [17th century]. Michelon, Oscar ed. Graz, Austria: Akademische Druck- und Verlagsanstalt.

Dürr, M. 1987. Morphologie, Syntax und Textstrukturen des (Maya-) Quiche des Popol Vuh. *Linguistische Beschreibung eines kolonialzeitlichen Dokuments aus dem Hochland von Guatemala.* Bonn: Mundus.

Eagle, Herbert J. 1981. Verse as a semiotic system: Tynjanov, Jakobson, Mukarosky. *Slavic and East European Journal* 25(4): 47–61.

Edmonson, Munro S. 1970. Metáfora maya en literatura y en arte, in Verhandlungen des XXXVIII Internationalen Amerikanistenkongresses: Stuttgart-München, 1968. 2: 37–50.

1973. Semantic universals and particulars in Quiche. In *Meaning in Mayan languages: Ethnolinguistic studies,* ed. Munro S. Edmonson. The Hague: Mouton. 235–46.

1982. *The ancient future of the Itza: the Book of Chilam Balam of Tizimin.* Austin: University of Texas Press.

1986. *Heaven-born Merida and its destiny: The Chilam Balam of Chumayel.* Austin: University of Texas Press.

Edmonson, Munro S. and Victoria R. Bricker. 1985. Yucatecan Mayan literature. In *Supplement to the Handbook of Middle American Indians,* Vol. 3, ed. Munro S. Edmonson. Austin: University of Texas Press. 44–63.

Farriss, Nancy. 1978. Nucleation vs. dispersal: the dynamics of population movement in colonial Yucatan. *Hispanic American Historical Review* 58: 187–216.

1984. *Maya society under colonial rule.* Princeton, NJ: Princeton University Press.

1987. Remembering the future, anticipating the past: History, time and cosmology among the Maya of Yucatan. *Comparative Studies in Society and History* 29(3): 566–93.

Fought, John. 1976. Time structuring in Chorti Mayan narratives. In *Mayan Linguistics,* ed. Marlys McClaren. Los Angeles: University of California American Indian Study Center. 228–42.

　　1985. Cyclical patterns in Chorti (Mayan) literature. In *Supplement to the Handbook of Middle American Indians,* Vol. 3, ed. Munro S. Edmonson. Austin: University of Texas Press. 147–70.

Freidel, D. and L. Schele. 1989. Dead kings and living temples: Dedication and termination rituals among the ancient Maya. In Hanks and Rice, eds. 233–43.

Garibay, Angel Maria. 1953. *Historia de la Literatura Nahuatl.* 2 vols. Mexico City: Porrua.

Gates, William. 1937. *Yucatan before and after the conquest by Friar Diego de Landa with other related documents, maps and illustrations.* Maya Society Publication No. 20. Baltimore, MD: The Maya Society.

Gonzalez Cicero, Stella Maria. 1978. *Perspectiva religiosa en yucatán, 1517–1571.* Mexico: El Colegio de Mexico.

Gonzales Navarro, M. 1970. *Raza y tierra: La guerra de castas y el henquen.* Mexico: El Colegio de Mexico.

Goodman, N. 1976. *Languages of Art.* Indianapolis: Hackett Publishing Co. 1978. *Ways of Worldmaking.* Cambridge, Hackett Publishing Co.

Gosner, Kevin. 1989a. Caciques and conversion: Juan Atonal and the struggle for legitimacy in post-conquest Chiapas. Paper presented at the XV Congress of Latin American Studies Association, Miami.

　　1989b. Conceptualizing community and hierarchy: Recent views of colonial Maya political organization in the highlands. Paper presented at the annual meeting of the American Anthroplogical Association.

Gossen, Gary H. 1974. *Chamulas in the world of the sun: time and space in a Maya oral tradition.* Cambridge: Harvard University Press.

　　1985. Tzotzil literature. In *Supplement to the Handbook of Middle American Indians,* Vol. 3, ed. Munro S. Edmonson. Austin: University of Texas Press. 65–106.

Gruzinski, Serge. 1988. *La Colonisation de l'Imaginaire, Sociétés Indigènes et occidentalisation dans le Mexique Espagnol XVI-XVIII siècle.* Paris: Éditions Gallimard.

　　1992. *Painting the Conquest: The Mexican Indians and the European Renaissance.* New York: Flammarion-Abbeville Press.

Hammond, Norman and Gordon R. Wiley, eds. 1979. *Maya archeology and ethnohistory.* Austin: University of Texas Press.

Hanks, William F. 1984a. Sanctification, structure and experience in a Yucatec Maya ritual event. *Journal of American Folklore* 97(384): 131–166.

　　1984b. The interactive basis of Maya divination. Paper presented at the Eighty-Third Annual Meeting of the American Anthropological Association, Denver, CO.

　　1985. Letter of Maya nobles to the Spanish Crown, March 19, 1567, Archivo General de Indias, Mexico 359 [unpublished transliteration and translation of document 138 lines in Maya; Department of Linguistics, University of Chicago].

　　1986. Authenticity and ambivalence in the text: a colonial Maya case. *American Ethnologist* 13(4): 721–44.

　　1987. Discourse genres in a theory of practice. *American Ethnologist* 14 (4): 668–92.

　　1988. Grammar style and meaning in a Maya manuscript. *International Journal of American Linguistics* 54(3): 331–64.

　　1989a. Elements of Maya style. In Hanks and Rice, eds. 92–111.

　　1989b. Rhetoric of royal address. Paper presented at the symposium on the Colonization of

Language, University of Pennsylvania [unpublished ms. 66 pages; Department of Anthropology, University of Chicago].

1989c Text and textuality. *Annual Reviews of Anthropology* 18: 95–127.

1989d. Word and image in a semiotic perspective. In Hanks and Rice, eds. 8–21.

1990a. *Referential Practice, Language and lived space among the Maya.* Chicago: University of Chicago Press.

1990b. Temporal orientations in Maya shamanic performance. Paper presented at October workshop on La formación de Otro, Trujillo, España.

1992. Intertexualité de l'espace au Yacatán. *L'Homme* 122–24, 32 (2–3–4): 153–74.

1993. Metalanguage and the pragmatics of deixis. In *Reflexive Language: Reported Speech and Metapragmatics.* ed. J. Lucy. Cambridge: Cambridge University Press, pp. 127–57.

Hanks, William F. and Don S. Rice, eds. 1989. *Word and image in Maya culture: Explorations in language, writing and representation.* Salt Lake City: University of Utah Press.

Harvey, H. R. and Hanns J. Prem, eds. 1984. *Explorations in ethnohistory: Indians of Central Mexico in the sixteenth century.* Albuquerque: University of New Mexico Press.

Hawkins, John. 1984. *Inverse Images: The Meaning of Culture, Ethnicity and Family in Post-Colonial Guatemala.* Albuquerque: University Of New Mexico Press.

Hopkins, Nicholas A. 1987. The Lexicon of Maya hieroglyphic texts. Oral presentation at the 86th Annual Meeting of the American Anthropological Association (session 3–023).

Hunt, Marta Espejo-Ponce. 1976. The processes of the development of Yucatan, 1600–1700. In *Provinces of Early Mexico, variants of Spanish America regional evolution,* eds. Ida Altman and James Lockhart. 33–62.

Iser, Wolfgang. 1989. *Prospecting: From reader response to literary anthropology.* Baltimore: Johns Hopkins University Press.

Jakobson, Roman. 1960. Linguistics and poetics. In *Style in Language,* ed. T. Sebeok, Cambridge: MIT Press. 350–77.

1985. *Verbal art, verbal sign, verbal time.* eds. Krystyna Pomorska and Stephen Rudy. Minneapolis: University of Minnesota Press.

Jauss, Hans Robert. 1982. Toward an Aesthetic of Reception. trans. T. Bahti (from German). *Theory and History of Literature, Vol 2.* Minneapolis: University of Minnesota Press.

Jenny, Laurent. 1982. *The strategy of form.* In Todorov, ed. 34–63.

Jones, Grant D., ed. 1977. *Anthropology and history in Yucatan.* Austin: University of Texas Press.

Jones, Grant D. 1989. *Maya resistance to Spanish rule: Time and history on a colonial frontier.* Albuquerque: University of New Mexico Press.

Jones, Grant D., Don Rice and Prudence Rice. 1981. The Location of Tayasal: A Reconsideration in Light of Peten Ethnohistory and Archeology. *American Antiquity* 46:530–547.

Josserand, Kathryn J. 1987. The Discourse Structure of Maya Hieroglyphic Texts. Presented at the Annual Meeting of the Anthropological Association.

Justeson, John S. and Lyle Campbell, eds. 1984. *Phoneticism in Mayan hieroglyphic writing.* Institute for Mesoamerican Studies, State University of New York at Albany, Publication no. 9.

Karttunen, Frances. 1982. Nahuatl literacy. In *The Inca and Aztec states 1400–1800: Anthropology and history,* eds. G. Collier, R. Rosaldo and J. Wirth. New York: Academic Press.

Karttunen, Frances and James Lockhart, eds. 1987. *The art of Nahuatl Speech, The Bancroft Dialogues.* Nahuatl Studies Series, 2. Los Angeles: UCLA Latin American Center.

Kelley, David H. 1976. *Deciphering the Maya Script.* Austin: University of Texas Press.

Klor de Alva, J., H. B. Nicholson and E. Quiñones Keber, eds. 1988. *The life and work of Bernardino de Sahagún: Pionneer ethnographer of 16th century Aztec Mexico.* Albany: SUNY Press.

Landa, Fray Diego de. 1985. Relación de las Cosas de Yucatan. Edición de Miguel Rivera. *Cronicas de America* 7. Madrid: Información y Revistas S.A.

Léon-Portilla, Miguel. 1985. Nahuatl literature. In *Supplement to the Handbook of Middle American Indians,* ed. Edmonson. Vol. 3. Austin: University of Texas Press. 7–43.

Levinson, S. 1983. *Pragmatics.* Cambridge: Cambridge University Press.

Lizana, Bernardo de. 1893 [1633]. *Historia de Yucatan: Devocionario de Nuestra Señora de Izamal y conquista espiritual.* 2d ed. Mexico: Museo Naciona.

Lockhart, James, Frances Berdan and Arthur J. O. Anderson. 1986. *The Tlaxcalan Actas, A compendium of the records of the cabildo of Tlaxcala (1545–1627).* Salt Lake City: University of Utah Press.

Lounsbury, Floyd G. 1980. Some problems in the interpretation of the mythological portion of the hieroglyphic text at the Temple of Cross at Palenque. In *Third Palenque Roundtable, 1978, Part 2,* ed. Merle Greene Robertson. Austin and London: University of Texas Press 99–115.

——— 1984. Glyphic substitutions: homophonic and synonymic. In Justeson and Campbell, eds. 1984. 167–84.

——— 1989. The names of a king: hieroglyphic variants as a key to decipherment. In Hanks and Rice, eds.

Love, Bruce. 1984. Wahil kol: A Yucatec Maya agricultural ceremony. *Estudios de Cultura Maya.* Vol. 15. Mexico: UNAM. 251–300.

——— 1986. Yucatec Maya Ritual: a Diachronic Perspective. PhD. dissertation, Department of Anthropology, University of California at Los Angeles.

——— 1989. Yucatec sacred breads through time. In Hanks and Rice, eds. 336–50.

Marcus, Joyce. 1976. *Emblem and state in the classic Maya Lowlands: An epigraphic approach to territorial organization.* Washington, D.C.: Dumbarton Oaks.

Martinez Hernandez, Juan. 1926. *Cronicas Maya, Cronica de Yaxkukul.* Mérida, Yucatán.

——— 1929. *Diccionario de Motul, Maya-Español Atribuido a Fray Antonio de Ciudad Real.* Mérida: Talleres de la Compania Tipografica Yucateca, S. A.

Mathews, Peter. 1984. Appendix A. A Maya hieroglyphic syllabary. In Justeson and Campbell, eds. 311–14.

McQuown, Norman A. 1967. Classical Yucatec (Maya). In *Handbook of Middle American Indians.* Vol. 5, *Linguistics.* Austin: University of Texas Press. 201–47.

——— 1979. *A modern Yucatec Maya text.* IJAL Native American Texts series, no. 3, Mayan texts II, ed. Louanna Furbee Losee. 38–106.

Miller, Arthur G. 1989. Comparing Maya image and text. In Hanks and Rice, eds. 176–88.

Miller, Arthur G. and Nancy M. Farriss. 1979. Religious syncretism in colonial Yucatan: The archeological and ethnohistorical evidence from Tancah, Quintana Roo. In Hammond and Willey, eds. 223–41.

Mitchell, W. J. T. 1986. *Iconology, Image, Text, Ideology,* Chicago: University of Chicago Press.

Molina Solís, Juan Francisco. 1904–1913. *Historia de Yucatan durante la dominación española.* 3 vols. Merida: Imprenta de la Lotería del Estado.

Morley, Sylvanus G. and George Brainerd. 1983. *The ancient Maya.* Revised edition by Robert J. Sharer. Stanford: Stanford University Press.

Morson, Gary Saul. 1981. *The Boundaries of Genre: Dostoievsky's Diary of a Writer and the Traditions of Literary Utopia.* Austin: University of Texas Press.

Nash, June. 1975 [1971]. *Bajo la mirada de los antepasados, creencias y comportamiento en una comunidad maya.* Mexico D.F.: Instituto Indigenista Interamericano.

Norman, William M. 1980. Grammatical parallelism in Quiche ritual language. In Proceedings of the sixth annual meeting of the Berkeley Linguistic Society. 387–99.

Panofsky, Erwin. 1976. *Gothic Architecture and Scholasticism: An Inquiry into the Analogy of the Arts, Philosophy and Religion in the Middle Ages.* New York: New American Library.

Perez, Juan Pio. 1866–1877. *Diccionario de la lengua maya.* Merida: Imprenta Literaria de Juan Molina Solís.

Phelan, John Leddy. 1970. *The millenial kingdom of the Franciscans in the New World.* Berkeley: University of California Press.

Quezada, Sergio. 1985. Encomienda, cabildo y gubernatura indígena en Yucatán, 1541–1583. *Historia Mexicana* Vol. 34(4): 662–84.

Reed, N. 1964. *The Caste War of Yucatan.* Stanford: Stanford University Press.

Ricard, Robert. 1947. *La conquista espiritual de México.* trans. Angel María Garibay. Mexico: Editorial Jus.

Riese, Frauke J. 1981. Indianische Landrechte In *Yukatan um die Mitte des 16. Jahrhunderts.* Hamburg: Museum für Völkerkunder.

Roys, Ralph, L. 1943. *The indian background of colonial Yucatan.* Publication 548. Washington DC: The Carnegie Institution.

——— 1957. *The political geography of the Yucatan Maya.* Publication 613. Washington DC: The Carnegie Institution.

Roys, Ralph L., ed. and trans. 1965. *Ritual of the Bacabs.* Norman: University of Oklahoma Press.

Roys, Ralph L., ed., 1939. *The Titles of Ebtun.* Washington: Carnegie Institution.

Sanchez de Aguilar, Pedro. 1937 [1613]. *Informe contra idolorum cultores del obispado de Yucatan dirigido al Rey N. Señor en su Real Consejo de la Indias.* 3d ed. Merida: Imprenta Triay e Hijos.

Schele, Linda. 1982. *Maya Glyphs: The Verbs.* Austin: University of Texas Press.

Schele, Linda and Mary Miller. 1986. *The Blood of Kings: Dynasty and Ritual in Maya Art.* New York: George Braziller, Inc.

Scholes, Frances, V. and Eleanor Adams. 1936–1937. *Documents relating to the Mirones expedition to the interior of Yucatan,* 1621–24. Maya Research 3: 156–76; 251–76.

Scholes, Frances, Carlos Menendez, J. Rubio Mañé and E. Adams. 1938. *Documentos para la historia de Yucatan.* Vol. 2, *La iglesia en Yucatan.* Mérida: Compañia Tipografica Yucateca.

Scholes, Frances V. and Ralph L. Roys. 1968 [1948]. *The Maya Chontal indians of Acalan-Tixchel: A contribution to the history and ethnogarphy of the Yucatan penninsula.* 2d ed. Norman: University of Oklahoma Press.

Searle, J. 1976. *Speech Acts: An Essay in the Philosophy of Language.* Cambridge: Cambridge University Press.

Sharer, Robert J. 1983. *The Ancient Maya.* Stanford: Stanford University Press.

Sherzer, Joel and Anthony C. Woodbury, eds. 1987. *Native American Discourse: Poetics and Rhetoric.* Cambridge: Cambridge University Press.

Solis Acala, Ermilo. 1949. *Códice Pérez.* Mérida: Liga de Acción Social.

Sosa, J. 1986. Maya concepts of astronomical order. In *Symbol and Meaning beyond the closed community, Essays in Mesoamerican ideas.* ed. G. Gossen. Albany: SUNY Press. 185–96.

Stross, Brian. 1983. The language of Zuyua. *American Ethnologist.* 10(1): 150–64.

Stuart, D. 1985. The Yaxha emblem glyph Yaxha. *Research Reports on Ancient Maya Writing.* No. 1 Washington, D.C.: Center for Maya Research.

Sullivan, Paul. 1989. *Unfinished conversations: Mayas and foreigners between two wars.* New York: Alfred A. Knopf.

Taussig, M. 1987. *Shamanism, colonialism, and the wild man: A study in terror and healing.* Chicago: University of Chicago Press.

Tedlock, Barbara. 1982. *Time and the highland Maya.* Albuquerque: University of New Mexico Press.

Tedlock, Dennis. 1983. *The spoken word and the work of interpretation.* Philadelphia: University of Pennsylvania Press.

——— 1987. Hearing a voice in an ancient text: Quiché Maya poetics in performance. In Sherzer and Woodbury, eds. 140–175.

Thompson, John, Eric S. Sir. 1974 [1970]. Maya history and religion. Norman: University of Oklahoma Press.

Thompson, Philip C. 1978. Tekanto in the eighteenth century. Ph.D. dissertation, Tulane University.

Thompson, R. A. 1974. *The Winds of Tomorrow: Social Change in a Maya Town.* Chicago: University of Chicago Press.

Todorov, T. 1984. *The conquest of America.* New York: Harper and Row.

Tompkins, Jane P., ed. 1980. *Reader Response Criticism, from Formalism to Post-Structuralism.* Baltimore: The Johns Hopkins University Press.

Tozzer, Alfred M. 1977 [1921]. *A Maya Grammar.* New York: Dover Publications.

Tozzer, Alfred M., trans. and ed. 1941. *Relacion de las cosas de Yucatan, by Fray Diego de Landa.* Cambridge: Peabody Museum of American Archeology and Ethnology, Harvard University.

Vicenta Cortés Alonso. [1984]. ¿ La escritura y lo escrito, España y América en los siglos XVI y XVII.? Manuscript distributed at 1984 Summer Institute, Newberry Library.

Villa Rojas, Alfonso, 1945. *The Maya of East Central Quintana Roo.* Washington D.C.: Carnegie Institution, Publication 559.

——— 1978 [1945]. *Los Elegidos de Dios: Etnografía de los Mayas de Quintana Roo.* Série de Antropología Social, 56. Mexico: INI.

Warren, K. 1978. *The symbolism of subordination: Indian identity in a Guatemalan town.* Austin: University of Texas Press.

Watanabe, John. 1983. In the world of the sun: A cognitive model of Mayan cosmology. *Man* 18(4): 710–28.

——— 1984. We who are here: The cultural dimensions of ethnic identity in a Guatemalan Indian village, 1937–1980. Unpublished dissertation, Harvard University.

Watts, Pauline Moffitt. 1991. Hieroglyphs of Conversion: Alien Discourses in Diego Valadés's Rhetorica Christiana. In *Memoriae Domenicane,* n.s. 21. 1–29

White, Hayden. 1987. *The content of the form: Narrative discourse and historical representation.* Baltimore: Johns Hopkins University Press.

Woodbury, Anthony C. 1987. Rhetorical structure in a central Alaskan Yupik traditional narrative. In *Native American discourse: Poetics and rhetoric,* eds. Joel Sherzer and Anthony C. Woodbury. 1–51.

Zimmermann, Günther. 1970. *Briefe der indianischen Nöbilitat aus Neuspanien an Karl V um die Mitte des 16. Jahrhunderts.* Munchen: Kommissionsverlag Klaus Renner.

Credits

Chapter 2: W. F. Hanks. 1990. Extract from *Referential Practice: Language and Lived Space among the Maya.* Chicago: University of Chicago Press: pp. 81–134.

Chapter 3: W. F. Hanks. 1993. "Metalanguage and Pragmatics of Deixis." Reprinted from *Reflexive Language: Reported Speech and Metapragmatics,* John Lucy, ed. Cambridge: Cambridge University Press. pp. 127–57.

Chapter 4: W. F. Hanks. 1986. "Authenticity and Ambivalence in the Text: A Colonial Maya Case." Reprinted from *American Ethnologist.* 13(4):721–44.

Chapter 5: W. F. Hanks. 1987. "Discourse Genres in a Theory of Practice." Reprinted from *American Ethnologist.* 14(4):64–88.

Chapter 6: W. F. Hanks. 1989. "Text and Textuality." Reprinted from *Annual Review of Anthropology.* 18:95–127.

Chapter 7: W. F. Hanks. 1993. "The Five Gourds of Memory." Reprinted from *Mémoire de la Tradition,* ed. Aurore Becquelin Monod and Antoinette Molinié (avec le concours de Daniel Dehouve). Recherches Thématiques Numéro 5. Nanterre: Sociéte d'Ethnologie. pp. 319–45.

Chapter 8: W. F. Hanks. 1993. "Copresence and Alterity in Maya Ritual Practice [originally published as *Copresencia y Alteridad en la Práctica Ritual Maya*]." Reprinted from *De Palabra y Obra en el Nuevo Mundo,* Vol. 3, ed. Miguel Léon Portilla, Manuel Gutierrez Estevez, Gary Gossen, and J. Jorge Klor de Alva. Madrid: Siglo XXI de España Editores, S. A.

Chapter 9: W. F. Hanks. 1992. "Intertextuality of Space in Colonial Yucatan" was originally published as "L'Intertextualité de l'Espace au Yucatan" in *L'Homme* 122–124 (avr.-déc. 1992): XXXII (2–3–4), pp. 53–74.

Chapter 10: W. F. Hanks. 1996. "Language and Discourse in Colonial Yucatán." Reprinted from *Le Nouveau Monde, Mondes Nouveaux: L'Expérience Américaine.* Sous la Direction de Serge Gruzinski et Nathan Wachtel. Paris: Coédition EHESS/Editions Recherche sur les Civilisations. pp. 238–71.

Index

discourse analysis, 11, 274
discourse genre: asymmetric, 49–50; *carta,*
    113–14; colonial documents, 13–14,
    103–27, 138–44, 281–99; conversa-
    tional, 49–61; definition of, 135; doctri-
    nal discourse, 299, 300; and footing,
    61–62; instrumental, 56–61; and inter-
    textuality, 111, 267–68, 275–76, 280;
    letters, colonial, 103–27 (*see also*
    Yaxkukul documents); official Maya, 114,
    125, 127, 144, 256–58; and practice the-
    ory, 133–61; prayer, 232; ritual speech,
    224–25, 274, 276, 277; structure of,
    136–37; symmetric, 49, 52. *See also* genre
discourse structure: boundary markers in,
    297–98; of colonial documents,
    138–43; and habitus, 145; macro- ver-
    sus micro-level, 184; views of, 166–68
divination, 228–29, 234, 237, 238 *See also*
    t'iič'k'aák'
doctrina 'doctrine', 287–92, 290 fig. 10.2
Doctrina Cristiana: by Beltran, 288–91; by
    Coronel, 288–90, 292
doctrine, Christian, 287–92
Documentos de Cacalchen, 297, 298
documents, colonial: authenticity of,
    103–27; and discourse genres, 133–61;
    and intertextuality, 135, 249–68; list of,
    135 table 5.1; value of, 104
Don Seéb, 197–216; ritual performance
    of, 228–29, 231, 232, 233, 234–35,
    237, 246; as ritual specialist, 222–23,
    229–30, 231, 232, 235, 236, 237, 243,
    246

ecstasy, in shamanic experience, 201–204,
    207, 213
Edmonson, M., 250, 272
ek 'black', 122–24, 125
elicitation, 72, 73, 75, 84, 96
embodiment: of reference, 23, 62–63; and
    ritual, 232–34. *See also* body
empiricism, 2–3*encomenderos,* 108, 109,
    258, 266. *See also* Pech, (Don) Alonso;
    Pech, (Don) Pedro
engagement: and ritual discourse, 224–28;
    and textuality, 169, 173–74, 266–67

enlightenment, and the Franciscan mission,
    119–26
ethnography, 3–4
event frames, 84–85
event framework, 83–84
event, objective, 144
experience, 205–7, 221, 225

Farriss, N., 126, 134, 154, 161n1, 260,
    272, 295
features, prosodic, 81–82
field, corporeal: definition of, 7, 22; and
    -iknal, 28–29; and reference, 29–31, 60,
    61, 62–63; of ritual performance,
    239–44; vs. *schéma corporel,* 6–7, 62–63
field, deictic, vs. *-iknal,* 94. *See also schéma
    corporel,* embodiment, body
field, perceptual, 25–26
field, spatial: in colonial documents,
    154–57; and deixis, 89–94
field, temporal: of colonial documents,
    157–58, 160; of ritual performance,
    238
Fillmore, C., 70, 75, 98n4
finalization, 144
five, significance of, 214, 215–16
footing: in colonial documents, 150; defini-
    tion of, 76; and ritual copresence, 233;
    and textuality, 168
form: vs. function, 175; vs. use, 70
formalism, 170, 180–81
frame, participant. *See* participant frame
frames: definition of, 70; deictic, 71,
    85–88; vs. frameworks, 70; and meta-
    language, 72, 94–95, 96–97, 147–50,
    158–59; schematic, 20, 70, 71–72, 73;
    spatial, 225, 232–33; and textual inter-
    pretation, 168, 178, 181
framework, 69–72; definition of, 69, 70; vs.
    frame, 70
framework, interactive: and deixis, 95–96;
    and gesture, 88–89; and *-iknal,* 92–94;
    and metalanguage, 95–97
framework, participant. *See* participant
    framework
framework, spatial: and boundary marking,
    302n10. *See also* space

Ingarden, R., 12, 173–74, 180, 182, 183
innovation, in colonial discourse, 281–83
inquisition, 104–5, 108, 109, 292
inspection, of boundaries, 264–66
instrumental speech. *See* speech, instrumental
intentionality, and ritual, 231–32
interpretation: and context, 168, 178–79;
    and genre, 135–36; global vs. local,
    178–79; of texts, 168–69, 174, 175,
    176–79
intertext, definition of, 13
intertextuality: and ambivalence, 127; of
    boundary counting, 258; of colonial
    documents, 13–14, 110–15, 123–24,
    126, 128n2, 135, 159, 275–76,
    280–81; of the cross, 298; definition of,
    111, 280; and genre, 111, 267–68,
    280; and maps, 253, 255, 280–81; of
    space, 249–68; and Spanish borrow-
    ings, 112; and textuality, 168; and
    translation, 14
invocation, 153
irrealism, 252
Iser, W., 180

Jakobson, R., 176, 180–81
Jameson, F., 169, 176
Jauss, H., 180
Jenny, L., 111
Johnson, M., 20, 21
Jones, G., 272
"A Judgement", 176–77

kahtalil, 'homestead', 31–32
k'ay 'song', 207, 214
Kayapo, myths of, 185
k'èey (*k'èeyik, k'eyah*) 'bawl out', 49–50, 203
keys, in footing, 76
king, Spanish, letters to, 103–27. *See also*
    documents, colonial
kinship terms, Maya, 38–39, table 2.1
k'oób'en 'kitchen', 42, 46

labor, 45–46, 56–60
lamination, of frames, 96
land, and inheritance, 32–33
land surveys, 252ex, 275, 280, 295, 296.

See also Yaxkukul documents, Sotuta
    documents
Landa, Fray Diego de, 104–5, 108–9, 292
landmarks: crosses as, 295; in land surveys,
    141–42
Langacker, R., 70
language: and the body, 4–5; social ideolo-
    gies of, 9–10; and social practice, 5; *See
    also* discourse genres; genres, speech
Lee, B., 186
letters, colonial Maya, 103–27; of 1560s,
    109, 275–76, 280, 282. *See also* letters
    of 1567
letters of 1567, 104, 105–27, 135 table 5.1,
    138, 139–40, 143, 146, 147, 149,
    150–51, 155, 159, 249; authenticity of,
    105–10, 146, 249; intertextuality of,
    110–15, 249, 275–76; of lords of Mani,
    106, 107, 108, 282; royal address in,
    115–22; secular clergy in, 122–26
liik'sik k'aák' 'raising up fire', 237
Lizana, Bernardo de, 292
Lopez Medel, Tomas. *See* Lopez, Oidor
    Tomas
Lopez, Oidor Tomas, 133, 157, 160, 273
Lopez *Ordenanzas. See Ordenanzas*
Lu Xun, 177
Lucy, J., 98n13, 177
Lyons, J., 66n23

maákó'ob '(old) people', 199, 205, 206, 240.
    See also spirits
"A Madman's Diary", 177
Mani: chronicle of, 138–39, 160; map of,
    253–55, 254 fig. 9.1, 295–96
map of Yaxkukul, 252, 256
maps: intertextuality of, 280–81; of Mani,
    253–55, 254 fig. 9.1; participant frame-
    works of, 253, 255; perimeters in, 255
Marxism, 169, 185
Maya, Yucatec, 1–2. *See also* official Maya
meaning: and concretization, 12; double, 54;
    and motivation, 4. *See also* interpretation
Medvedev, M., 172, 180, 182–83
memory: and consciousness, 202, 203; and
    experience, 205–207; and the five
    gourds ceremony, 197–216; loss of,

201–202; and prayer, 208, 213–14; and time, 205. *See also* history, memorial

mention, 73–74, 260

Merleau-Ponty, M., 6–7, 8, 12, 19, 20–21, 62, 64n8, 66n23

metalanguage: in colonial documents, 277; and concretization, 277; vs. direct speech, 72–73, 92; and ideology of language, 9–10; and pragmatics of deixis, 69–97; structural resources for, 76–84; and textuality, 170, 175–78

metatextuality, 177–78

metonymy, and head of household, 34

Morson, G., 134–35, 275

Munn, N., 65n20

nah 'house, home', 41, 42, 91

naming, in colonial documents, 262–63, 278–79, 302n10

narrative, and reported speech, 114–15, 148, 199

Nash, J., 64n4, 65n19

Naum Pech. *See* Ah Naum Pech

nobility, Maya: ambivalence of, 103, 104–5, 160–61, 258–59, 282; and boundary marking, 264–65; status of, 115, 125, 160–61, 258–59, 282

Norris, C., 182

objectivism, 252

"official Maya", 256, 268, 273–74. *See also* discourse genre, genre

officialization, 145–46, 149, 158

ojo 'eye', 26, 64n7

-oól 'will', 24–25

Ordenanzas, 133–34, 155, 160, 273

orientation: bodily, 26–27, 27, fig. 2.1, 30; ritual, 238–44; spatial, 21–22, 26–27

Oxkutzcab, market of, 46–47

paˀ ˀiik 'exorcism', 24, 226, 231, 233, 238, 246, 277; transposition in, 238

Panofsky, E., 23, 281

parallelism, 119–21, 125, 139–40, 150, 156–57, 162n6, 175

paraphrase, 94, 95, 98n3

participant frame, 9

participant framework: ambiguous, 154; in colonial documents, 13–14, 151, 153–54, 263–64, 273–74, 278–80; definition of, 9; and maps, 253, 255; of royal address, 116; of shamanic ritual, 223, 224, 231, 237–39. *See also* voicing, deixis, footing, participant reference

participant reference: ambivalence of, 282; in colonial documents, 263–64, 263ex, 278–80, 282; rule of succession in, 263 ex, 279

participant roles. *See* deixis, participant framework, footing

participants: in colonial discourse, 258–65; in discourse, 76; symmetry of, 57–60

patriline, and inheritance of land, 32–33

payal či ˀ tˀàan 'summons mouth speech', 209–10, 213–14, 300

Pech, (Don) Alonso, 251, 261 fig. 9.2, 262 fig. 9.3, 263, 264–65, 266Pech, (Don) Pedro, 251, 261, 262 fig. 9.3, 263, 264, 265, 266, 278

Pech patriline 260–63, 261 fig. 9.2, 262 fig. 9.3, 266, 267, 268n8, 279. *See also* Pech, (Don) Alonso; Pech, (Don) Pedro

perception: and deictic frame, 85–88; and *prise de conscience,* 30; verbs of, 25–26

Peres, Juan Pio, 235–36

performance, ritual: and memorial history, 227–28; and metalanguage, 277; and orientation, 231–33; paraphernalia of, 232, 233; participants in, 224–26; *sakab* offering, 197–216; temporal framework of, 230, 236–37

performance, verbal, 179. *See also* prayer, cruciform, shamanism, etc.

perimeter: in colonial documents, 255, 263–66. *See also* space, perimetal

persignarse, 288ex, 289ex

place names: cross in, 296; Western Apache, 183

place of discourse, in colonial documents, 154–57

places, cardinal, 241 fig. 8.2, 242 fig. 8.3

play speech. *See baášal tˀàan*

poetics: and social practice, 144; sociological, 136–37

About the Author

William F. Hanks, Milton H. Wilson Professor of the Humanities at Northwestern University, is the author of *Language and Communicative Practices* and other noted works on language.